Toward Nationalism's End

The Tauber Institute Series
for the Study of European Jewry

JEHUDA REINHARZ, *General Editor*
CHAERAN Y. FREEZE, *Associate Editor*
SYLVIA FUKS FRIED, *Associate Editor*
EUGENE R. SHEPPARD, *Associate Editor*

The Tauber Institute Series is dedicated to publishing compelling and innovative approaches to the study of modern European Jewish history, thought, culture, and society. The series features scholarly works related to the Enlightenment, modern Judaism and the struggle for emancipation, the rise of nationalism and the spread of antisemitism, the Holocaust and its aftermath, as well as the contemporary Jewish experience. The series is published under the auspices of the Tauber Institute for the Study of European Jewry—established by a gift to Brandeis University from Dr. Laszlo N. Tauber—and is supported, in part, by the Tauber Foundation and the Valya and Robert Shapiro Endowment.

For the complete list of books that are available in this series,
please see www.upne.com

*A Sarnat Library Book

TOWARD

NATIONALISM'S END

An Intellectual
Biography of
HANS KOHN

Adi Gordon

Brandeis University Press · Waltham, Massachusetts

BRANDEIS UNIVERSITY PRESS

An imprint of University Press of New England

www.upne.com

© 2017 Brandeis University

Manufactured in the United States of America

Designed by Eric M. Brooks

Typeset in Parkinson Electra by Passumpsic Publishing

For permission to reproduce any of the material in this book,
contact Permissions, University Press of New England, One Court
Street, Suite 250, Lebanon NH 03766; or visit www.upne.com

Cloth ISBN: 978-1-5126-0086-5

Paper ISBN: 978-1-5126-0087-2

Ebook ISBN: 978-1-5126-0088-9

Library of Congress Cataloging-in-Publication Data
available upon request.

5 4 3 2 1

Contents

Acknowledgments

Written mostly in Amherst, Massachusetts, in 2014, this book is the final product of a rather nomadic decade, in which I studied the life and times of Hans Kohn, first in Madison, Wisconsin; then in Jerusalem and Haifa; and later in New Orleans, Louisiana, and Cincinnati, Ohio. I owe much to scholars who, during my very first steps in graduate school—long before the current book was even conceived—encouraged and inspired me. Those include Guy Miron, Amos Goldberg, Henry Wassermann, Jakob Hessing, Moshe Zimmermann, Dan Diner, and, especially the late Gilad Margalit. I am profoundly indebted to my *Doktorvater*, Steve Aschheim, an extraordinary teacher and an inspiring scholar. I cherish his friendship and advice. This book literally owes its existence to him. It was Steve who first introduced me to Kohn and later suggested I write this biography. Though fascinated by the drama of Kohn's break with Zionism, I—unlike my *Doktorvater*—was initially rather unimpressed with Kohn. Kohn's youthful pathos left me cold, and his later work struck me as almost trite, lacking any critical edge. It took me time to get hooked, and even more time to gain a deeper understanding of the significance of Kohn's turbulent life and career. I hope something of my *Doktorvater*'s inquisitive, ironic spirit is present in this book.

I am not the first scholar to discuss chapters in Kohn's life. As a biographer, I have learned a great deal, for example, from the works of Craig Calhoun, Hillel J. Kieval, Taras Kuzio, André Liebich, Dieter Riesenberger, and Ken Wolf. Furthermore, I was lucky enough to meet and occasionally befriend many of the finest scholars who dealt with Kohn in one way or another. These include Michael Enderlein, Romy Langeheine, Hagit Lavsky, Zohar Maor, Noam Pianko, Shalom Ratzabi, Dimitry Shumsky, Anja Siegmund, Brian Smollett, Scott Spector, Yfaat Weiss, and Christian Wiese. I have learned much from all of them, but the one from whom—and with whom—I learned most about Kohn is my friend Lutz Fiedler.

I am very grateful to Kohn's son, the late Immanuel "Ike" Kohn, for an illuminating interview in his Lower Manhattan office in late 2007. Ike was invaluable in providing me with a sense of his father's private, social, and family life and in correcting a few preconceived notions I had. One of Hans Kohn's former students, Stanley Moses, generously shared his memories of Kohn during the 1960s. I thank him for the stories and the interest he has shown in this book. I am also obliged to Daniela Tal and her lovely family. Our conversations acquainted me with the personal life of Robert Weltsch, who was her father and Kohn's closest friend.

This book owes much to the kind professionalism of librarians and archivists in multiple countries. I would like to mention especially the librarians at the National Library of Israel, Jerusalem (particularly in the atypically quiet General Reading Room); the University of Wisconsin-Madison's Memorial Library (particularly the Interlibrary Loan office); the Klau Library of Hebrew Union College, in Cincinnati (particularly Israela Ginsburg and Laurel Wolfson); and Amherst College's Robert Frost Library (particularly Dunstan McNutt and Steve Heim). Among the many archivists who assisted me along the way, some of the most supportive were in Jerusalem, including people at the Central Archive for the History of the Jewish People, the Central Zionist Archives, and the Archives Department of the National Library of Israel. Exceptionally generous have been Dana Herman, of the American Jewish Archives; and Frank Mecklenburg, Director of Research and Chief Archivist at the Leo Baeck Institute, whose kind assistance made a tremendous difference in my ability to study Kohn. Michael Simonson, archivist and registrar at the Leo Baeck Institute, has always been extremely helpful. I also thank the friendly team at the Yad Tabenkin Archives in Ramat Efal, Israel, for granting me permission to use a photo from their collection.

Wherever life took me during the years I worked on this project, I was fortunate to find erudite interlocutors, colleagues, and friends who were generous with their time. I have benefited greatly from discussing Kohn and this book with colleagues, including Ari Finkelstein, Hanan Harif, Jason Kalman, Ethan Katz, Michael A. Meyer, Till van Rahden, Haim O. Rechnitzer, Sven-Erik Rose, Sarah Wobick-Segev, and Stefan Vogt. I am particularly grateful to the boldest ones, who read the manuscript in whole or in part and provided me with valuable insights. These include Ofer Ashkenazi, Aaron Berman, Nellie Boucher, Frank Couvares, Andy Donson, Arie Dubnov, Catherine Epstein, Judy Frank, Sergey Glebov, Udi Greenberg, Malachi Hacohen, John A. Hall, Nitzan Lebovic, Ted Melillo, Monica Ringer, Willard Sunderland, Bill Taubman, Jesse Torgerson, and April Trask.

In a way, this book grew out of my doctoral dissertation, which I began writing as a George L. Mosse Fellow at the University of Wisconsin-Madison. I thank the George L. Mosse Program in History—and especially its tireless manager, John Tortorice, for his boundless generosity, kindness, and great sense of humor. In Madison, David J. Sorkin was remarkably generous with his time and ideas. Multiple fellowships allowed me to pursue this long project. I thank the Zalman Shazar Center for Jewish History for granting me the Jacob Katz Prize; the Dinur Center for Research in Jewish History for granting me the Dinur Prize; the Leo Baeck Institute, Jerusalem, for granting me the Grunwald Grant; the Mandel Institute of Jewish Studies, and especially Otto Dov Kulka, for granting me the Erich Kulka Prize; and the Hebrew University's Faculty of Humanities and Rector's Office for granting me the Dean's and Rector's Distinction Prize. I thank the Richard Koebner Minerva Center for German History at the Hebrew University for offering me an ideal academic home. I am especially obliged to its past director, Moshe Zimmermann, for his generosity and wit. I thank the Studienstiftung des deutschen Volkes for awarding me the Leo Baeck Fellowship in 2007, and for its truly enlightening fellows' seminars. I thank the Franz Rosenzweig Minerva Research Center for a postdoctoral research fellowship in 2009. I thank my friends at the Simon Dubnow Institute for Jewish History and Culture at Leipzig University—especially its past director, Dan Diner —for glorious weeks in the summer of 2010. The memory of a visit to the Völkerschlachtdenkmal remains with me as I think about nationalism. I thank Brian Horowitz and the Department of Jewish Studies at Tulane University for a colorful, indeed unforgettable, year. My three years at the University of Cincinnati were a blessing in many ways. There I found not only an untapped and invaluable archival collection of Kohn's Zionist papers that enriched this manuscript, but also many wonderful people who enriched my life and that of my expanding family. I thank my dear friends in the Departments of Judaic Studies and of History, as well as my friends at the Hebrew Union College. From the very first day, they all made my family and me feel at home in the Queen City.

A stroke of good luck brought me to Amherst College in 2013, when I was roughly the same age as Kohn when he joined the faculty of nearby Smith College. As Kohn did eighty years before me, I count my blessings and am very taken with my new neighbors. Amherst College is like no other place I have known before, with colleagues and students who never cease to impress me. My department, the Department of History, is a small wonder of collegiality, professionalism, and intellect. Many colleagues in the Five College Consortium —including Jay R. Berkovitz of the University of Massachusetts–Amherst, Justin Cammy of Smith College, Jeremy King of Mount Holyoke College, and Aaron Berman of Hampshire College—went out of their way to welcome me to western Massachusetts. Special thanks are due also to the participants in the Five

College History Seminar, who generously asked me stimulating questions that improved this book.

I am grateful for my brilliant student assistants—Bailey Romano, Yvonne Green, and Rebecca "Becky" Konijnenberg—who became real partners in this endeavor and had their own unique, irreplaceable impact on the book. Thank you for your hard work and good questions and for being who you are. Special thanks go to my former student Lukas Nievoll and to Mario Rewers, who assisted me tremendously with the Dwight Macdonald and William Ernest Hocking collections.

It is a great honor to have this book included in the Tauber Institute Series for the Study of European Jewry, alongside works by some of my favorite scholars. I am truly grateful to Jeanne Ferris for her thorough and smart copyediting. Her insightful questions helped me clarify my thoughts and arguments. I thank Phyllis Deutsch, editor-in-chief of the University Press of New England, for her feedback and support. It has been wonderful to be guided by someone as experienced, knowledgeable, and friendly as Sylvia Fuks Fried, executive director of the Tauber Institute. Thank you for your ongoing support and steady hand. Eugene Sheppard has been an ideal editor, combining breadth of knowledge, sharp critical thinking, warmth, humor, and the rare ability to keep even rigorous work immensely enjoyable. My friend Erin Holman greatly improved this book with a preliminary edit. My colleague Andy Anderson generously and professionally created the map in chapter 2.

Finally, I would like to thank my family, the Gordons, Noys, and Walkers. It is great to be part of a big family in which everyone is such an original. My siblings may not know just how much they helped with the book. Dana assisted with the first draft of a map, Aya helped with the photographs, and Ori supported me throughout with his visits.

I dedicate the book with love to Vanessa, who makes all adventures—this book included—much more fun and worthwhile, and to our children, Asher, who (though mistaking Tom Waits for Cookie Monster) taught me how to sing; and Maya, whose confident smile melts me anew every morning.

Toward Nationalism's End

INTRODUCTION

Nationalism is becoming a
question of personal ethics,
personal shaping of life; it
is becoming questionable. It
is faced with new problems.
Things close to it are now
remote. Certitudes are
questionable.
Hans Kohn, "Nationalismus"
("Nationalism")[1]

I was always impressed by
Lucanus' retort to Cato's
words . . . "The victorious
cause pleased the gods,
but the defeated cause
pleased Cato." Even the
gods apparently have often
changed their minds in history,
and what was heralded as the
victorious cause has become
sooner or later . . . the cause of
the vanquished.
Hans Kohn, *Living in a World
Revolution*[2]

The life work of Hans Kohn marks the beginning of nationalism studies as we know it. In the period between the two world wars, his scholarship historicized nationalism and insisted not only on its modernity but also on its constructedness. Nationalism, Kohn was one of the earliest to argue, was "first and foremost a state of mind."[3] In the 1930s, in attempting to explain why nationalism developed in such diverse ways, Kohn famously sketched an extremely influential distinction between two archetypes, or families, of nationalism: Western, or civic, nationalism and Eastern, or ethnic, nationalism. Even though scholars have long criticized this dichotomy—challenging its geographic validity and even the notion of mutual exclusion—it "proved to be the longest-living, and probably most influential, typology in the field of nationalism studies."[4]

This book is both a biography of Kohn and an exploration of theories of nationalism in the twentieth century analyzed through the turbulent life of a leading scholar-activist. What renders Kohn's lifelong struggle with nationalism ideal for such an exploration is not just his stature as a scholar but also his position as a politically outspoken public intellectual whose life crossed continents and ideologies yet always took place at the meeting of scholarship and politics. Kohn wrote his major works on nationalism during and after his slow and painful break with Zionism, his own national movement. The break "gave me a better understanding of the pitfalls and self-deception inherent in most national movements," he explained in his memoirs.[5] Indeed, my work on this biography began with an exploration of that break but led me to a much broader understanding of this important theoretician of nationalism. No single chapter in his peripatetic life—not his Habsburg youth, his Zionism, or the break —wholly determined his work. Kohn was a child of his times; his concept of nationalism evolved radically over his lifetime, reflecting the changing world around him. His political agendas initially generated his interest in nations and nationalism, but his evolving understanding of the essence of nations and nationalism then transformed his political agendas. Indeed, Kohn went through many ideological conversions in addition to his break with Zionism: a central figure in international pacifism, he became a hawkish Cold Warrior; a socialist in the 1920s, he became a member of the Mont Pèlerin Society, the think tank of Friedrich Hayek and Ludwig von Mises and the birthplace of neoliberalism. As he faced the catastrophes of the twentieth century, he took very different political stances, but always in his capacity as the great authority on nationalism, "the most prominent investigator of nationalism."[6] This book thus demonstrates how myriad ideologies and agendas constituted and relied on ideas of nations and nationalism.

The book includes seven chronological chapters that roughly parallel Kohn's theoretical and personal positions. The first chapter (1908–1914) details Kohn's upbringing, socialization, and young adulthood in Habsburg Prague and his earliest Zionist writings. As a young Jew from a highly assimilated family—he himself described his parents' home as such—he found in nationalism a way for his generational revolt against his parents' and grandparents' Jewish "ideology of emancipation."[7] It was a quest for authentic identities—grounded in the historical realities of that place, time, and milieu—that brought the young Kohn to Jewish nationalism. This chapter argues that he adopted illiberal central European assumptions regarding the essence of nationalism but flatly rejected the prevalent nationalist politics of the feuding national movements around Bohemia.

The second chapter (1914–20) explores Kohn's dramatic wartime odyssey and political and intellectual transformation. Kohn welcomed the outbreak of World War I, but he spent most of the war as a prisoner in Russia. In hindsight, he labeled the five years of war, revolution, and civil war he spent in Siberia, Central Asia, and the Russian Far East as "the decisive years of my life":[8] they politicized him, sensitized him to the dynamics of colonialism, and turned him into a staunch opponent of the nation-state model. It was as a prisoner of war that he wrote his first systematic studies of nationalism and committed himself to transforming Zionism from within, turning it away from the nation-state model and a colonial relationship with the Arab world. His first efforts to theorize nationalism—rather than accept it as a given—emerged from his attempt to redefine a place for Jews in a world radically transformed by World War I.

The following three chapters discuss the years 1919–34—which Kohn spent in Western Europe and around Palestine and during which he radically and completely committed himself to translating his newly acquired understanding of nationalism into both political action and scholarship. His political action—analyzed in chapter 3—was rooted in a categorical rejection of the nation-state model and the idolatry of national sovereignty in the wake of the Wilsonian Moment, when ideas about national self-determination as a key component of the postwar international order captured the world's imagination.[9] The ideology of the nation-state, in his view, constituted an unjustifiable hierarchy between a dominant nationality and "minorities."[10] Thus, it spawned future irredentist wars. Kohn became an important voice in the international pacifist movement in the late 1920s. Furthermore, throughout the 1920s he fought tirelessly for an alternative Zionist vision, rejecting the idea of a Jewish nation-state and advocating instead the creation of a binational Arab-Jewish state. In those same years Kohn emerged as a scholar of oriental political modernities—and especially of Arab nationalism—and as a prolific commentator on Jewish political thought. Chapter 4 analyzes his scholarship and Jewish thought in 1920–34 and argues that both were rooted in his rejection of the nation-state. That rejection was so central to Kohn's thought that it would ultimately cause him to break with the Zionist movement, as he concluded that Zionism would henceforth aspire to nothing but a Jewish nation-state. Chapter 5 studies this break and its significance.

In 1934, Kohn left Palestine for the United States, where he became a professor of history at Smith College, in Northampton, Massachusetts. Chapter 6 (1934-48) analyzes Kohn's Americanization, academic breakthrough, and ideological transformation during his time at Smith. Advocates of the nation-state model in the 1920s tended to be self-proclaimed liberals. In the 1920s, however, Kohn often aligned himself with antiliberals—communists and conservatives alike—who shared his rejection of the nation-state model (the notorious doyen of interwar German geopolitics, Karl Haushofer, often presented as an intellectual father of the Third Reich, saw Kohn as one of his protégés). Following Hitler's ascension to power, however, Kohn underwent a liberal turn. His eclectic radicalism gave way to a post-catastrophic adherence to liberalism. Nazism transformed the nature and purpose of discussions about the essence of nationalism, and thus it is perhaps not surprising that 1944 set the stage for his academic breakthrough—revealed in his magnum opus, *The Idea of Nationalism*. Contemporaries read it as a response to the questions of why German nationalism deteriorated into Nazism and whether all nationalisms had a similar potential. Kohn's response was his familiar distinction between ethnic and civic nationalisms, which dominated his writing henceforth. Only civic nationalism, Kohn asserted, retained a universal horizon and an innate propensity to form federations greater than itself. Faced with "the totalitarian crisis," Kohn ceased to be a pacifist and became a vocal anti-isolationist, a proponent of collective security, and an advocate for democratic world federalization.[11]

The seventh chapter, which begins with Kohn's move in 1949 from Smith to City College in New York City, discusses Kohn's Cold War career. His theory of nationalism—distinguishing between a positive Western type and a negative Eastern one—became useful in American soft power in the Cold War: he eagerly joined in US efforts to Westernize, democratize, and reeducate West Germans; was active in the Congress for Cultural Freedom; and, with the young Henry Kissinger, participated in the Foreign Policy Research Institute. Kohn's 1953 *Pan-Slavism* rejected Soviet claims of anti-imperialism by pointing to the disparity between the Soviets' creed and actual policy. Soviet continental imperialism simply abused pan-Slavism to establish the hegemony of the Soviet Union. His 1957 *American Nationalism*, however, had nothing of that critical edge of juxtaposing creed and policy. There, Kohn found "the United States . . . the most 'modern'; and most 'western' nation."[12] In all, Kohn's writing during the Cold War analyzed nationalism through the self-serving prism of modernization theory. It appears that Kohn wanted to be a conformist in Cold War America. However, as this book's coda demonstrates, he found himself strongly opposed to America's special alliance—and American Jewry's unique bond—with the State of Israel. Ironically, it was the Jewish Question that stood in the way of his full identification with the United States.

.   .   .

Kohn was ahead of the curve in challenging nationalism's claim of self-evidence by insisting on its constructedness and modernity, but—in spite of his own bitter experiences with nationalism—he never rejected nationalism outright, as Elie Kedourie and Eric Hobsbawm did.[13] Instead, he stubbornly insisted that nationalism could also be good or benign; indeed, he insisted that originally it was a positive, liberating force that became corrupted in certain places and historical settings. His imperative, then, was to struggle against nationalism's corruption. Though Kohn's concept of nationalism evolved over time, his good nationalism consistently retained some qualities: it was always a means to a higher human goal; its horizon was always humanity and never just a nation; and it was always seen as ultimately leading to its own evolution into "higher forms of integration."[14] Kohn thus saw his mission as working toward nationalism in two ways: protecting its higher goal and pointing to its transcendent supranational culmination. Kohn's theory epitomized what Partha Chatterjee aptly dubbed "the liberal rationalist dilemma in talking about nationalist thought": as a liberal, Kohn "accepts nationalism as an integral part of the story of liberty," and his way to overcome the mounting evidence to the contrary (such as the existence of racism, fascism, and

Nazism) was to offer a useful, yet somewhat dubious, distinction between civic nationalism (seen as heir to the political legacy of the Enlightenment) and ethnic nationalism (seen as heir to the opponents of the Enlightenment).[15]

Chatterjee's observation points precisely to this biography's argument: Kohn's dichotomy could not have been purely academic but rather was ultimately grounded—for better or worse—in a personal political commitment to liberalism. Theorizing nationalism always emerges out of a certain political agenda, and thus the critical study of nationalism theories should analyze texts in their historical, political, and ideological contexts. Especially in the age of Brexit and Trump—when nationalism again overtly frames the course of the future—it must make explicit what Perennialists, and Modernists, and Ethno-Symbolists talk about when they talk about nationalism, why their theory of nationalism matters, and how it related to the world around them.[16]

· · ·

Though focusing on theories of nationalism and how they served twentieth-century political ideologies, this book is ultimately a biography. As such it will analytically reconstruct the story of a life—of a single man's triumphs and tragedies, achievements and failures—and it will tell that story with equal measures of criticism and empathy. Kohn deserves both. Additionally the book will examine the stories of the various intellectual or political organizations in which Kohn participated, including the Prague Bar Kochba Association before the Great War, organizations of international pacifism and binational Zionism in the 1920s, anti-isolationist policy research organizations in the 1930s, and idealist Cold War intellectual organizations in the 1950s. Each of these groups addressed the challenges of nationalism in some way, and most of them were failed projects, markers of many roads not taken.

At times I found it much easier to reconstruct Kohn's endeavors and struggles, positions and beliefs, and fears and hopes than to capture his personality. Who was Kohn, a man whom T. S. Eliot admired as "a brilliant talker as well as a charming person" and whom Gershom Scholem derided as "Ober-Quatscher" (a windbag)?[17] One of Kohn's former students, Stanley Moses, remembers him as a professor who stood out for "his great cordiality, openness, availability and responsiveness as a human being."[18] Lewis Mumford remembered Kohn as "a heavy-set man, with a kindly pasty face, an earnest pessimistic air. He talked volubly, but with great dialectic skill, real insight, well-supported arguments, and unshakable moral conviction."[19] Nothing in Kohn's personal papers indicates a good sense of humor or lightheartedness. "I never danced or drank after 1914; I never learned to swim, or to ski," he noted in his memoirs, explaining that "this was not my style of life."[20] Yet he was always a very social man, liked and admired by many people, who throughout his adult life hosted many friends multiple times a week. Kohn was always extremely driven, both intellectually and politically, as is evidenced by his unfathomably vast body of publications, correspondence, and public lectures and the long paper trail of his political life. He really never stopped, and during the hardest years of his life he redoubled his efforts, as if to numb his fears and channel his anguish into a sense of accomplishment and selfhood.

This recurrent pattern—channeling his personal tribulations into political and scholarly work—is related to an increasingly sharp split between Kohn's public persona and his inner emotional life. His childhood friend Robert Weltsch—one of the greatest Jewish journalists of the twentieth century and one of the leaders of German Jews under the Nazis in the 1930s—may have been the only person with whom Kohn regularly shared his true feelings. "He never lost his cool," was the first thing Kohn's son, Ike, told me in our interview.[21] But in spite of his cool exterior, Kohn—as his diaries and letters attest—went through some extraordinary dramas. In the 1920s, he radiated confidence externally, while confiding in his diary that "a sense of proximity to death" had hung over him ever since he arrived in Palestine: "Almost every [waking] hour I must think of death."[22] In the mid-1940s, the contrast grew between the optimism of his published work and the unrelenting melancholy and pessimism of his diaries. His memoirs, written in the mid-1960s, occasionally exposed that melancholy spirit, especially in the concluding chapter. Yet Kohn's overall insistence on a Panglossian outlook fooled even the brightest of readers. "The dominant impression made on me by the book," Arnold Toynbee told him, was that "here is someone who has no chip on his shoulder, no grievance against life."[23] This, alas, was not the case.

Kohn's writing always included both razor-sharp critiques of state ideology and seemingly naïve and uncritical idealizations of peoples, civilizations, and polities. For instance, he idealized the Soviet Union in the early 1920s and the United States in the 1950s: the critiques remain fresh even today, while the idealizations seem to contain as little intellectual rigor now as they did at the time. A few examples of Kohn's immunity to state ideologies will suffice: Questioning the Czechoslovak state ideology in the late 1920s, Kohn proclaimed, "the Czechs need an army not for war against external enemies but rather to suppress the Germans at home."[24] Challenging American state ideology in the 1930s, he boldly rejected the apologetic presentation of lynching as isolated exceptional cases disrupting the prevailing order. On the contrary, he proclaimed, lynching creates America's racial order: it is "the basis of unequal treatment be-fore the law meted to the different races. . . . Racial inequality is thus conducive not only to the destruction of democracy and liberty but also to the undermin-ing of justice and law."[25] And he declared the Soviets' pan-Slav ideology in the 1950s to be nothing but a cynical manipulation designed to establish the hege-mony of imperial Russians over other Slavs.

Kohn's political commitments have determined and polarized the manner in which his intellectual and ethical legacy is presented. The key moments in this regard are his defiance of political Zionism and later the State of Israel, on the one hand, and his Cold War service on behalf of soft power used by the United States and the North Atlantic Treaty Organization (NATO), on the other hand. Both of these actions attracted admirers as well as detractors. In 1958, Karen Brutents, a Soviet specialist on Third World affairs at the Communist Party's Central Committee, set out to expose Kohn's theory of nationalism as nothing more than an "apology of colonialism."[26] Lesser Soviet commentators followed suit, denigrating the books on Russian history by "Mister Kohn" as little more than propaganda but stressing that the books "are not his affair only. They are published, read and publicized. Kohn's ideas are shared by scores and hundreds of bourgeois 'Russian Experts.' The Kohns are a social phenomenon, they serve a definite policy."[27] During and after the Cold War, much of the criticism of Kohn's East-West concepts was grounded in the critique of Cold War ideology and its residues. At the end of the Cold War, the Scottish New Left political theorist Tom Nairn pointed to Kohn's legacy as the root of what he saw as an oversimplified and self-congratulatory Western demonization of East European nationalism. Nairn argued that it was Kohn's "conventional wisdom of the day before yesterday" that has "come back to haunt and distort Western interpreta-tions of what is happening." Kohn embodied "the creaky old ideological vehi-cles trundled out to cope with the post-Soviet and Balkan upheavals"—which, however, "explain nothing whatever about their subjects." The legacy of Kohn's Cold War service as an advocate of the use of US and NATO soft power was that of a retrograde self-congratulatory denigration of the East.[28]

However, for those who admired Kohn as a vocal opponent of the Jewish state, he remained a model—almost a Cassandra-like prophet—of progressive self-critique.[29] In 1945 the anti-Zionist American Council for Judaism proudly broadcasted the rejection of Israel and Zionism by "the world's greatest author-ity on Nationalism."[30] In 1958 the Egyptian diplomat Tahseen Basheer praised Kohn as a man who "lives up to the old tradition of Arab-Jewish harmony that typified for many generations the relationship between these Semitic peoples."[31] "The words of Hans Kohn," commented Jacqueline Rose almost half a century later, "could just as well be describing the politics of the preemptive war on terror today." She referred to the concluding paragraph of Kohn's 1922 essay "Nationalism," which cautioned against "the suggestiveness of national faith, which permits and excuses anything." She found Kohn to be an articulate dissenter and a sharp-eyed critic of the Jewish state's core failure.[32] Somewhat similarly, Judith Butler recently found in Kohn—as she did in Hannah Arendt, Martin Buber, and others—an intellectual who "called into question the narrative that is part of the legitimating discourse for the State of Israel."[33]

Rather than taking sides, I wish to underscore Kohn's remarkable appropriation by what seem to be groups at two ends of an ideological spectrum—groups that are both familiar with one facet of Kohn's life and arguably oblivious of another facet. Rather than making Kohn's two positions harmonious, I will evaluate Kohn's inner tensions and theoretical irresolvability in his biographical and historical contexts. The resulting degree of incoherence in his views is not to be confused with the maturing of his thought, particularly his understanding of nationalism. Rather, Kohn's story is one of nonarrival. As a septuagenarian —regardless of what his published work proclaimed—Kohn expressed as much doubt and confusion about the future of nationalism and his own political allegiances as he had as a young adult. Kohn's nonarrival, however, is inherent to the questions raised by nationalism, whose content, impact, and historical context is ever changing.

It would be wrong to see Kohn's theory of nationalism as ultimately grounded in his Habsburg experiences, and to present his later career as an attempted application of those Central European experiences to other settings. Nor was his theory shaped exclusively by the Great War. When Alain Locke and W. E. B. Du Bois encountered Kohn and his theory of nationalism in the mid-1930s, they were struck not only by its affinity with their concept of black nationalism but also by the fact that, in Locke's words, Kohn's "basis was a generalization of the Jewish experience as well as of the Soviet program for minorities."[34] Seen through the broadest biographical lens, they were both right and wrong. Kohn's exploration of nationalism was rooted in central European Jewish sensibilities and was profoundly affected by the Soviet doctrine on nationalism, but later historical forces—Nazism, World War II, and decolonization—continued to shape his concept of nationalism to no lesser degree. Though he tended to deny it, Kohn was a rolling stone that gathered no moss. Although his theory and its motivation constantly changed, Kohn never abandoned or completed his journey toward nationalism's end.

AUTHENTICITY & POLITICAL RUIN, 1908–1920

PART ONE

A TURNING INWARD

Kohn's Youth in Multinational Late Habsburg Prague

It is in general a necessary condition of free institutions that the boundaries of government should coincide in the main with those of nationality.

John Stuart Mill, *Considerations on Representative Government*[1]

The [gentile] nations have drawn political boundaries around themselves and have neighbors beyond their borders who are their enemies; the Jewish nation has its neighbors in its own breast.

Gustav Landauer, "Sind das Ketzergedanken?"[2]

"In the summer of 1908, when I was seventeen years old, I became a Zionist," Hans Kohn wrote. "As far as I remember I made this decision quite suddenly, without much soul-searching. I was about to enter the *septima*, the penultimate class, in the gymnasium at the time. And so for the last two years there and during my four years at the university, I was a zealous member of the association of Jewish university students which called itself Bar Kochba." Zionism would become the center of Kohn's social and spiritual life for many years, rendering his becoming a Zionist the starting point of his intellectual biography. In those years, at Charles-Ferdinand University in Prague and in Bar Kochba, Kohn began several lifelong intellectual and spiritual explorations, learning, writing, publishing, and occasionally lecturing on myriad themes. Here also some of his most formative relationships—with Robert Weltsch, Hugo Bergmann, and Martin Buber—began to ripen. "It was," he would comment in old age, "intellectually and morally as outstanding a group of men as I have met."[3]

This chapter deals with Zionist ideology in the context of Central Europe around the beginning of the twentieth century. What was Kohn looking for, and what did he find, in Zionism? After all, his upbringing had little to no Jewish cultural or religious aspect, nor did he experience persecution. What brought him to Zionism, I would argue, was a quest for authentic identities, grounded in the historical realities of that place, time, and milieu. It was a generational sensibility; he and his friends had grown increasingly skeptical of their parents' liberal worldview and particularly of how the older generation understood its Jewishness. For the young, authentic identity seemed to be grounded in nationhood, understood in the terms of that place and time as anchored in blood, soil, and a distinctive national culture. Kohn and his Bar Kochba friends struggled with these ostensibly objective factors and discerned the limits of their authenticity or, at the very least, the limits of their applicability to the Jewish nation. Their spiritual Zionism stayed clear of the aggressive practices of the feuding national movements around them. In fact, they avoided politics altogether, seeing it as not only a shallow, "minor matter" but also as a hazardous distraction from the true goal of their "nationalism of inwardness," which sought a Jewish

previous page:

Figures 1.1a and b Hans Kohn, February 1913. Hans Kohn among his classmates in Prague, 1907. Courtesy of the Leo Baeck Institute, New York.

spiritual renewal and a transformation of the way they lived.[4] The Prague Zionists began seeking different formulations of nationalism; yet in the final analysis, the allure of primordiality still dominated even their concept of nationhood before the Great War.[5]

This chapter follows Kohn from his teenage years to young adulthood, stopping before his twenty-third birthday, and is set solely in Prague. Its purpose is threefold: First, it will introduce the historical setting of late Habsburg Prague and show that setting's bearing on Kohn's later work. Second, it will explore Kohn's prewar Zionism in the Bar Kochba Association under the mentorship of Martin Buber, paying special attention to the concept of Jewish renewal and its relation to German idealism and *Lebensphilosophie* (philosophy of life). Finally, it will explore the discussion of national soil, national blood, and national culture in Bar Kochba.

But Kohn was still an intellectual neophyte, clearly influenced by Buber and Hugo Bergmann, "the leaders of our ethical community."[6] Only around 1913 —when Kohn became Bar Kochba's chairperson and de facto coeditor (with Buber) of the volume *Vom Judentum* (On Judaism)—would he develop a more distinctive and independent voice. For this reason, this chapter, more than later ones, will present Kohn's voice as part of a larger chorus. In their ruminations on the Jewish renaissance, the young members of Bar Kochba were also debating the essence of nations and nationalism, and these debates had a lifelong impact on Kohn.

The Omnipresence of Nationalism:
The Formative Late Habsburg Setting

Kohn grew up in the "sheltered home atmosphere" of a middle-class family in Prague. His father, Salomon, who was fifty-two in 1908, was a rather unsuccessful traveling salesman, "a man of little formal education" and of "old-fashioned chivalry," who wished his first child to have a life of middle-class security and stability. Kohn "did not feel especially close to" either parent, but he seemed more attached to his mother, the more culturally and intellectually curious Berta. She was a homemaker, eleven years younger than her husband and very engaged in fostering her eldest son's *Bildung*. When Kohn entered the university, she was diagnosed with breast cancer, which claimed her life ten years later. Kohn had three younger siblings: Fritz, two years his junior, was fifteen in 1908; Franz was only six; and the youngest, Grete, was four. Completing the Kohn household was the Christian Czech cook and maid, Marie "Mařenka" Vrbová, who stayed with the family for over forty years.[7]

"The very air of Prague made me a student of history and of nationalism," he reflected nearly fifty years after his departure from the city.[8] By that point, he was a distinguished American scholar and a septuagenarian. This connection between his early experience of the multinational hometown and his later interest in nationalism, however, should come as no surprise to anyone even remotely familiar both with Kohn's *oeuvre* and the nationality conflicts in late-Habsburg Prague and their impact on the city's Jews.[9] Remarkably, however, Kohn's writings from prewar Prague do not seem to focus on, or even directly address, any theory of nationalism or advocate any multinational federation. His direct attempts to theorize nationalism in light of his experience, however, would occur overtly only much later. In the six years before the outbreak of World War I, Kohn was a young Zionist fascinated with issues such as modern literature, postliberal philosophy, and especially theology.[10]

What was it, then, in prewar Prague—where Kohn spent the first twenty-three years of his life—that so unmistakably shaped his worldview? It was, first and foremost, the multiethnic composition of the city and the surrounding Bohemian lands, where Czechs, Germans, and Jews still lived side by side. At least in retrospect, Kohn found this multiethnic setting enriching, lending the city a cosmopolitan air. But the groups did not only live side by side: for more than two generations, Czech and German nationalists in Kohn's hometown had been

Figure 1.3 Hans Kohn (*right*) with Ernst Mueller in 1907.
Courtesy of the Leo Baeck Institute, New York

Figure 1.4 Hans Kohn (*right*) with his brother Fritz, before World War I.
Courtesy of the Leo Baeck Institute, New York

engaged in a "bitter, implacable struggle."[11] The outnumbered, once influential German population was in a steady decline, while the Czech majority was increasingly asserting its dominance. Growing up in this setting exposed Kohn to both the practices of an escalating national conflict and key nationalist concepts. Both would inform his academic and political careers.[12]

The strife between Czechs and Germans that shaped the Prague of Kohn's youth existed all over Bohemia and (though to a lesser degree) in the other Crown Lands, Moravia and Silesia. It was indeed part of the broad nationality problems of the late Habsburg monarchy. Both Czech and German nationalist activists—"ethnonational entrepreneurs," as Rogers Brubaker called them[13]—constructed and advocated clear, unhyphenated ethnic identities. The feuding sides struggled for nationalization of territories and clashed especially fiercely on the multilingual, multiethnic "language frontiers," where local people quite often identified either with both nationalities or with neither.[14] The ongoing conflict was based on the assumption, liberal in origin, that the nation had the right to self-government in a fixed territory. The subsequent assump-

Figure 1.5 From *left to right*: Grete, Franz, Berta, and Salomon Kohn, probably during World War I.
Courtesy of the Leo Baeck Institute, New York

tion was that lands rightly belonged exclusively to a particular national group (and hence not to others): one national group was ostensibly more rooted in the land than another. In this context, political rights clearly seemed to depend on demography, and thus being a member of a minority group was politically dangerous. Simultaneously, as in much of Europe, feuding national movements understood themselves more and more in primordial terms of blood and ethnic differences, ostensibly manifested in local history since time immemorial. This was the dominant language of nationalism, and when Kohn became a Zionist, he had to come to terms with the concepts of both national territory and blood.

Kohn would later describe this nationalist discourse of rootedness and the reality of voluntary ethnic segregation—an Iron Curtain of sorts—as strange. Notably, however, in his memoirs this state of affairs seemed neither intolerable nor too alarming:

The German-speaking minority among whom I grew up maintained a fully developed, separate cultural and social life of its own. We [members of that minority] did not feel isolated. We felt perfectly at home in Prague and in the Czech countryside around the city. All this was our land, too; we breathed its air and loved its contours. . . . Thus, the German minority did not feel the lack of "roots" in Prague. Our roots were there. We even accepted without much reflection the strange fact

that in Prague the two national groups lived strictly separated lives. There was little, if any, social or cultural contact between them. Each had its own schools and
universities, theatres and concert halls, sport clubs and cabarets, restaurants and
cafés—in all fields of life and activity there reigned a voluntary segregation, a kind
of tacitly acknowledged "iron curtain" which separated two worlds living side by
side, each one self-contained, scarcely communicating.[15]

Given that the Austro-Hungarian Empire collapsed during World War I and
disintegrated into national successor states, many standard histories have depicted it as doomed in the face of the mighty rise of national movements all over
its territory. The previous generation, however, saw a major revision in historiography, which both qualified the appreciation of nationalities as natural and solid
and questioned the empire's ostensible inability to create a supranational identity. Kohn's own understanding, as both a witness and a historian, fits this new
historiography. That supranational identity was ingrained in him. "Prague was
my home," he wrote in his memoirs, "the Austrian monarchy my fatherland,
and, not unreasonably, I felt a sentimental loyalty toward both."[16] Indeed he repeatedly described the last days of the empire not with nostalgia but with melancholy about needlessly missed opportunities:

> This experience of my youth predestined me . . . to develop an awareness of the
> importance of nationalism. Rationally, the conflict between Germans and Czechs
> in Bohemia should have been solved by compromise. Economic considerations
> and geographic reality were in favor of such solution. In two Austrian provinces
> —in Moravia, where Czechs and Germans lived together much as they did in Bo-
> hemia, and in the small province of Bukovina, which was populated by three na-
> tionalities, Ukrainians, Rumanians, and Germans—such compromise solutions
> were found (as compromise solutions were found after World War II for Tri-
> este and for Cyprus). But in the case of Bohemia such reconciliation of opposite
> claims, which would have been in the ultimate interest of both groups and would
> have assured a common future on a reasonable basis, was frustrated by visions and
> ambitions carried over from the past—and often from a narrow interpretation of
> the past—and by the emotions aroused by such visions. History was too powerful
> to allow sense to prevail.[17]

When Kohn sarcastically wrote that "history was too powerful," he was pointing to the force of nationalist historical narratives. He was even more specific
regarding the nature of the broader solution to the empire's acute nationalities
problem. The Austria of his childhood, he wrote, was "on the way to becom-

ing a *Vielvölkerreich*, a truly multinational state. Yet the nationalist groups in Austria, eager for the panoply and power of full sovereignty, and equally eager to achieve dominant position at the expense of other nationalities, continued to complain and press for special privileges," and under this pressure "the monarchy disintegrated."[18]

Kohn's formative experiences in prewar Prague consisted not only of the polarizing ideas and practices of aggressive "ethnonationalist entrepreneurs." They also contained the multiethnic coexistence that defied any nationalist visions of purity and exclusivity. Most importantly, his youth in Prague exposed him to the plans for a federative solution that promised to accommodate the various national movements through the monarchy's transformation into "a truly multinational state."

A multinational Austrian federation would have been—to quote the title of Adolf Fischhof's 1869 essay that advocated this path—"the Guarantee of Austria's Existence."[19] Kohn was certainly aware of the Austromarxist expansions of this idea of a multinational Austria, which already included the key component of nonterritorial national autonomies. Karl Renner offered a classic account of this "Personality Principle" in 1899: "The nations should be constituted not as territorial entities but as personal associations, not as states but as peoples, not according to age-old constitutional laws, but according to living national laws."[20]

Such visions offered an alternative to the ideal of full political national sovereignty, which imagines ethnic homogeneity where there is none and thus strives toward the partition of a territory into nation-states. Furthermore, since the thorniest arena of the national problem appeared in the most richly mixed regions, the principle of nonterritorial autonomies could allow for national self-government without the human tragedies of partition. More profoundly, according to the "Personality Principle," nationality is an act of choice by individual citizens: citizens alone determine the nationality of which they wish to be a part. Therefore, these plans ran counter to the prevailing notion of primordial national identity as a matter of fate and blood.

The location of Prague Jews (or Bohemian Jews in general) between Czechs and Germans was a vital part of the setting into which Kohn was born and in which he spent his early life. The age of emancipation for the Jews of Prague and Bohemia spanned the years between 1781 (when Kaiser Joseph II issued the Edicts of Toleration) and 1867 (when, with the creation of the dual monarchy of Austria-Hungary, Jews were finally granted full legal emancipation). As in other lands, Jewish inner life and core values were transformed during and by the protracted struggle for full emancipation. In the case of Jewish Prague, "the ideology of emancipation" included the adoption of an unmistakably German cultural identity.[21] When Czech nationalism increased in the mid-nineteenth century, however, "Jews faced the dilemma of reconciling an essentially German acculturation with the reality of an ethnically divided society."[22] A "secondary acculturation"—to borrow the term from Hillel Kieval's classic work —took place and had changed the profile of Prague Jews by the 1870s, as more and more of them integrated into and identified with Czech society and culture.[23] However, recent scholarship reveals that rather than being torn between two very clearly defined nationalities, in addition to their polarized cultural national identities many Jews and other Bohemians had less clear and more sophisticated constellations of identity, ranging from various combinations of both cultures to "national indifference."[24] At least theoretically, Jews could also opt to reclaim an unhyphenated Jewish cultural identity.

On the face of it, Kohn seems to have presented his own Jewish milieu rather unequivocally as "the German Jewish circle"—that is, as a Jewish minority within Bohemia's German minority.[25] This presentation exemplifies the persistence of German cultural identity among Prague Jews as portrayed in Gary Cohen's standard work, *The Politics of Ethnic Survival*. Indeed, much in Kohn's biography supports that view: German was his mother tongue, the language of his correspondence and of his early publications; like his closest friends, he went to a German school and studied at the German university; and he and his friends "participated fully in the German and European life of the period." Even his writing career began (at age fourteen) in German, when he reported on the German soccer league.[26]

However, Kohn and many others in his "German-Jewish circle" were no strangers to Czech culture and society. Indeed, their sociocultural setting defies the simple category "German-Jewish." Like Franz Kafka, Bergmann, and others, Kohn belonged to the first Prague-born generation of families that came from the Czech countryside. His mother was from Kralupy, and his father was from Nová Cerekev; although German was their primary language, both were bilingual. Furthermore, as Dimitry Shumsky has shown, Kohn's family was registered in the 1910 census as Czech speaking (their first names were even registered in the Czech version: Hanuš, rather than Hans, and so on).[27] Though Kohn must have had a fairly good command of the Czech language, his prewar university transcripts indicate that he took three university courses in Czech as foreign language (as he had also done in high school).[28] Rather than prove his German cultural identity—for had he been truly bilingual, he wouldn't have needed to take such courses—this may indicate his wish to enhance his understanding of and involvement in Czech life. It seems, then, that even though young Kohn "accepted without much reflection the strange fact that in Prague the two national groups lived strictly separated lives," Czech life was never really foreign to him, and in this regard he may be representative of the many people of that place and time who defied the crude nationalist (and Jewish integrationist) imperative to commit exclusively and fully to one of the nationalities. Though Kohn, especially as he grew older, played down antisemitism's impact on him and his prewar circle, he did acknowledge, albeit in passing, that "the Czechs on the whole were unfriendly to the Jews, and many of the German students who came to the Prague University from the Sudentenland were racist and pan-German."[29]

Though the social circles of Kohn and his family were overwhelmingly Jewish, his formal Jewish upbringing was quite minimal. His father attended synagogue only for the obligatory high holiday services. His mother did not even do that. Kohn had a very broad education and studied eight years of Latin, in addition to French and Greek. Yet "none of the Jewish children among my acquaintances knew Hebrew or Yiddish or had anything more than the most superficial knowledge of Jewish history or religious literature. The official and compulsory religious education in the public schools, given by rabbis, did little to foster Jewish tradition or sustain its deeper religious sentiments." Kohn, it seems, may not have even been exposed to this minimal instruction, as his parents sent him to an excellent private Catholic school run by the Piarist Fathers. This elementary school was "mostly frequented by Jewish children" (among its famous Jewish graduates were Max Brod, Egon Erwin Kisch, Fritz Mauthner, Leo Perutz, Felix Weltsch, and Franz Werfeland). The Catholic fathers never attempted to convert their many Jewish pupils, but of course they offered no Jewish curriculum.[30]

"In Bohemia and Moravia," Kohn wrote in old age, "the political situation of the Jews toward the end of the nineteenth century became increasingly difficult, since they were torn between the deeply hostile Czech and German camps. As a way out of this difficulty, some Jews after 1890 took the step of refusing to consider themselves either Czech or German. Renouncing integration into either of the two camps, they declared themselves members of a separate Jewish national community."[31] When Kohn became a Zionist, he and his peers adopted Central European assumptions about the essential nature of nations and nationalism yet stayed clear of any combative nationalist practices of their time and place.

A "Nationalism of Inwardness":
Postliberal Spiritual Zionism

With the implied intent of achieving a position in the civil service, Kohn enrolled in the faculty of law and political science at the German Charles-Ferdinand University in Prague. However, his heart and about a half of his courses were in the humanities. He took multiple courses of philosophy: metaphysics, practical philosophy, and logic with Anton Marty; philosophy of religion and science with Christian von Ehrenfels; and metaphysics with Oskar Kraus. He also took Hebrew and biblical studies with Isidor Pollak and Arabic and Islam with Max Grünert.[32]

In those years, his Zionist student association, Bar Kochba, was an intellectual powerhouse. With the future philosopher Bergmann as its chairperson starting in 1903, the association's cultural, educational, and intellectual activity intensified, and through its publications and public events, it reached well beyond Prague and became the voice of young postliberal spiritual Zionists throughout central Europe. The ubiquitous distinction in Central European Jewry between Zionist and liberal Jews relied on the overlap of political, cultural, and religious divides, but most members of the first generation of Central European Zionists—with Theodor Herzl being the prime example—were liberal in their worldview, rationalism, belief in progress, and trust in the state.[33] Kohn and his Bar Kochba Zionists proudly rebelled against the "Liberal Age":

> This era of Liberalism, which was nothing but a cheaper repetition of the era of Enlightenment of the eighteenth century, brought forth an absolute domination of materialist ideals. Thus, it exerted a particularly strong influence upon the Jew who took part in its development for the first time since he had been torn up by his very roots. . . . The Jewish community is disintegrated and debased. There is no human being whose sole liberal individualism conquers as triumphantly as the Jew's. His interests are exhausted in a continuous skirmishing about actual enforcement of the rights granted to him on paper. The stream of life flows no longer. The Jew is bent upon producing the fiction of life. He becomes an actor, a counterfeiter, a liar.[34]

Bar Kochba reached its zenith in early 1909, when Buber attended a meeting as the association's guest to deliver an address titled "Der Sinn des Judentums" (The meaning of Judaism, later published as "Judaism and the Jews"). "Why do we call ourselves Jews?," he bluntly asked the audience, challenging them to make any substantial response grounded in the authenticity and actuality of their own lives. He went on to brutally refute all conventional responses, leaving many in his audience astonished and enraptured. Buber's address—which Kohn would see as a turning point in his life, to his *Menschwerdung* (becoming human)—formulated their Jewish Question—"the personal Jewish question, the root of all Jewish questions, the question we must discover within ourselves, clarify within ourselves, and decide within ourselves."[35] "All that we call Zionism," Kohn stated, echoing Buber's focus on the personal, "is grounded on the deepest problems of our self (*unseres Ichs*) and of our time."[36] Only a few years older than the members of the association, Buber—with his broad intellectual universe, charisma, Nietzschean worldview, and bold antiliberalism—knew how to appeal to the young Prague Zionists "eager for deeper spiritual experiences." The association "discovered its master teacher and advisor in Martin Buber," and the highlight of their collaboration was the 1913 volume *Vom Judentum*.[37] Twenty years later, Kohn elucidated the sensibilities of his postliberal generation: "Science—mechanized and specialized—appeared cold, lifeless, and barren to the new generation. They wanted to return to the herd, to the dark wellsprings of being, which seemed to have flowed in the periods of heightened life feeling, of synthetic world sensation, in still-adolescent Greek philosophy, in mysticism, [the] Renaissance and Romanticism."[38]

Buber's lectures in front of Bar Kochba came to be known (and published) as the *Three Addresses on Judaism*, clearly an allusion to Johann Gottlieb Fichte's *Addresses to the German Nation* (published in 1808). Kohn and his Zionist friends were impressed by Fichte's *Addresses*, delivered in Berlin during the French occupation following the Prussian defeat by Napoleon's forces at the Battle of Jena. "To us," Kohn wrote, "the lesson was clear: The Jews of our time seemed to find themselves in a position similar to that of the Germans on the eve of the rise of their nationalism."[39] But there was more to that similarity: Kohn and his peers were thinking of their cultural Zionism in terms inherited from German idealism, particularly from Fichte.[40] However, Fichte was an unlikely prophet for cultural Zionists not only because of his brutal anti-Jewish statements and his emphasis on a common language and soil (which Jews could hardly share). He also was unlikely because the cultural Zionists—as opposed to the political Zionists—aspired not to a Jewish state but to a Jewish cultural renaissance, and Fichte, after all, was the political thinker who married the nation to the idea of the statehood. (A few years later Kohn would call him "the greatest theoretician of the nation-state.")[41]

Yet when Robert Weltsch, Kohn's closest friend, proclaimed, "we must all become little Fichtes," he did not find in Fichte's addresses a road map to a Jewish nation-state, but rather—as George Mosse put it—"signposts of how personal ethics might be reinforced through national commitment. National-ism was an ethical imperative, a means of developing one's own personality."[42] Though Kohn's understanding of nationalism clearly changed over time, he would remain indebted to Fichte in two crucial ways: he always understood na-tionalism in ethical terms ("Fichte's patriotism was a call to spiritual regener-ation") and as part of a society of nations.[43] Fichte's Jewish readers, Manfred Voigts showed, saw him as the voice of a "metaphysical people . . . existing as a metaphysical inwardness," in the words of the German Jewish socialist Fer-dinand Lassalle.[44] Kohn celebrated Fichte and the philosophers of German idealism from a century earlier for "renewing the German spirit" and believed himself to be witnessing a similar Jewish process—a Jewish Renaissance—under the guiding lights of Buber, Gustav Landauer, Henri Bergson, and Karl Joël.[45] "Zionism," Kohn wrote to Buber, "has its roots in an idealist philosophy, and for the present we ought to nourish these roots."[46] In another letter to Buber, Kohn expressed his insistent preoccupation with "the relationship between our Zionism and the new idealism of all peoples (or in other words, [that] it seems as if today it is not only a subterranean Judaism that awakes, but an entire subter-ranean humanity)."[47] This new idealism, according to the people Kohn named as its proponents, seems to be nothing but Lebensphilosophie: Georg Simmel and Wilhelm Dilthey (both Buber's professors), Bergson, Joël, and most prom-inently Rudolf Eucken—were all philosophers of life. (Indeed, Eucken named his life philosophy "New Idealism."[48]) "We [Zionists]," Kohn wrote in the lead-ing Zionist periodical in 1913, "are grateful to Bergson and Joël for granting us a philosophy that one can have only when one lives it; which dissolves . . . all which is fossilized or dead; a philosophy for which nothing is complete, but rather everything is a road, a task for us to become ever more complete, to al-ways grow taller than we are. A philosophy of increased force for action and life." Kohn thus fits the picture presented by Yotam Hotam of Zionist think-ers with an affinity for Lebensphilosphie, to the extent that the two schools of thought seem almost like twins—both theologically imaginative responses to very similar late-nineteenth-century crises.[49]

The student association's name evokes Simon bar Kochba, the leader of the Jewish revolt against the Romans who established a short-lived independent state. And yet there was not the slightest hint of militarism in the students' Zi-onism.[50] Bar Kochba was committed to "internal education and to the primacy of the spiritual."[51] In addition, its Zionism had nothing to do with Jewish state-hood, and it never aspired to the creation of a Jewish state in Palestine. It had little to do with antisemitism at home or with the plight of Eastern European

Jews. Rather, Bar Kochba's Zionism was focused on the dilemmas of a young generation of highly acculturated Central European Jews, specifically regarding the reclaiming of their own Jewishness, which they perceived as their authentic identity, and bringing about a Jewish spiritual renaissance.[52] They found in Ahad Ha'am's and Buber's concept of a Jewish renaissance the promise of a spiritual and intellectual exploration and a radical Jewish self-discovery. Asher Biemann's study of the idea of renaissance in modern Jewish thought beautifully highlights the contradictions underlying the concept. The yearning for a renaissance expresses the rejection of one's imposed identity and also of the progression of history. A renaissance envisions, by definition, a return that is also forward moving; a return that is also a beginning. The idea of renaissance "begins as protest against one's time" and becomes "a protest against one's place and oneself."[53] This contradictory idea of renaissance was not uniquely Jewish. The political philosopher John Plamenatz identified it as typical of all Eastern, or non-Western, nationalisms.[54] The art historian Inka Bertz has shown that the Jewish renaissance—with its pursuit of a radical reform of Jewish life—displayed an almost surprising Zionist affinity to the postliberal Central European *Lebensreform* (life reform) movements of the time, whose agendas ranged from vegetarianism and naturopathy to naturism and educational reform.[55]

However, the remarkable aspect of the pursuit of Jewish revival by Kohn and his highly educated young friends is that they had very limited knowledge of Judaism and Jewish history. In his "Letter to His Father," Franz Kafka very brutally expressed the limited Jewish identity and Jewish education that this cohort received from their parents. The letter paid great attention to "the weakness of your Judaism and of my Jewish upbringing," while depicting it as typical of the Jewish middle class in Prague during those years. Kafka stressed how utterly impossible it was for him to relate seriously to "the insignificant scrap of Judaism you yourself possessed." It was "a mere nothing, a joke—not even a joke."[56] Though eight years older than Kohn, Kafka had gone to the same high school (the Alstädter Gymnasium) and the same university (the German Charles-Ferdinand University), and he too was a friend of Bergmann. Thus, Kafka and Kohn belonged to the same milieu.

"In regards to things Jewish, we were ignoramuses," admitted Robert Weltsch, but "determined to conquer Judaism for ourselves and to do so in an entirely new fashion, expressing the core of our feeling (*Grundgefühl*)."[57] In an age of heightened nationalism, Kohn and his peers found the common self-understanding of liberal Jewish integrationists of their day ("Austrians of the Jewish faith") both unconvincing and inauthentic.[58] This imaginative reclaiming of Jewishness was founded on more than their feelings; it was stimulated by generational sensibilities and tensions in central European Jewry. If their parents and grandparents —late proponents of the ideology of emancipation—depicted a Judaism whose core values were remarkably similar to those of the dignified Central European Christian bourgeoisie, Kohn and his peers were drawn to a subversively wild and exotic Judaism. Thus, it is not surprising that Kohn's father had a "low opinion of Zionism and Zionists."[59]

Perhaps because of the young Zionists' illiteracy in all things Jewish, there was something uniquely creative about their appropriation of Jewish texts and history. Precisely because Judaism was an entirely new world for them, they could allow themselves to relish their imagined community and its invented traditions, to use anachronistic terms. Hence, Kieval stated that Bar Kochba's task "to build a modern Jewish cultural tradition de novo" relied heavily on its members' "own imagination."[60] The result was an abundantly essentialist discussion of all things Jewish. When Kohn and Buber coedited Vom Judentum, Kohn more than once eulogized a thinker as embodying the essence and voice of a new Jewish generation, only to discover from Buber that that those "model Jewish voices" were converts to Christianity (or their children) or Christians with no Jewish ancestry. To be sure, Buber's writing similarly essentialized Judaism and Jews. Kohn's first letter to Buber focused on the claim that Buber stretched "the boundaries of Judaism . . . too wide, indeed projects them ad infinitum and confuses that in us which is ethnically conditioned (*völkisch-bedingt*) with that which is humanly intrinsic (*menschlich wesenhaft*)."[61] Their repeated cautionary comments to each other only confirm how similar they once were in their rhetoric and thought patterns.

It is no coincidence that Kohn found his mentor in Buber, the religious thinker. If politics, in Otto von Bismarck's famous dictum, was "the art of the possible, the attainable," then for Kohn religion was precisely the opposite: it was the noble pursuit of the ultimately impossible and unattainable. Young Kohn's critique of contemporaneous diasporic Jewry related to its "godlessness," broadly defined, and his early texts and lectures consistently imagine the Jewish renewal as a religious renewal: "The life of the Jews in the West, Kohn diagnosed, is flawed, lacking any religiosity or 'vital order.' Only a Jewish reorientalization could mend it. In the Orient Jews once again become pure vessels of divine will, [standing] in awe of one another and boldly before God."[62]

His 1912 article "Der Zionismus und die Religion [I]," which conveys what one today would call postsecular sensibilities, sees religion as a form of unifying social experience, one that generates an identification with the nation and thus claims that the adequate form of Jewish life is religious. "Zionism will never be able to generate a renewal," Kohn proclaimed, "if it does not become a religious movement; that is, a movement which stirs the masses."[63] Thus, Kohn advocated a clear religious agenda for Zionism: it had to cease presenting religion as a private matter of personal beliefs and take up the battle against the traditional Jewish religion (both as the obvious enemy of any renewal and as an exceedingly corrupting factor). That anticipated religious renewal, it should be obvious, would not be a return to orthodox tradition, and certainly not a modernizing moderate religious reform. Following Buber, Kohn contrasted not only "official" and "subterranean Judaism" but, more broadly, religion (institutions and dogma) and religiosity (inner, personal, subjective): Kohn shared Buber's language, according to which "religion means preservation" while "religiosity means renewal."[64] The religiosity Kohn and his young friends found most attractive, and most absent in the present, was the irrational, ecstatic one. Indeed, Zohar Maor has found a central dimension of Bar Kochba to be mysticism.[65] In his youth Kohn was certainly fascinated by the idea of mysticism, even outside Judaism, reading extensively in Eastern mystical works and compiling an anthology of German mystical writings.[66]

What did a clean-shaven, tie-wearing Jewish law student in Prague have to do with ecstatic religiosity or mysticism? Though it is tempting to dismiss much of Kohn's youthful writing as merely an intellectual interest in a foreign (and hence exciting) idea, a very personal letter to Robert Weltsch attests to the urgency with which Kohn grappled with mystical ecstatic religiosity. "I believe I understand Buber now," he wrote. Buber "is not only a historian, but a prophet of a sect (*Bekenntnis*)" whose core is ecstatic mysticism. Though there will never be a nation of mystics, he went on, "I believe that every human owns the seed necessary to become an ecstatic (*Ekstatiker*)," and that within the Jewish Renaissance "these possibilities can (and should) be developed." This is not just an aestheticization of the mystical experience: "No! This is not the purpose of mysticism; one should not approach it if one is not driven by utter need to find God, oneself or life." Mysticism emerges as a pillar of the Jewish renewal. "To become more mystical," Kohn explained, "means to seek to fulfill the three tendencies" spelled out in Buber's addresses—the tendencies toward unity, toward deed, and toward the messianic future—as all of these rely on the individual's transcendence of consciousness and his or her subsequent expanded spiritual awareness. Kohn even envisioned a similarity between the ecstatic moment and Jewish national redemption.[67]

In Jewish messianism, Kohn found the prime example of a national idea

uttered in religious language. One of his most remarkable and personal publications from this period was dedicated to a radical reevaluation the seventeenth-
century false messiah Sabbatai Tsevi in the context of the Jewish renaissance.
Kohn's bold repositioning of the false messiah—moving him from the margins
of Jewish history and Judaism to the center—seems to have anticipated Gershom Scholem's magnum opus of a generation later. It most likely reflects Shai
Hurwitz's 1909 provocatively favorable historical judgment of the false messiah in *He'atid*.[68] Kohn insisted that Sabbatianism, rather than a nadir in Jewish
history, was a climax: indeed it was "the only moment of the whole Diaspora,
where the Jewish people lived a real life." Drawing thinly veiled comparisons
between Tsevi and Herzl, Kohn depicts Tsevi as a leader who managed to at-
tract many followers because at a time of deep crisis ("when official Judaism
could say no more"), he rekindled the old messianic idea, the desire to overcome the Diaspora and return to the ancestral land, and he promised a national
and religious renewal: "This was a moment of rare intensity in human history.
Had Sabbatai Tsevi died as a martyr [rather than convert to Islam], the moment
of supreme creative power for Judaism in the Diaspora would have come; [Ju-
daism] would have been renewed, would have gained contents, would have created a new religion, as it was at the time of Jesus Christ. The moment of will
[however] was over." Kohn did not even conceal his religious and historiographical agenda: conflating contemporaneous Reform Judaism and Tsevi's bold historic magnitude, he deridingly dubbed the former "*Reförmchen*" (petty reform).
The reform affiliated *Wissenschaft des Judentums* (science of Judaism) failed to
recognize the significance of Sabbatianism because that science was "born in
the time of the shallowest rationalism and for purely rationalistic purposes."[69]

Religion exposes the radically nontraditional, indeed transgressive, nature of
Jewish renewal that Kohn and his fellows envisioned. In Kohn's July 1912 Bar
Kochba lecture "On the Concept of Renewal," he depicted Jewish religious
history as a series of religious renewals, in each of which a religion ceased to
exist in its old form and was replaced by a profoundly redefined one: the covenant, the giving of the Torah, the beginning of rabbinic Judaism, and so on. He
had no qualms about including Jesus of Nazareth in this larger story of eternally
renewing Judaism, and he would also do so repeatedly in the edited volume
Vom Judentum.[70] True to form, Kohn systematically and repeatedly stated the
goal of revolutionizing Judaism, which must eventually result in the emergence
of a new religion.[71]

Though it seemed quite radical at the time, the religious conceptualization
of the Jewish renewal, I would argue, kept Kohn's Zionism "a nationalism of

Figure 1.6 Prague Zionist Student Association, Bar Kochba, February 1913.
Kohn, the chairperson, is in the middle of the first seated row.
Courtesy of the Leo Baeck Institute, New York.

inwardness." At least in hindsight it seems to have counteracted much of the
allure of ethnic nationalism and, arguably, would later facilitate his transition to
advocacy of civic nationalism. After all, the basic dimensions of civic nationalism—its voluntarism and shared laws, which bind a people together—are also
core attributes of religious life. A national renewal imagined as a religious one
could not be biologically determined.[72] Yet ambivalence and skepticism aside,
Kohn and his peers were seeking an authentic, primordial national identity.

Longing for Authentic Nationhood: "When Skepticism Mates with Longing, Mysticism Is Born"[73]

Young Kohn was taken with the works of Henrik Ibsen ("the greatest dramatist
of modern times," one of "the great emancipators of modern times"), and especially with *Peer Gynt*, which remained a point of reference for him throughout his life.[74] Peer Gynt was a man totally committed to being himself, yet he
was tragically clueless about his true identity. He repeatedly claimed that "being
oneself" was man's first duty and prided himself for having, indeed, "[given] up
my love, and power, and honors, simply and solely to be myself."[75] His refusal,
or rather inability, to become a troll (even with the promise of marrying the troll

king's daughter and thus becoming heir to his throne) was a case in point. Yet as the play's very first line indicates—"That's a lie, Peer!!"—his insistence that he remained himself does not capture the whole story. People, and especially the button molder, insist more convincingly, that Peer Gynt, in effect, "up till now [has] *never* been [him]self." *Peer Gynt* is a profound and bold exploration of genuine identities, of how impossible it can be to know oneself and to be oneself, and how easy it can be to confuse being oneself, becoming oneself, and losing oneself. As such, Ibsen's literary masterpiece resonated with Kohn in his pursuit of an authentic identity as a young Central European Zionist.[76]

Indeed, the ever-present drive underlying Kohn's early intellectual explorations and the prewar Zionism of Bar Kochba was the quest for authentic identities: individual, collective, and Jewish. Just as it did in interwar Germany—as shown by Michael Brenner—so the Jewish search for authenticity and wholeness generated the quest for renaissance in prewar Prague.[77] The pursuit of authentic identity was of course a quest born out of a sense that one's Jewish identity was either inauthentic or perceived as such. Zionism, then, was an attempt to patch together an identity for a fragmented self. Bergmann, arguably Bar Kochba's spiritual leader, openly expressed this impetus clearly in a letter to Franz Kafka, his friend and classmate. In the letter Bergmann attempts to explain, yet again, why he became a Zionist. His Zionism was not merely a laughable *idée fixe*, but "a piece (*Stück*) of my life. . . . It is pieced together and patched together from the shreds of my self."[78] His letter to the German philosopher Carl Stumpf expressed a similar sentiment, as Bergmann felt compelled to refute any accusation that there was something dishonest in being both a German philosopher and a Zionist.[79]

For Hans Kohn and his young Jewish friends in Prague, Zionism proposed nation and nationalism as the key concepts needed to understand the Jewish Question. Their Jewish question, however, was the personal one, grounded not in antisemitism and persecution but rather in an inescapable sense of emptiness, fragmentation, and inauthenticity among the highly acculturated young Prague Jews. Nations and nationalism were omnipresent in Kohn's Prague, but it was Zionism that first made him aware of and accountable to the power of nations and nationalism in his own life. The formative nature of this heightened and elevated encounter with the nation via Zionism is the point of departure for Kohn's lifelong struggle with nationalism.

In retrospect, it is clear that Kohn's early Zionist explorations and relentless examination of Zionism's actual essence and goals laid some of the foundations for his later theory of nationalism. Kenneth Wolf has aptly identified—probably based on conversations with Kohn himself—three enduring elements in Kohn's understanding of nationalism, which he received from Buber in prewar Prague: an appreciation of the ethical dimension of nationalism; its potential for reconnecting the modern individual to a community; and its potential to bring greater unity, rather than division, to the world (the sense of a shared nationality as a necessary step toward a sense of a shared humanity).[80] Given the nature of Kohn's later scholarship on nationalism and his statements regarding the formative impact of his experiences as a Jew in prewar Prague, one would expect that his earliest works—all conceptualized and written, delivered in lectures, and published in this particular Zionist framework—would consist of preliminary yet direct and systematic discussions of nations, nationalism, multinational federations, and internationalism. However, this was not the case. None of Kohn's early writings directly addressed nationalism and politics, narrowly defined. His written works, lectures, and correspondence before World War I focused on issues such as theology and gymnastics, neo-idealist philosophy and contemporary literature, and Taoism and mythology. These interests were, in fact, rather typical of Bar Kochba's members in those years, as evidenced by the association's abundant reports and publications.[81]

In other words, though Kohn's Zionist youth in multiethnic Prague certainly informed his developed theory of nationalism, if there was a line leading from the one to the other, it was neither straight nor obvious. Understanding Kohn's Bar Kochba Zionism both in the context of late-Habsburg nationalism and in the context of his emerging theory of nationalism requires identifying the concepts of authentic nationalism underlying Bar Kochba's activities and Kohn's early writings, even when these claimed to address other topics—ranging from gymnastics to Asian philosophy and contemporaneous European poetry. In all of these explorations, regardless of their subject matter, the association's members worked out the essences of their Zionism and the nature of nationalism.

Land or Territory

Land was a central concept across the spectrum of Zionist thought. Herzl's political Zionism was founded on the idea of Jewish homeland, be it a return to the ancestral land, Palestine or the Land of Israel, or a creation of a safe haven for Jews elsewhere, as suggested by the Uganda Proposal of 1903. Israel Zangwill and the Territorialists had radicalized the centrality of the land so as to transcend Zionism altogether and challenge it from without, coming to advocate the creation of a Jewish national home outside Palestine. Mainstream Zionists consistently claimed the Promised Land—all or part of it—based on historical rights. Religious

Zionists added an openly theological (theopolitical, or desecularized) dimension to the return to the Promised Land, and the labor Zionist followers of A. D. Gordon focused their ideology not so much on the return to the Promised or Ancestral Land as on the return of the overly urbanized diasporic Jews to a life of labor on the land—Boaz Neumann, for instance, has recently deepened our understanding of the centrality of this early Zionist desire to be one with the land.[82]

Kohn and his fellow Bar Kochba Zionists may have carried over into their concept of land, or national territory, the lessons learned from the aggressive practices of both Czech and German "ethnonational entrepreneurs" in claiming territory for their respective nations. Scholars have argued that Bar Kochba Zionists rejected this paradigm of national lands. Some suggest that Bar Kochbalism replaced physical territories with spiritual ones, while others claim that they had already envisioned their Zionism along the lines of nonterritorial national autonomies under a truly multinational federation.[83] A fair exploration of Bar Kochba's prolific document trail, however, reveals an ambivalence regarding territoriality.

Bar Kochba's statutes—enshrined long before Kohn joined the association—spelled out its three purposes, and one was "the encouragement of lawfully secured colonization of Palestine through Jews (Zionism)."[84] The association's members, then, took for granted the geographic imperative of classic political Zionism. From other documents, more indicative of the views of Kohn and others in 1908-14, three general approaches to the concept of national soil emerge: the first sees the return to the national soil as transformative, and hence as vital for the renewal of Judaism; the second defines the ancestral land as oriental; and the third challenges the myth of national soil, and questions the absolute necessity of national soil for full national life.

Herzl and his followers viewed the national land as a safe haven for persecuted Jews and probably also as a place where Jews could manage their own affairs. But for Buberian Zionists, the land created a people. Theirs, it seems, was an even bolder vision of individual and national transformation by the national soil. As long as "he is a member of a people that leads a secure, free, and full life on its own soil," Buber told the Prague students in his second address to them (in April 1910), the individual does not need to struggle with his national belonging. It was the rootlessness in the Diaspora that rendered the Jew's national bonds problematic. The diasporic Jew was not on his soil, and the soil that he was on was ostensibly not his. The primary function of the national soil, it followed, was to create a people and a new Jewish type. The union between the People of Israel and the Land of Israel would thus transform both—but of course the greater miracle would be the transformation of the diasporic Jew (*Golusjude*) into an elemental Jew (*Urjude*). True to form, Buber concluded that the Jewish renaissance could "only be accomplished on the ground of the homeland; the soul will be rejuvenated only where it originated from."[85]

A few months earlier, in the winter of 1909-10, Bar Kochba members had expressed the same conviction following a presentation by the founders of the Zionist art school Bezalel in Jerusalem. The visitors brought with them new Jewish art, created in and inspired by Palestine, which they presented to the young Prague Zionists as a beautiful testament to the allegedly transformative qualities of living on one's land. The diasporic Jew, the association's activity report proclaimed, had been "cured"; he overcame his tragic fragmentation and "became whole."[86] A Jewish cultural and aesthetic renewal, the report concluded, could take place "only in Palestine, where Jews are true to their roots." Buber's third address on Judaism to the members of Bar Kochba, in December 1910 ("Die Erneuerung des Judentums" [Renewal of Judaism]), imagined—in a language reminiscent of the rhetoric of eugenics—the role of the elemental Jews of Palestine in the renewal of Judaism, constituting "a nucleus (*Kernvolk*) of a healthy Jewish people."[87] Kohn expressed the same understanding in his June 1912 lecture "Über den Begriff der 'Erneuerung' des Judentums und unsere Gegenwart" (On the concept of the renewal of Judaism and our present), in which he insisted that Zionists "have to work in Palestine, so that the renewal would not be shattered but . . . find grounds over there, in freedom, and reside in our hearts."[88]

Benzion Mossinson's 1911 lecture to the members of Bar Kochba on "Palestine in Jewish History and Literature" expanded on this general notion of the transformative role of the national soil in the Jewish future. He offered the Prague students a Jewish history that had been ruled by geographic determinism since time immemorial. From Abraham to the present, from history to theology, all seemed determined by the geographic location of the Jewish people. The summary of the talk in the association's activity report stated unequivocally and as a matter of course that diasporic Jews never felt autochthonous in the respective lands.[89]

Integrationist Jews in Central and Western Europe took great pride in their Europeanness and Western cultural identity. It was in this context that Buber and the young Bar Kochba Zionists speculated about the orientality of the Jewish homeland. Provocatively yet sincerely, they stated that the Jew was and would always remain an oriental. Their denied, repressed, and ultimately forgotten origin would render the full integration into the surrounding society of even the most acculturated Jews an impossibility. Buber's three Bar Kochba addresses on Judaism spelled this out, layer after layer. In his first address, he noted that "the land [the Western Jew] lives in, whose nature encompasses him and molds his senses" doesn't belong to him. However, his tragedy is not only his rootlessness, but also his bond—even if forgotten or repressed—to the "homeland of his blood," Palestine.[90] In the second and third addresses, the "homeland of his blood" was given a location. That was in the orient, and hence the Western Jew was an oriental among occidentals. The national soil, according to this address, remained formative in the composition of the Jew.

In "Der Geist des Orients" (The spirit of the orient), Kohn's contribution to *Vom Judentum*, he delineated the path to a Jewish *Volksgemeinschaft* (an ethnic people's community) and to a Jewish renaissance, via the orient. Writing on behalf of a generation of young Zionists, he proclaimed that "[we] now carry within us the awareness of our kinship to the cultural entity of the orient" and also the knowledge that "the great collision of East and West is fast approaching." With youthful enthusiasm, he declared: "We Jews lacked living and practical order for hundreds of years. Only where our roots lie can we regain it: in the orient. There we will again become pure vessels of divine will, [standing] in awe of one another and boldly before God."[91]

Kohn's piece bears many similarities to Buber's speech "Der Geist des Orients und das Judentum" ("The Spirit of the Orient and Judaism"), given only a few months earlier.[92] His notion of a moribund occident is obviously reminiscent of a later, more famous (or rather infamous) postliberal text—namely, Oswald Spengler's *Decline of the West* (1918-23). Kohn's piece offered a very telling set of essentialized polarities: the West is plan and theory, while the East is deed and action; the West is "fragmentary and schematic," while the East is organic wholeness; the West attempts to reduce all to reason, while the East fearlessly embraces the ultimately irrational nature of life; the West is comfort and calculated concession, while the East lives dangerously and to the full; the occidental's life runs its course "indifferent and barren, restless and futile, without elevation or higher purpose," while the oriental is aware of his essence and purpose. "For the East," Kohn proclaimed, "the heart of the world is not located within the single individual, but within the community. There, the individual found his natural soil, his perpetuity, and eternity."[93] He constructed an ideal East in contrast to the ever-present Westernized (or de-orientalized) dimension of Jewish integration into Central Europe.[94] At the same time, these notions of East and West were undoubtedly influenced also by European orientalism and postliberal and sharply antiliberal schools of thought in Central Europe. Kohn's statements clearly indicated a broader phenomenon, which Paul Mendes-Flohr aptly called "orientalism and the aesthetics of Jewish self-affirmation."[95] However, even Kohn's friend Bergmann felt that Kohn's anti-occidentalism went too far, to the detriment of the anthology *Vom Judentum*—though Bergmann may have exaggerated when he claimed that "no one but Kohn identified with Buber's linking of Judaism and the spirit of the orient, and with the juxtaposition to the European spirit."[96]

While much of the essentializing mythology of the national soil seems to have come from without—Buber, Boris Schatz, and Berthold Feiwel (a prominent Zionist leader of the older guard)—the members of Bar Kochba emulated and even developed some of these notions. However, fairly soon they also started challenging the myth of the national soil: Are Jews really rootless in the Diaspora? Is Jewish territory, or national soil, necessary for cultural Zionists? Couldn't the national home be a spiritual and cultural one? Couldn't rootlessness be brought to Palestine too?

Bergmann's article "On the Meaning of the Hebrew Language to the Jewish Youth," which appeared in *Zionistische Briefe*, openly assumed that Jews would never achieve geographic unity and that a real "Ingathering of Exiles" —a biblical promise whose secularized version became a pillar of Zionist ideology—would never occur. Since that was the case, Hebrew, the language of the Jewish past, could help to create "a 'spiritual home' by allowing for a unified culture between the [Jews of the cultural center] in the homeland, and the Jews who remained among foreign cultures."[97] Interestingly enough, Bergmann— who seems to have advocated channeling the idea of national soil into the idea of language as "a spiritual home" in language or culture—was also the one Bar Kochba member who actually visited Palestine. After his return, in the winter of 1910-11, he shared with other members of the association his impressions of Palestine, both "positive and negative."[98]

In his article "Weltanschauung und Partei" (Ideology and party), published in *Zionistische Briefe*, Siegmund Katznelson too expressed this subsuming of "national soil" into "spiritual home in culture." Shifting his gaze from the "national soil," Katznelson talked about the inner Diaspora, which could exist even in Palestine and could be overcome even in Prague. Not only the homeland but also the Diaspora was de-territorialized.[99] Nathan Birnbaum's contribution to *Vom Judentum* (titled "Das Erwachen der jüdischen Seele" [The awakening of the Jewish soul]) completely refuted the territorial imperative:

Territory is likely to remain the most practical and the safest foundation for national cultures, for a long, long while. But it becomes obvious that increasingly—very slowly, but surely—they [national cultures] free themselves of the absolute necessity of large, contiguous territories. The rootedness (*Bodenständigkeit*) of the territory is needed less and less, and so their original and truly decisive base—their particular locality—grows advantageous. Modern transportation becomes increasingly capable of merging native, local cells of the [respective] culture into a joint nationwide cultural work. And it is precisely the Jews who are already most experienced in this respect. Everything points to this sort of inter-territorial united culture.[100]

In 1912 Kohn joined those who were more skeptical of the transformative qualities of the national soil. He questioned the rootlessness paradigm and insisted that Jews also lived harmonious lives in nature in the Diaspora—not only in Palestine—using the early Hasidim as his prime example.[101] Kohn's definition of Zionism as "*unsere Heimat im Geist*" (our homeland in spirit), in an article about Jewish philosophers,[102] is remarkably similar to the notion of metaphysical nationalism Jewish readers found in Fichte's *Addresses to the German Nation*: "The German people has no territory! A solitary spirit encircles this people, the German people, consisting of a purely mental inwardness and a thirst for a reality, a postulate of the future! To the metaphysical people, the German people, by means of its entire development and in history, there has fallen this highest metaphysical lot, this highest world-historical honor existing as a metaphysical inwardness, of creating out of the purely mental national concept a national soil, a territory, thereby producing out of the thought an entity."[103]

In a similar vein, Kohn wrote to Buber about the necessity of keeping Bar Kochba metaphysical in times when the Zionism of some of its newer members became more soil-driven.[104] Weltsch stated the idea most clearly when he proclaimed that they simply "reached the conviction that the meaning of our efforts cannot be settling a few people, or even a people, so that they will externally resemble other nations."[105]

Blood or Race

Blood, race, and racial self-depiction have recently drawn a lot of attention in Jewish historiography.[106] The provocative, even iconoclastic, appeal of the topic seems obvious: Jews have been the victims of racial ideologies, policies, and regimes. What, then, does it mean that Jews were some of the most engaged in modern racial thought? What does it mean—to quote Gil Anidjar—that "race enslaved, but it also emancipated; it stigmatized, but it also became a medium of self-understanding, indeed, an almost indispensable instrument of thought?"[107] The centrality of the concept of blood for the Bar Kochba members cannot be denied or dismissed. But they interpreted the concept in many different ways.

While some have taken blood at face value and concluded that Bar Kochba's ideology represented a protofascist Jewish variation of Central European Volkism, most had interpreted the blood rhetoric more benignly.[108] A decade later, Franz Rosenzweig would also celebrate the authenticity of a Jewish nationalism defined by blood: "The community of the same blood alone feels even today the guarantee of its eternity running warmly through its veins." Yet the philosopher, and arguably Kohn's circle, celebrated Jewish blood nationalism as a "spiritual" alternative to the ubiquitous non-Jewish soil nationalism: other nations "cannot be satisfied with a community made up of the same blood; they put forth their roots into the night of the earth . . . and appropriate from its permanence a guarantee of their own permanence. Their will to eternity clings to the soil and to the soil's dominion, the territory." Rosenzweig's "blood," then, meant above all "not soil."[109] In their correspondence, activities, and especially publications, Kohn and other Bar Kochba members expressed a similar ambivalence about the mythology of blood. Though the idea of blood is prominent in their writings and activities, they generally rejected both race theory and any notion of racial hierarchy.

In spite of the patent proximity of the concepts of blood and race, it seems Kohn and his cohort used blood as a signifier of one's own primordial traits, which were beyond one's choice, control, or even comprehension. If blood was a mysterious inward-looking prism, race was a cold scientific category that was measured from without. Hence, race was approached with much greater caution, though not necessarily completely and unanimously rejected. Jews and Zionists, after all, did participate in the racial discourse of their time and place (which was never limited to protofascists but also included socialists and self-proclaimed liberals). Jewish scholars took it as a Jew's duty "to respond to the ongoing debate about 'the Jewish Race' and to racial antisemitism by producing scientific studies of their own."[110] The young Zionists of Bar Kochba understood their Jewish calling differently: they were lured by the concept of blood but rather repelled by that of race. Both Kohn (in his introduction to *Vom Judentum*) and Weltsch (in an article titled "Concerning Racial Theory") explicitly rejected racial categories and race theory.[111] It is fascinating to see, however, that both proclaimed blood as the determining factor in one's life.

On the evening of January 20, 1909, Buber gave a lecture to the members of Bar Kochba that would become known as his first address on Judaism. Before

Buber took the stage, the poet Hugo Salus recited his "Das Lied des Blutes" (Song of blood):[112]

> You, brother in darkness, what draws me to you?
> And what draws you, I feel it, to me too?
> You do not know me, nor do I know you,
> Yet in our hearts something speaks:
> He is your brother! Love him!
>
> And this cannot be anything from yesterday or today,
> Thus I could have been neither victor nor prey!
> Different from friendship and love and loyalty,
> From the primeval beginning and yet new again:
> Your blood and my blood are brothers!
>
> Five thousand years ago—reflect on that!
> My ancestor and yours carried the yoke of slaves!
> And three thousand years in torment and distress,
> Don't you think anymore? Your ancestor offered
> Mine the drink of love!
>
> Brother, how darkly rushes the blood of my heart!
> I feel it, like your ear eavesdrops on my whisper,
> And we both hear the same song,
> As back then, when an ancestor kneeled by another:
> A God loomed over both from heaven!
>
> And the storm blows away, the ember goes out
> And pain becomes pleasure, yet blood remains blood!
> And a drop in me, and a drop in you,
> Know: we are brothers,
> Brothers coming from the same darkness.[113]

Blood here refers to ethnic bonds beyond one's choice, inherited traits and sensibilities beyond one's understanding, and inherited attraction even against one's will. But somehow (not unlike religious devotion), acknowledging blood and succumbing to it is an act of will. Salus's blood, however, is dark, frightening, and oddly transgressive. Its dream is a dream of darkness, not light. Its longing is for slavery, not freedom. Its beauty is abject, and its desire incestuous.

Buber's address—which transformed Kohn and his friends into devoted disciples—continued where Salus's poem ended. The address, "The Meaning of

Judaism," also focused on the concept of blood: as an inner component of the self and as a Jewish nature (*Innerlichkeit*), standing in contrast to European or Western nurture (*Umwelt*). Blood was one's inheritance from previous generations (*das grosse Erbe der Zeiten*). Blood created the inborn national archetype (*nationales Urbild*). Through thousands of years of (alleged) rootlessness in their Diaspora, the Jews' alternative roots were in blood. Seen from the other angle, it was this very blood that kept even the most acculturated Jew from ever becoming, or being perceived as, native anywhere in the diaspora. It was the blood that generated a "split, a duality, a tension (*Zwiespältigkeit*) in the Jewish soul" between Jewish nature and European nurture.[114] Blood was slightly less central yet still present in Buber's third address, "Renewal of Judaism," where it was not so much an anchor to the national past as a tie to the future (*das Blut verbürgte es und Gottes Herz verbürgte es*).[115]

The Jewish students in Bar Kochba—including Kohn—were captivated by the subversive allure of this blood rhetoric. Blood was subversive because it countered liberal integrationist aspirations and rational individualism. After Buber's addresses, the rhetorical concept was integrated more fully into their activities and publications. For example, the reader is hard pressed to find a single essay among the twenty-eight collected in *Vom Judentum* that does not allude to blood in some form. A few additional examples will suffice: Discussing the Jews' history in Bar Kochba's periodical, Willy Stein stressed that their historical consciousness was generated by nothing less than "invigorating pulses of [their] blood (*kräftigende Blutswellen pulsen*)."[116] And when Weltsch published "A Letter to a Jewish High School Graduate," he reminded the young addressee that—with all due respect to one's nurture—his blood remained the determining factor: "*Dein Blut bestimmt.*"[117] The most macabre illustration of this sanguinary rhetoric was a collection of Jewish blood poems titled "Stimmen des Blutes" (Voices of the blood) in Bar Kochba's *Zionistische Briefe*. The collection included Salus's "Song of Blood" as well as Richard Beer-Hofman's "Schlaflied an Mirjam" (Lullaby for Miriam) and Stefan Zweig's "Singendes Blut" (The singing blood).[118] Even Kohn's essay "Der Geist des Orients" (Spirit of the orient) succumbed to the language of blood: "We are Jews today. Jews in our ancestry (*Abstammung*), in our history, in our thought and emotions, determined by the factor of blood."[119]

At least some members of Bar Kochba were genuinely interested in Jewish race theory, among them Leo Hermann and Oskar Epstein (the association's chairman for the academic year 1909-10). During the winter semester of 1910-11, Bar Kochba hosted a talk by one of the greatest Jewish race theoreticians of the day, Ignaz Zollschan, "Kulturwert der jüdischen Rasse" (The cultural value of the Jewish race), which the association's activity report hailed for adding scientific basis to Bar Kochba's aspirations.[120] The association had addressed Zollschan's work even prior to his visit.[121] In its association Epstein published a two-part article titled "Was bedeutet die Rasse für uns?" (What does race mean for us?), which was primarily a review of Zollschan's book *The Race Problem*. Epstein tried to walk the line between two claims: on the one hand, he assumed the existence of races, which shaped both Jewish history and the life of the Jewish individual, and on the other hand, he refuted race science altogether—or at least race science as it was then known—pointing to its glaring cultural biases. The most interesting element in Epstein's article was his Lamarckian propensity to see race as changing, the outcome of long historical processes of the collective. Rather than determining history and society, in Epstein's eyes, race was shaped by social and historical forces.[122]

The best articulated discussion of racial theory that emerged from Bar Kochba in those years was Weltsch's article "Concerning Racial Theory," published in 1913 in the main international publication of the Zionist movement, *Die Welt*:

> I have an insurmountable mistrust of any attempt to trace back an intellectual or spiritual disposition to material causes; the same holds true for all racial theories, which derive consciousness from anthropological facts and thereby seek to ground consciousness in natural science. . . . It was one of the most pathetic errors of an age, worshiping natural science as its false god, to seek to explain the wonder of the human spirit by means of Zoology. . . . Zionism is not something that can be explained "scientifically." We know that Judaism lives in us; this knowledge is the most powerful proof of Judaism's hold. . . . Zionism is not science, it is a way of life; it does not require knowledge, but spirit; it is above all not about cognition, but about will. . . . The great works of mankind have all been the product of the spirit, not the result of materialist developments. In the realization of such great works, such as the renewal of Jewry, one requires the powerful force of an idea. . . . Zionism is the faith in the spirit that exists in us. Zionism is enthusiasm.[123]

Beyond flatly rejecting the scientific basis of any racial theories, Weltsch presented them—in a voice that was mature beyond his twenty-two years—as diametrically opposed to the Zionist spirit. Kohn occasionally praised a recent work of biblical studies for its "racial-psychological perspective," but on the whole he remained immune to racial theory.[124] As a matter of fact, his words in the introduction to *Vom Judentum*, which reiterated his understanding of Zionism as a life-reform movement, were almost identical to Weltsch's: "Zionism is not science. It is not a logical conceptual system. It has nothing to do with race theories or definitions of nationalities. It is impossible to win someone over to Zionism through arguments, and all of the discoveries of race biological or sociological research leave us cold. Zionism lies in a completely different plane of being. It is not science, but life."[125]

National Culture versus Assimilation: Lordship and Bondage

The concept of national culture, one would assume, should have been the least contested among spiritual cultural Zionists such as Buber, Kohn, and the other members of Bar Kochba. In addition, at least at first glance, the concept raises hardly any ethical or political concerns—compared, say, to race or nationalist appropriation of territories. Yet in discussions of national culture, contradictions of cultural Zionism in Central Europe and the West became most evident, arguably verging on the absurd: Central European cultural Zionists advocated the reversal of acculturation, a certain retreat from the surrounding culture, but they did so using the German language and German (and often Christian) cultural references. Indeed, their entire concept of nationalism and of what authentic national culture looked like was unambiguously borrowed from Germans and Czechs. Scholars have long explored the inner contradictions of Zionist cultural production in Central Europe.[126]

If we take a closer look, we will see that the constructed aspect of the clear boundaries of national cultures had already become evident to Kohn and his peers in Bar Kochba. That did not render the need of a Jewish cultural revival any less urgent, but it did make them develop a more sophisticated concept of assimilation than the majority of Zionists had. The general understanding of assimilation and its relationship to Jewish national culture and identity that Kohn shared with several other followers of Buber could be summarized in the following arguments: First, Zionism and assimilation are opposites, but even when Zionism aspires to return to the orient, it does not intend to build a fence around Jews or Judaism. Second, Zionism is committed to the affirmation of Jewishness and of Jewish distinctiveness. Zionists thus must engage with their Jewish cultural legacy and make it their own. This, however, does not have to mean a withdrawal from the non-Jewish cultural world around them. Indeed, the very idea of such a withdrawal is quite impracticable. Third, Zionism—as an affirmation of Jewish distinctiveness—allows for more sincere participation in the surrounding, non-Jewish, culture. It not only deepens Jewish participation in the life of the mind but also broadens it beyond participation in liberal circles. The opposite of cultural ghettoization, Jewish self-affirmation, allows the modern Jew greater openness in his exploration of the non-Jewish world. Assured of his Jewish commitments, the Zionist may more freely discover Asian religions and even reevaluate Jesus of Nazareth. Fourth and last, assimilation is the denial of Jewish essence. It is thus a matter not of cultural exposure but rather of intent. But as Ahad Ha'am has stated, political Zionism could be quite ineffective at combating assimilation. Much worse, Herzl's political Zionism may be seen as inherently assimilationist if, wittingly or unwittingly, it denies or rejects Jewish distinctiveness.

Kohn's ambivalence about cultural identities is best exposed by highlighting three distinct approaches to the challenge of national culture and assimilation: first, more or less banal manifestations of cultural patriotism and the notion of an endangered national culture; second, multiple unorthodox redefinitions of assimilation; and finally, the multiple ways Kohn and his circle challenged the notion of the purity and independence of national cultures, and thus put the discussion of cultural identity and assimilation on an entirely new level.

In Bar Kochba's publications and activity reports, Jewish culture (broadly defined) and assimilation clearly stand out as the association's main concerns.[127] The association held countless events related to the nature of cultural self-assertion and feelings of patriotism toward one's endangered culture. The most readily available reservoir of authentic Jewish folklore came from Yiddish-speaking Eastern European Jews, and members of the student association not only read and learned Yiddish literature, in German translation, but they also organized many Eastern European evenings. In those festive events, Eastern European Jewish performers would recite popular tales or shorter works of Yiddish literature, followed by German translations, and later the group would sing Yiddish folk songs (transliterated Yiddish lyrics circulated ahead of time, since most of the Prague students could not read Yiddish).[128]

In an otherwise highly unorthodox essay in *Vom Judentum*, the Zionist leader and historian Adolf Böhm declared quite simply that Zionism is the act of "turning away from assimilation (*die Abkehr von der Assimilation*)."[129] Members of Bar Kochba spelled out an even starker juxtaposition of Zionism and assimilation. Whereas Zionism was commitment to Jewish renewal, stated Katznelson, assimilation was "the deliberate objective of a life not according to Jewish content." As such, the two are diametrically opposed. For Weltsch, assimilation meant first of all living a lie, whereas Zionism was the return to honesty ("the [assimilated] Jew desires the pretense of life. He becomes an actor, a faker, a liar"). And Ernst Klinger saw a collision between Jewish *Kultur* (Zionism) and non-Jewish *Zivilisation* (assimilation).[130] Feiwel developed these same old notions in a January 18, 1910, lecture to the members of Bar Kochba on "The Impact of the New Jewish Movement on Judaism." In that rather uninspired talk, he attempted to draw an allegorical mental map of the Jewish world, with spiritual Zionists at its core and converts and assimilationists on the margins. The Jewish cosmopolitan may not be a problem, Feiwel stated, but cosmopolitanism constituted a real danger.[131] Integrationist assimilation was also presented as a threat in Stein's discussion of the battlegrounds of Jewish historiography between the Wissenschaft des Judentums and the Zionists. The paradigm was that of an irreconcilable tug of war between Jewish liberals and nationalists over the proper framing of Jewish knowledge. Zionists, it seemed to Stein, needed to combat the bias of many decades of the science, which ostensibly presented Judaism as a historical relic rather than as a living thing, a vibrantly evolving people.[132] Kohn also presented himself as a patriotic member of an endangered Jewish culture. He did so, for example, in an October 1912 article on Chinese philosophers, which he began by asserting that the similarity between Jewish and Chinese thought is not in the ostensibly shared ideas and patterns of thought but more in the shared threat of being intellectually, spiritually, and culturally overrun by the modern, rationalistic, secular, and utilitarian civilization of the West. In both the Chinese and Jewish cases, this calamity unfolds due to assimilation, or people's wrongheaded willingness to culturally conform with the modern West. As mentioned above, for Kohn the alternative was not returning to old tradition but rather its radical renewal.[133] This rejection of Westernization is central to Kohn's prewar Zionism. By claiming a Jewish oriental primordiality grounded in the blood, Kohn and his friends rejected the claims of a singular occidental modernity, which they saw as threatening Judaism.

However, at the same time, these cultural Zionists also expressed a more complex and more nuanced understanding of the term "assimilation." Indeed, they contested its very meaning. Bergmann's "Über die Bedeutung des Hebräischen für die jüdische Jugend" (The meaning of Hebrew for the Jewish youth) distinguished between external and internal assimilations. According to Bergmann, external assimilation refers to the great number of Jews who drift away not only from Judaism but also from any Jewish identification; internal assimilation, in contrast, refers to those who identify themselves as proud, even national, Jews yet are ignorant of any Jewish knowledge. The dichotomy of assimilation versus Zionism thus collapses, as Zionists acknowledge the impact of assimilation even in their own camp.[134] In his contribution to *Vom Judentum*, Moritz Goldstein blurred the distinction between assimilation and Zionism even more.

"If we draw today from Europe the conclusion simply to become a nation like all others and nothing more," he wrote, "then our Zionism constitutes a terrible assimilation into this Europe—a most dangerous one, because we commit it naïvely and unconsciously."[135] Following Ahad Ha'am's critique of Herzl, Goldstein raises the alarming prospect of political Zionism becoming assimilation on a national scale.

Kohn's questioning of the Zionist-assimilationist dichotomy led him down a different path: while presenting the goal of Jewish revival in contrast to Jewish assimilation, he was eager to trace the often unnoticed or denied Jewish quality that may exist within assimilation and learn Jewish lessons from more conflicted Jewish intellectuals, including some of the most conspicuously assimilated ones. Kohn's critical appreciation of Heinrich Heine, Jakob Wassermann, Arthur Schnitzler, and probably even Otto Weininger can be traced back to his Bar Kochba days, and all of them would remain influences on Kohn's reflections on the Jewish Question throughout his life. Kohn favorably reviewed Schnitzler's 1908 novel *The Road into the Open*, which depicted the predicament of young Jews and other liminal Viennese in a disintegrating society that seemed to be closing in on them. Indeed, it is the assimilated Jews in the novel who best articulate the general crisis of the time. The entire Viennese society experiences the crisis, but, in the words of John Toews, "it is the Jews who theorize, politically and philosophically, the meaning of . . . homelessness, the . . . inability to produce oneself objectively in art or society as a solid, essential identity, and the ambivalence of 'freedom' in a world without anchors where all are strangers within their own homeland."[136] Though Schnitzler is often assumed to have had his the assimilationist protagonist, Heinrich Bermann, serve as his alter ego, Kohn's review stresses that the book's strength is Schnitzler's complete identification with all its tormented figures, assimilated and Zionist alike. "Schnitzler has some of his flesh and blood in all of the Viennese Jews," Kohn wrote. "He endows them all with a quiet touch of the pain, because he has too felt all of their pain. And whatever the position regarding the Jewish question, all are marked by rootlessness; all know they are homeless—even the assimilationist. . . . They all seek a way out of this fragmentation, also the young Zionist."[137] Kohn identified with Schnitzler's meta-ideological empathy. Though Kohn's review insisted that the Zionism of the protagonist Leo would be "a road into the open," note how similar rhetoric of Kohn's (and Buber's) personal Jewish Question is to the words in which the character Bermann rejects the Zionist formula: "Maybe there really are people who have to move to Jerusalem. . . . I'm just afraid that many who arrive at their imagined goal would only find themselves more lost than before. I don't believe at all that such journeys to free-dom can even be taken together, since the roads to our destination do not run through the outside world, but lie within ourselves. It's up to each person to find his own inner way."[138]

Kohn's review encouraged his fellow Zionists to learn a lesson in home-lessness from assimilationists. According to Kohn, they are key participants in the greater Jewish renewal, even against their will. He was similarly impressed with Jakob Wassermann's work in general, and particularly with the discussion of assimilation in Wassermann's 1910 booklet titled *Der Literat; oder, Mythos und Persönlichkeit* (Man of letters; or, myth and character). In his review of the work for the Zionist *Selbstwehr*, Kohn emphasized the notion that truly cre-ative people are always grounded in their community.[139] Kohn even included in *Vom Judentum* the pertinent chapter of Wassermann's booklet—a chapter that included this passage on assimilation: "We know them, dear friend, and are ag-onized by them, by thousands of the so-called modern Jews, who gnaw at all foundations because they themselves are without foundation; those who dis-card today what they conquered just yesterday; those who vilify today what they loved just yesterday; those for whom betrayal is a desire, dishonor is a thing of beauty, and negation is a goal."[140]

Yet Wassermann was never a Zionist. As Gershon Shaked has shown, he is interesting precisely because he defies the dichotomous categories of assimila-tion and Jewish self-affirmation. Yet he shares the assessment of assimilation of the proponents of a Jewish renewal—as the severing of ties to one's community, assimilation constitutes a major problem for Jewish creativity.[141] Bar Kochba's most unlikely interlocutor in this regard was Otto Weininger—the most noto-rious, pathological, and occasionally brilliant, exemplar of Jewish self-hatred. Bergmann named Weininger as a major inspiration for the Prague Zionists, and Epstein even delivered two talks on Weininger in the winter of 1910-11, "Buber and Weininger" and "Weininger and the Jewish Ethic."[142] Kohn would write about Weininger only years later, but Weininger's metaphysical critique of contemporaneous Jews, which focused on the accusation that "the Jew be-lieves in nothing, either within himself or outside,"[143] strikingly resembles (and may have directly influenced) many of Kohn's early writings. Precisely because Kohn was committed to Jewish self-affirmation, he could not have overlooked Weininger's self-negating challenge. Indeed, Paul Mendes-Flohr has already shown that Buber—as he was writing his three addresses on Judaism—was con-sulting Weininger's writing, including the assertion "that Judaism is utterly be-reft of any competence for mysticism or religious mystery."[144]

Similarly, Kohn and his fellow Zionists saw problems in the very notion of a distinct national culture. Buber's first address to the members of Bar Kochba—which was supposed to examine the question of assimilation—ended up offering a telling definition of Jewish cultural identity by discussing that which is beyond culture (namely, blood). Buber pointed to a schism in the Jewish condition, in which the Jew is torn between two inner forces: his Jewish origin (his blood) and his non-Jewish cultural environment: "Neither the land he lives in, whose nature encompasses him and molds his senses, nor the language he speaks, which colors his thinking, nor the way of life in which he participates and which, in turn, shapes his action, belongs to the community of his blood; they belong instead to another community. The world of constant elements and the world of substance are, for him, rent apart. He does not see his substance unfold before him in his environment; it has been banished into deep loneliness, and is embodied for him in only one aspect: his origin."[145]

It is easy for the Jew in the Diaspora, especially in the modern West, to forget about the existence of the blood and hence about this inner schism, but "in the stillest of hours when we sense the ineffable, we become aware of a deep schism in our existence. . . . [T]he insight that the blood is the creative force in our life has not yet become a living, integral part of us. To attain unity out of division we must become aware of the significance of this blood within us. . . . We must come to a decision; we must establish a balance of powers within us."[146] Those attending the address were led to believe that Buber would ask them to follow their blood—the world within them—and achieve unity by discarding the world around them. However, it was not the choice that Buber advocated:

> Choice does not mean that one must expel, relinquish, or overcome the one or the other; it would be senseless, for instance, to try to shed the culture of the world about us, a culture that, in the final analysis, has been assimilated by the innermost forces of our blood, and has become an integral part of ourselves. We need to be conscious of the fact *that we are a cultural admixture*, in a more poignant sense than any other people. We do not, however, want to be the slaves of this admixture, but its masters. Choice means deciding what should have supremacy, what should be the dominant in us and what the dominated.[147]

Neither Kohn nor Buber, then, ever entertained the idea of national cultural purity. Their Jewish renewal was always conceived of as a balanced cultural synthesis, because national cultures in general are amalgams. Cultural purity is thus neither attainable nor desirable: "What matters for the Jew is . . . that he purify himself from the dross of foreign rule, and that he find his way from division to unity."[148]

Bar Kochba's own Bergmann expressed with even greater clarity similar notions about the essence of Jewish national culture in an article, which may have predated Buber's address: "We should think of this unfolding of the Jewish peculiar character (*Eigenart*) as a great synthesis between the Jewish spirit and European culture. Both have to work together, to complement one another, to grow into each other. The fresh air of modern Jewish creativity will fill the abstract, insubstantial (*wesenlos*) and false cosmopolitanism of the emancipated Jews, and rejuvenate fossilized Judaism through the influences created by others."[149]

If Buber merely accepted that the Jew would always remain "a cultural admixture," Bergmann has turned that view into a normative statement. The Jew aspires to a Jewish peculiar character (*Eigenart*) that, by definition, has to be a cultural synthesis. Kohn and his fellow members of Bar Kochba never aspired to a complete retreat from the culture around them–rather, they sought a better synthesis with it. The intent was not to narrow their Jewish horizons but to broaden them much further. It is precisely in this context that we should understand their exploration of Asian philosophies: their heightened Jewish sensibility allowed them to develop spiritually and intellectually beyond the confines of Europe.

The final, and most striking, text that Kohn included in *Vom Judentum* is Gustav Landauer's essay "Sind das Ketzergedanken?" (Are these heretical thoughts?). This essay has taken Buber's understanding of Jewish national culture quite a few steps further: Buber accepts that "it would be senseless . . . to try to shed the culture of the world about us," which has long "become an integral part of ourselves," but he insists that Jewish blood would be dominant over that culture. However, Landauer flatly rejects any superiority.[150] Furthermore, where Buber sees the burden of schism, Landauer sees the blessing of a "multifarious unity":

> The mother tongue of some of my offspring will perhaps be Hebrew, perhaps; it
> does not affect me. My language and the language of my children is German. I
> feel my Judaism in the expressions of my face, in my gait, in my facial features, and
> all these signs assure me that Judaism is alive in everything that I am and do. . . .
> [T]he expressions "German Jew" or "Russian Jew" sound odd to me, just as would
> the terms "Jewish German" or "Jewish Russian." The relationship indicated by
> these terms is not one of dependency and cannot be ascribed by means of an

adjective modifying a noun. I take my fate as it is, and live accordingly: my being a Jew and a German at the same time does not do me any harm, but actually a lot of good, just as two brothers . . . are loved by their mother—not in the same way but with equal intensity. . . . I experience this strange and yet intimate unity in duality within myself as something precious and do not distinguish one element of this relationship within myself as primary and the other, secondary. I have never felt the need to simplify myself or to create an artificial unity by way of denial; I accept my complexity and hope to be an even more multifarious unity than I am now aware of.

. . . Perhaps one day things would develop so that our Jewishness would grow and crush our Germandom or our Russianness; perhaps Hebrew Judaism would come and destroy Yiddish Judaism. But whoever acknowledges himself to himself; whoever senses in his diversity both his singularity and his mission for humanity— could he wish to bring that about? . . . The [gentile] nations have drawn political boundaries around themselves and have neighbors beyond their borders who are their enemies; the Jewish nation has its neighbors in its own breast.[151]

Landauer's "heretical thoughts" are ultimately not unrelated to Homi Bhabha's notion of hybridity half a century later. Kohn was not enthusiastic about including Landauer's piece in *Vom Judentum*, yet it does frame the broader discussions of national culture and assimilation in which Kohn participated in the prewar years.[152] Buber, Bergmann, and Landauer made it clear that the Jewish renaissance was culturally open to the world, seeking new exchanges and new forms of consciousness to expand Judaism culturally rather than hoping to narrow it.

A recurring pattern emerges in the spiritual Zionist discourse that Kohn participated before World War I. Though clearly taken with idea of a national land, Kohn and his peers found in that notion primarily an intellectually stimulating idea for the Jewish spiritual renewal. Kohn's Zionism, to use his own terms, remained "metaphysical" and at best saw Zionist settlement in the "national land" as a means to a spiritual end. Likewise, his undeniable fascination with the idea of blood as biological nationhood never challenged the preponderance of the spiritual and the metaphysical in his Jewish renewal: "Zionism," he wrote, "lies in a completely different plane of being." His early concept of national culture, we can see, also fits this pattern. Though—as "Der Geist des Orients" attests—his early Zionism was grounded in the cultural juxtaposition between the Jewish and the European, it is evident nonetheless that his Jewish renewal sought greater and bolder exchanges with non-Jewish civilizations, and not a retreat from them. Furthermore, in the final analysis, the discussions that Kohn participated in as a young man at the very least accepted the idea that Judaism is, in Buber's terms, "a cultural admixture."

Bar Kochba's members' ruminations about nations and nationalism included additional elements, such as national language and national history. The lack of a living national language spoken by all Jews was often brought up as a challenge to the Jewish claim to nationhood. Quite similarly, in Central Europe many looked to linguistic borders as the clearest indicator of the borders of national lands. Dimitry Shumsky depicted Bar Kochba as an association of Czecho-German Jews—that is, people who were bilingual and also culturally literate in both the Czech and German worlds. This characterization has been seen as a sign that they transcended the politics of unilingualism also in the context of their Zionism.[153] But even if their lives in Prague were bilingual, the concept of a Hebrew revival had an undeniable appeal to Kohn and his fellow members of Bar Kochba. Fully aware of the pitfalls of the allure of national unilingualism, they were nonetheless mesmerized by the myth of the national language. For example, some *Vom Judentum* essays warned against Hebrew unilingualism (those by Landauer and Birnbaum), others (Kohn's introduction and the essay by Böhm) celebrated the revival of the Hebrew language as a "great wonder" symbolizing "our struggle with the people and for the people."[154] But the idea of a national language appealed to Kohn and his peers only to the extent that it complicated and enriched their Jewish renewal. Hebraization had very limited appeal to Kohn as a supreme Zionist goal or even as practical path to Jewish renewal.

Finally, Bar Kochba's debates on the meaning of Jewish history offered another way to critically examine the essence of nationalism. "Historians," Eric Hobsbawm once said, "are to nationalism what poppy-growers in Pakistan are to heroin-addicts: we supply the essential raw material for the market."[155] His witty dictum certainly applies to both Habsburg Prague and to Zionism's radical rereading of the course of Jewish history. Though very little in Kohn's early writing indicates that he would become a historian, many of his own writings and those of his Bar Kochba peers addressed not just Jewish history but historiography. The clearest calls by members of Bar Kochba for a robust Zionist historiography that would challenge generations of denationalizing scholarship by the Wissenschaft des Judentums came from Stein.[156] That plea to nationalize historiography to provide the Jewish nation with clear historical boundaries indeed fits Hobsbawn's quip. Kohn, too, spoke along those lines. His 1912 article "Books on the History and Literature of Judaism" decried the influence of

Protestant Christians, on the one hand, and Orthodox Jews, on the other hand, on the scholarship about Jewish history and literature. As a result, he found that the scholarship failed to understand "that Judaism, like any other nation, is a living process, and [an] organic spiritual development." He thus concluded his article as follows: "And above all, we have to create in Palestine, on the terrain of that history, an institute whose mission would be to provide us finally with a *Jewish* 'Jewish Studies.'"[157] But, at the same time, in his early historical meditations Kohn frequently provoked national sensibilities: he repeatedly claimed Jesus Christ and earliest Christianity as Jewish—not only biographically, but essentially—and celebrated the false messiah Sabbatai Tsevi, a villain in the eyes of most Jews, as a flawed national hero. In Hobsbawm's terms, then, Kohn's divisive vision of history hardly presented a "poppy" to the "heroin-addicts" of nationalism.[158]

Beyond Objective Dimensions of Nationhood

Blood, national culture, land, national history, and language were commonly seen as the objective dimensions of nationhood in Central Europe around the beginning of the twentieth century. Nevertheless, the members of Bar Kochba, though drawn to these dimensions, clearly discerned the limits of their authenticity—or, at the very least, the limits of their applicability to the Jewish nation. This, I would like to suggest, is why their Zionist discourse remained anchored primarily in intangible, metaphysical terms of a national idea and a national soul or psyche, and why their nationalism, or Jewish renewal, was conceptualized principally in religious terms.

These five dimensions were all key attributes of the ethnic romantic nationalism that Kohn, as a scholar of nationalism, would so forcefully reject by the interwar years. That his youthful Zionism—all ambivalence notwithstanding—was never entirely free from such romantic nationalist paradigms sheds valuable light on this point of departure from his lifelong struggle with nationalism. This, admittedly, is hardly news. After all, he wrote in his memoirs:

> Buber was influenced—and we, in turn, by him—by the German thought and style of the period. . . . Blood, destiny, and the organic Volk-community then played a great part in nationalist German thought, and these fateful words, opposed to the spirit of the age of enlightenment, shaped our thought, too. . . . The implications of this emphasis on blood and ancestral heritage as the determining force of human life were not fully clear to me at the time. Some of my friends went so far as to believe that a man of Jewish ancestry and cultural heritage could never become or

be a true German, Italian, Frenchman, or Dutchman. He could never be fully integrated into the life of any "host" nation; he was and must remain an alien everywhere except on his own "ancestral" soil, by which we mean . . . ancestors, real or imaginary, of fifty generations past. . . . [O]f course, such a belief in biological determinism ran counter to the spirit of the enlightenment, but my young friends proudly rejected the heritage of the Age of Reason.[159]

At the end of the day, primordiality still dominated Kohn's concepts of nationhood before the Great War, without distorting the ethical dimensions of his "nationalism of inwardness." However, in attributing Bar Kochba's members' youthful romantic nationalism naïveté, Kohn appears to be a somewhat unreliable narrator.

Ultimately, it seems that the setting that rendered these conceptualizations of nationalism so desirable to him was also the one that allowed him to sense their constructedness: as a Jew whose national land, in Palestine, he had not yet seen, the bond of the land was an idea or a fantasy; and the condition of un-hyphenated Jewish cultural identity also had to be a fantasy for an exceedingly assimilated Jew—intimate with the German culture and initially disconnected from the Jewish one. What could have replaced land or culture as vessels of Jews' nationhood? Blood was an even more abstract fantasy than the previous ones, and even religiosity seems to have been analyzed and not experienced by Kohn. He did not say so at the time, but his and his friends' Zionism seem to have been anchored simply in the desire to be a nation. It was, in the terms that the older Kohn would use, "a state of mind."[160]

The emphasis on the emotional and psychological foundations of nationalism—which did not contradict the paradigm of primordiality—was one of the few unvarying elements in Kohn's otherwise radically transformed theory of nationalism. Its roots can be traced to his discussion of the Jewish soul in the prewar years, as was laid out by Buber, Weininger in his 1903 *Sex and Character*, and Daniel Pasmanik in his 1911 *Die Seele Israels: Zur Psychologie des Diasporajudentums*. In addition, the budding process of the future theoretician can be seen in Kohn's early enchantment with theology. Tellingly, Kohn—a perfectly secular man with postsecular sensibilities—would somehow remain surrounded by religious thinkers from Jakob Wilhelm Hauer to Reinhold Niebuhr and would frequently revert to theological language.

In the prewar years, Kohn wrote extensively about religion but often did not feel the need to compare it clearly to nationalism. This comparison, however, would become central to his analysis of nationalism after the Great War. As mentioned above, voluntarism and the shared laws that bind people together are, after all, the sine qua non not only of religious life but also of civic nationalism. In this regard, the religious conceptualization of the Jewish renewal may have been influential in Kohn's conversion from ethnic to civic nationalism (indeed, official Judaism, which Buber's and Kohn's Jewish renewal was hoping to dethrone, was, as Leora Batnitzky has recently shown, a child of the nation-state).[161]

Kohn's religious thoughts in the prewar years, however, were not yet framed in quite those terms. Rather, he was drawn to religion and religious thought as a means of imaginatively broadening both Judaism and his world. The reimagined boundaries of Jewishness—according to Kohn's circle's very unorthodox notions of what is Jewish, and what isn't—stood at the heart of *Vom Judentum*. The anthology appeared in August 1913, and the religious Zionist and artist Hermann Struck attacked it in the plenary session of the World Zionist Congress in early September. He cited the book's many admiring depictions of Jesus of Nazareth, in which Jesus was embraced as integral part of the Jewish tradition. Struck was received with loud applause when he accused *Vom Judentum* of containing a systematic denigration of Jews and glorification of Christianity. "But," he stated, "we who feel ourselves to be proud descendants of the old aristocratic race, who revere the old Jewish traditions and law—we cannot love our enemies; we cling to the old truly Jewish phrase, 'Love your *fellow* as yourself.'"[162]

But parallel to the assault by some members of the Zionist old guard—who were alarmed by this kind of charting of the boundaries of Jewishness and Judaism—many a young Zionist in Central Europe received the anthology enthusiastically. Kohn, who was finishing up his university coursework, and Buber made up their mind to turn *Vom Judentum* into a yearbook and started working on the second volume. Buber's goal was to achieve greater coherence and have the yearbook become the mouthpiece of an actual intellectual circle (*Kreisbildung*).[163] He was also hoping to include the works of more Eastern European Jewish national intellectuals, such as David Frischmann and Chaim Zhitlowsky. All these plans, as well as Kohn's university graduation and his planned anthology of German mystical writings, were put on hold on June 28, 1914, with the assassination of Archduke Franz Ferdinand. Kohn heard the news that Sunday afternoon, a few months before his twenty-third birthday, as he was meeting with a friend in the Radetzki Café in Prague, his hometown.

"THE DECISIVE YEARS"

The Great War and the Waning
of the Imperial World Order

CHAPTER TWO

Everything begins in mysticism
and ends in politics.
Charles Péguy, *Notre Jeunesse*[1]

Incipit vita nova
[a new life begins]!
Martin Buber to Hans Kohn,
September 30, 1914[2]

The last days of Austria
were perhaps not the last
days of mankind, but they
were the last days of the
old, civil Europe.
Hans Kohn, *Karl Kraus, Arthur Schnitzler, Otto Weininger*[3]

"Rejuvenating Force": Into the War

More than simply a chronicle of the historical events he witnessed and the political transformations around him, Kohn's war journal offers an account of his own reactions, actions, and emotions. With literary details, he depicts the imperceptible funnel that led an unsuspecting young protagonist from the comfort of his hometown into combat:

> I can still remember the beginning vividly. It was June 28th. Norbert Adler and I sat at Radetzki Café, . . . a business that has been around for centuries. A Sunday afternoon, around four. Most people were away on vacation. Only a few regulars in the café: typical Austrians, clerks, families. We discussed the rigidity of the German criminal law. Not a cloud on the political horizon. And then the headwaiter came to our table. Old and shivering, tall and with an aggravated expression. An old and worn-out Austrian civil servant who belonged here more than anyone. He is paler than ever. He growls a few words, which one hardly comprehends. We hear "Ahhtchook." We have to ask him to repeat that. And once more, and then we understand: our archduke and his spouse were assassinated in Sarajevo. Which archduke? We had no idea that the heir to our throne was in Bosnia. Still—our crown prince.
>
> Amazing how it hit us. The color drained from our faces. . . . It hit us somewhere we never knew existed: as Austrians. Somehow we too were hurt. People started crying for "revenge," even before knowing any facts. I asked for a copy of the special edition [of the newspaper]. A printed edition of the *Prager Tagblatt* appeared within minutes, with a short message, confused and riddled with internal contradictions. The assassin, at any rate, was a Serb: Slavic (nationalistic) motivations. We got up and left at once. Kleinseite Square was quiet, but downtown you could sense that people were hurt, gloomy, restless. As a matter of fact, it was the Slavic element of the whole affair that unsettled everyone. . . . Prague was shocked, the train stations were filled to capacity, but nowhere were there riots, commo-

tions, demonstrations. Disciplined activeness. The declaration of war, on the 28th, surprised no one. [Kaiser Franz Joseph's] manifesto "To My Peoples" was well phrased. On the 31st a general mobilization [was announced,] and it became evident: a world war. People listened alertly to Germany. The swift resolve left a deep impact: A twelve hours' ultimatum! We were not used to that. The Czechs spoke of a done deal: Austria became a German outpost.[4]

This chapter, covering the years 1914-20, deals with concepts of nationalism and internationalism during the Great War and in its immediate aftermath. In the wake of the Great War—under the impact of war, captivity, the disintegration of the Austro-Hungarian Empire into its national components, and the encounter with brutalities of colonialism and revolution—Kohn made his first attempts at a theory of nationalism. However, the war profoundly changed his Zionism and concept of nationalism. Zionism and, more importantly, nationalism now were Kohn's response to entirely different questions: no longer was nationalism his response to the question of inauthenticity. The urgent question was whether it was nationalism that had brought about the war and its horrific outcomes. The root problem of the age, Kohn would determine by 1919, was the nation-state model, which had led Europe and the rest of the world down the path of chaos and endless wars. True nationalism, he would insist, had nothing to do with state sovereignty. The ideology of the nation-state and nationalism, he contended, were two distinct creeds. The imperative, as he would spell out by 1919, was to separate nation and state and thus save both from themselves. In the 1920s, Kohn would formulate political platforms and a suitable mode of operation to implement this imperative.

.   .   .

The importance of the war's outbreak in Kohn's biography lies in how it engulfed him in the political, forcing him to succumb momentarily to the passions of politics, initially prompting his enthusiastic enlistment and later, following the tribulations he experienced during the war, leading him to diametrically opposed political commitments. The war politicized Kohn, and with that politicization, nationalism became as much the problem as the solution.

"When I had just finished my courses at the university," Kohn later recalled, "history and my life took an unexpected turn: the First World War broke out."[5] On the day of Austro-Hungary's declaration of war against Serbia, Kohn wrote "Ode an Mein Volk" (Ode to my people), a Zionist variation on the general conceptualization of the war as a historical turning point and on the notion of a regenerative war. The poem's key motif was Jewish national renaissance and the return to history through war by forging of a new law. Using many of the familiar watchwords of Bar Kochba Zionism—generationality, religiosity, and renewal—Kohn's poem depicted a moment of transcendence: "Man awakes. Out of the blue, youths ascend and see a new world, glowing with light. . . . God speaks[:] 'I have chosen you to forge new destinies (*zu schmieden neue Geschicke*) out of the ancient people of hallowed force. Shake off the disgrace. Create a new law (*Recht*) / Long enough you were only enslaved, you who are destined to greatness. Finally the time has come. . . . It is up to you now to build upon this new experience.'"[6]

Participating in the general euphoria and seeing the war as a personal trial and a longed-for historical breakpoint, Kohn enlisted in the infantry in August 1914, the first month of the war. Historians have long come to see the initial enthusiasm about the war and the so-called spirit of 1914—in which inner divisions and strife disappeared and a nation of various origins and beliefs united in protection of the fatherland—as largely a useful, mobilizing myth crafted early in the war and abused decades later.[7] Be that as it may, Kohn genuinely embraced the outbreak of war enthusiastically. He and his closest friend, Robert Weltsch, were assigned to the same Prague infantry regiment. A month into basic training, Kohn confided in his diary that he "welcomed the war's outbreak" and "couldn't wait to be enlisted, to be allowed to participate. I had the joy of youth. The thought of war—the very idea—had a rejuvenating force." Above all, he continued, "a people rose here to sublime unity, and while this people was not mine, I have, looking at Germany, felt awe, felt drawn, felt as if my ego (*mein Ich*) somehow expanded. For ultimately it was about fulfilling duty where it is the hardest, about self-sacrifice for a higher thing, [about surrendering] the part for the whole. And also at present, I know I could die with dignity."[8]

The double impression of German nationalism is quite evident. Kohn's Jewish sense of nationalism was elevated by what he perceived to be a transformation of the German people, but even the notion of nationalism as an expanded selfhood—which he took as almost self-explanatory—was taken from Johann Gottlieb Fichte's *Addresses to the German Nation*. Kohn's expectations of war followed a familiar pattern of Nietzschean affirmation of war, in which combat was seen as an extreme inner experience, an act of will, and a crucible for spiritual renewal.[9] But Kohn's military service began in a reality devoid of pathos, in long and exhausting months of basic training far from the front line. Alfred Kraus, a friend from Bar Kochba, was already at the front, and from there—a week before he fell—he wrote a striking letter to his and Kohn's friend Robert Weltsch:

Dear Robert! . . . I too see that this war—the dimensions and effects of which one cannot yet comprehend—lent us, the youth of all nations, magnitude and glory, and primarily it allowed us Jews to understand again the meaning of *activitas*, and in it we experience something vital. . . . Life is a joy! . . . [U]nfortunately I have not yet participated in anything serious . . . but I hope for glory in a murderous battle-field. . . . [F]or you, for Hans Kohn and for a few other members of our association a soldier's life would be a redemption. I see a new race of Bar Kochba members rising from it. . . . [M]y young friend and brother in arms, in march through life! We'll see each other again joyfully, here or there. Alfred.[10]

Kraus saw around him only birth, blooming, and life: war was a burst of vitality; enlistment was liberation. He assumed that military life would be "a redemption" for Kohn too, and Kohn seems to have expected nothing less. With such expectations, it is hardly surprising that the unromantic reality of prolonged training turned out to be "a big disappointment."[11] Concerned, Kohn wrote in his diary about the absence of the volunteering spirit, of the lack of commitment and self-sacrifice in his Prague, and hence primarily Czech, regiment. He seems to have shared this disappointment with Martin Buber, who responded a few days later:

What you told me about the general mood has rather disappointed me. Here things are entirely different: never has the concept of peoplehood (*Volk*) become such a reality to me as it has during these weeks. Among the Jews, too, the prevailing feeling is one of solemn exaltation. . . . For everyone who would like to save himself in these times, the words of the Gospel of John apply: "He who loves his life loses it." . . . If we Jews could feel, really feel, feel through and through, what this means to us: that we no longer need our old motto, *Not by might but by spirit*, since force and spirit are now going to become one. *Incipit vita nova!*[12]

In the future, Kohn would have a hard time forgiving Buber's uncritical slogans—evoking first the Hebrew Bible, then the New Testament, and finally Dante—and his proclaiming might as spirit and war as duty. At the time, however, the slogans affirmed his own thoughts, expressing the expectation of a regenerative war that would transform and purify Jewish consciousness and accentuate Jewish national sentiment. The motif of a Jewish war of liberation in Eastern Europe stood at the heart of a handwritten programmatic poem from the time that Kohn kept in his papers: "Not only for the fatherland does the Jew reach today for his weapons." He also fights "today's decisive battle . . . for the liberation of Jews the world over." Only hope can revive "the desperate and repressed [Jews] in Russia." The war is to break their shackles. We Jews "will all leave the strange land Diaspora (*Golus*) had given us as a home, and will roll to the shores of the land of Israel." Indeed, already "today—in [our] happiness and human dignity—we are free again."[13]

Seeing Germany's war as a Jewish war of liberation, Kohn, Buber, and other Central European Zionists emphasized the spiritual bond between Germans and Jews. Buber even went so far as to view Germany's war as the war for the liberation of the orient from colonial yoke (and the redemption of Zion was to be a part of that oriental liberation).[14]

In October, Kohn's and Weltsch's infantry regiment was transferred from Prague to Salzburg.[15] There, as university students, the two became military cadets in the officers' training school. A harsh letter from Mirjam Scheuer, a young Zionist friend, gives a vivid impression of Kohn's worldview during these months, and of its resemblance to the ideas conveyed by Buber and Kraus. She ridiculed Kohn for his "incomprehensible mixture of arrogance—which probably stems from the status of death candidacy (*Todeskandidatur*)—and a much more comprehensible melancholy," while also discussing his "claim that the war will 'establish the real ancestral Jewish kingdom (*das eigentliche Urjüdische Reich*),'" which Kohn dubbed "the kingdom of love." What Scheuer found especially ludicrous was Kohn's assertion that "war—and especially this war—was not mutual murder but a deed committed by the union of a nation and out of the wholeness of a spiritual bond!" There was, she continued, no spiritual bond between Jews and the Germans, and "if we were already in our ancestral land," no Jew would have even considered enlisting to fight Germany's war.[16]

In stark contrast to Kohn's pathos and heroic mood, his months in Salzburg prior to deployment were relatively easy and like civilian life in all but name. On February 1, 1915, after four months of officer's training, Kohn volunteered to join a platoon soon to be deployed to the Carpathian front against the Russians. His diary suggests that his decision to volunteer may have been influenced by peer pressure and was not made lightly. This is apparent in such sentences as "Glad I have volunteered. Otherwise I would have been forever ashamed and humiliated. Sure: my enthusiasm gave way before long, but this is a moral question anyway. And I hope to stand the trial."[17] At first, according to his letters, nothing much happened.[18]

In his memoirs, Kohn claimed to have experienced the battles as "not altogether unpleasant" and added that "though [he] realized the absurdity and futility of war, [he] did not then experience a strong reaction to them."[19] But a close inspection of his war diary gives the impression that he did not participate actively in any battle before March 20, 1915, when he was taken captive in a Russian attack before dawn.[20] Even that combat is depicted in quite a pitiful manner: Kohn and his soldiers failed to identify the Russian attack ahead of time; as they fired back, Kohn sank into the mire, causing his rifle to malfunction: "I hardly stepped out [of the mire] when a Russian grabbed me forcefully by the hand. Above him stood two others with primed guns. I am helpless. They push me forth while shouting. My officer's rank is indiscernible. At dawn I see virtually my entire platoon. . . . [W]e are led forth, through the barbed wires. . . . Then began the torment of the monotonous Galician road. The towns partly ruined, all Jewish houses and businesses wrecked, all inns are shut. . . . [A]ll is so sad. When will we take [conquer] the place again?"[21] At the beginning of his captivity, as one of the 2.11 million Austro-Hungarian prisoners of war (POWs) in Russian captivity, Kohn thus witnessed the catastrophe that had befallen Galician Jewry in the initial wave of pogroms that followed the Russian occupation.[22] At the Russian military headquarters to which he was brought, he saw Czech Austrians who had defected to the Russian side, and he assumed that the Russians had formed multiple defectors' battalions. The defectors he saw probably belonged to the Czech Company (Česká Družina), the foundation of the future Czechoslovak Legion, which Kohn would encounter again in his wartime odyssey.[23] Prisoners, almost as much as the fallen soldiers, became mobilizing symbols of sacrifice to the nation. However, Alon Rachamimov's study of Austro-Hungarian POWs on the Eastern Front found that prisoners on the whole tended to be much less nationalistic than previously assumed.[24]

Captivity and Growth
Samarkand, Gulcha, and the Lessons of Defeat and Colonialism (April 1915–June 1916)

For Kohn, fighting ended in March 1915, but his wartime odyssey had just begun. After his capture, he spent five years in the Russian sphere (see the map of Kohn's route as a soldier and a POW). In his memoirs, Kohn would claim that these years "brought for me a continuing personal encounter with the three historical forces of our time—war, revolution, and colonialism. In many ways, I am inclined to regard my years in Russia as the decisive years of my life. They changed my outlook and redirected my life into paths I could hardly have foreseen in 1914." After his capture, the Russians marched Kohn and his fellow POWs for eight days along dusty Galician roads—and Kohn was deeply impressed by his captors ("I quickly came to like the Russian people and the Russian language") and the sights. They marched from the Carpathians to Lvov

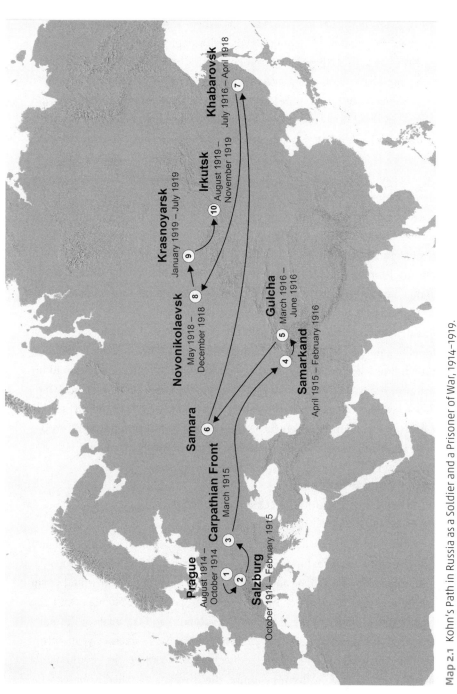

Map 2.1 Kohn's Path in Russia as a Soldier and a Prisoner of War, 1914–1919.
Map by Andy Anderson, courtesy of the author.

(Lemberg) and then went on to Kiev, where they were put on slow trains to remote Samarkand.[25]

Kohn was a wreck in the first weeks: "When I arrived here [Samarkand] I was so exhausted and worn out from the physical and nervous strains of the front and from the depression of captivity, that I gave the impression of a completely broken man: I could hardly walk and used a cane; when forced to walk more quickly, I had to sit down; I was constantly dizzy; my stomach was upset; I could not rid myself of diarrhea and bronchial catarrh; I lay indoors apathetically the whole day, unable even to write home."[26] The POW camp he reached in April 1915, about two miles from Samarkand, housed some twenty-five thousand Austrian prisoners. Hygiene there was poor, but the camp security was lax enough that Kohn was even able to visit the city and acquaint himself with Samarkand's Jews.

The camp was divided according to nationalities. However, Jewish POWs did not constitute a separate national category and were instead scattered among the Slav, German, and Hungarian subcamps. Inner Jewish life in the camp, then, was voluntary.[27] "Misery here is great," Kohn noted in his diary, but at least he, as a cadet, had better living conditions than enlisted men did. Officers like Kohn received a sufficient monthly allowance of twenty Russian rubles, but regular POWs were wretchedly poor ("*arme Teufel*") for the most part.[28] The camp was constantly plagued with deadly malaria and typhus—both of which Kohn suffered from during much of his time there. "Mortality," he noted in July 1915, "amounts to 8–12 men a day." Though he had sufficient money, finding quinine proved impossible.[29] Russia, a signatory of the 1899 and 1907 Hague Conventions, tried to provide suitable conditions for its POWs, but shortages, limitations, and the terrible logistics created dismal circumstances for millions of prisoners.[30]

"And so we live here . . . so my life passes away. 'Life'! It's revulsion, boredom, . . . physical and spiritual," Kohn observed.[31] In September 1915 he wrote to his parents "on my twenty-fourth birthday in Samarkand. All is so sad."[32] In October he mentioned in his diary that out of the twenty-five thousand Austrian prisoners, some three thousand had already died due to poor sanitation.[33] Two months later he wrote to his parents: "Dear ones, [I] am healthy. I think of lost time and the future years. . . . [O]nly after being confined for months on end in the house of the dead (*Totenhaus*), one learns to properly cherish the value of life with movement, the value of intellectual and spiritual activity. Lucky is the man who does not need to learn this lesson. Lucky is the man who survives it unbroken and unreduced!"[34] After half a year in the camp, he decided to escape.

Kohn's encounter with Samarkand and its local population forced him to see things in new ways. It gave him a new understanding of the impact of colonialism on subjugated groups and forced him to revisit his earlier notions regarding Jewish orientality. The local Jewish community, which he visited frequently, consisted of an Ashkenazi minority (estimated to contain fifty families), and a Sephardic "Bukharian" majority (some twelve thousand people). These were Jews of a kind he never encountered before, endlessly more eastern and foreign than the exotic Eastern European Jews praised by Bar Kochba on the eve of the war. This encounter may have challenged, rather than confirmed, Kohn's prewar notions regarding Jewish orientality: Samarkand Jews were oriental; he, admittedly, was not. Kohn's diary takes note of their foreign language (Sart), looks, home décor, dress, teenage marriages, food, and dining etiquette. Yet foreign as they were, they were his Jewish brothers, as he would note a couple of years later: "In Turkestan, in the heart of Asia—under a totally alien sky, in entirely different customs, in a colorfully bizarre world, saturated with sun and profoundly foreign to us—we enter the Jewish quarter, and lo and behold: we are among brothers, who welcome us as brothers, whom we understand, and who share with us, all which lies most deeply within us from [the ancient] past."[35]

To encounter the "Bukharian" Jews of Samarkand, Kohn had to go off the beaten track: "We walked not in the so-often seen streets of the bazaar. . . . Rather we went through narrow, winding alleys, where hardly a single business, a single wagon, or a single European can be seen. Into the actual residential area of the Sart [Muslim] city." This division of a single town between two populations—a Muslim Sart Samarkand and a Christian Russian one—should have been familiar to Kohn from Prague. This may be why the tension and divisions between Russian Samarkand—built and populated by Russian settlers—and Sart (Muslim) Samarkand fascinated him. In his diary, he noted: "I go to the town more frequently. One has to admit that the Russians set up their quarter in a very cozy fashion. (They certainly care very little for the Sarts; one would be amazed how few people know Russian in a place that is only a few miles away from the train. One can get anything. Imported goods at high prices.) Two [international] bookstores . . . , a municipal library . . . , a local museum, music and theater societies (they stage comedies . . . Carmen, Tosca, The Demon); very good high schools for both girls and boys . . . , three movie theatres . . . , telephones are common."[36]

The populations living side by side seemed centuries apart. The relationship between Christian Russians and Muslim Sarts was colonial, and "the realities of colonialism, which I saw in Samarkand for the first time, were unknown in

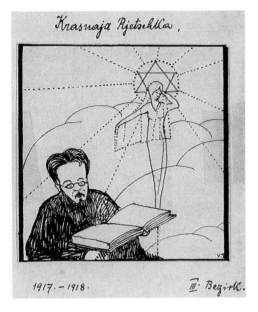

Figure 2.3 Hans Kohn's self-portrait in his Krasnaia Rechka prison notebook, 1917.
Courtesy of the Leo Baeck Institute, New York.

Prague. . . . They made me sensitive to the difficulties that arise when a people try to govern peoples of another race and culture. In Prague there had been a bitter [national] enmity, but it was one between nationalities that shared a similar racial and cultural background. Now in Samarkand I witnessed the clash of two different civilizations, a relationship not of rival peers, but of master and subject, which expressed itself in countless ways."[37] In Samarkand it became evident to Kohn that a colonial setting gives nationalism an entirely different meaning, one that he would soon reflect on in his writing about Zionism and nationalism in general.[38]

Relying on their money; their relative freedom of movement, and colonial dynamics—which meant Russians did not go into much of the old city—Kohn and some of his friends planned an escape from the camp in September 1915 and even purchased local traditional Sart clothes for the purpose. After repeated postponements and ten months in Samarkand, Kohn escaped in February 1916, hoping to cross the border to Afghanistan. After three days of wandering, completely exhausted, he was recaptured.[39] Now, along with ninety other so-called dangerous prisoners, he was sent to an even more remote site near the Chinese border, from which escape was virtually impossible. The prisoners began their journey by train, going first to Andijon, currently in Uzbekistan. From there, they were brought by high-wheeled ox-drawn carriages to the town of Osh (currently in Kyrgyzstan). They continued to their final destination with five days of horseback riding, during which Kohn suffered from a very harsh attack of malaria. Finally, they arrived at a remote post near the small mountain town of Gulcha in the Pamir Mountains, currently in Kyrgyzstan.[40] Thanks to the favorable weather, Kohn soon regained his health, and—now isolated and with plenty of free time on his hands—he committed himself to an increasingly systematic and broad self-education, beginning with acquiring new languages. Looking back later, he claimed that these "were lovely months, in which I read a lot."[41] Much of his reading in Gulcha and beyond reflected the new lessons he had learned about defeat and colonialism.

Krasnaia Rechka and the Preponderance of the Political (July 1916–April 1918)

In June 1916, some four months after arriving in Gulcha, Kohn and the other POWs were evacuated. After a thirty-two-day westbound journey on painfully slow trains, they reached Europe's border, only to turn back east and take the Trans-Siberian Railway to its easternmost end, near the Sea of Japan.[42] Kohn would stay there for two years in the POW camp of Krasnaia Rechka, near Khabarovsk, Russia. The world would change dramatically during those two years, and so would Kohn. For example, he would receive news of the death of Kaiser Franz Joseph, in November 1916; the Russian revolutions of February and October 1917; the Balfour Declaration, in November 1917; President Woodrow Wilson's Fourteen Points, in January 1918; and the Treaty of Brest-Litovsk, in March 1918.

When they arrived in Krasnaia Rechka, Kohn and other "dangerous prisoners" were isolated from the rest of the camp and incarcerated in a *Strafpavillon* (penal pavilion)—Kohn's occasional use of the term "solitary confinement" was probably a misnomer. With his great intellectual drive, his learning intensified during his time at the camp. Through the Red Cross, he received a constant flow of books from his parents and friends. As of August 1916, he could also receive Russian and international newspapers, which gave him a fair sense of current affairs.[43] The life of the mind became his sole escape; the world of learning, his inner liberation. The breadth of his reading in these months is staggering.[44] Another POW in Krasnaia Rechka at that time was the author Heimito von Doderer, who would share much of Kohn's wartime journeys. Interestingly, von Doderer also found his intellectual calling in those years of captivity.

From the isolation of the camp Kohn wrote to Weltsch, in a tone reminiscent of his prewar "Spirit of the Orient," that "in the East one survived only together, it [the East] is stronger than the lone man. . . . It is now fourteen months that I have not left the camp's premises! And how much longer will it last?" Not without pride, Kohn detailed his academic achievements: "In a year I will have perfect command of French, very good command of English, and satisfactory command of Russian, Hebrew, Arab, Turkish, and Italian. With utmost patience I have taught myself political economy (*Nationalökonomie*) and [about] social problems. . . . As soon as I return I would like to complete the *juris doctor* [law degree], and later maybe a doctorate in Semitic or Oriental studies . . . I [write] a little bit. Some of it is even ripe for the press. Some of it is different from our yearbook [the 1913 anthology *Vom Judentum*]."[45] Kohn's letters home focused now on book orders, and occasionally he felt compelled to apologize to his parents: "Don't be irritated that I keep asking you for books, but it is truly horrible here, and so arid. And especially now in the winter! Send me books frequently and by multiple routes. My friends from Bar Kochba have not written a thing. Tell them I am very sad. Everyone should write me. I am so lonely here."[46]

The results of Kohn's reading and introspection were channeled into his war notebooks—a mélange of poems, reading notes, drafts for lectures and essays, and a number of commentaries on current affairs and the future postwar order.[47] In early November 1916, in the wake of the Brusilov offensive, Kohn wrote a remarkable set of notes titled "Zur Lage" (On the state of affairs), in which he envisioned a bright future consisting of multiethnic federations, not of nation-states, and it was precisely in this modernized imperial setting that Kohn imagined Jewish national aspirations would be best addressed.[48]

Though already "uninterested in a German victory over the Western states," Kohn saw a "complete victory over Russia and Rumania" as "necessary for our people, for the Jews." The Austrian victory he imagined would facilitate the creation of a greater Austrian federation. "In my dreams," Kohn wrote, "I imagine the shape of the future as follows: Austria annexed the territory of Poland, Lithuania and Volhynia . . . and Rumania." This vast new empire "would be transformed federatively into an intra-Austrian complex of Hungarians, Czechs, Polish, Lithuanians, Ukrainians, Romanians, and South Slavs."[49]

His main interest, however, remained the Jews: "By annexing the provinces that are predominantly inhabited by Jews, we provide them [the Jews] with more than the opportunity for free political, economic, and cultural development. . . . Like all national minorities, [the Jews] would have their own national assemblies (*Kurien*) with certain communal and educational autonomy—[and indeed] would constitute the unifying glue" of the new federation. Without a claim on any of its lands, the Jews of multinational Greater Austria would never aspire to independence by breaking away from it: they "would be loyal to Austria solely and absolutely." Austria's victory, would thus, revolutionize the Jewish world: "The masses of the Jewish people will be concentrated in two countries, where they enjoy [the] possibility of free development as respectable and active [members]—in America and in Greater Austria. What a tremendous turnaround in the situation of the Jews!" But as a Zionist, Kohn had dreams that went even further, and he imagined that in this triumphant situation, a land swap would allow Turkey to grant the Jews "Palestine as an autonomous free state under Ottoman suzerainty and an American protectorate regarding the military and customs, but not regarding its comprehensive legislation."[50]

In his notes, Kohn clearly acknowledges that these are, at least in part, merely "dreams." Yet the importance of this document lies precisely in that quality: very soon, dramatic historical changes would render such scenarios unimaginable, and hence Kohn ceased mentioning them in his interwar alternatives to the nation-state model. However, one should keep his wartime ruminations in mind when seeking to fully understand his emerging political agenda.

The idea of a semiautonomous Jewish region in Palestine under international and imperial aegis frankly resembles Theodor Herzl's vision. Much more important, however, was Kohn's vision for Central and Eastern European Jews in the multiethnic federation of Greater Austria. This vision follows the Austro-marxist prescription of national and cultural autonomy on the basis of the personality principle, as Jews are imagined to have national assemblies without geographic coherence. The creation of the Kingdom of Poland (1916–18) by the Central Powers a few weeks later—even though it was only a puppet state— alarmed Kohn because it took up the language of nation-state and national sovereignty, rather than that of multinational federations. On November 25, 1917, he wrote: "The creation of a new Poland as well as the unspecified autonomy of Galicia were quite unfortunate steps, and made me realize fully how disastrous for us would be a victory of the Entente in Eastern Europe."[51] On the occasion of the old kaiser's death, Kohn clearly noted that the attachment to the Austrian idea only intensified in exile and captivity: "How unfamiliar must everything at home have become."[52]

Facing the increasingly inevitable collapse of the world order in the Great War, Kohn became interested in seeking principles for international order. In 1917, he read Charles Saint-Pierre's *Project for Perpetual Peace* and Immanuel Kant's *Toward Perpetual Peace*, which he found to be "a bright and thoughtful text that could be applied also regarding the current war."[53] Saint-Pierre's 1712 text was the first formulation of the ideal of an international arbitration forum along the lines of the League of Nations or the United Nations. Though Kant was writing about republics, not democracies, his seminal 1795 essay is considered an early statement of sorts of the democratic peace theory. In the essay Kant discussed the "Preliminary Articles" for perpetual peace, and especially its three basic assumptions, the "Definitive Articles": first, "the civil constitution of every state should be republican"; second, "the law of nations shall be founded on a federation of free states"; and third, "the law of world citizenship shall be limited to conditions of universal hospitality."[54] Fichte—who greatly influenced Kohn's concept of nationalism—famously praised Kant's essay for showing "that the Idea of perpetual peace is contained, as a task, within pure reason, . . . that this idea will become more than a mere concept and that it will be realized in the sensible world. . . . Nature itself pledges this."[55] It is in early 1917 that internationalism—as a political idea that aspires the institutional coordination among polities and among nations—becomes an increasingly central dimension of Kohn's concept of what nationalism is or should be.[56]

In late February (or early March, according to the Gregorian calendar then used in Russia) 1917, a revolution began that would soon bring down the war-weary, three-hundred-year-old Romanov dynasty. Russia's capital, Petrograd (today's St. Petersburg)—thousands of miles west of Kohn's POW camp—was transformed by strikes, demonstrations, and mutinies. In early March, the czar abdicated, and a democratic provisional government was formed. This revolution also brought Kohn's confinement to the penal pavilion to an end, and after eight long months, he and his cellmates could once again interact with their fellow POWs.[57] His sense of liberation was enormous. Cultural life in the POW camp flourished: with the help of the Red Cross and other philanthropic bodies, the camp was home to two choirs, two orchestras, at least one theater group, and even an organization known as "the peasant university"—a college of sorts that offered POWs an assortment of courses, ranging from Esperanto to paleontology. The lecturing POWs had been faculty members in various Central European universities before the war.[58]

At that unique moment, Kohn's rigorous blending of soul searching, intensive learning, and essay drafting turned outward. With ever more books sent by family and friends and with an astounding intellectual drive, Kohn and some friends created a parallel Zionist college of sorts. This college, in which Kohn was the prominent lecturer, catered to several hundred POW-students. A fellow POW attested that "after the Balfour Declaration [November 1917] Zionist groups sprang up in most prisoner camps," creating a greater student body than had existed before in the camps. The Zionist college in Kohn's camp offered lectures on a variety of topics, ranging from philosophy to literature and Russian culture. Most of its activities, however, focused on Jewish learning.

Over time, the "college" allowed Kohn to discover both his individual Zionist agenda and his "vocation as a teacher." In his memoirs, he recalled this period as "the beginning of a new life,"[59] and it is hard not to compare this to Buber's promise to Kohn in the summer of 1914 that in this war "a new life begins."[60] Kohn may have hoped to find in this Zionist college a continuation of his activities in Bar Kochba in profoundly different circumstances, and he named its handwritten newspaper *Vom Judentum*, the title of his 1913 volume. In the face of dramatic world events, however, a mere continuation of his prewar Zionism was impossible, and his wartime Zionism gained a new emphasis and agenda.

Before the war, Kohn and his friends had been influenced by Ahad Ha'am's notion of Jewish renaissance but were unimpressed by his old-fashioned liberal style. While Ha'am's Zionism was grounded on cultural heritage and ethical ideas, Kohn and his friends were drawn (albeit not in a naïve way) to a nationalism imagined as grounded in land and blood. But as Kohn wrote in an August 1917 letter to the members of Bar Kochba, it became obvious that Ahad Ha'am was right: "justice is Judaism's primary trait," and it also had to be "the ultimate yardstick" of Jewish nationalism. By this, it should be stressed, Kohn meant political justice; it was in this direction that his Zionism had developed during the war. He continued: "Humanity's social question has merged into it [his spiritual Zionism]. . . . Now I see human suffering in greater clarity and feel with greater rage the shackles tying us to any human question."[61] With considerable wishful thinking, Kohn claimed that the tension between Herzl's political Zionism and Ahad Ha'am's spiritual Zionism had been resolved through synthesis. Herzl provided the means ("bringing the Jews together under the blue-white flag"), while Ahad Ha'am's view had prevailed ("ethical and intellectual renewal of Judaism"). Thus, Kohn could even claim that Ahad Ha'am's ideas were able "to turn a political and economic movement into a spiritual and cultural one."[62]

In late October (early November) the second Russian revolution unfolded, and following the famous storming of the Winter Palace, the Bolsheviks claimed to control Russia. This revolution, and the brutal civil war that followed in its wake—between the communist Reds and the anticommunist Whites—had a profound impact on Kohn's life, worldview, and concept of nationalism. The new Soviet Russia had a truly global vision and voiced a new and challenging concept of international relations and a critique of imperialism that Kohn could hardly resist. The concept of national self-determination as a war goal had first been articulated by the Russian provisional government in April 1917.

For the Bolsheviks this formula was very effective; it was "an important tool for undermining the capitalist-imperialist world order and, more specifically, for destabilizing the older regime in Russia and gaining the support of non-Russian minorities for the revolution. As early as March 1917, Lenin declared that [the Soviet] peace plan would include 'the liberation of all colonies; the liberation of all dependent, oppressed and non-sovereign peoples.'" When President Wilson appropriated the Soviet concept of national self-determination and integrated it into his American war aims, Trotsky was quick to charge him with hypocrisy: "The imperial powers, [Trotsky] said, could not claim to be fighting for the rights of small nations in Europe while at the same time oppressing other national groups within their empires."[63] These fundamental inquiries into the questions of national rights and colonialism were certainly of the utmost concern for Kohn. His exposure to the Soviet perspective on those issues would become deeply engrained in his political thought. Here—as in so many key junctions that would follow—Kohn's struggle with the idea of nationalism was entangled with the question of colonialism on the one hand and that of capitalism on the other hand. A letter to Buber in November 1917, after probably three years of silence, allowed Kohn to chart his intellectual growth:

> In the last three years I have been through a lot—through much more than in the preceding 23 years. I have seen, and learned a lot, read and thought, and all this has ripened and enriched me, and made me more earnest in a way. I have experienced the orient, learned languages, and acquired some skills for life. During 15 months of solitary confinement (*einsamer "Haft"*), I had time to confront myself, God, and the world and have indeed become a different person, for upon "liberation" [from the penal pavilion] two months ago, I could exert on my fellows greater influence than I would have ever believed; [I was able] to direct them out of the murkiness of the swamp, from a mood of suffering to the pure air of the "inner autonomous" kingdom.... I have created here—with success I myself cannot explain—a Zionist circle, at the center of which I stand.... I edit a journal called *Vom Judentum*, deliver lectures, seminars, Hebrew classes.... I have first and foremost ripened as a fine speaker, and also improved and enriched my style; partially through encountering foreign cultures, but partially also from reading rewarding works of sociology and economy.[64]

Beyond this personal change in him and his Zionist activity in the camp, Kohn elaborated on the transformation of his worldview, particularly of his Zionism. The physical distance imposed on him by captivity allowed for more critical introspection, and he had ample time for extensive learning, both of

which made Kohn "increasingly aware that we need to move from 'conversations with God' to influencing the tenets of society and that we must intensify
the political and social direction of our Zionism." Juxtaposing cosmos, or order,
and chaos, Kohn believed that he had "become more radical, the great chaos
of the Russian Revolution influenced me."[65] His politicizing imperative, in spite
of his best intentions, remained unfocused in the next two years. Isolated from
his Prague circle, he was processing the collapse of the old world and imagining
what Zionism could and should be in the new one.

And so, all of his proclaimed politicization notwithstanding, most of Kohn's
lectures and essays from Krasnaia Rechka still dealt—albeit more critically
—with the old, less political questions about authentic nationhood raised by
members of the Bar Kochba before the war. In February 1918 he wrote a major
essay on "Das kulturelle Problem des modernen Westjudentum" (The cultural
problem of western Jewry), which he would later republish in *Der Jude*). No
western Jew, he claimed, could truly ever rid himself of the "un-Jewish, foreign"
element within him: "We do not believe that land, language, and habits are
something merely external. . . . [T]hey too are an integral part of our core; . . . I
speak and think in multiple languages, but my innermost feelings and thrills appear in German words; I have seen many landscapes and still, the terraced Bohemian landscapes surround my dreams, always subconsciously there like the
habits of my parents' home." Kohn's position was now identical to that of Gustav Landauer in 1913. Kohn did not wish "to abolish any dimension of our dual
or multifarious being, nor to doctrinally obliterate our plurality." Challenging
the oversimplified denunciation of Jewish assimilation, he would henceforth
integrate this notion into both his Zionism and understanding of nationalism:
"Our nationality (*Volkstum*) turned from a natural fact (*Naturgegebenheit*) to a
purpose, an act. Here nationality means more than race and soil." Nationalism,
thus, was not about being but about becoming.[66]

Homeward Journey Interrupted:
Novonikolaevsk (April–December 1918)

In April 1918—some two years after arriving in Krasnaia Rechka, and a couple of
weeks after the signing of the Treaty of Brest-Litovsk between the Bolsheviks
and the Central Powers—Kohn and his fellow POWs were taken on cattle cars on
a slow westbound train through the seemingly endless Siberian steppes. Kohn's
diary referred to the trip as a "*Heimreise*" (homeward journey),[67] but the complicated circumstances of the early stages of the Russian Civil War prevented
Kohn's anticipated return. Having arrived in Samara in the west, the POWs were

sent back deep into Siberia, to a camp near the city of Novonikolaevsk (now Novosibirsk), where they were to await the proper POW exchange as stipulated in the Brest-Litovsk Treaty. Kohn wrote: "We were so close to home—closer than we had been for a very long while; many already saw their dreams fulfilled, all the beauty and love that awaited them at home. And now we are again banished indefinitely; deprived of our loved ones and peaceful social life, which alone creates values and endows merit to our toil."[68]

In late May, Kohn's camp was captured by the Czechoslovak Legion, which closed off any prospect of an imminent return. Though Kohn's memoirs—written in Cold War America—did not clearly state this, his homeward journey was under Red (Soviet) auspices, while his devastating reimprisonment was at the hands of White (counterrevolutionary) forces. The Czechoslovak Legion, containing some forty thousand men at that point, consisted primarily of Czech and Slovak soldiers who had switched sides after being captured (the legion accounted for some 16 percent of the Czechs and Slovaks captured by the Russian army). Kohn happened to encounter the legion at a turning point in its history: on its eastbound journey, which should have gotten the legion out of Russia, it clashed with the Red Army in May 1918 in Chelyabinsk, near the Ural Mountains. The Red Army, still quite unorganized, failed to disarm the legion, which then managed to defeat the Red forces and take control of the Trans-Siberian Railway. Kohn and the POW train, then, were captured by the legion very shortly after it began its active participation in the Russian Civil War, fighting with the White forces against the Reds.[69]

Kohn and the POWs were held for seven months in the most primitive of conditions in a camp in the vicinity of Novonikolaevsk. As a Habsburg loyalist and an officer, Kohn described these months as exceptionally hard: "The Legion . . . too began to show disquieting signs of brutality in its actions. The Czech Legion was hostile to the Austro-Hungarian prisoners of war, especially to the officers. After the Legion took over in Novonikolaevsk, we were not treated too well."[70] But even there Kohn continued his Zionist and intellectual activity. With Hugo Knoepfmacher—a fellow POW who remained a friend for life—he translated modern Hebrew poetry into German and, having received the author's permission, translated Joseph Klausner's *History of Modern Hebrew Literature* from the Russian original. Kohn delivered multiple large lectures on Zionism and Herzl, taught a course on Jewish history (twice a week, with 120 registered students), ran seminars titled "The History of Zionism, Its Organizations, Theories, and Methods" (twice a week, with 116 students); and led a Bible reading group.[71]

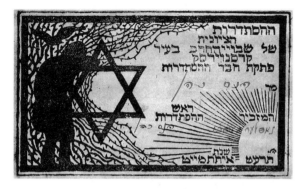

Figure 2.4 Hans Kohn's Krasnoyarsk Zionist POW Association membership card. Courtesy of the Leo Baeck Institute, New York.

"War imprisonment," he wrote at the time, "has robbed us of the possibility of free actuation of our essence. The web of bondage traps us here more than anywhere else. It is a time of no progress in our outer lives, and in our impact on the shaping of the outside world. . . . We are dependent upon conditions beyond our control. We do not have the capacity for any creative force and activity based on our true and absolute self—we hardly even recognize that self anymore." The prisoner, however, should never agree to become "a pawn of external contingencies."[72] In another essay from those months, Kohn developed another imperative for the POW: rather than letting captivity diminish him, the POW must turn it into a rare opportunity for introspection and "spiritual growth," so as to eventually return home "a new and better person." Kohn—who had initially seen war as regenerative and rejuvenating—now believed that society at home had been so morally and materially degraded by the war that it needed its POWs to return as better people who could restore the country.[73]

An album that Kohn's fellow POWs gave him as a present for his twenty-seventh birthday attests to his centrality among the prisoners. One of them praised Kohn in festive and archaic Hebrew as "a priest," a model of selfless dedication to the cause, and a dedicated "rabbi" who taught them "Zionist thought and a unique Jewish perspective."[74]

The November 1918 collapse of the Austro-Hungarian Empire "meant to us a 'crisis of loyalty,' we didn't know where we belonged," wrote Knoepfmacher.[75] From this moment on, Prague and Central Europe lost their appeal to Kohn, and emigrating to Palestine became a paramount goal. A few weeks after the empire's demise, writing Leo Hermann about the prospects of an administrative position in the Zionist movement, Kohn was unequivocal about his resolve to make Aliyah (to emigrate to Palestine). Boasting about his "perfect command of Hebrew," Kohn stressed that he and his fellow POWs "have but one thought

Figure 2.5 Hans Kohn's bookplate from Krasnoyarsk. Courtesy of the Leo Baeck Institute, New York.

—to get to Palestine as soon as possible." They had left their European homes so long ago that they were no longer homesick. They were ready for a new life in Palestine.[76]

Rejecting the Approaching Nation-States and Growing Red in White Siberia: Krasnoyarsk (January–May 1919)

There was a staggering disparity between Kohn's rigorous studies and other activities and his wretched situation as a POW of a country that had ceased to exist and of a war that had first ended and then morphed into a ruthless civil war. A few days after Kohn sent his letter to Hermann, in the freezing cold, his group of POWs was dispatched eastward on the Trans-Siberian Railway, to Krasnoyarsk. In his captivity diary, next to the date January 25, 1919, and the name Krasnoyarsk he scribbled two Hebrew words "*Begalut Kfula*" (doubly exiled), which was also the title of an improvised newspaper he and his fellow prisoners produced.[77] In this camp, Kohn endured not only extremely harsh living conditions but also the terrorizing regime of the Czechoslovak Legion, which included the arbitrary execution of Hungarian officers. In late January 1919, there were about ten thousand POWs in the camp, primarily from the Austro-Hungarian army, and about a fifth of them would die from various typhoid fevers. Typhoid and terror notwithstanding, the camp seems to have been "a town by itself," with "all kinds of businesses—restaurants, laundries, barber shops, a theater and an orchestra of 35 players," and "some kind of self-government" with an "elected body of representatives of the prisoners" took place even prior to Kohn's arrival.[78]

Kohn managed to maintain equilibrium in his life through his dedication to Zionist and intellectual activity.[79] The members of his Zionist circle were integrated into the new camp's Jewish POWs' Association, and Kohn soon became head of the Zionist Association of POWs in Krasnoyarsk, with 367 members (more than a half of the camp's Jewish POWs). In addition to the familiar topics, many courses now focused on preparation for the pending Aliyah, among them agricultural training; principles of export from the Levant; geography, geology, and botany of Palestine; and conversational Hebrew, Arabic, English, and French. Furthermore, Kohn's activities gained a clearly political dimension, with courses such as "The Jewish People and Contemporary World Affairs," "Collectivist Settlement," "The Collectivist Idea," and "Judaism and Socialism." Indeed, Kohn and his friends had actually "established, on socialist-collectivist principles, a Jewish workers' collective named *Nemala* [ant]," consisting of 189 of the Zionist prisoners.[80] Kohn was clearly growing Red in White Siberia, and he would remain pro-Soviet for many years. His reading lists and personal correspondence indicate the growing sway that utopian or anarchist socialism had on him.[81] "I am an anarchist and an absolute antistatist (*Staatsgegner*)," he told Weltsch very plainly.[82]

Anarchist socialism was but one element—not even the key element—of Kohn's new political outlook, which began emerging in White Siberia in 1919. Other elements were pacifism and the rejection of the nation-state model. Whereas the anarchist socialist dimension in Kohn's work would dissipate after his return from Russia, his pacifism and the rejection of the nation-state—which were grounded in his internationalist agenda for the postimperial world order—shaped the next decade of his life. "From the First World War on," he wrote, "I distrusted power, officialdoms, and brass, and I abhorred the excesses of national pride and self-righteousness, the brutalization and inhumanity inherent in war." In his memoirs, he linked becoming a pacifist not to military service or wartime captivity per se but mainly to the manner in which the war ended, in revolutions and the disintegration of old empires: "The world events of 1917 to 1920, which focused my attention to history, also made me a pacifist."[83] His pacifism would reach its peak in the late 1920s.

Kohn's "Das Wesen des Nationalismus" (The essence of nationalism) lecture, delivered in Krasnoyarsk in April 1919, marks the obscure beginning of his illustrious career as a scholar of nationalism and of his political agenda in the 1920s.[84] This twenty-four-page essay was written half a year after Austro-Hungary's disintegration into its national components—that is, from the perspective of the end of the war, with the seemingly inevitable emergence of a world of nation-states. This essay also marked the beginning of Kohn's long and creative confrontation as a Habsburg patriot and a Habsburg Jew with the postimperial order. As a European, he wished to challenge the claim that this new political pattern, which was a nightmare in his eyes, somehow fulfilled the promise of nationalism or proclaimed its triumph. As a Jewish nationalist, he wished to disprove the perception that the calamitous World War I was an indictment against nationalism as a whole.

The essay begins with a detailed laudatory discussion of Fichte's equally postcatastrophic *Addresses to the German Nation*. Kohn's essay retained a few assumptions that he would later contest: "Nation is something one is born into. As its name suggests, it is a natural fact," and "Nationality has always existed. Not only science attests to it, but history . . . and not only nationality, but also national consciousness." Yet, the definition of "nation" (*Volk*)—which he spelled out in this essay for the first time—was already not unlike his famous one from the mid-twentieth century: "A nation," stated Kohn in 1919, "is a community based on common descent and spirit, which must live and perform a mission in the world; and like the individual, it has a purpose (*Sinn*) to fulfill, and it is truly alive only so long as as it fulfills that purpose." Common national descent, then, was secondary to the national mission, or, as he more frequently called it, "the national idea." For a national idea to be viable, Kohn wrote, it had to transcend narrow national interests. Thus, authentic nationalism is inherently supranational (*übernational*), cosmopolitan, and international—Kohn still used the three terms interchangeably. Conversely, a policy or an ideology that merely follows narrow self-interest cannot be true nationalism: "The first to provide the German people with a profound philosophically based nationalism, were also [Germany's] first cosmopolitans. One need only read Fichte to see how Germany's greatest nationalist man was its biggest cosmopolitan." Nationalism, thus, is "an extension of our humanity," and national consciousness is "the passage point toward panhuman consciousness, and only through it is it feasible to organically attain all-human consciousness."[85]

Having outlined his definition of what nationalism is, or is not, Kohn ended the essay by tying these general definitions to contemporaneous events: the ruin of Europe and the emerging postwar world order. Kohn's definition of nationalism as cosmopolitan set a clear boundary between true nationalism, on the one hand, and the ideology of the nation-state, on the other hand: "If the World War was fought with reasons and pretexts of nation-states," Kohn wrote there, "then this is the worst spiritual blindness, and does not express true nationalism." Not only are nationalism and states two different things—Kohn alluded to Fichte at this point—but they "contradict one another, diametrically opposed like *Geist* and *Ungeist*" (roughly, the juxtaposition of the human spirit and the spirit of inhumanitity). True nationalism doesn't aspire to have a state or a nation-state, but rather to accomplishing "a spiritual ideal, unconstrained by self-interest":

> The state is merely an instrument serving its temporary, practical aims in the spirit of the time. But a nation is an eternal entity, carried by the spirit, which does not divide people, but rather unites them. It presents an ideal . . . that ties one man to his brother, and provides him also with the meaning of the essence of other individuals and of foreign nations. But the state . . . separates, and does not unify. It generates wars. . . . [T]he World War was generated not because people were too national, but because they were not sufficiently national [in Fichte's original meaning, which was supranational, cosmopolitan, and international].[86]

The essay's final sentences address Zionism. Kohn stopped short of saying explicitly that Zionism should reject the goal of a Jewish nation-state. But although he was personally committed to moving to Palestine, Kohn already knew full well that—in the post-Balfour era and the Wilsonian Moment—his understanding of the nation-state would force him to boldly take some unpopular positions within his movement. "I don't care how I am going to make a living there [in Palestine]," he wrote Weltsch a couple of months later. "there is a lot I have to do there. I can already sense that it would not cease being a battle, and nowadays, aware of the narrow chauvinistic egoism of our people, I know that there is no other place to struggle for humanity than among us."[87]

Moving to Irkutsk (May–November 1919): Zionism and Postwar Internationalism

Months had elapsed since the collapse of the Austro-Hungarian Empire and the end of the war, but Kohn was still in Siberia, still a POW of sorts. The ongoing Russian civil war blocked his way home, and at least initially the Czechoslovak Legion, the captors of Kohn and the other prisoners, "saw to it that we [officers who had been loyal to the Austro-Hungarian Empire] should not get home before they did."[88] In the spring of 1919 he left the Krasnoyarsk POW camp to visit Irkutsk as the representative of the POWs in the institutions of Siberian Zionism. "Soon," he wrote, "I will most likely move to Irkutsk as secretary of the Zionist office, and as vice editor of the [Russian-language Zionist] periodical *Jewish Life*."[89] It was at that time that, for lack of any better option and for practical considerations, he applied for Czechoslovak citizenship.[90] Kohn was not intending to return to Prague permanently anyway, but rather to settle in Palestine soon.

His move to Irkutsk took place in the summer. Bidding farewell to their "president," the members of the Krasnoyarsk Zionist association thanked Kohn for showing them "in these days of confusion and general brutalization . . . the ethical path, which leads to our people."[91] As a new Czechoslovak citizen, Kohn joined—as a civilian rather than a soldier—the Culture and Information Department of the Czechoslovak Legion's headquarters in Irkutsk, where he served as a deputy librarian. In addition, as he told his mother, "I have a position, as a Czechoslovak subject, on the editorial board of a paper named *Heimat*, and I also coordinate the Zionist activity here and edit a Russian Zionist paper named *Jewish Life*. I have a lot of money. I hope to be home in a few months."[92] Kohn never fully explained this crucial yet elusive moment, in which he ceased being a POW and began working for his former captors, the Czechoslovak Legion. After so many years of captivity, it was a remarkably anticlimactic moment of liberation—which for him, as Habsburg loyalist, must have been tainted by loss of identity and arguably of integrity as well.

The legion paid him a salary, and his Zionist activity satisfied many of his spiritual and intellectual needs. At the legion's headquarters he befriended the Czech writer Josef Kopta and helped him edit the "independent . . . paper *Vykřik* [Outcry], . . . bear[ing] witness to our fervent though confused hopes in 1919, our overestimation of the power of good intentions, our refusal to face the unpleasant realities of human nature and the follies of governments." Kohn did not hesitate to condemn Kopta and his Irkutsk Czech friends harshly, writing "that the Czechs served their 'national interests,' and French imperialism, and combated the Soviets." Zionism, Kohn hoped, would not go down that path, but would instead take the one on which ethical ideas outweighed "national interests" and that was not aligned with imperialism.[93]

On July 14, 1919, almost four and a half years after they had been separated by the war, Kohn wrote a pensive letter to his close friend Weltsch. It may have been the looming prospects of liberation and homecoming—whatever that term could now mean—that prompted Kohn to reflect on the personal and the ideological, the emotional and the intellectual, and the past and the future. Though impatient to leave captivity, he stressed that he was no longer homesick or nostalgic for Prague. He took pride in his academic learning and Zionist leadership, yet he also admitted feeling intellectually stuck (he said he was "undergoing a minor crisis now").[94] The lessons he learned during the war were hard and unforgiving, and he used unprecedentedly harsh language to convey his deep concern that Zionism had not learned those lessons and might therefore be doomed to repeat the same mistakes:

> When the war started, I was 23 years and, at the end of the day, was allowed [such] stupidities. That is to say, I was certainly not allowed, and I remorsefully say *pater peccavi* [Father, I have sinned], as I have already often said. But that men like Buber or Bergmann—the leaders of our ethical community—could fall like that! . . . And in this swamp of filth Zionism swims and splashes and seems quite content. . . . The most gruesome is this: everything, Zionism included, is governed by *right or wrong—my country*, or my nation, or my class. . . . [T]he clearer I see our complicity in the world chaos—the lonelier I become.[95]

Engulfed by the Bolshevik Revolution, Kohn believed he had become "much more of a leftist than [he] would have been in Vienna." Though it would have been impossible for him as a pacifist to truly identify with Soviet Russia, the emergence of the socialist state struck him as a sign of tremendous historical progress: "It is a world that trembles with joy, full with the spirit of spring. It is good even if it attests to shortsightedness." Indeed he—who never became a Marxist—aptly proclaimed, "Now I understand the great impact the French Revolution had on Kant."[96]

New Order: Hans Kohn's Emerging Political Agenda

In Irkutsk in the summer of 1919, Kohn wrote several essays for Buber's new monthly magazine, *Der Jude*. The remarkably lucid writing in these essays is a culmination of his wartime politicization and contains the key components of the intellectual and political quest he would embark on in the ensuing decade. "Perspektiven" (Perspectives), Kohn's first contribution to *Der Jude*, began with his critique of prewar spiritual Zionism—a criticism Buber was already familiar with given Kohn's letter to him in November 1917.[97] Though "sufficiently deep," Kohn wrote, "their [prewar Zionists'] old Zionism was not wide enough; it focused too much on the individual, and thus paved the Zionist path only to the modern man."[98] Prewar spiritual Zionism failed to address the major social and political challenges of the present, so Kohn tackled the greatest issue of the time—namely, the Paris Peace Conference, which was then taking place, and more broadly, the tenets of the postwar world order.

Looking at the negotiators at the Paris Peace Conference (who "recognized the Jewish nation and its vital rights"), many Zionists hoped that the cataclysm of the war would reveal itself as a blessing in disguise, eventually creating a better world for the Jews and the rest of humanity. Kohn had sobering words for such Zionists: though the Great War had been a catastrophe for Jews, the world order being created in its wake (which in his eyes promised "chaos") had the potential to be even worse.[99] Kohn wrote:

> The [Paris] Peace Conference proved to be a conference of hatred and greed and the cradle of future wars. Ignoring the voices of the peoples, diplomats sat and toyed with the fate of mankind. . . . The Peace Conference neither constructed peace nor sowed love. It fulfilled the demands of the strong and disregarded the voices of the weak. The battle is over but war prevails everywhere: an open bloody struggle or and even fiercer clandestine, subterranean one. The fruits of hatred ripen in the endless civil war in Russia—in which Cossacks go incomprehensibly wild . . . , in Central Europe and the Balkans, where one bully state (*Raubstaat*) was replaced by a dozen smaller ones—in Egypt and India, in Ireland and Korea. And obviously the fruits [of hatred] ripen also in Poland and the Ukraine, where so much of our flesh and blood dwells. And our blood in Wisła is as red as that of the unfortunate Arabs, Indians, and Koreans for whom "Order" was established.[100]

Standing boldly against the tide, Kohn offered a contentious, razor-sharp analysis of the emerging world order. His outlook may have been bleak, but it was based on clear parameters and related to multiple arenas. His analysis did not emerge out of thin air: it merged his Habsburg sensibility, with its distaste for nation-states, with the ethical language of Ahad Ha'am and Buber and— most clearly—with the early Soviet perspective on international affairs. After all, Kohn was writing in the midst of the Russian civil war, where he was living among the Whites yet identifying with the Reds. Having laid bare his broader analysis of the Paris Peace Conference and its political ideas, Kohn then asked where Zionism stands—and where it should stand—in this global drama.

Blinded by "national interests," Zionists "followed the lead of power and the powerful," eager for the Paris Peace Conference to "give" them what they desired: guarantees for Zion. They failed to recognize, wrote Kohn, that the pogroms against Jews all over the new borderlands were epiphenomena of the very same "chaos of national sovereignty" that underlay the conference. Zionism should have "stood up explicitly and selflessly against the world abomination

(*Weltgreuel*)," but instead, it "betrayed morality for the sake of crumbs from that spirit of inhumanitity (*Ungeist*)."[101] Here we can see how Kohn returned—now in a concrete setting—to the key argument of his "Essence of Nationalism" —namely, that for Zionism to be viable, it must be based on ideals transcending its narrow "national interests"; it had to be anchored by a supranational ethical idea.

Kohn was probably aware that, with the demand that Zionism constitute something like a "concrete messianism," he raised the movement's moral bar unrealistically. Whether as a religious imperative or as a religious allegory for a political and ethical imperative, Kohn envisioned a Zionism that was true to "the Jewish messianic mission, as the servant of God, carrying the yoke of the kingdom of heaven."[102] This religious rhetoric was actually right in line with Kohn's prewar conceptualization of Zionism as religious renewal. "Zionism will never be able to generate a renewal," he had proclaimed in 1912, "if it does not become a religious movement."[103] Before the war, he had already understood messianism as a national idea uttered in religious language, and Buber's early addresses spoke of the cosmic dimension of that Jewish redemption. But politicization transformed Kohn's religious terms as well: the "concrete messianism" he envisioned in the wake of the Great War was not "traditional messianism, but a new and unique fruit of that old tree. This messianism needs a concrete form. . . . [It cannot] be individualistic, and has to be socialistic"—or, more specifically, anarchistic in Landauer's terms. This "concrete messianism" was bound up with the rejection of the aspiration for a nation-state (which Kohn dubbed "the mechanistic and diplomatic solution for the Jewish Question") and was needed "precisely in the days of the new triumph" of this questionable solution.[104] Zionism, he reminded his readers, was always something else: "a reflection on Judaism's deep sources."[105] After all, he continued, it was the legacy of assimilation to idolize the state and citizenship in it. Statehood and national political sovereignty in the conventional sense are neither Zionism's goals nor its guarantees:

> Messianism and anarchist socialism will turn Palestine into Zion. No charter or Peace Conference resolution would provide the guarantees for that. The contemporary world is ruled by chaos, which renders the future uncertain, and which is bound to generate new catastrophes in a few decades, which, in their collapse, would also wash our achievements away. Only we can create the guarantees: through steadfast struggle against the global effect of that which I have dubbed chaos. . . . But the end of that struggle lies in the eternal future: in the creation of a state, which is already no state at all, a rule which is already no rule at all.[106]

The enigmatic, paradoxical concept of Zionism is paradigmatic of Kohn's insistence to fuse antistatist, anarchist socialism with Zionism. He was certainly not the only anarchist within the Zionist movement, nor was he more radical than the great Labor Zionist ideologue, A. D. Gordon.

. . .

"I may have ceased being a Zionist in the common sense," Kohn confided in Weltsch in the fall of 1919, "between *Miklat Batu'ach* (assured home) as it stands in Hebrew in the Basel Platform which I can still justify well, and the 'State,' which the Peace Conference brews for us, there is quite a difference."[107] The aspiration for a state lent Zionism's Arab Question new urgency, and this challenge became the focus of Kohn's Zionist activity from this moment on. His new approach to the significance of this question and its essence is rooted in his experiences as a POW in the East. What he had seen in Samarkand had made him "sensitive to the difficulties that arise when a people try to govern peoples of another race and culture," generating a "clash of two different civilizations, a relationship not of rival peers, of master and subject." Beyond all ethical qualms, Kohn's "experiences in Turkestan, and [his] interest in Palestine, led [him] to question the generally accepted premise that the colonial empires . . . would last."[108] For both ethical and practical reasons, then, it became clear to Kohn that in the looming clash between the colonial powers and the Arab world, Zionism should never stand in the way of Arab self-determination.

Many early Zionists, acutely concerned about the international endorsement of Zionism, remained remarkably silent regarding the Arab population of Palestine. But certain Zionists did raise their voice on that fateful matter. Ahad Ha'am's 1891 "Truth from the Land of Israel" accused fellow Zionists of thinking of the Palestinian Arabs as easily manipulated "desert savages." This, he warned, was profoundly misguided, and when Zionism would reach "the point of encroaching upon the native [Arab] population, they will not easily yield their place."[109] Yitzhak Epstein's 1907 "Hidden Question" had already addressed the question on ethical grounds—not only practical ones—pointing to the human tragedy that Zionist settlement had brought, even against Zionists' will, to many Palestinian Arabs. Epstein's prescription was to settle Jews in Palestine only on unpopulated and uncultivated land.[110]

Thus, Kohn's essay "Zur Araberfrage" (On the Arab Question), written in the summer of 1919, was not the first Zionist writing on the centrality of the Arab Question.[111] Nor was it even the first discussion of the matter in Buber's *Der Jude*.[112] However, all essays before Kohn's still relied on at least one of the two prevalent types of Zionist wishful thinking. Kohn avoided, first, the romantic belief in a cultural and racial affinity between Jews and the Palestinian Arabs. Ironically, this kind of wishful thinking developed from a very European discourse among Zionists, the wish to reaffirm Jewish distinctiveness by embracing and imagining an ideal aesthetic oriental identity—in short, Zionist orientalism.[113]

The second kind of Zionist wishful thinking absent from Kohn's essay was the notion that Arab opposition to Zionism came primarily from the effendis—the few Arab noble and landowning families. According to this line of reasoning, socially progressive Zionism constituted no threat to the Arabs but rather that Zionists were natural allies of the fellaheen, the Arab have-nots or quasi-serfs. Zionism had a lot to offer them. It was only the wealthy and reactionary effendis, their oppressors, who had reason to fear and resent Zionism and to stir up the emotions of the uneducated masses. The appeal of this effendis thesis was its presentation of a zero-sum national conflict as a social problem.[114]

Kohn's essay presented fellow Zionists with a much more alarming situation. In a tone remarkably similar to those of Ahad Ha'am and Epstein, he claims that the Great War made Zionists recognize "the great problems that lie dormant in Eretz Israel, indeed problems that cry out in a loud voice and burden our conscience." The greatest of these is the Arab Question. Many Zionist catchphrases had been used in an attempt to brush this problem away, but

> no matter how unwelcome this may be for us, Palestine is now an Arab country. The population consists of five-sixths Arabs, and that makes an overwhelming majority. This majority is greater than that of the Great Russians in the Russian state of 1914. The country's past, as far as it is relevant ethnographically and economically at the present time, is Arab. The country's language is an Arab dialect; the costumes and way of life (insofar as they have not been superseded by a pretty inferior European import) are Arab. All around live Arabs who are related by language and customs. Geographically Palestine is self-contained, but it belongs orographically [that is, according to the formation of mountains] and geologically to Syria, an Arab nation. Thus today Palestine is rightly and in fact an Arab country.[115]

Kohn wrote these words some six years before Arthur Ruppin's famous speech to the fourteenth World Zionist Congress ("Palestine will be a state of two nations").[116] Kohn saw absolutely no relevance to the Zionist claim of a historical right over the land. "Historical rights" in general seemed fundamentally dubious to him: "Time has advanced. It has swept away everything that was and has built anew. History continues to have an effect on us, but it does not give us rights. Only the living present gives us rights, . . . [hence] we have no historic right to Palestine." But neither do the Arabs: "No nation has a right to a country in such an exclusive sense. The country belongs to those who make it so fertile through the strength of their minds and their hands that they can make their living there." The Jewish right for a national home in Palestine, as Kohn saw it, was grounded in the Zionists' love of the land—a relatively sparsely populated one—and their wish and ability to contribute to it and to all its inhabitants. "This does not, of course, give the Jews the right to take the country from the Arabs, but to settle beside the Arabs on uninhabited land."[117] A prerequisite for building Zion—following Epstein's prescription—would be a certain voluntary segregation in settlement, but even that would not be enough:

> Once there will be a Palestinian state, [. . . it] will not be a national state (*National-staat*) for an indefinite period, but a multinational one (*Nationalitätenstaat*). If we do not realize this in all seriousness, we shall always suffer from the Jewish-Arab problem.
>
> We need a peaceful and friendly accord with the Arabs. . . . Judaism has recognized justice as one of its basic principles, and we ourselves have proclaimed justice as one of the foundations of our movement. If we were to oppress or drive out the Arabs, this would be acting against our innermost being, destroying our true nature, and paralyzing our strength. . . . We undermine the ground beneath our feet by "chauvinist imperialist" actions, by behaving like a "nation-state" (*Staatsvolk*) toward the Arabs . . . [and against such conduct a] purely practical reason must be added. . . . We will always live in the midst of a numerically far larger Arab population. Almost only Arabs live to the north, the east, the south, and only Arabic is spoken. Enmity with them would put us in a state of constant arming and preparation for war.[118]

Those sentences are probably the first clear Zionist call for a multinational —or, rather, a binational—state in Palestine. Kohn reiterated the tenets of coexistence that would prevent the national problem in Palestine from deteriorating into the "serious disease" that has recently affected and indeed destroyed "other states" (namely, the successor states in Central Eastern Europe): the Jews have to combat the chauvinism in their midst and the dangerous assumption that the country "belongs" to them; one "must give both Jews and Arabs the broadest autonomy and self-determination so as to diminish friction"; one has to establish the political mechanism that would enable the coexistence of "two non-territorial, noncoherent, sovereign national communities (*zwei unterritoriale, unzusammenhängende souveräne Nationalgemeinschaften*)." Kohn applied here the Austromarxist prescription of national and cultural autonomy on the non-territorial basis of the "personality principle."[119]

Figure 2.6 Hans Kohn (*second from right*) at the Great Buddha in Kamakura, Japan, on his journey back from Russia, 1920.
Courtesy of the Leo Baeck Institute, New York.

He tied the political and ethical principle at the basis of his plea for a binational Palestine to the path of Jewish history: "The Jews, who have themselves learned what it means when one nation considers itself the ruler within a state (*das herrschende staatliche Volk*), may not and can not set themselves up over the Arabs as the ruling nation in Palestine." The sole guarantee to the success of the Zionist endeavor—as Kohn stressed repeatedly—was not diplomatic, economic, or military. Rather, it was the purity of Zionist action:

> None of the powers of the present-day world, built by dint of law or the accident of history and maintained by force or idleness, can give us any guarantees. . . . The Arab question is difficult. . . . It will never be solved by the dictators of the peace conference, nor by us alone, but only by an agreement between both peoples, Jews and Arabs. . . . Let us not allow ourselves to be beguiled by national chauvinism. Let us, the slaves of yesterday, not become tomorrow's imperialists. Jewish nationalism was always a moral nationalism; it is based on duties, not rights, and on responsibility in the face of humanity. Let us remain serious, prepared, and true to ourselves. Let us beware of all fetishism, let us beware above all of the fetishism of a national master race (*Herrenvolk*)![120]

Figure 2.7 A bearded Hans Kohn on September 20, 1920, shortly after his return to Prague.
Courtesy of the Leo Baeck Institute, New York.

Though Kohn seems to set an exceptionally high moral bar for Jewish nationalism, it should be noted that he attempted here to chart a universal principle, one that is based neither on exclusive rights nor on exclusive duties. Thus, he stressed that these words hold good for the Arabs as well.

Even some friends and colleagues in Kohn's closest circle—like Siegmund Katznelson, a fellow member of Bar Kochba—disapproved of Kohn's essays on the Arab Question. In a harsh essay titled "Jüdisches und arabisches Selbstbestimmungsrecht" (Jewish and Arab right of self-determination), Katznelson presented Kohn as completely out of touch with Zionist reality, attributing to him "overly dogmatically doctrinarism." Kohn, Katznelson wrote, was a "bleeding heart" and was "righteous" (*gerecht*; Katznelson put the term in quotation marks) to the extent of self-destruction; even worse, he "did not wish to discuss the practical and political side of the problem, only its ethical dimension."[121] Kohn's Zionism, it seemed, faced a protracted uphill climb.

Back to Europe

During Kohn's months in Irkutsk, great transformations continued to unfold in the international arena—especially in Russia, where the Red Army grew stronger and seemed close to a full victory. In mid-November 1919, after the Reds had taken Omsk, the fall of Irkutsk seemed inevitable. With alarming news of his mother's deteriorating health, and with sufficient funds for the journey home, Kohn made preparations to leave Siberia.[122]

At the end of the war, "we modern civilizations," wrote Paul Valéry, "have learned to recognize that we are mortal like the others. We feel that a civilization is fragile as a life."[123] Kohn sensed the same thing, long before he could put it into words. The twenty-eight-year-old Kohn returned to Europe a changed man. "The myth of this war," he would conclude ten years later, "was the bourgeois national state." For him the most formative element of the war was his own initial culpability—the fact that he and his mentors had been so uncritically drawn to war in 1914 and thus "all share[d] the guilt (*alle mitschuldig*)." His broadest political conclusion was simply how "necessary it is to be critical (*Es ist notwendig, kritisch zu sein*)."[124] Kohn returned to Europe politicized: his Zionism still spoke the language of religious renewal, but its urgency lay clearly in the realm of a new world order, in questions of war and revolution and in the twilight of colonialism. Kohn returned to Europe a scholar in the making, having devoted most of his years of captivity to self-education, developing his skills as a lecturer, and drafting essays (even, as he told his friends, "entire books").[125] At least in hindsight, it is apparent that his wartime works addressed the essence and historical development of nationalism. The Great War exposed Kohn to nationalism's unimaginably destructive force. His reaction—which would remain the hallmark of his theory of nationalism—was to distinguish between the benign and malignant: between true nationalism, on the one hand, and its degeneration into the ideology of the nation-state, on the other hand. Whereas he still saw in nationalism noble qualities and functions that had to be protected, he now believed that the ideology of the nation-state was inherently destructive and needed to be challenged.

With these formative experiences, plans, and new political ideas, Kohn embarked on a homeward journey that took some four months. Instead of traveling westward—through areas under Red control or the battlefields of the Russian civil war—he began his journey by going eastward, taking the Trans-Siberian Railway to the Pacific port city of Vladivostok, a route through White-controlled territory. From far eastern Russia, Kohn sailed to Japan, where he spent five weeks visiting Kyoto, Tokyo, and Yokohama. Then he sailed southwest, traveling through Shanghai, Hong Kong, Penang, and Colombo. After that he went across the Indian Ocean to the Red Sea and through the Suez Canal to the Mediterranean, landing in Marseille in late March 1920. From there, after a few hours by train, he reached Prague, his hometown.[126]

SEPARATING NATION & STATE, 1919–34

PART TWO

TO TAME EMPIRE, NATION, AND MAN

Political Agenda in the 1920s

The end of that struggle lies in . . . the creation of a state, which is already no state at all, a rule which is already no rule at all.
Hans Kohn, "Perspektiven"[1]

The Bolsheviks are right to see each and every national movement as a bourgeois movement. Nationalism in its current political form is the religion of the bourgeoisie.
Hans Kohn to Robert Weltsch, November 6, 1922[2]

Pacifist convictions are only worth something if maintained when one's own interests are at stake. . . . Hence I am happy that we Jews, returning to Palestine, are not coming to an unpopulated land and can maintain . . . the seriousness and sense of reality of our principles as well as the meaning of Judaism.
Hans Kohn, "Aktiver Pazifismus"[3]

n late March 1920, Hans Kohn entered the Prague railway station after five years of war and captivity. In mid-May 1934, en route to America, he left Palestine for good. Kohn's concepts and agenda, which clearly evolved throughout this fourteen-year period to a politics that fundamentally rejected the nation-state model, were part of a contemporaneous counterdiscourse on nationalism and internationalism. This chapter of Kohn's life was shaped by his struggle against the nation-state model in multiple parallel arenas: as a Jewish thinker, he pointed to the nation-state foundation underlying the Jewish Question; as a Zionist, he fought for a binational Palestine; as a scholar of non-Western nationalisms, he pointed to the ultimate superiority of multiethnic federations; and as a pacifist, he grounded all effective pacifism in a deep understanding of nation-state dynamics.

This rejection of the nation-state was so central that it would ultimately cause Kohn to break with the Zionist movement after twenty years, once he concluded that Zionism would henceforth aspire to nothing but a Jewish nation-state. In the 1920s, many of the advocates of the nation-state model, espousing the principles of "self-determination" and "national sovereignty," were self-proclaimed liberals. During that decade, Kohn had no qualms about engaging with and even learning from nationalist conservatives or communists who shared his rejection of that model. It would only be after Adolf Hitler's accession to power that Kohn would undergo a decided, if not surprising, liberal turn.

In Western Europe (1920–25)

Kohn's reunion with his family, after five years of separation, was bittersweet— perhaps more bitter than sweet. His mother, who had struggled with breast cancer for ten years, was dying. His younger siblings, only children when he left, were now teenagers. He had not been there to see them grow or to assist them through their mother's illness. The years 1914–19 were not only the "decisive years" in his life, they were also years stolen from him as a son and a brother.[4] Since the collapse of the Austro-Hungarian Empire, in his letters and diaries

previous page:
Figure 3.1 Hans Kohn in Palestine (probably at the passport control at the port of Jaffa) in 1927.
Courtesy of the Leo Baeck Institute, New York.

Kohn had expressed complete disinterest in returning to Prague. Homecoming, in this regard, lived up to his low expectations:

> Nothing of what I saw in the weeks following my return was much of an inducement to stay in Central Europe. Prague, now a capital city, has lost much of its captivating quiet charm. The new Czechoslovak government was building on faulty foundations: it identified the new state with a single ethnic group, at the expense of the other groups [mainly the Germans and Hungarians] living in what was now the new Czech state. A similar narrow nationalism had taken hold in the whole of Central Europe. . . . A decade earlier, I had expected to live my life in Prague; in 1920, I now felt something unhealthy and restrictive in the unsettled atmosphere of Central Europe. . . . In Central Europe the experiences of the war had in no way lessened the nationalism that had led to the war. Quite the contrary. Thus the prospects for democracy and peace appeared dim.[5]

Kohn did not stay long in Czechoslovakia, which he clearly saw not as a multinational state—Slovak and Czech—but as a nation-state of sorts, created at the expense of its local minority populations.[6] A letter from Prague to a friend from Kohn's years of Russian captivity documented the deeper personal and cultural dimensions of his homecoming experience.[7] Kohn felt alienated from the culture "at home" and a surprising degree of nostalgia for life in Russian captivity: "I believe that returning is a bitter disappointment to anyone who comes back to Central Europe after years of absence." He continued: "The war, which was hoped to bring about catharsis and purification, to terminate egoism and nurture sincerity—generated the complete opposite. . . . [S]omehow everything deteriorated." What he saw around him in Prague was "disgusting libertarianism" and "false and sterile idealism": "Inevitably we [returning POWs] became strangers." This generated a homesickness for the life he had in Russia as a prisoner of war—a life that now seemed more real and freer than life at "home," he explained: "it is hard not to yearn for Russia," where "one lives more forcefully, and with greater contact with reality." He especially missed the openness and depth of human interaction there: "Here one approaches another from the outset with suspicion. A barrier stands between people." Oddly, what he missed most of all was a certain freedom and audacity of the mind, which had become impossible for him as a free man at home: "I do not know yet what the end would be; but I have the steady consciousness that—may all perish around us, may Europe continue to mangle herself during a last flinching of agony—in the East, in Asia there will remain the possibility of true life."[8]

Uninterested in—even disgusted by—decaying Europe, Kohn was drawn

Figure 3.2 Hans Kohn (*top right*) circa 1920, reunited with Prague friends, among them Robert Weltsch (*to his left*), Pepi Wien (top left), Leo Herrmann (*middle*), and Lise Weltsch-Kaznelson (*to his left*).
Courtesy of the Leo Baeck Institute, New York.

to Asia. Similar notions in his letters from Russia written over the previous two years were always linked to the promise of an impending Aliyah to the Land of Israel. Indeed, only days after his return from Russia, he participated in the Prague conference of the socialist Hapo'el Hatza'ir, alongside Martin Buber and many Bar Kochba friends. Hapo'el Hatza'ir, founded by A. D. Gordon, would ostensibly become Kohn's political home in postwar Zionism. However, in spite of proclamations about his imminent Aliyah, he would not leave Europe quite yet.

Paris, the Comité des Délégations Juives, and the French Intellectuals

In May 1920, just two months after his return to Prague, Kohn moved to Paris, where he would live for a year and a half, holding a secretarial position in the Comité des Délégations Juives (Committee of Jewish delegations). The committee had been founded through a Zionist initiative in an attempt to create a unified representation for Jews at the Paris Peace Conference, where various Jewish organizations represented different positions. Very little is known about

Kohn's work there; this is especially regrettable because the committee—now known primarily as defender of the rights of Jews in Central Eastern Europe between the world wars—was a vocal advocate of national minority rights at the time.[9] This aspect of its activity seems remarkably well aligned with Kohn's feeling that the power of the nation-state must be curtailed. That goal was achieved to a considerable extent in the League of Nations' Minority Treaties, in the creation of which the committee was famously instrumental.[10]

To be sure, though rightly identified with the principle of national minority rights, the committee's position on national sovereignty was neither simple nor coherent, and neither impartial nor academic. Its leaders, who included some rather hawkish Zionists such as Menachem Ussishkin and Pinhas Rutenberg, advocated for the national minority rights of Eastern European Jews but felt no need to tone down their demand for a national home for the Jewish people in Palestine. This is probably why Kohn wrote so little about his role in the committee. "Nothing," he wrote in a letter, "draws me to the *Comité*. I hate these people with their petty vanity, with their pushiness, with their fluffing of something that is not there, with their lust for power."[11] The tension between restraining the model of the nation-state and aspiring to have a nation-state for their own people was not unique to the Jewish representatives at the Paris Peace Conference, and it was typical of the tension between principle and self-interest in the conference in general. The League of Nations never granted the principle of minority rights universal validity, and calls to apply it to the Irish or the African Americans (a Japanese initiative) were rejected out of hand.[12]

For such reasons Kohn saw the immediate postwar moment as hypercolonial, even before he went to Paris. As shown in the previous chapter, influenced by the Soviet critique of western policies, Kohn called the Paris Peace Conference "a conference of hatred and greed and the cradle of future wars," which simply "fulfilled the demands of the strong and disregarded the voices of the weak"—the Irish, Indians, Koreans, and Arabs.[13] Even decades later, his basic understanding of the period remained unchanged:

The end of the war had brought a new scramble for the spoils of empire. Britain, by gaining German East Africa, fulfilled Rhodes' dream of a trans-African Cairo-to-Cape-Town link. Britain also thought to hold Egypt, promised Palestine to the Zionists, and secured the land route across Arabia to India as well as the oil to be found along the route. France enlarged her African holdings and realized in Syria and Lebanon the aspirations of the Crusaders, which she claimed as her heritage. The United States, while looking askance at European "imperialism," competed with British oil interests, kept a tight rein on Cuba, Puerto Rico, and the Philippines, and took a dim view of the socialist revolution in Mexico, finally intervening with armed forces in 1916.[14]

Beyond Kohn's deep moral aversion to this kind of imperialism, he simply found it unattainable. Old colonial Europe would not be able withhold the backlash of subject populations. Apparently, however, Europe was not yet aware that its domination of the globe was effectively over.

There was a clear divide between Kohn's secretarial work for the committee and his aspiration, which grew clear during these Parisian months, to become a critical voice within Zionism, engaging his people and his movement through loyal but harsh opposition. Kohn—whose sense of political commitment is best summarized by Proverbs 27:6: "Faithful are the wounds of a friend"—was inspired by contemporaneous French intellectuals, whom he found quite unlike their Central European counterparts.[15]

Tellingly, Kohn mentioned in his memoirs that in Paris 1920 he "discovered Charles Péguy, [Georges] Sorel, [Pierre-Joseph] Proudhon, and the generation of the Dreyfus affair, Charles Maurras and Maurice Barrès, Daniel Halévy, and Romain Rolland, Roger Martin du Gard, and André Spire. I became well acquainted with Spire and Jean-Richard Bloch." All in their way embodied the ideal of the politically committed intellectual, yet the broad ideological spectrum of these men is quite baffling. It was to be expected that Kohn would be impressed by the Zionist poet Spire and by Rolland's humanist, internationalist pacifism. And as Kohn was pro-Soviet at the time, it may not be surprising that he became close to the communist novelist Bloch. Péguy was a pacifist and an anarchist socialist—also like Kohn at the time. However, Sorel was a militant and antisemitic anarchist-syndicalist. Equally antisemitic was the nineteenth-century anarchist Proudhon. Barrès was not only an antisemite but a militarist ethnonationalist. The counterrevolutionary Maurras—leader and ideologue of the Action Française—extends the political spectrum much further. More than anything, it must have been Kohn's discovery of Péguy (and his magazine, *Les Cahiers de la Quinzaine*) that paved his way to these ideologically diverse writers, including some of the staunchest opponents of liberal democracy: "The conflicts which Péguy discussed were made real to me each morning because I regularly read *Action Française*, the lively organ written by Maurras, Léon Daudet, and Jacques Bainville (though its vitriolic attacks on the Republic became monotonous after a time). The other French papers seemed vacuous and boring to me."[16] Throughout the 1920s Kohn would engage reactionary modernists and counterrevolutionary thinkers with a surprising degree of curiosity and openness —occasionally even with critical admiration.

Kohn's political activity and writing from that time on were clearly inspired by two not dissimilar models: that of modern French intellectuals and that of the ancient Hebrew prophets. The prophetic role here denoted not a supernatural ability to predict the future but rather the prophet's ability—as a person separated from political power and establishment—to voice critical judgment of one's people and ruler; to speak truth to power; and, when necessary, even to sling hurtful words at one's own party.[17] So, following the San Remo Conference (April 1920) in which the League of Nations made the Balfour Declaration its business by demanding that the British implement the declaration, Kohn's article "Der Augenblick" (The moment) was quick to rain on the Zionists' parade, warning against triumphalism: neither the British Empire nor the League of Nations offered a lasting foundation for Zion.[18] He depicted Zionism as a self-satisfied movement that had lost its critical edge, had gone technocratic, and did not even recognize the meaning of the challenges ahead: "Where are the few who love their people and its revival deeply, whose reason can crumble [empty] phrases, and who stay away from the suggestions of the masses? Why are they silent?"[19]

These few, for Kohn, would be the modern incarnations of the Hebrew prophets. His search for fellow prophets in postwar Zionism was almost inevitably tied to the conceptualization of the Zionist movement as now, after its first decisive victory, consisting of suggestible masses:

> These people are honest, but their gaze does not go deep. They easily succumb to suggestion. They are exposed to the natural, animalistic feelings—which are so deeply burned into us, and which tell us that *our* instincts are good, and the ones of the *others* run counter to the laws of ethics—and to the atavistic feelings of togetherness, which perceive the stranger as foe. They do not read the papers, but . . . are likely to believe their lies. They have the ability for enthusiasm, and for dedication, but their reason does not rise to the uncompromising critical inquiry needed to penetrate the whole truth. . . . Hence I fear that their enthusiasm may one day be sacrificed on impure altars.[20]

In September 1921, in a critical report from the twelfth World Zionist Congress at Carlsbad, which he attended and described as "a disappointment," Kohn explained what he meant by "impure altars." The Zionist movement's political achievements, he asserted, were merely a byproduct of British imperial and foreign policy, yet this policy was dynamic and volatile, and it might very

Figure 3.3 Hans and Jetty Kohn around the time of their marriage, 1921.
Courtesy of the Leo Baeck Institute, New York.

soon turn toward the Arabs, potentially pulling the rug out from under the Zionist project: "In a matter of years, maybe even months, we may be obliged to build our whole project on entirely new ground . . . but [in the Congress] one sees no acknowledgement of such a possibility . . . [and in such a case] things may end up in despair, like in the days of Sabbatai Tsevi."[21] Here Kohn used the seventeenth-century false messiah Sabbatai Tsevi, whom he had provocatively praised on the eve of the Great War, to warn against what Kohn now saw as the perversion of the Zionist idea. This historical allegory would serve him throughout the period between the world wars.

London and the International Dimensions of British Scholarship and Politics

Kohn's fifteen months in Paris were "some of [his] happiest."[22] In the summer of 1920, while visiting London, Kohn met his future wife, Jetty (later Yetty) Wahl, at the house of his Bar Kochba friend Leo Hermann (Jetty was Her-

Figure 3.4 A formal photo of the married couple, 1920s.
Courtesy of the Leo Baeck Institute, New York.

mann's sister-in-law). Kohn and Jetty married on April 16, 1921, and that summer Kohn joined her in London, where they would spend the next four years. His position in London was with the newly established Keren Hayesod (Foundation fund), the chief Zionist fundraising organization, where he would serve as head of the Press and Propaganda Section (replacing none other than Vladimir Jabotinsky).[23] There was always a contradiction between Kohn's position as a formal representative of the Zionist movement and his vocal criticism of it. Though Kohn's position was an important one, the value of these years for Kohn clearly lay outside the office.

Deeply impressed with British political culture, he came to view his London years as a complement to his time in Russia, understanding Russia and Britain as the poles of Europe: "Russia is the link between the East and West, belonging fully to neither," while "Britain is the heartland of the modern West." His impression of the rising chauvinist authoritarian spirit in Europe only confirmed the radicalizing impact of the revolutionary process in Russia on Kohn's politics. "The strength of the democratic process" in Great Britain, however, had a deradicalizing effect. Excited about the formation of the first Labor government, Kohn joined both the Independent Labour Party and the Fabian Society. He also joined the War Resisters' International and would later become one of its leaders. Both the democratic, orderly transition of power and the advance of "non-doctrinaire democratic socialism and pacifism" indicated to Kohn that "democracy was a way of life" in Great Britain.[24]

Though the extent of his engagement in British politics may be somewhat surprising, the appeal of the Fabian Society makes sense given his view of politics and his potential role therein. Kohn clearly identified with the Fabians as "children of the Enlightenment and radical Liberalism" who, rather than appealing to their tribal passions, appealed to the people's critical reason. More importantly, he praised them as a prime example of how a small group of intellectuals could reframe political debates.[25]

In addition to what he saw as the strength of the British democratic process, in London Kohn found himself living in the capital of what was then the world's greatest empire, a metropolis with a truly international horizon, and he was impressed with the wide global perspective of "the British periodicals . . . [that] took the whole world for their subject matter."[26] Compared with this British global perspective, Central European horizons seemed narrow and alarmingly self-referential. But there was something confusing going on in England, to which Kohn alluded very subtly in his memoirs and that is documented in his intellectual trajectory in the interwar period: in spite of their global perspective, the British, as victors in the Great War, were mostly oblivious to the end of their world dominion brought about by that war. In general, Kohn believed, the British were under the false impression "that they were still living in the world that existed before 1914. . . . The foundations of Western society had been profoundly shaken. The German and Italian nationalists and Russian communists knew it. But Great Britain and the United States remained unperturbed."[27] Based on his experiences in Turkestan and his interest in Palestine, Kohn was "one of those who saw that the 'unchanging' East was changing rapidly."[28] This knowledge, which transformed his Zionism, also defined his early academic pursuits. In the next decade, Kohn would establish himself as a student of modern Eastern politics and a scholar of nationalism in "the Middle East, from Egypt to India." Kohn, along with Arnold Toynbee, was a pioneer in the field, and the two men were in communication as of the late 1920s. Serving as a Middle East correspondent for both the *Neue Zürcher Zeitung* and the *Frankfurter Zeitung*, Kohn also analyzed the same questions in a nonacademic fashion (in this regard, too, he resembled Toynbee, who was the *Manchester Guardian*'s correspondent). Kohn spent much time during his London years in the British Museum Reading Room, conducting the research he would use to produce many future academic works.

By the early 1930s Kohn would have published seven books and many shorter publications on non-Western political modernity. Impressive as his scholarship was, however, in those years he was equally committed to multiple similarly massive undertakings, to each of which he brought a great sense of urgency: Kohn published eight books and scores of essays on Jewish political thought. He waged an uphill battle for a binational Palestine (cofounding the Brith Shalom association and serving as its secretary). Similarly, he struggled to invigorate international pacifism (playing a considerable role in the War Resisters' International in the late 1920s). Kohn's parallel political and intellectual careers between the mid-1920s and early 1930s profoundly informed each other and shaped his emerging theory of nationalism.[29] Precisely for this reason, it is vital to explore those careers to appreciate their importance in Kohn's life.

The Struggle for Binationalism in Palestine

Kohn neither abandoned nor scaled down the daunting task he spelled out in Irkutsk 1919: to redefine Zionism and direct it away from the nation-state model. In the wake of the Great War, the Balfour Declaration, and the San Remo Conference, this could no longer be done based on prewar spiritual Zionism alone. Kohn felt the need to explore this overwhelming mission and advocate a new political and ideological agenda with like-minded Zionists. Buber had already made such an attempt in 1918, in a society he called Tsvat (the Hebrew word for "pliers" and also the Hebrew acronym for "Zion shall be redeemed with judgment" [Isaiah 27:1]). Still a POW at that time, Kohn could not take part in Tsvat, but immediately after his return from Russia he explored the creation of similar opposition groups within Zionism. He hoped, as he told Robert Weltsch in 1920, "that somehow, from our old friendship a group of independent [intellectuals] would arise."[30]

It took Kohn several years to settle on a platform, a suitable mode of operation, and most vitally, on the right partners. Though Kohn was clearly ahead of the curve—arguably due to his unique war experience—many of his postwar political sensibilities were shared by Buber and his Zionist circles. In London in 1921, Kohn attempted to create a group called the Jüdische Gesellschaft für Internationale Verständigung (Jewish society for international understanding). The proposed society would—as a representative of the Jewish people— collaborate with like-minded intellectuals of other nations on a vitally needed "*menschheitlicher Aufbau des Völkerlebens*" (panhuman construction of the lives of nations).[31] The political and ethical reform of Zionism, moving it away from the nation-state model, would lend universal importance to the small national movement of the Jews, which would become an exemplar of a new type of nationalism and a model of national peaceful coexistence. The proposal to create such a society unmistakably resonated with—and can indeed be seen as an attempted implementation of—essays on nationalism written by Buber in September 1921 and Kohn in 1922.[32] Variations of this idea would run through Kohn's career in the 1920s. However, he failed to turn the idea of the society into a reality, though he wrote letters in 1921 and 1922 on behalf of the society to Haim Arlosoroff, Hayim Nahman Bialik, Jacob Klatzkin, and two dozen other leading Zionist intellectuals.[33]

The Arab Question was central to Kohn's postwar Zionist concerns, and it also made for a more effective rallying call than the abstract goal of international understanding. As noted above, Kohn was not the first Zionist thinker to view the treatment of the Arabs as the movement's moral and political touchstone. He was, however, the first to bundle it with a principled critique of the nation-state model and to prescribe, as early as 1919, a multinational Palestinian state.

His multinational vision was grounded in concepts from the late Austro-Hungarian Empire, and especially in Austromarxist theories of nationalism. Yet in the early 1920s, parallel formulas of multinational empire were taking center stage, broadening and reinforcing his political imagination. Soviet nationality policy, which Kohn explored most favorably in two books, promised a new model of liberation of subject nations, turning them not into feuding nation-states but into a multinational, ostensibly anticolonial, empire.

Kohn was similarly impressed by the alternative British liberal model that inspired the creation of an international commonwealth on a global scale through the reform of the British Empire along the lines of the Round Table Movement. Theirs, as Jeanne Morefield has demonstrated, was an imperialist project through and through, yet "they wanted a universal theory that was also specifically Anglo-Saxon in origin . . . that would tie their evolving vision of commonwealth to a particular English form of liberty."[34] In the wake of the Wilsonian Moment, these concepts gained greater urgency for some, as disillusionment among members of non-European subject nations "helped to displace the liberal, reformist anticolonialism that failed in favor of the more radical, revisionist nationalism."[35] This seemed like the last chance for any such multinational reform.

Many of Kohn's Zionist associates spoke out with increasing clarity and urgency about the gravity of the Arab Question. But while they engaged the subject through a variety of ethical questions ranging from the modes of settlement to the moral threat in an alliance with European imperialism against Arab nationalism, Kohn remained focused on one goal: a multinational state in Palestine.[36] Indeed, he seems to have remained the only one to explicitly prescribe this path. For him, the clear divide between nation-state and multinational state was the key moral and political distinction. This distinction was somewhat similar to his principled pacifist stands: he did not believe in just wars but in the abolition of war; and similarly he did not believe in a just nation-state but in the abolition of the nation-states. Kohn's rigid a priori rejection of the nation-state, especially the new nation-state, is not trivial. After all, some nation-states were more inclusive and liberal than others. Be that as it may, Kohn resisted the tide of national self-determination as he developed his scholarship, his Jewish political thought, and his political agendas and consistently denounced the nation-state model and its underlying assumptions.

In 1922 Kohn told every Zionist who was willing to listen that rather than informing the Palestinian Arabs that they came in peace, Zionists needed to declare that they did not seek the establishment of a Jewish state.[37] In the summer of 1923 Kohn visited Palestine for the first time, traveling all over the land, meeting many members of the Yishuv and its leaders. He was taken with Jerusalem's "uncanny (*unheimlich*) beauty" and even delivered lectures in Kibbutz Heftziba.[38] Things were slowing down in the Yishuv, after the major breakthroughs of the Balfour Declaration of 1917 and the euphoria about it and its ratification by the League of Nations in the San Remo Resolution of 1920. In 1923 the Yishuv, whose population was less than a hundred thousand, was experiencing more than an economic crisis. A year earlier, the Churchill White Paper of 1922 had made clear that the British never intended to make Palestine "as Jewish as England is English." Among other things, it presented the principle of limiting future Zionist immigration based on "the economic capacity of the country at the time to absorb" new immigrants, so as not to "deprive any section of the present population of its employment."[39] These British guidelines alarmed many Zionists, but from Kohn's perspective, they seemed to chart a fair path forward. Only two years after his first visit to Palestine, Kohn moved to Jerusalem along with the Keren Hayesod main office—a move that had seemed so self-explanatory and imminent to him five years earlier finally took place.

In the early 1920s, Kohn had been in contact with the Austrian journalist Eugen Höflich (later known as Moshe Ya'akov Ben-Gavri'el), who was on a similar mission to fundamentally reform Zionism. Whereas Kohn's catchphrase was "multinational state" (and a Zionist rejection of the nation-state model), Höflich's was "Pan-Asianism" (and a Zionist rejection of the European self-conception and alliances). In 1925, not long before leaving London for Palestine, Kohn and Höflich were considering ways "to create an active group, espousing an agreement (*Verständigung*) with the Arabs." Letters Kohn sent to Höflich in April articulate the mission, proposed activity, and even members of the binationalist Brith Shalom association a good half-year before its inception.[40] "In recognition of the actual conditions of the country and the changes in the political world of the Orient," Kohn wrote, "we do not want the creation of a Jewish state in which a Jewish ruling majority stands opposite to a less entitled second nation in Palestine. . . . Palestine must become a binational commonwealth (*Gemeinwesen*), in which there is no dominant state nationality, and where two peoples can address their respective national needs with complete equality."[41]

Several other Zionists of similar background started working toward very similar goals at roughly the same time. In late 1924 Arthur Ruppin, head of the Zionist Palestine Office and one of the foremost Zionist leaders, corresponded with Robert Weltsch and others about establishing a "society for the improvement of Jewish Arab Relations."[42] And on June 10, 1925, Ruppin hosted Weltsch and others in his Jerusalem home for concrete discussions about the creation of a "league for Jewish-Arab understanding."[43]

En route from London to a new life in Jerusalem, Kohn attended the fourteenth World Zionist Congress in Vienna, where Ruppin famously addressed the plenary session in an overt appeal for a binational Palestine. "Palestine," Ruppin said, "will be a state of two nations. Gentlemen, this is a fact, a fact which many of you have not yet sufficiently realized. It may also be that for some of you this is not a pleasant fact, but it nonetheless remains so."[44]

Settling into Jerusalem in the summer of 1925, Kohn never intended to become a full-time Zionist functionary. His academic agenda included the completion of a book he tentatively called "History of National Movements in the New East"; his Jewish publication agenda included both a biography of Buber and a book tentatively titled "The Jewish Man: His Essence and Path." In addition, he asked Buber to reach out to his acquaintances at the *Frankfurter Zeitung* and help get Kohn a position as Middle East correspondent.[45] In a letter to Buber a few months later, Kohn sounded invigorated: "We have already settled in here in Jerusalem, it offers a wide panorama, its air is free and open, and it hosts a distinctive mélange of the most colorful types of people, like no other place." In December 1926, Kohn would become a father (he and Jetty would name their son Immanuel Hananiah, after Immanuel Kant). And soon after the move to Jerusalem, Kohn started working for the Zionist press in a position par-

allel to the one he had in Keren Hayesod. His research and writing were moving steadily along. But his most important update for Buber was that "with Ruppin, Hugo Bergmann, Radler-Feldmann and others, we also work here on a group for Arab-Jewish agreement, about which you will hear more soon."[46]

The group that Kohn cofounded was a binationalist association, which would soon receive the name Brith Shalom (Covenant of peace). Ruppin would be its chairperson, Joseph Lurie his deputy, and Kohn the secretary-treasurer. The editorial in the first volume of its magazine, *She'ifoteinu* (Our aspirations), spelled out a vision: "Brith Shalom wishes to create here, in the Land of Israel, a state inhabited jointly by the two peoples living in this country under complete equality or rights, as the two elements that jointly and equally determine the destiny of this country, without regard for . . . which of the two is, at any particular time, numerically superior."[47]

Transcending the "abnormal condition of being in a minority" and acquiring "the normal condition of being a majority," as Israel Zangwill put it, had long been a preoccupation of many Zionists.[48] The distinction between minority and majority became overtly political in the interwar international arena, with demographic majorities seen as justified in their domination of ethnic minorities. Victor Jacobson was expressing that view when he told Buber that "we [Zionists] must create by all means a majority in the country [Palestine] as soon as possible."[49] A Jewish majority, it was believed, would solidify the Zionist claim for Palestine. But, as Kohn had noted in 1919, there was a majority in Palestine, and an overwhelming one at that, and it was Arab. Indeed, attempts to nationalize lands through such demographic means, Kohn had learned in Bohemia, never pacified national conflicts but rather caused them to escalate out of control. Brith Shalom rejected the Zionist aspiration to create a Jewish majority. As one association member put it, Zionism could have many different goals and principles, but not "this pitiful principle." Zionism needed to be rescued from this zero-sum game; the binational state was their formula, and the task was to work out the constitutional structure, the international guarantees, and the popular support for this endeavor.[50]

The association, which never had more than several dozen supporters and members, was a remarkable group of Zionist intellectuals. In addition to Ruppin, Kohn collaborated there with some larger-than-life figures: Yehoshua Radler-Feldmann, "the Zionist pioneer and orthodox Jew who lived for almost half a century in Palestine and wrote under the pen name Reb Binyomin," in whom Kohn saw "a great moral and intellectual strength"; Yitzhak Epstein, a veteran Hebrew educator and author of the 1907 essay "The Hidden Question," on the Arab Question; the educator and philosopher Ernst Simon; and Gershom Scholem, the pathbreaking scholar of Jewish mysticism.[51] "Scholem," Kohn confided in his journal, "is a strange man. His makeup is even more peculiar than ours: a faithless theologian, and hence, by essence, unproductive. Yet he is someone who one day could write a major philosophical work.... In many regards he is a medieval demonlike monk, without the humanity of [Albert] Schweitzer or [Leonhard] Ragaz, yet deeper than them metaphysically. All in all, he is a man of the metasphere.... [T]here is something ghostlike, demonic about him." In a later entry, Kohn noted: "Scholem is an honest man, but not a good one. His self-love and disrespect [of others] are frequently grotesque."[52]

The association included several prominent officers of Zionist organizations —people like Ruppin, Haim Margaliot-Kalvarisky, and Jacob Thon—who were instrumental in Zionist land acquisition and settlement. As members of Brith Shalom, they decried the systematic injustice caused by Zionist settlement in Palestine. As functionaries of Zionist organizations, however, they can be seen as the architects of that policy. The association's meetings were usually hosted in private homes, but sometimes they took place in the offices of the Palestine Land Development Company, where Ruppin and Thon worked, and that major colonizing organization also occasionally gave the association money.[53] This was much more than ironic; in fact, it represented an existential contradiction. On some level the members of Brith Shalom were torn. So was Kohn, whose task at Keren Hayesod was to present Zionism and its colonization project in a positive light, but whose role as a founding member of Brith Shalom was to expose the negative and dangerous impact of the Zionist policy.

Kohn was a central figure in the association. For example, he seems to have been the one who suggested its name and a coauthor of many of its key declarations and publications, and he constantly pushed for its transformation into a politically active group.[54] Indeed, within Brith Shalom, Kohn belonged to a subgroup known as the Radical Circle, which included his Bar Kochba friends Bergmann and Weltsch as well as Scholem and Simon. Whereas Ruppin wanted Brith Shalom, at least initially, to "act as a Fabian-style research and study association," the members of the Radical Circle insisted that Brith Shalom become a political actor within Zionism—the association was not only to launch a debate but to actually participate in it and, if possible, frame it.[55] Kohn was the model advocate of that approach: as early as November 1925 he urged the association to come out with a bold and binding public declaration.[56]

Initially, the dominant line in the association was the more cautious one, advocated by Ruppin. In late November 1925, Kohn attended a meeting between the association's representatives and several leaders of the Yishuv, including Haim Arlosoroff, Meir Dizengoff, Yosef Sprinzak, Berl Katznelson, Moshe Beilinson, and David Ben-Gurion. Ruppin's statements at that meeting were typical of the cautious line he championed: "People think that we [the association] will negotiate with the Arabs," he began. "No! First we have to clarify for ourselves the possibilities of shaping the relation between us and the Arabs." "We do not wish to go into political action," he would repeat throughout the meeting. "We merely wish to assist the Zionist Executive Committee."[57] But Ruppin's conciliatory tone did not appease Ben-Gurion, who stated his antagonism to the "Biational State formula." "Is it not enough," he asked, "to have the one 'National Home' formula which no one understands, that you wish to add yet another meaningless formula?" Ben-Gurion insisted that a binationalist restatement of Zionism's goals would fail simply because the Jewish people would never be interested in it: "There are vital historical needs of the Jewish masses which support Zionism, and the Jewish people will not follow you. The Jewish people want to be free and independent in its land, and this means a Jewish state. Obviously states can have different characters. One may aspire to a Prussian state, or a czarist state. . . . We, workers, aspire to a socialist state that oppresses no one, and in which no man rules another."[58]

At the time—to the dismay of Kohn and the other members of the Radical Circle—Ruppin's cautious line remained dominant, and though Brith Shalom clearly advocated binational Zionism, it presented itself as little more than an advisory policy research organization. When Kohn and other members of the association met again with leaders of the Yishuv—Ben-Gurion, Zalman Rubashov (later Shazar), Moshe Shertok (later Sharett), Katznelson and others —Ruppin stressed once more that Brith Shalom did not intend to initiate direct negotiations with Arabs, it sought only to facilitate a clarification of the Zionist position on the matter. Yet Ben-Gurion was not convinced: "I am opposed to the Brith Shalom Association. . . . [I]nstead of educating both sides to mutual understanding and respect, you are becoming a political party. I have nothing against what your platform includes, but I have much against what it does not include: *there is no Zionism in it.*"[59] Such meetings exposed Brith Shalom's precarious position. With prominent leaders like Ruppin, it was still tolerated and treated with respect, yet when it tried to address policy questions, it was marginalized. Ben-Gurion's hostility in that meeting and Katznelson's dismissive attitude boded ill for Brith Shalom's hope of beginning an open discussion of possible Zionist stands regarding the thorny question of constitution and popular representation in Mandatory Palestine. Two days later, Ruppin confided in his diary that the Labor Zionist leaders had expressed misgivings not so much about Brith Shalom's agenda as about the personalities of Kohn, Bergmann, and Radler-Feldmann, whom they derided as "ideologues and dreamers."[60]

Kohn's hopes for Brith Shalom, then, were bound to lead to conflicts within the association. In late 1925 he urged Ruppin commit the association to a binding platform and make it public, even at the expense of reducing initial support for Brith Shalom.[61] The association did make its views heard on current affairs, but it still shied away from addressing the big questions in a detailed platform. Accordingly, in 1926 Kohn worked with the Hebrew poet Mordechai Avi-Sha'ul on a thirteen-point "outline for an Arab-Hebrew understanding."[62] Their outline went well beyond the Zionist consensus in certain regards—such as the question of a legislative council—but remained within it on Jewish immigration, which they saw as repatriation that should be virtually unconstrained. However, this outline was not accepted by the association or made public.

In the 1926 article "The Political Future of Palestine," Kohn spelled out his binationalist vision, not on ethical or distinctly Jewish grounds but in practical political terms.[63] In it, he addressed the burning questions on which he had wanted Brith Shalom to take a stand. The essay, which Kohn wrote as a political scientist, acknowledged the significant particularity of both Palestine and Zionism but pointed to many multiethnic precedents—from the past and present, and from East and West—to learn from. Those people pursuing a binational state in Palestine could find real assistance in the lessons of these precedents. Moreover, much of Palestine's uniqueness could actually help the creation of this admittedly singular state mechanism.

Following the Austromarxist formula and his own 1919 essay "On the Arab Question,"[64] Kohn envisioned two essentially extraterritorial national autonomies in Palestine. Above those two, there was to be a Palestinian government, a central authority "with a minimum of interference and regulation."[65] This authority, however, was to be administered by the British on behalf of the League of Nations. For Kohn, though, the true guarantee for the success of this state mechanism lay not above the national autonomies but beneath them, at the most local levels:

> The focus of civic political will should occur within the communities, it should develop from the bottom to the top, and any interference from the top should be limited to cases of absolute necessity. There should be a far-reaching decentralization, the head administration should not constitute the main pillar in shaping [civic] life, which assigns certain responsibilities to the communities and regions, but rather communities and regions should ascertain the matters of immediate concern to the daily life of the citizens, and should in turn assign parts of their authority to the head administration; a process that would require a general regulation. Today the communities' ethnic identity is already largely clarified, almost without exceptions in the villages, and in part in the cities.[66]

The underlying assumptions of this decentralized political structure, as the historian Yfaat Weiss has noted, are telling.[67] Given that interethnic fusion might prove volatile—as would be manifested a few years later, in the 1929 riots—Kohn built his binational vision on the more solid small community or region, whose ethnic identity is overt and hence less contested. Concentrating political life at this communal level would be sure to keep, and even increase, the ethnic profile of the smaller community. At the lowest community level, this policy would sustain and even intensify ethnic segregation. Moving from the regional level to the national one, Kohn saw the representative bodies of the respective nationalities as allowing both nationalities unhindered autonomy to develop as they wish. However, the actual scope of this autonomy, as Kohn described it, did not exceed the rights stipulated by the League of Nations' Minority Treaties.

Kohn assumed that the national aspirations of both Zionists and Arabs could be scaled down to that level. Finally, moving to the state level, he proposed multiple regulatory mechanisms to limit the power of the demographically superior ethnic group over the demographically inferior group, but he placed this central authority firmly under the suzerainty of the League of Nations. Binational Palestine, it follows, would never aspire to full (joint) sovereignty and would always remain under the stewardship of an empire, albeit a benevolent one. Kohn's vision of the political future of Palestine might have been a hard sell for many Zionists, yet it demonstrated—or attempted to demonstrate—that different solutions were available and that, given the necessary political will, a suitable multinational formula could be negotiated and accepted.

As a key figure in Brith Shalom, Kohn got to collaborate and converse with Arab nationalists. In January 1928, he worked with Habib Khoury and Mussa el Alami on a series of lectures for an audience of Arabs and Jews, delivered by both Arab and Jewish speakers. The suggested format matched an Arab chairperson with a Jewish speaker, and a Jewish chairperson with an Arab speaker. The plan did not materialize, perhaps because several Arabs saw it as a "Zionist maneuver."[68] In June Kohn, Itzhak Epstein, and Yizahk Ben Zvi participated in a conversation "with Ihsan B. Jabarin, the famous leader of the Syrians, with Auni abdul Hadi [of Istiklal] of Jerusalem, and one leader of [the] Haifa Arabs in the home of Mussa al-Alami in Sharafa outside Jerusalem. All participants share[d] the impression from the three-hour discussion that Arabs are ready for [a negotiated] agreement if they were to receive a sincere Jewish declaration to the effect that Jews aspire to neither a Jewish state nor a majority but rather genuinely aspire to live as their [Arabs'] equals."[69]

Set on bringing the binational idea closer to the stage of practical discussions, in March 1928 Kohn spearheaded Brith Shalom's attempt to draft a binational constitution for Palestine. He presented a rough draft containing eight articles, on basic rights, parliamentary representation, regulation of the language question, local autonomy, education system, judiciary and court system, defense and police, and economic development. Joseph Lurie and Kohn then took it on themselves to flesh out the wording dealing with the thorny issues of basic rights and parliamentary representation, and Ruppin added a ninth article, on the regulation of immigration, which he wrote in full.[70]

That spring, Kohn and other members of the Radical Circle started expressing grave concerns about what they saw as Brith Shalom's inactivity. On May 26, Kohn and Bergmann had a hard conversation with Ruppin, which left the latter "rather depressed." Their demand that "Brith Shalom adopt a stand in favor of a constitution for Palestine" and become a political actor within Zionism worried and embarrassed Ruppin, who believed it "ought to be a study or discussion circle" only.[71] Kohn followed up with a letter to Ruppin that included a draft of the proclamation to the press: "We declare that we principally look favorably at the idea of a Palestinian constitution and the establishment of popular representation. We trust that negotiation toward agreement on the details of the constitution and popular representation in Palestine would be to the benefit of both peoples."[72] Ruppin responded two days later in a very thoughtful letter. Brith Shalom, he said, had not yet fulfilled its vital task of proposing well-thought-out and developed measures according to which Zionism could be realized without either conflict with the Arabs or resorting to conquest of some sort. If Brith Shalom became a political actor, it would forever abandon that most vital of tasks. As for the constitution, Ruppin pointed to the fundamental conflicts of interests between Zionists and Arabs and stressed quite convincingly that "under the circumstances, a constitution deserving of the name must inevitably lead to a situation in which the Arabs will make use of the rights that the constitution has granted them as the majority to prevent any economic progress of the Jewish minority. That would quite simply mean the end of the Zionist movement."[73] The members of the Radical Circle did not heed the cautionary words of the association's chairperson, however. In October, while Ruppin was out of the country, a new issue of *She'ifoteinu* was published in spite of his explicit request, and in December Kohn's declaration regarding the constitution was published on behalf of Brith Shalom.[74] Though Kohn ultimately esteemed Ruppin as a man who carried the full burden of the contradiction between his commitments to Zionist achievement and to human ethics, the two men could not see eye to eye regarding Brith Shalom's task. In Kohn's eyes, "Ruppin's scandalous inactivity" placed a grave moral burden on the association.[75]

NATION AND STATE IN KOHN'S SCHOLARSHIP AND JEWISH THOUGHT

Judaism is not a nation like other nations; it is somewhat unique, and has thought of itself as such since the days of Moses and the prophets. Its 2,500 years of spiritualization, stripping itself of statehood and territoriality, may be "abnormal," and yet it is nothing to deplore; it follows its own laws and it may even constitute a higher development.

Hans Kohn to Robert Weltsch, December 21, 1925[1]

The infant nationalism of the East already gives evidence of all the weakness of its elder brother. The national states in Asia, such as Turkey, are becoming oppressors of every alien nationality . . . like the newly created national states in Middle and Eastern Europe.

Hans Kohn, *A History of Nationalism in the East*[2]

Jewish Political Thought and the Nation-State

"The entire problem of the Jews exists only within national states," remarked Friedrich Nietzsche, quite cryptically.[3] This observation, Kohn would have argued in the 1920s, was not confined to Jews' legal status alone. The European nation-state profoundly shaped modern Jewish thought and theology, as Leora Batnitzky has shown with remarkable clarity and breadth in her introduction to modern Jewish thought, *How Judaism Became a Religion*. The very concept of religion as personal belief or faith, which Jews increasingly took for granted, was a modern—indeed, a Protestant—one, she stressed, "created in tandem with the modern nation-state."[4] Citizenship and legal equality in such nation-states would ostensibly not be limited by the individual's faith and personal belief. Thus, Jewish thinkers of the age of emancipation—most prominently men of the Reform movement and the Wissenschaft des Judentums—invented and developed the idea of a Jewish religion in that new Protestant meaning. This is why it was vital for Gabriel Riesser, the advocate of Jewish emancipation, to underscore in 1831 that "religion has its creed, the state its laws." "The Jew," the 1844 Reform Rabbinical Conference at Braunschweig thus proclaimed, "acknowledges every man as his brother. But he acknowledges his fellow countryman to be one with whom he is connected by a particular bond, a bond forged by the effort to realize common political purposes (*Staatszwecke*)."[5]

Some two generations later, however, Martin Buber and Kohn's Jewish renaissance rebelled precisely against such a concept of Judaism and all it stood for. In their unorthodox ways, both men would even uphold Samson Hirsch's orthodox insistence that "Judaism is not a mere adjunct to life: it comprises all of life."[6] Thus, they sought Jewish experienced religiosity rather than proclaimed religion, a subterranean Judaism rather than the official one. As a member of Bar Kochba before the Great War, Kohn may not have been fully aware of the importance—indeed, omnipresence—of the nation-state in his earlier explorations of Judaism and religion. However, his Jewish political thought between the world wars tackled the nation-state head on.

previous page:

Figure 4.1 Hans Kohn in Heidelberg, Germany, August 12, 1928.
Courtesy of the Leo Baeck Institute, New York.

Kohn and his colleagues had been planning a sequel to the 1913 *Vom Juden-tum* ever since its publication. Before the Great War, he had thought of the work as a yearbook; during the war he named his POW periodical *Vom Juden-tum*, and after returning from captivity he collaborated with Robert Weltsch and others on a second volume.[7] Tellingly, nothing came of it. That failure aside, the publication of his and Hugo Knoepfmacher's translation of Joseph Klausner's *History of Modern Hebrew Literature*, only months after his return from Russia, signaled Kohn's commitment to return to publishing his Jewish works without delay.

Kohn's Jewish and Zionist publications in the 1920s and 1930s amounted to more than an ongoing series of commentaries: they added up to a significant and rather cogent body of Jewish political thought, which compares in scope and content to his scholarly work on oriental political modernities. In addition to a stream of essays in Jewish and Zionist publications like *Der Jude, Die Ar-beit, Palästina, Jüdischer Almanach, Hapo'el Hatza'ir,* and *She'ifoteinu,* Kohn's published Jewish works in this period included his 1924 *Die politische Idee des Judentums* (The political idea of Judaism) and three volumes of his collected essays.[8] He also wrote some of the key entries for the 1927-30 *Jüdisches Lexikon.*[9] In 1929-30, he published a slim double volume titled *Prakim Letoldot Hara'ayon Hatzioni* (History of Zionist thought). Together with Hugo Bergmann he coedited two anthologies of political writings. Perhaps most impressive of his works on Jewish thought was a four-hundred-page biography, *Martin Buber, sein Werk und seine Zeit: Ein Versuch über Religion und Politik* (Martin Buber, his work and time: an essay on religion and politics), which appeared in 1930.[10]

Careful readers would note the modus operandi that allowed Kohn to be so prolific: in the interwar years he wrote his Jewish works primarily as essays, which he published first in periodicals and later translated into a variety of languages and used as building blocks for volumes with slightly different conceptual frameworks. Repetitions aside, this was a wide-ranging body of work addressing a variety of topics, yet the focal point remained roughly the same: a Jewish critique of the model of the sovereign nation-state. Indeed, it was primarily in his interwar Jewish political thought that Kohn developed his early concepts of nationalism. Noam Pianko correctly situated the work of Kohn and several other Zionists within a much broader contemporaneous exploration of "the relationship between nationality, sovereignty and international politics," opposing the nation-state model and the paradigm of political sovereignty as self-determination. However, Pianko's application of Rogers Brubaker's term "counter-state" to Kohn's Zionism overlooks a crucial point: that Kohn sought the creation of a state—a just and multinational one.[11]

In 1922 Kohn published *Nationalismus: Über die Bedeutung des Nationalismus im Judentum und in der Gegenwart* (Nationalism: on the meaning of nationalism in Judaism and in the present), which collected his recently published essays on Jewish affairs—almost all written after the Great War and previously published in *Der Jude*. The book's epigraph—from Gustav Landauer—presented nationalism as the only force that could save people from the state, wars, and exploitation and marked Kohn's general agenda. In his introduction, Kohn presented the nation as "only a means" to the desired end, which is "the elective affinity of humanity," a panhuman "community that may be stronger than blood relationship."[12] The concluding essay, which gave the volume its title, was Kohn's most important essay from this time.[13] Though influenced by Buber's address at the twelfth World Zionist Congress in September 1921 (also titled "Nationalism"), Kohn's essay differed in several significant ways and was more clearly based on his lectures during his Russian captivity—primarily his "Das Wesen des Nationalismus" (Essence of nationalism) from Krasnoyarsk in April 1919.[14]

At the core of Kohn's essay is a historical comparison, which he may have borrowed from Simon Dubnow or Lord Acton:[15] just as people formerly went to war in the name of religion, today people wage war in the name of the nation. But it did not have to be that way, for true religion and true nationalism have nothing to do with wars. In an unfortunate historical process, religion was used by policies of power and narrow interest to the extent that it was integrated into the state's political power. The Peace of Westphalia and the principle of *cuius regio, eius religio* (whose realm, his religion) marked the zenith of religious intervention in politics but also the end of that intervention—and the end of the age of religious wars in Europe. At the end of the Great War a similar principle of *cuius regio, eius nato* (whose realm, his nationality) emerged, but this was not the face of the future. The postwar age, Kohn claimed, would appear as a time of transition in which nations and nationalism would undergo a process similar to what religion experienced after the Peace of Westphalia—a process of maturation, distillation, and liberation from the bonds of power and interest. This process would bring to an end the age of national wars in Europe. In the chaos at the wake of the Great War, nationalism was already "becoming a question of personal ethics, personal shaping of life; it is becoming questionable (*fragwürdig*). It is faced with new problems. Things close to it are now remote. Certitudes are questionable." The future was promising, but the present was still very bleak. Instead of defending nationalism's genuine manifestations, Europe tore itself apart into a patchwork of small, feuding, and unviable states—the surest recipe for continuing wars:

> In the face of its most absurd consequences, people are thinking up palliative devices, such as national-minority rights. They are gradually starting to realize that nation and state are distinct and that the nation in its vital utterances, in its culture and development, must be protected even without national independence, without the nation-state. The nation-state principle has been applied to the point of absurdity. Europe has created economically unviable, mutually threatening minor states, . . . thereby prolonging national warfare and the illusion of nation-states, until mankind, having grown weary of such politics, will find it as incomprehensible as religious wars, and witch trials. The solidarity of men will bring them together in larger and larger state alliances, which will be able to grant greater freedoms to communities and groups, federations and parishes.[16]

This postwar transformation in the international order was, by definition, bound up with a transformation in the vision of nationalism: "The time will come when 'national sovereign independence'—the object of political nationalism—will vanish because mankind will have realized that, just as individual men can never be fully sovereign, and must be bound by myriad of dependencies and obligations and, for the sake of solidarity, must put up with restrictions and temporary suppressions, so national independence." The cataclysm of the Great War thus marked not the birth or fall of nationalism, but its maturation. Nationalism's "first youth" was over, and it moved, through "elevation and purification," to a stage of transcending the passions and suggestiveness of mass politics, so that now it "yields to moral laws; eternal valuations; it dares to look into its own eyes with ultimate clarity, thereby salvaging its justice and truth."[17]

In spite of the unambiguously Jewish and Zionist setting of its publication, the essay marks a milestone in Kohn's career as a critical scholar of nationalism. At the time, however, even his closest friends read it strictly in terms of the inner debates of postwar Zionism. For example, Bergmann did not like the essay because he thought it set Jewish nationalism an exceptionally high—and hence unfair—moral bar and by so doing might harm Jewish nationalism in the Diaspora. Kohn attempted to convince his friend that the essay was primarily a general, elemental work on the nature of twentieth-century nationalism, but of course he did not deny its critical edge: "As far as Eretz Israel is concerned, I am convinced today more than ever that Zionism will be attainable [only] once one overcome[s] the level of territory and state."[18]

Kohn's principal book of Jewish political thought was his 1924 *Political Idea of Judaism*. This dense, sixty-six-page essay bridged the conceptual, ideological, and methodological distances between his prewar works and the later ones. It argued that a certain idea guides Judaism through the ages, defining its essence, history, and teaching. Kohn boldly set out to define that idea through an exegesis of Jewish texts from antiquity to his own day. Arguably, his central text was Exodus 19:6, which described the chosen people as "a kingdom of priests, and a holy nation" (countering the prevalent political Zionist biblical imaginary of the Kingdom of Israel, with its emphasis on sovereignty and warriors). Kohn's understanding of Judaism on the basis of prophecy, universal justice, and Kantian principles clearly echoes Hermann Cohen's 1919 *Religion of Reason*. This is noteworthy because of both Cohen's vocal rejection of Zionism and his heated public debate with Buber, Kohn's teacher.[19] In an interview with the London *Jewish Chronicle*, Kohn spelled his argument out in a relatively straightforward fashion: "The principal contribution which Judaism made to humanity is not merely a religious conception but primarily a political conception of the regulation of human society based on the idea of absolute justice. I suggest that this idea was original to Judaism, that it originated in a special characteristic of the Jewish mind. . . . In this sense we can speak . . . of the Jews as a people with a feeling for political justice."[20] The Jewish idea of political justice is absolute and distinct in the sense that it was not narrow or self-serving, but rather universal.

Kohn attributed another related, essential characteristic to Jews and Judaism: "I believe that the Jews are a people specifically of the ear, whereas the Greeks were a people of the eye. . . . The ear is the organ of inner experience, whereas the eye is the organ of external sensation. . . . [Jews] were a people with a most highly developed sense of history because the ear is the organ of time perception."[21] Whereas in prewar Prague Kohn had made this distinction to stress Jewish orientality, now it allowed him to underscore Jewish universalism. It was not a narrow national history that Jews had a "highly developed sense of," but rather a global, universal history in which they as a nation had a role to play.[22] Kohn's selective reading allowed him to find in the Jewish messianic idea the clearest expression of panhumanity: "Here the distinction between Israel and the [other] nations ends. . . . There are no barbarians. All ultimately constitute a single unity; all are equal; all are related. This realization places the Jewish teaching not only well ahead of its time but also ahead of the present day in which national, racial, and color differences also evoke differentiating evaluation" of humans along those biological lines. Hence Jews and Judaism were the agents of the idea of a unified world historical process. Kohn saw the idea of the covenant as playing a dramatic role in the history of later Christian nations, claiming that "here lie the roots of modern democracy and the slogans of the French Revolution" and of American federalism.[23]

However, the political idea of Judaism was more than a single idea. According to Kohn, it combined at least the idea of human unity and that of political justice. These, he claimed, reemerged in new forms throughout history, and their impact was almost as universal as their content.[24] The political idea of Judaism that Kohn put forth, however, was intriguingly unconvincing. In making his case for Jewish universalism, for example, he was extremely selective with his sources. He did not mention the famously uncompromising ethnic boundaries of Judaism conveyed by Nehemiah's expulsion of foreign women (Nehemiah 13) or the *Kuzari*'s (1:115) notion of Jewish biological superiority (according to which the convert into Judaism was deemed "not equal to the native-born Jew"). He did not address even such a central text as the *Aleinu* prayer, supposed to be recited three times a day ("It is our duty to praise the master of all, to ascribe greatness to the author of creation, who has not made us like the nations of the lands, nor placed us like the families of the earth; who has not made our portion like theirs, nor our destiny like all their multitudes"). Instead, Kohn's exegesis focused on selected biblical sources, especially the prophets (for example, Isaiah 2:2), but —claiming Jesus as a Hebrew prophet—Kohn had no qualms about using the New Testament to support his interpretation. This universal mission, the emphasis on justice, and the celebration of the prophets as sworn enemies of the state and statehood, all make Kohn's proposed idea very similar to that of early Reform Judaism, which he so often derided.[25] As we shall see in some of his later works, Kohn however unwillingly had to reevaluate the legacy of liberal Judaism.

Regardless of its validity or originality, the most important thing about Kohn's *Political Idea of Judaism* is that it served him as a model of civic nationalism: a people united not by land, blood, or language but by allegiance to a political idea. "Our people, the Children of Israel," said Saadya Gaon, "are people only by the virtue of our laws."[26] The covenant, Kohn stressed, marked the *Volkswerdung* (birth of the nation). The Jew serves as a model in that he "is not rooted in factual condition (*Gegebenheit*), but in his goal," in his higher ideal. Kohn, it becomes evident, found this to be true of all nations: "The particularity of an individual or a nation cannot be grasped through external causes. The essence of a nation is never determined by external formal dimension (*Moment*), neither language, nor land. Only its inner nature is decisive," and "a people is not definable by the possession of definite characteristics, but by its tendency to emphasize certain characteristics."[27]

The notion of Judaism being defined by its striving toward an eternal ideal was central to Buber's prewar address "Renewal of Judaism" and to Kohn's Bar Kochba writings.[28] Yet *The Political Idea of Judaism* was Kohn's first work to really point to the distinction between civic and ethnic nationalism (without using those terms).[29] In 1924, however, Kohn still seemed to have thought of civic nationalism only in terms of universalism and of ethnic nationalism as state nationalism.

How Kohn's early typologies of nationalism related to his political agenda at the time was mostly left implied in this essay, but he did make an exception for Palestinian binationalism. The political idea of Judaism, he stressed, lent truly global significance to Zionism's treatment of the Palestinian Arabs: "Precisely the presence of a large non-Jewish population provides the construction of our [Zionist] commonwealth (*Gemeinwesen*) with unique tasks, whose solution could be significant for humanity afflicted by the madness of nationalism. This is a hardship that is simultaneously both curse and blessing. We welcome this fact, because it provides us with twice the opportunity to preserve the political idea of Judaism." "All this leads me to the conclusion," Kohn told the *Jewish Chronicle*, "that in reestablishing their nationhood on the soil where their original conceptions of life were evolved they should not create a state like all other states, but that Palestine must become Jewish, not by imposing Jewish nationality upon any other race, but as a unifying entity among the peoples according to the ideas of Justice and brotherhood and humanity, which the highest Jewish thought [has] evolved."[30]

In 1925 Kohn wished to publish, together with Bergmann and Weltsch, a volume "that would constitute a restatement of Zionist ideology." He summarized the outlook he assumed that he shared with the other two men as "modernized Ahad-Ha'amism linked to that concept we have reached of the essence of nationalism." Though stillborn, this project's ten-point outline, written in broken sentences, captured the broad contours of Kohn's Jewish political thought at the time.[31]

Kohn's first point was that "Judaism is not a nation like other nations." It has undergone "2,500 years of spiritualization (*Vergeistigung*), stripping itself of statehood and territoriality." The spiritualized Jewish nationalism "follows its own laws and may even constitute a higher development" compared to other nations. The second point in Kohn's outline offered a more sophisticated understanding of assimilation. Here, Kohn raised the "positive value of assimilation for us," which lies in its ability to expose the Jewish Question fully, and often quite creatively. Assimilation is no more and no less than "denial of

[Jewish] distinctiveness (*Eigenart*)." Thus, it followed in his third point that Zionism could also become assimilation if, as a national movement, it uncritically betrayed its spiritualized distinctiveness: "Though seen as a turn away from assimilation, Herzl's [political] Zionism is really its continuation. It renounces [Jewish] distinctiveness and leaves nothing of it (compared to assimilation, in which [some Jewishness inadvertently] remains intact). Judaism [according to political Zionists] should become like all other nations; should become a political nation and [regain] statehood."[32]

Faced with "nationalism's deficiency in ethical and human terms," Kohn's fourth point was simply a call to challenge the apparently self-evident nature of Jewish nationalism: not only "the essence and meaning of modern nationalism" need to be critically analyzed, but also "its effect on Judaism." His fifth point pointed to Zionist expectations of transcending the Jews' diasporic condition. These expectations were not only utopian ("The Diaspora will always remain") but wrongheaded, overlooking "the virtue of Diaspora." The sixth point stressed the mutual existential dependence of the Diaspora and the Jewish cultural center in Palestine. The only objective of Jewish settlement in Palestine, Kohn stated in his seventh point, should be that cultural center: Jews are "not aspiring to a Jewish state, no minor new nation-state. Judaism gladly overcame statehood," and that should "also shape its relations to the Arabs." The eighth point rejected Zionism's promise to solve the Jewish Question: Zionism "is clearly not a comprehensive solution to the Jewish Question or the Question of Judaism. No such a question exists. We [simply] have to continue carrying the yoke. The decisive solution will occur in the days of the messiah, when the lives of nations and men will be governed by justice. The solution of the Jewish Question is intertwined with the human question and the two can be solved only simultaneously."[33]

Whereas Theodor Herzl's *Jewish State* famously insisted that the Jewish Question "is a national question which can only be solved by making it a political world question,"[34] Kohn's ninth point claimed that "the Jewish problem is a spiritual problem. A problem of balancing world-openness and circumscription. A question of language and religion." "The practical consequences of such an attitude," Kohn's tenth point proclaimed, will be manifested in "the relation to the Arabs," and in the way this relationship will shape "the political future of Palestine." Cryptically, he closed that final point by stating: "East and West. We are equally homeless (*heimatlos*) and native (*beheimatet*) in both."[35]

These ten points summarized much of Kohn's Jewish agenda in the 1920s. His 1927 *Zionist Politics: A Series of Essays*, coauthored with Weltsch, was a collection of recently published essays, primarily from the *Jüdische Rundschau* (where Weltsch was editor in chief). Kohn's contributions to this volume were part of his greater ongoing projects: his previously discussed binational Zionism and his history of Zionist thought, which will be discussed in the following chapter.[36]

As noted above, Kohn was a major contributor to the *Jüdisches Lexikon*. Taken together, his essays for this work constitute a substantial yet forgotten chapter in his Jewish oeuvre, offering a window into his Jewish worldview. Jewish history, he stated in his essays on Jewish culture and on assimilation, has always been and will forever remain the history of Jewish cultural exchange with surrounding civilizations. The complex dynamic of this ongoing exchange shaped modern Jewish life in many ways. Often, he noted, "Jewish culture operated through manifestations borrowed from foreign cultural spheres," and in the nineteenth century "this indirect impact [even] became characteristic of [Jewish culture]."[37] Kohn also rejected the contrast between assimilation and Zionism as false. Reiterating an ambivalent approach that he had taken since his Bar Kochba days, Kohn presented assimilation not as a catastrophe, but rather as an unavoidable and salutary transition: assimilationist Jewish thinkers often maintain their distinctive "Jewish note," and many of them even become participants—though perhaps against their will—in the Jewish national renaissance: "Precisely Assimilation, with the conflicts and with the inner problematic it generated, led to a deeper insight into Jewish essence [and] to a more conscious affirmation of Jewish belonging."[38] Many of the leaders of modern Jewish nationalism, he reminded his readers, were disillusioned assimilationists. Jewish assimilation and Jewish cultural revival, intersected, and quite often resembled and complemented one another.

Though Kohn saw assimilation as a constant feature of Jewish history, nineteenth-century assimilation rendered the absence of a Jewish cultural center a clear threat for the survival of Judaism. The problem, it seemed to Kohn, was not only the scope of assimilation but its essence: modern Jews assimilated not into a "a 'panhuman' civilization (*Weltkultur*) . . . , but rather into the national culture of the surrounding people, and soon also into its political and national life."[39] Assimilation, then, became a threat during and because of the age of nationalism and nation-states. The threat posed by the nation-state, Kohn maintained, was not only a cultural one. The political Jewish Question, he and Weltsch wrote, was primarily an outcome of the nation-state—because "the state and the nation dominating it demand that Jews relinquish in as much as possible all national and religious features."[40]

Though published by the Zionist He-Halutz World Federation, Kohn's *History of Zionist Thought* clearly maintained its critical edge. Kohn managed to craft a remarkably compelling and cogent book out of content that had mostly been published previously as essays. The book's chapters are of two distinct sorts: several address the broader context from which, and in contrast to which, the Zionist idea emerged—assimilation, Eastern European Haskalah, and liberal Judaism—while most chapters analyze and discuss Zionist thinkers such as Moses Hess, Ahad Ha'am, Herzl, Nathan Birnbaum, Buber, and A. D. Gordon. Kohn emphasized elements of their thought that matched those in his own. "The true objective of the nationalism of the Jew," he concluded, "is not mere biological self-assertion, unrelated to a sense of moral values; not territorial, political, or economic aggrandizement; but the social education of the entire human race. This is in essence also the thought of [Moses Hess and] those great figures who came after [him], Ahad Ha'am and Martin Buber."[41]

Kohn foreshadowed his future academic career by discussing not only the agendas of these thinkers but also their underlying theoretical concepts of nations and nationalism. He noted, for example, that "for Hess, a nation was an organic, natural entity," yet that Hess also maintained that "a nation is not an end in itself. The historical and social process of complete national self-fulfillment points to a united and liberated humanity as the ultimate goal. This goal and the furtherance of its culture and mission justify the existence of a people; the mere fact of its existence as a separate entity does not sufficiently justify it."[42] Even more reflective was his discussion of Birnbaum's though:

> Birnbaum developed a new concept of nationalism, which, albeit vaguely, points to the future. . . . Birnbaum separates the idea of nationalism from the idea of political territory. . . . Land is the natural element in the life of men and collectives. But the "normal" peoples, in their "normal" development turned this natural element into something artificial, to an idol of sorts—territory, political and geographic unity, state. . . . Precisely the new European civilization—precisely the new nation-states—are not defined by the land at all . . . but by territory. . . . And so Birnbaum's thought leads us to a new understanding of the concept of nation—an anarchic concept, oriented toward the prophets, toward the kingdom of God; a state without borders; an extraterritorial, internal state; a state entirely within us, within our terrestrial lives, and first and foremost—in our soul.[43]

Virtually all of the Zionist thinkers whom Kohn discussed demanded the creation of a model Zionist society, with at least the implied sense that such a society would be a "light unto the nations." Kohn's discussion of Buber's Zionism, however, brings this notion to another level: Zionism's universal mission is to embody a model of nationalism for a humanity plagued by exaggerated nationalism. Paradoxically, then, Zionism is a nationalism destined to cure nationalism.[44] As we shall see, Kohn was already on the ideological margins of Zionism when he wrote this book, and this fact may explain why its most original chapters deal with non-Zionists such as Birnbaum—with a focus on his work after his break with Zionism—and with liberal Judaism. It is hardly surprising that Kohn, with his increasing emphasis on nonstate nationalism, the distinctiveness and ethical foundations of the Jewish political idea, and Judaism's universal mission, would feel compelled to reevaluate liberal Judaism. Reform and liberal Judaism, after all, seemed to have always asserted very similar commitments. On an abstract plane, liberal Judaism may have many ideas in common with Kohn, but, as he insisted, liberal Judaism was never serious about its proclaimed creed and ultimately always ended up being the lackey of its nation-state.[45]

The primary importance of *The History of Zionist Thought* was in its exposing Hebrew Zionist readers in the Yishuv to broader, unfamiliar, and probably marginalized elements and contexts of Zionist thought. In those years, Kohn published, together with Bergmann, two additional slim Hebrew anthologies with the same intended function—of broadening the Zionist pantheon and Labor Zionism's ideological horizons. The first volume, *Lezikhro shel Gustav Landauer* (In memoriam Gustav Landauer), commemorated, ten years after his assassination, the German Jewish anarchist who influenced so many Central European Zionists. The second volume, *Am-Adam: Divre Hamatzpun Ha'enoshi: Kovets Ne'umim Uma'amarim* (Am Adam: words of humanist conscience), was an "anthology of humanitarian, liberal pacifist literature," divided along national lines—French, American, Russian, German, English, and Jewish—and addressing those nationalities' ethical and political commitments to an ultimately unified mankind.[46] This emphasis on pacifism is clearly indicative of Kohn's activities at the time. Many of the thinkers discussed in the volumes stressed, as Kohn and Bergmann did throughout, that (in the words of Hess) "not only does the nationalism of the Jew not preclude any unity of all mankind and civilization, it actually requires it."[47] The book's title was borrowed from Gordon, an excerpt from whose writing concludes the volume. Am Adam is Hebrew for "the 'man-people,' guided in its relations with other peoples as a man is guided in his relations with his neighbor—by ethical considerations."[48]

Kohn's broadest and most impressive work of Jewish thought was his four-hundred-page biography of Buber. This was largely an official biography in the sense that it was written under Buber's supervision, and Buber censored parts of the work, such as that about his heated debate with his friend Landauer during and about the Great War.[49] The biography was, Kohn told Buber on its publication, "a book that was not conceived or written as a confession and yet became one."[50] More than a biography in the conventional sense, it was "conceived of as an intellectual portrait of a generation in German-speaking Central Europe," which allowed Kohn—on the eve of his break with Zionism—to critically engage with the ideas that had formed his Zionist youth.[51] Finally, in the summer of 1931 Kohn published his final Jewish book for a long while: the French volume *L'humanisme juif* (Jewish humanism).[52] Consistent with Kohn's usual modus operandi, it consisted primarily of previously published essays and hence stayed within the methodological and conceptual framework discussed above.

On the whole, this entire body of work, albeit in varying ways, offers a threefold contextualization of the Jewish present: within, first, the general political philosophies of its day; second, broad Jewish historical developments, and finally, distinctive Jewish historical traditions. Each of these hermeneutic dimensions had a critical edge. Though Kohn's various Jewish works addressed a wide range of topics, one main theme emerges throughout—namely, the nation-state, seen as purveying Jewish assimilation, being diametrically opposed to the most vital Jewish political traditions, and most importantly distorting the goal and essence of Kohn's Zionism.

Scholar of Oriental Political Modernities

"The Bolsheviks," Kohn noted unambiguously in 1922, "are right to see each and every national movement as a bourgeois movement. Nationalism in its current political form is the religion of the bourgeoisie and it is through the bourgeoisie that it came to the throne. If we search out those whom national independence serves, we see that it serves only bourgeois capital and the bourgeois intelligentsia. . . . It serves neither the feudal aristocracy nor the proletariat. With the end of the rule of the bourgeoisie, to which the Bolsheviks aspire, nationalism's myth of political independence will also have to end."[53] The deep impression that Soviet Russia made on Kohn's concepts of nationalism, internationalism, and imperialism holds a key to understanding Kohn's scholarship and politics in the 1920s. It should not, then, come as a surprise that his first non-Jewish book —the 1923 *Sinn und Schicksal der Revolution* (Meaning and fate of the revolution)—dealt with the Bolshevik revolution. Though no longer a revolutionary, as his Fabian Society membership indicates, Kohn wrote an exceedingly pro-Soviet book. It was a slim volume (a hundred pages long), written for a general audience, and based on very little research. Its Austrian publisher, E. P. Tal, has made several contributions to Central European discussions of the postwar order, including a book on President Woodrow Wilson's peace plan by the Austrian jurist and statesman Heinrich Lammasch and an anthology on the League of Nations by the pacifist and Nobel laureate Alfred H. Fried. Kohn's pro-Soviet book must be understood in this context.

Not just singing the revolution's praise, Kohn claimed it was virtually inevitable: the misery of the Russian war brought about the revolution and though the ensuing chaos begot the counterrevolution; once the civil war began, only the Bolsheviks could effectively promise the people what they demanded. The people, Kohn repeatedly stated, "does not know, it demands." Whereas the Bolshevik revolution followed and implemented with integrity and resolve a certain idea—perhaps a dangerous one, but an idea nonetheless—counterrevolution at home and abroad was always someone's lackey: "From the longing for cosmos [an orderly system], the counterrevolution was born. Its tragedy, however, is that its fair-minded hankering immediately stepped into the service of the greed of generals, of big business, of landowners, of their whores and wives. A witches' dance ensued, which threatens to crush the desired cosmos from the get-go. . . . From the very beginning, the representatives of the foreign ruling class, the diplomats of the Entente, sabotaged all sincere efforts of the Bolshevik government to bring about peace."[54]

Contrary to the claims of counterrevolutionists in Russia and abroad, Kohn insisted unequivocally on the ultimate legitimacy of the Soviet government:

> Here [in Soviet Russia], for the first time the people (*das Volk*) created its own state, just as knighthood built its feudal state and the bourgeoisie its republic in the French Revolution. No one can say that a handful of politicians or even a secret organization of comrades alien to the people (*volksfremde Gesellen*) has imposed this state on the Russian people. . . . [In this book] I have tried to show that it was no coincidence that the *Bolsheviki* assumed power in the autumn of 1917, that they had to assume it in the name of the people, and that what took place here was the flesh and blood of the Russian people.[55]

Though a consistent pro-Soviet apologist, Kohn was not entirely blind to the brutality of the Soviet dictatorship. Yet this book, intended for a non-Soviet readership, was especially critical of what he saw as an exaggerated and self-righteous condemnation of the revolution by the self-congratulatory liberal West:

> But here we [Westerners] face the spots and ugliness in a sharper and more critical way; we are already so used to the injustice of the old states . . . that we have grown estranged from the pathos of indignation; but over there, where we expected

something new, better, good, toward which we have looked with longing we turn away severely disappointed, when we become aware of what is necessarily tied to the state, forcible order and education according to a social plan, especially in critical times. . . . But how much unconscious hypocrisy, how many ludicrous lies are contained in all the indignation of the liberal bourgeoisie.[56]

The book's relevance in the context of the postwar order, then, seems to lie in seeing anti-Bolshevism as restraining the much-needed Western self-criticism—indeed, as serving old imperial interest and "the representatives of the foreign ruling class."

However, *Meaning and Fate of the Revolution* was also Kohn's surprising entry point to the study of oriental political modernities. It is surprising because —with the exception of its conservative adversaries, to whom "oriental" was a derogatory term—the Bolshevik revolution was hardly considered an oriental phenomenon. This, however, was Kohn's central argument: "Russia is an inextricable mix of East and West, and with it Bolshevism too is a mix of West and East, in which elements of both fuse." Kohn's Russia, however, was not a perfectly balanced mixture; rather, it remained more Asian than European, and more Eastern than Western. His essentializing characterization of what that actually meant, however, was almost identical to his prewar discussion of Jewish orientality in *Vom Judentum*—indeed, it openly borrowed from that earlier work.[57] Since before the Great War Kohn had seen unrestricted Westernization —the universal claims of a singular occidental modernity—as a major threat, endangering Judaism and other minor cultures. In Soviet oriental modernity Kohn found one possible response to that threat.

Kohn presented the Russian revolution as a tale of collisions and mergers between Asian and European ideas. Marxism and socialism were Western European ideas, which made their way into Russian life through the mediation of Westernized Russian intellectuals who, in Kohn's depiction of them, bore a striking resemblance to assimilated Jews. For many generations, however, these Westernized Russian intellectuals had no impact on the Russian masses: "The multitudes of farmers remain untouched by these European ideologies. Of mingled Slavic and Asian blood, the Russian lives in the timelessness of the orientals. The value of time as a field of action, the usefulness of that organizational constraint, is alien to him. . . . Such is the Asian soul of Russia: timeless, immeasurable, and limitless."[58]

It took the cataclysm of the Great War to fuse these separate, parallel worlds of Asian Russian masses and Europeanized Russian revolutionary intellectuals: "In November 1917, the union took place and the mass brought into it all of Asia's fervor, endurance, softness, and cruelty." For the revolution to be implemented in Russia, Kohn insisted, it had to be orientalized. Its ruthlessness, for example, is understood in these broader geocultural terms. However, after 1917, the revolution's Westernizing drive became "one of its most prominent traits." But in the final analysis, Kohn found the East-West fusion underlying the Russian revolution to be a crucial guarantor of the revolution's truly universal horizon: "One can already note the progress from the French Revolution to the Russian one; the former [revolution] was a Western European affair, whereas the latter, situated at the intersection of Europe and Asia, has a universal character; it turns eastward as much as westward."[59]

.   .   .

Starting in the mid-1920s Kohn served as Middle East correspondent for the *Frankfurter Zeitung* and *Neue Zürcher Zeitung* and wrote regularly for Zionist papers, such as the Hebrew *Hapo'el Hatza'ir*, on Arab nationalism and Arab and Muslim politics in general. In addition, he published articles on those issues in the US *Foreign Affairs* and in scholarly journals including *Zeitschrift für Politik, Archiv des öffentlichen Rechts*, and *Jahrbuch des öffentlichen Rechts*. Before and especially during his London years (1921–25) Kohn worked on his massive *History of Nationalism in the East*. In 1926, two years before publication of the original version in German, he published an excerpt from it in Hebrew as *Toldot Hatnu'ah Hale'umit Ha'arvit* (History of the Arab national movement) —a stand-alone book released by the press of the Labor Zionist Hapo'el Hatza'ir. Though this work is an integral part of the broader, later book, its earlier publication date and intended Zionist readership call for their own discussion.[60]

Kohn offered his Zionist readers a geographically, intellectually, and chronologically broad vista into Arab nationalism, encouraging them to speculate about its future trajectory and its probable ramifications for Zionism. The Hebrew book analytically presents the historical development of Arab nationalism, with a clear emphasis on its interaction with European ideas and colonial policies. Kohn emphasized the diversity of approaches among the actors in the Middle East: Zionists, representatives of colonial empires, and Arab nationalists. He distinguished clearly between two separate populations that had their own distinctive patterns of the development of Arab nationalism: the city dwellers by the eastern Mediterranean, especially in Syria, and the Bedouins of the Arabian Peninsula. In the wake of the Great War, the two groups' nationalist movements had started along a path that seemingly led inevitably toward an eventual merger into a unified pan-Arab national movement.[61] Kohn allowed his readers to reflect on, among other things, the nature of nationalism and co-lonial policy—both, it becomes evident, can take either progressive or reaction-ary paths. Furthermore, Zionist readers were likely to notice the similarities between the challenges faced by Arab and Jewish nationalists and to ponder the political ideas that affected both national movements. This is especially the case in Kohn's detailed description of the secular and progressive dimensions of Syrian Arab nationalism and of the centrality of language, literature, and higher education in that movement.[62]

Kohn's discussion of Westernized Arab nationalism was, on the whole, sympathetic, and even when he expressed dismay at certain Wahhabi actions and practices, he remained evenhanded in his discussion of Wahhabism and presented Ibn Saud as not only "the strongest personality in Arabia" but as "a far-seeing realist in statecraft."[63] Tellingly, however, Kohn's critique of the nation-state model—which had shaped his Zionist agenda, his concept of na-tionalism, and his insights into contemporaneous European politics—is also present in his study of the modernizing Arab world:

> Rooted in political nationalism is the fatal tendency to erect strong national states, and this prevented the Young Turks, just as it had prevented the Germans in Austria, from setting about their task in the right spirit and saving the empire through a policy of decentralization that would have met the demands of cul-tural nationalism; with such a policy the empire might have stood, rejuvenated, strengthened, and united, as a firm bulwark to block the advance of Western im-perialism. The nineteenth century was dominated by the tendency to identify the state and the nation, a tendency that has to run its fateful course through succeed-ing decades before men come to realize that the function of the state is to regulate economic activities and make provisions for the peace and prosperity of all its in-habitants, while the nationality of the various groups of inhabitants no more con-cerns it than their religious faith, for it is the duty of the national community, not of the state, to foster national culture and speech.[64]

Judy Tzu-Chun Wu's concept of radical orientalism is remarkably suitable for explaining Kohn's position in the 1920s and early 1930s. "Radical oriental-ists," Wu explained, "continued an orientalist practice of cultivating ideas and fantasies about the Orient as polar opposite of the Occident and using these projections to more clearly define themselves. Their romanticization of Asia dif-fered from traditional Western conceptions of the feudal, stagnant and exotic orient. Instead . . . they highlighted the progressive, revolutionary East and contrasted it with the capitalist and militaristic West."[65] Though the nation-state idea was taking greater hold on Arab nationalists, Kohn claimed, the vision of pan-Arab federation kept it in check. An even bolder eschewal of the national state model, he stressed, was felt, albeit with some differences, by both Syrian Arab nationalists, who imagined the Arab renaissance under the aegis of a profoundly reformed Turkish empire, and Brith Shalom Zionists, who imagined the Jewish renaissance in a binational Palestine in which Arabs and Jews had equal rights and no ethnic group claimed exclusive privileges as the sole state nationality. Though nationalism would only grow stronger in the Middle East, its future, Kohn emphasized, did not have to be imagined as divided between sovereign nation-states.

Finally, Kohn's Hebrew book highlighted the West's enormous role in the evolving drama of Arab nationalism. The latter would have been inconceivable without Arab appropriation of Western political ideas, like popular representation, democracy, national state sovereignty, and nationalism itself—even if these ideas were frequently applied against European imperialism. Understandably focusing on the British Empire, Kohn elucidated the impact of the decades-long struggle between the "two schools of British policy in Arabia, the Anglo-Indian and the Anglo-Egyptian." Though sympathetic in tone regarding both Zionists and Arab nationalists, Kohn did not fully mask his criticism of colonial European empires' politics in the Middle East. He went into considerable detail about the practice of dirty politics in Iraq, shady alliances, systematic uninformed misjudgments of the region, and a pattern of contradictory promises.[66] His tone would change considerably in his later books.

Almost a decade in the making, Kohn's *Geschichte der nationalen Bewegung im Orient* (A history of nationalism in the East) was completed around the spring of 1927 and appeared a year later in German. In some five hundred thoroughly researched and eloquently argued pages, Kohn analyzed nationalism between Egypt in the West and India in the East, with regional chapters on Turkish, Persian, Afghani, and Arab nationalisms. The chapter on the Russian revolution and the orient discusses the nationalities Kohn had encountered a dozen years earlier in Turkestan as a POW. Beyond these regional focuses, other sections of the book discuss broader issues, such as reformation and renaissance in Islam, pan-Islamism, and Great Britain and the Orient—the last in a chapter that a prominent reviewer hailed as "truly masterful."[67] The book was received by many as the authoritative work in the field. *Foreign Affairs* found it "one of the few really outstanding books on the recent developments in the Near East." The *Times Literary Supplement* praised its remarkable objectivity, and the *Her-*

ald Tribune hailed it as "one of the most important books on world politics that has been written since the end of the world war."[68]

The book was written out of profound, though tacit, identification with the peoples explored. On the opening page, Kohn described the Great War's transformation of Eastern peoples in a manner strikingly applicable to his own war experience: "In the world war . . . for the first time Asiatic and African peoples played a part and helped decide the destiny of Europe. . . . [T]he masses became politically conscious, their sufferings sharpened their ability to detect cause and effect not otherwise observed in everyday life, they came in contact with alien countries and conditions, and all this roused the desire for a thorough-going change in existing conditions." Nationalism in the East—which had become apparent since the beginning of the twentieth century, and dramatically so in the wake of the Great War—was largely a reaction to the dominion of European colonialism, but it was also an incorporation and internalization of a European political idea. "Europe," Kohn aptly noted, "became not merely the adversary but the schoolmaster." The key concepts of his 1922 essay "Nationalism" loomed large here as well: nationalism supplanted religion as the governing principle; the cultural concept of nationalism deteriorated into a political one and into a part of the idolatry of the sovereign national state. These European developments from some eighty years earlier have now, in the 1920s, reached the East:

> The principle of political nationalism is penetrating the East. There, as formerly in Europe, it brings a fresh impetus, a fuller consciousness of self, a richer sense of values. But in Europe it was speedily transformed into a destructive principle, bringing arrogance, hostility, and suspicion in its train and making its own ambitions the supreme standard of human conduct in the name of its *sacro egoismo*, and the infant nationalism of the East already gives evidence of all the weakness of its elder brother. The national states in Asia, such as Turkey, are becoming oppressors of every alien nationality . . . like the newly created national states in Middle and Eastern Europe.[69]

Kohn qualified the developmental notion of different stages in an identical historical process only moderately, claiming that "the European historical phases of the past two centuries . . . will appear in the East in a new and characteristic form," but he concluded the book with the vision of a world of "uniform political and social outlook." Having earlier seen Jewish and other oriental nationalisms as qualitatively different from (indeed, superior to) Western nationalisms, Kohn has come to view them as embodying different stages in a single drama. This amendment is important as it points to the direction in which Kohn's concept of nationalism would evolve in years and decades to come. The volume indeed constituted a significant new development of his general theory of nationalism. Though clearly addressing ideas and, more specifically, cultural and religious aspects of nationalism, his theory of nationalism emerged for the first time as relying on socioeconomic patterns. If not Marxist, this updated theory of nationalism was unmistakably socialist:

> The feudal system and the dominance of the great landed proprietors made way for industrialism and the dominance of the middle classes, who attained their new and preponderating influence, economic and political, through the revolutions in England, America, and France. . . . Along with the shifting of the social centre of gravity, new cultural conditions arose. Protagonists of historical materialism might say that the middle classes brought with them their own myth, the myth of nationalism. Side by side with the representatives of large-scale finance and industry, the intellectuals, the professional classes, erected the theoretical superstructure of the new economic system. In a way they took the place of the priesthood of earlier days. . . . The wars that were now waged were, in conception, national wars of liberation; socially they were competitive struggles for monopoly in exploiting a certain territory or labour supply or certain natural resources.[70]

The book found an unlikely publishing house. Vowinckel Verlag was affiliated with the German right-wing radicals of the interwar period, with conservative revolutionaries and especially with German exponents of *Geopolitik*.[71] "In the early part of the twentieth century," Gearóid Ó Tuathail stated, "geopolitics [was] a form of power/knowledge concerned with promoting state expansion and securing empires." Yet some of its aspects could apparently also have appealed to anti-imperialists like Kohn because "geopolitics addresses the 'big picture' and offers a way of relating local and regional dynamics to the global system as a whole."[72] Karl Haushofer—the notorious doyen of interwar German Geopolitik, and often seen as an intellectual father of the Third Reich—saw Kohn as one of his protégés. Haushofer was a teacher and friend of Rudolf Hess and in 1924 had regularly visited Adolf Hitler and Hess in Landsberg Prison. He took a personal and intellectual liking to the Zionist pacifist Kohn, writing him letters of recommendation, inviting him to contribute regular articles on Middle Eastern affairs to his *Zeitschrift für Geopolitik*, and volunteering to write a cordial and admiring introduction to Kohn's book.[73]

Haushofer's introduction found Kohn's analysis of Eastern nationalism applicable and vitally important to Germany (as Haushofer put it, to "*Inner- und*

Mitteleuropa"): Germany could attain greater freedom of action and renew its position and national prestige by harnessing the tides of Eastern nationalism. But to do so, Germany needed to study that mighty movement in the East and incorporate it into its understanding of world affairs, and Germany's place in it. Given the publisher's clear ideological profile, Haushofer found it necessary to explain why it would be a Jew—indeed, a Zionist—rather than an "Aryan" who would teach the German reader this important lesson: "Only a man hailing from a stock which, Janus-faced, overlooks both orient and occident, can do both justice."[74] Kohn had to censor passages in the introduction that were "too nastily German nationalistic." One example referred to the "shrewd Anglo-Saxon politicians who played the Orient off against Central Europe." Another long and especially offensive segment compared the German "*Volk ohne Raum*" (people without space) and the Jewish "*Volk ohne Land*" (people without land), and called for German compassion toward political Zionism and Jewish sympathy for German expansionism.[75]

Kohn's pacifism, socialism, and Jewishness notwithstanding, his principled aversion to any nationalization of territory—present in his political agendas and rooted in his Bohemian upbringing—should have rendered him a foe of Geopolitik. Strangely, this was not the case, and his affinity to Haushofer was not even an isolated instance. In the 1920s and a bit later, Kohn and certain conservative revolutionary intellectuals had an undeniable mutual interest, fascination, and probably even critical respect. The divide between the academic and the political could not explain away this remarkable affinity, because for Kohn—an outspoken public intellectual—no such divide ever existed. Yet even during his year in Paris (1920–21), Kohn had relished the rigorous intellectual challenge of *Action Française*. In the late 1920s, he collaborated not only with Haushofer and his largely right-wing radical circle but also with Adolf Grabowsky, a prominent German geopolitician of more moderate political leanings.[76] Kohn thought very highly of the publisher and intellectual Eugen Diederichs long after the latter and his circle, publishing house, and magazine had gone *völkisch*. As a matter of fact, Kohn hoped that Diederichs would publish Kohn's biography of Buber.[77] After the biography was published, Kohn named the readers of the conservative revolutionary journal *Die Tat* as one of the "three circles that would have an interest in the book."[78] Kohn read the issues of *Die Tat* closely and occasionally expressed his admiration to its radical editor, Hans Zehrer—who, though not a Nazi, participated in the Kapp Putsch.[79] The German radical right-wing intellectuals who took an interest in Kohn may have done so because of his outspoken rejection of the postwar order and his harsh critique of the hegemony of what he called the Anglo-Saxon fellowship and of the self-congratulatory liberal Western democracies. Certain of these German intellectuals found their own national situation comparable to that of the postwar have-nots analyzed in Kohn's books. In turn, Kohn appreciated their bold *Fragestellung* (interrogation) and their ability to ask the hardest questions about the postwar world order. He may have hoped their answers would gradually come closer to his, if they could only transcend what they perceived as national self-interest.

The author of a favorable review of Kohn's book in the conservative revolutionary weekly *Der Ring*, with the telling title "Europe's Nationalism in the Orient's Mirror," was struck by Kohn's acknowledgment of the conservative legacy—parallel to the liberal one—underlying modern nationalism in both East and West. The reviewer, Heinrich Rogge, saw a conservative essence in phenomena that Kohn described primarily as liberal. Indeed, he took issue with Kohn precisely on that point, attributing to him a one-sided theory that "seems to regard such national romanticism rather as an accident of backward-looking folk." Conservatism, Rogge insisted, is the core of the nationalist drama. Abhorring chauvinism, Kohn identified with the moderates among the nationalists in the East. The conservative reviewer Rogge, however, identified with the Turks —who, after reconnecting with their past, attained "*Stolz einer Herrenrasse*" (pride of being a master race). Whereas Kohn's analysis of progressive peaceful Eastern nationalism seemed starry-eyed to him, Rogge stated: "European nationalism developed as a state ethos of a free people under arms. . . . One should not whitewash the facts with logical and moral speculation and toward value judgment: the legal and conceptual complement of the Turkish national democracy is the Armenian Question—that is, not merely secession, but oppression and destruction of foreign national elements in their own state."[80] Kohn confided his positive impression of this review in his diary: "An interesting discussion of my book by the German nationalist *Ring*: They rightly [pointed to] the connection, which now constantly grows, between nationalism on the one hand and corporate-conservative economic idealism and antiparliamentarism on the other; while originally in Europe—and today in the Orient—nationalism went hand in hand with Enlightenment, democracy, and industrialism."[81]

In 1931 Kohn published *Nationalismus und Imperialismus im Vorderen Orient* (*Nationalism and Imperialism in the Hither East*). Whereas his previous book had focused on the road to the Great War, this one—based on his years as a Middle East correspondent—focused on the developments in the 1920s. More than the previous book, Kohn intended this one "as a contribution to the endeavour to understand the historical and sociological character of nationalism and of the forces which are determining the history of our own day."[82] With chapters dealing with various regions and aspects, the book's heart was its fourth chapter, "Imperialism and Nationalism."

Kohn offered a closer look at both imperialism and nationalism and their interaction in the East. Written after Kohn's break with Zionism, the book manifested this profound change in its broadest contours. Compared to Kohn's earlier, more idealist work, it was less wholesale in its criticism of British imperial policy, and somewhat less sympathetic toward Eastern nationalists, and it ultimately saw all actors as participating in a historical drama much larger than their designs. Nationalism and imperialism are inherently interlocked everywhere: imperialism nationalized the subject peoples, but once their nationalism was attained, they too became imperialist "in the wider sense."[83]

No imperial policy could ever denationalize a people, so the task of the forward-looking empire was to grant its Eastern peoples full home rule, yet somehow "keep them within the . . . sphere of imperial political power." The British Empire—though it still practiced many unsavory and ultimately ineffective old imperial methods (such as divide and conquer)—clearly had begun to adjust and tame itself, as indicated by growing instances in which the empire "confronted colonists of her own . . . as the protector of the natives." Rather than defeating empire, Eastern nationalism could tame it. So, whereas Kohn's previous book presented Europe as both adversary and teacher of Eastern nationalists, the new book inverted, or complicated, this picture: "The *East* has become the schoolmaster of the West, has widened the [Westerners'] field of vision and forced them into serious self-examination."[84] The way forward, it seemed, was the path of mutual adjustment. The old empire's worst enemy, therefore, was not only rigidity but also the perils of self-righteousness and false consciousness: "What is peculiar to the present era is that more than ever those who apply such [brute imperialist] methods cloak their lust for power beneath a veil of morality, and that instead of pleading the instinct of self-preservation, the impulse to expand, and the extension of national power, they put forward the appeal—consciously or unconsciously untruthful—to justice and benefits to be conferred on the other party. It is the age of propaganda."[85]

Relying on the work of Karl Renner, Kohn expanded on his claim that in the West nationalism had degenerated into the fiercest self-destructive force of the present, while in the East it might still be progressive. Kohn's basic understanding of nationalism, its means, and its ends, however, had changed. In his previous book, he did not present the path of national revival as inherently violent, and he emphasized that not all nationalists aspired to a nation-state. This was no longer the case: "Nationalism strives to unite the members of one nation, politically and territorially, in a state organization."[86] Noticeably, nationalism was the quest of political rather than cultural revival, and thus Kohn's new concept no longer recognized even spiritual Zionism as nationalism. His understanding of the necessary means of national struggles had also changed: "History shows that suppressed nations and classes won their freedom only through movements of violence and insurrection. So long as they remain quiet no attention is paid to their demands; and indeed people often point to the calm prevailing in the colonies as proof that all is well. . . . It is only when bloodshed and riot occur that public opinion is forced to pay attention and give ear to the grievances expressed by the riots." Kohn, at the time a committed pacifist, could no longer identify with any of the belligerent parties. Sympathetic as he was to Eastern nationalism, he began to see it as part of the problem; and critical as he was of the British, he started to see them as part of the solution. He concluded the book with a ray of hope: "The historical trend in Arab civilization toward unity," Kohn assured his readers, though often thought of as a deepening rift between it and Europe, was ultimately a part of a looming East-West rapprochement. Hope, he concluded, lies in the constant adaptation of both East and West.[87]

This notion of a deeper East-West rapprochement under the surface of escalating conflicts was the leitmotif of Kohn's elegantly written *Orient und Okzident* (Orient and Occident). This short book, actually just an essay, summarized very broadly many of the insights in his previous two books: "This Europeanization of mankind, a spiritual victory of the dynamic civilization of the West over the static civilization of the East, turns politically and economically against the West and its hegemony which was based on the exclusive mastership of its civilization." All across Asia and North Africa, Kohn saw a national, democratic, and social revolution taking place. Essentially, this work was an essay about the new global stage as the end of the age of Empire and European trusteeship approached: "The twentieth century is the age of modern displacement of the economic and colonial centers of the world. . . . [The] center of gravity is now beginning to shift toward Asia and America. Politics, still continental and European a hundred years ago, are becoming more and more transcontinental and oceanic."[88]

Having established himself as a leading scholar of Arab nationalism, Kohn formed rather cordial relationships with some Arab nationalist scholars and intellectuals. Ameen Rihani—whom he had cited as early as 1926 in his *History of the Arab National Movement*—was a case in point. As Aaron Berman has shown, Kohn "admired Rihani's writing, particularly his portrait of Ibn Saud," and found in him "a kindred soul," whose "narrative of Arab nationalism ... emphasized the transcendence of religion." Kohn's sympathy for pan-Arabism, Berman argued, was mediated through Rihani's work. Indeed, Rihani offered "to write a short introduction to the Arabic translation" of Kohn's *Nationalism and Imperialism in the Hither East*, which he found "most comprehensive, . . . impartial, and sympathetic."[89]

Even though the bulk of his scholarly work dealt with oriental political modernity—as noted above, similar to the works of Arnold Toynbee—Kohn's readers quickly recognized his contribution to the study and theory of nationalism in general. While his first works spelled out his concept of nationalism as if in passing, later ones (such as *Imperialism and Nationalism in the Hither East*) were conceived of as studies of nationalism broadly defined. Only a few scholars studied nationalism before the end of World War II. "The early writings of historians like Hans Kohn, Carleton J. H. Hayes, Louis Snyder Alfred Cobban, and E. H. Carr," explained Umut Özkirimli, "were pioneering in that they treated nationalism as something to be explained, not merely defended or criticized."[90] Among these early pioneers, it was only Kohn, Alfred Zimmern, and especially Hayes—in his pathbreaking *Essays on Nationalism*—who published theoretical studies of nationalism as early as the 1920s.[91]

In the summer of 1931, the *Frankfurter Zeitung* sent Kohn as a correspondent to the Soviet Union. After his return, Kohn published *Der Nationalismus in der Sowjetunion* (Nationalism in the Soviet Union), with the original edition appearing in 1932. This second of his books on Soviet Russia was more academic than his *Meaning and Fate of the Revolution*, written almost a decade earlier. As the title of the new book indicated, it focused on the Soviet doctrine and early policy regarding nationalism, which contained many elements that still resonated with Kohn's vision of twentieth-century international order.

"Russia's new revolutionary government," noted Terry Martin, "was the first of the old European multiethnic states to confront the rising tide of nationalism and respond by systematically promoting the national consciousness of its ethnic minorities." Assuming government leadership over "the inevitable process of decolonization," the Soviet policy "supported the national forms of minorities, rather than majorities. It decisively rejected the model of the nation-state and replaced it with a plurality of nation-like republics."[92] Little wonder, then, that Kohn was so taken with this Soviet endeavor. In stark contrast to the nation-states, he found the Soviet Union to be a polity committed to a political ideal truly larger than itself. Kohn saw the Soviet Union—which in many ways resembled a multinational federation—as a progressive alternative to the nation-state model he found so corrupt. Vladimir Lenin, he stated, "had no idea of dividing up the surface of the earth . . . into a multiplicity of rigidly isolated states. His goal was the rapprochement of the peoples and their fusion into [an] association . . . of world-wide dimensions." The Soviet Union "effects a fundamental change conceived at the outset for the whole world. Communism no longer sees in the nation and the national state a life-giving force, the determinant of the course of history." Communism, Kohn's book emphasized, did not deny the existence of nations or the legitimacy of nationalism, and rather than repressing nationalism, it was committed to taming it and harnessing it to the higher, supranational ideal:

> This recognition will give nationalism a relative character, in place of the absolute character which it had during the last century and a half, as a final goal of political, social, and cultural activity, a fulfillment of nationhood for its own sake, for the sake of its sublimity and its historic mission. Nationalism will become a means to a higher end, will be judged by its appropriateness to that end, and will be given its place in the unified complex of the coming humanity, a complex which it threatened in its absolute form to hamper or even to rend asunder.[93]

Furthermore, the pronounced opposition to colonialism of the Soviet Union created an alternative to Western colonial empires. Sovietization did not mean Russification. According to Kohn, "the socialists of the dominant people were to stand for the abrogation of all national privileges and for the oppressed peoples' right of secession from the state or empire." His book discussed the formation of Soviet republics not according to old imperial borders but rather along ethnic lines.[94] Even beyond the Soviet borders, the revolution, as he had stated in earlier books, played a tremendous role in the emergence of Eastern national movements. Kohn's critical edge emerged finally in the book as he referred to the difference between doctrine and the actual impact of Soviet policy. The inspiring proclamation of commitment to fostering the national life of the various Soviet populations (*Korenizatsiia*) is rendered meaningless once the regime intervenes to ensure the political appropriateness of the respective national heritages. Thus, the Soviet Union

> destroys the bonds that unite the life of the people with the past. That means death to the national cultures, especially among peoples with a culture that is particularly strongly rooted in history and gives vivid expressions to the consciousness

of that history. . . . The Soviet government has no desire at all for the assimilation or the extinction of the Jewish people, it envisages in the future a Jewish, Yiddish-speaking people as vigorous and as thoroughly imbued with the communist idea as Russians or Tatars or Buriats. But the Jewish people of the Union must be entirely dissociated from Judaism; instruction in the Hebrew language and the perpetuation of Jewish religious culture—as it has been developed through more than three thousand years, forming and giving outward expression to the characteristic spirit of the Jewish people—are forbidden. The Jewish people is thus cut off entirely from the sources of its culture. The same experience has fallen to the lot of the Mohammedan peoples of the Soviet Union.[95]

Though this paragraph seems to invert Kohn's assessment of nationalism in the Soviet Union, on the whole this beautifully written book remains disturbingly uncritical of the regime of terror in the Soviet Union, the brutality of Soviet collectivization, and its ethnic dimensions. Kohn chose not to problematize the Soviet doctrine or probe the endurance of Russian national or pan-Slavic sensibilities (say, in the choice of Moscow as the Soviet capital and the Kremlin as the seat of power). This is disappointing, since Kohn clearly recognized that "more [was] at issue than the struggle between two economic systems: Communism and Western civilization stand face to face as divergent conceptions of the meaning of life and of human values," so he aspired to present "the mentality of the Soviet citizen, of the Communist 'theology' and the way in which it has tried to make its peace with the 'theology' of nationalism that dominates the world to-day." This book, it becomes evident, was intended not to challenge Soviet nationality policy, but rather to challenge Western readers through discussion of the progressive Soviet ideal. Indeed, Kohn stressed that "so long as that 'great society' remains unattained, Communism challenges the West . . . to an examination of the Western system of life."[96]

In 1934 Kohn published his final book on the Middle East. The rather dry and descriptive *Die Europäisierung des Orients* (Europeanization of the orient) was translated into English as *Western Civilization in the Near East*. In this book, Kohn addressed the seemingly paradoxical situation in which Europe, precisely at its moment of deep crisis, did not relinquish its influence in the Near East but rather seemed to exercise it more than ever. His argument was that the institution of mandates, because of their imperial affiliation, slowed down the process of modernization rather than accelerating it.[97] The Europeanization of the Middle East is part of Kohn's broader notion of different stages in a single historical process—a notion that he would have rejected in previous years. Elizabeth

MacCallum, author of the 1928 *Nationalist Crusade in Syria*—who cherished Kohn as one of the few writers who offered American readers studies of the modern Arab world written with both academic rigor and sympathy—praised the book, but few others took note.[98] This was a rather anticlimactic ending to his work as a pioneering scholar of oriental political modernities.

"A DISILLUSIONED LOVE"

Break with Zionism

Zionism is completely and openly an oppressive, antisocial, freedom-suppressing movement. . . . In this regard, the good will of a few . . . does not change a thing.

Hans Kohn's diary, August 29, 1932[1]

I gave up my position and was out of work four years . . . and it was quite uncertain, that I will become a professor in the USA. . . . But I am not made a martyr; more perhaps than my friends, but not much more; and so I walked away.

Hans Kohn to Robert Weltsch, July 2, 1936[2]

"What Grows There Runs Completely Counter to My Intentions"

In the fall of 1929 Hans Kohn resigned from his position in the Zionist Keren Hayesod and stated that he was doing so for reasons of conscience. He could not see a way to bridge the gap between his worldview and that of official Zionism, and therefore he could no longer represent it. Kohn continued his activity in the binationalist Brith Shalom association for an additional year, but in September 1930, he retired from it, too, claiming that the association did not take its own principles seriously. Brith Shalom had compromised where it shouldn't have, Kohn said, and it had systematically bypassed the key problems of Zionism and Palestine, instead wrapping itself "in a cloud of innocence." His primary concern, he continued, was that "from this cloud there is no possibility of influence."[3] Kohn, who lost his livelihood when he resigned from Keren Hayesod, was now determined to find his place in academia. The more radical his critique of Zionism, the greater became the gap separating him from the other members of his social circle. And the more he distanced himself from them, the more he drifted from their ideological worldview. For a couple of years he spent much of his time abroad, often separated from his wife and son, on research trips across the Middle East and to Europe and the Soviet Union (he visited that country in 1930), or on lecture trips to the United States (in 1931 and 1933). After enduring years of frustration as he failed to obtain a solid academic position, in late 1933 Kohn accepted a position as professor of modern history at Smith College. Months later, he left Palestine and started a new life in the United States.

Kohn's break with the Zionist movement provides a sense of the demarcation of the ideological boundaries of Zionism. The binationalist Brith Shalom association, after all, advocated the most dovish position within the wide ideological spectrum of Zionism. As the experiences of the late 1920s further radicalized his worldview, Kohn—the most dovish member of that association—effectively found himself beyond the ideological boundaries of Zionism. Published in the mid-1960s, Kohn's memoirs described this break and his subsequent emigration from Palestine in an almost dispassionate manner.[4] However, his diaries and

previous page:

Figures 5.1 and 5.2 Hans Kohn (undated).
Courtesy of the Leo Baeck Institute, New York.

Figure 5.3 Hans Kohn with his son (probably on the beach at Tel Aviv in the late 1920s). Courtesy of the Leo Baeck Institute, New York.

countless letters to Zionist and non-Zionist colleagues testify to his experiencing a great emotional and ideological upheaval. His colleagues recalled that he "left brokenhearted. Suddenly he recognized this path was wrong," and he actually abandoned it "out of despair."[5] The political and intellectual crisis that turned Kohn away from, and ultimately against, the national movement with which he had identified for twenty years propelled him into what eventually became a brilliant career as a critical and comparative scholar of nationalisms. Not only did his academic work fill the void left when his Zionist activities ended, but his research on nationalism was also inspired by his need to explain his own break with Zionism: he had to write about it.

Kohn's prominent post in Keren Hayesod, his friendship and collaboration with many Zionist leaders, his impressive body of Zionist publications, even his Brith Shalom activity—all somehow disguised the fact that he had held a genuinely liminal position in Zionism since 1918. Friends may have not taken him as seriously as they should have when he told them again and again that he was

Figure 5.4 Hans Kohn and Mirjam Scheuer in Ein Karem (outside Jerusalem), 1932. Courtesy of the Leo Baeck Institute, New York.

probably no longer a Zionist, not in the prevalent understanding of the term. In terms of philosophy, Kohn tried to use his political thought to sublimate his core concerns with Zionism, when he called in 1919 for "a state, which is already no state at all, a rule which is already no rule at all."[6] Moving from the philosophical to the political, Kohn used binational Zionism as a desperate attempt to cling to Zionism, a final attempt to ethically salvage a movement that he— as well as some of his colleagues—could no longer justify. Binational Zionism corresponded with so many of his other intellectual and political commitments —his critical theory of nationalism, his empathetic study of the modern Middle East, and his pacifism—that, daunting as the task was, it seemed to hold his life together. It was to allow him to combine commitments that otherwise seem contradictory. But his project began to fracture, and doubt seeped through the cracks. In his mid-thirties, Kohn finally ceased believing that the circle could ever be squared. His slow and painful break with Zionism inevitably coincided with a broader ideological conversion: when, after twenty years, his Zionism gave way, many other things also fell apart.

In 1927 Kohn's diary betrayed a new melancholy, a certain nostalgia for Europe, tied to an increasing sense that Zionism was now beyond repair—none of which he had yet shared publicly. According to his confessions, Kohn genuinely did not seem to belong to this society of Zionists who celebrated their rootedness and the birth of a new Jewish life away from Europe. When Rainer Maria Rilke died, Kohn noted: "I loved him very much. . . . He was homeless and cosmopolitan (*Heimatlos und Weltoffen*). Strange: since arriving in Palestine, [and particularly] since the end of October 1925 I have had a sense of impending death (*Todesnähe*)." When Ahad Ha'am died, just a few days later, on January 2, Kohn wrote, "All could have still been saved if there were a determined minority ... grounded on Ahad-Ha'am's thought."[7]

In 1928 Kohn's crisis about Zionism became even more tangible. Kohn and the Radical Circle failed to convince Arthur Ruppin to turn Brith Shalom from an advisory policy research organization to a politically active party in the Yishuv, and since neither gave up, the confrontation between Ruppin and Kohn escalated.[8] On the night of June 8, 1928, two Arabs passing Kohn's home in Jerusalem were murdered—apparently in retaliation for recent assaults on Jewish girls. Kohn, who heard the shooting, wrote in his diary about a neighbor who instructed him to say nevertheless that the murderers were Arabs.[9] He wrote to Robert Weltsch:

> We have degenerated in a horrible way due to our nationalism. . . . One can say today that 95 percent of the Yishuv supports such murders. . . . Here innocent people were murdered, passersby. Even the Germans did nothing like this. The French intelligentsia was in turmoil about the Dreyfus Affair. Here the murder interests no one. Who can afford to be a part of this? Just like in the world war, each barbarity, like this barbarity, is presented as a necessity. Beyond the moral level, I see also the practical problem in such a position. Where does it lead? [Yitzhak] Ben Zvi [one of the Yishuv's leaders and later Israel's second president] claimed it will scare the Arabs. I claim the exact opposite. . . . An indescribable racial hatred takes place here.[10]

After this event, his relations with the Yishuv changed.

Kohn was in Europe when riots broke out in Palestine during the summer of 1929, and he followed reports about them with great concern. "News from Palestine on the general uprising of the Arabs," he wrote in his diary. "That which I have feared has come into being. It had to come sometime. And we are to blame; for we did not practice any other policy!"[11] That same day, in an oft-quoted letter, Kohn urged Martin Buber not to stop at proclamations ("declarations simply do not do the trick") and to act immediately, for "if we do not act, act 'unconditionally,' i.e., without considerations for the self-interest of groups ... it will soon be too late."[12] In those days, Kohn oscillated between utter despair and the hope that a new awareness and a new Zionist policy would arise out of this crisis. He hoped the new policy would show that the Zionist movement understood how to transform itself to assist, rather than oppose, the Arab national movement. Days later, Kohn wrote Judah Magnes, chancellor of the Hebrew University in Jerusalem, who was also a binationalist: "We are faced by the 'national revolution' of an oppressed people. The Arab mob is fighting for a nation, or a nationalistic idea [and] ideal, just as our people, or the Sinn Féin did. And there are only two ways left now: either to oppress the Arabs and to keep them down by a permanent display of strong military force, a colonial and imperial militarism of the worst form—or Zionism must discover ultimately its true face, which has nothing to do with state, majority, [or] political power."[13] The policy of the Zionist executive, he noted in his diary the next day, was worse than what he could have ever conceived, and thus he "must not be there or be a part of it. We will secede then slowly! Silence and parting!"[14] A day later his resolve to "abandon Zionism as political Zionism, as an organization" had only grown stronger. He wrote: "I cannot partake in the responsibility. It means sharing the guilt for a crime. I want to retire from Keren Hayesod in the winter, without drama. We shall need to limit ourselves [economically], but I shall be able to breathe freely!"[15] On September 18, matters had progressed to the extent that he wrote Weltsch "a farewell letter of sorts to the twenty-one years of my Zionist activity, which was so intertwined with my friendship with him, that the things merged one into the other. . . . As far as Zionism is concerned, [Weltsch] cannot draw my conclusions. He is also more materially dependent. But I cannot be there any longer; for what grows there runs completely counter to my intentions, and my activity in the group [Brith Shalom] is used only to conceal and support that which should neither be concealed nor supported."[16]

Kohn's resignation, however, was forced on him. Even before his return to Palestine in the summer of 1929, the Labor Zionist newspaper *Davar* had attacked an article that Kohn had published in the *Frankfurter Zeitung*, in which he criticized the supporters of the British iron fist policy. Weltsch "was notified that on the basis of the *Davar* article, the [right-wing] revisionists in Palestine have begun collecting signatures demanding that the officials of Keren Hayesod fire Hans Kohn."[17] Shmuel Sambursky, a Brith Shalom member, recalled a meeting when a superior of Kohn's in Keren Hayesod asked permission to investigate Kohn: "He is waiting only for a letter from the public, and then he would initiate an investigation against Hans Kohn. He requested that Bodenheimer write such a letter."[18] At the end of those months, therefore, Kohn did not really decide to resign from Keren Hayesod—rather, he was forced to leave.

On October 22, 1929, Kohn sent a letter of resignation to his superior, Arthur Hantke, claiming he realized that his "heretical Zionist conceptions" might damage "the smooth functioning of the office." Toward the end of the restrained letter, Kohn wrote: "Today I am almost forty years old, twenty of which —the very best years—I have devoted purely to Zionist work and thought. In a certain sense, thus, I feel orphaned. I also do not know where to begin, and integrating into a new world will not be easy for me, but it had better happen now rather than in a couple of years when integration would be even harder."[19] A month later, in a letter to Berthold Feiwel, Kohn detailed the motivation for his decision:

> Lately, I have become increasingly aware that the official policy of the Zionist organization and the opinion of the vast majority of Zionists are quite incompatible with my own convictions. I, therefore, feel that I can no longer remain a leading official within the Zionist organization. The Zionism that I have championed since 1909 was at no time political. I and a group of my friends regarded Zionism as a moral and spiritual movement within which we could realize our most fundamental humane convictions: our pacifism, liberalism, and humanism. . . . The reality of the Zionist movement and of Jewish settlement in Palestine is far from all this. You know that for years I have been fighting the battle for those ideas which to me represented the very meaning of Zionism. Eventually these ideas acquired focus in the so-called Arab Question. For me, this question became the [moral] touchstone of Zionism. . . . It has, alas, become increasingly clear to me that, in this respect, the Zionist organization has failed utterly. The decisive experience was the Arab national uprising in August 1929. . . . We pretended to be innocent victims . . . but we are obliged to look into the deeper cause of this revolt. . . . The Arab national movement is growing and will continue to grow. In a short time it will be much more difficult for us to reach an agreement than it is today. Increasing our numbers by tens of thousands will not make it any easier. I believe that it will be possible for us to hold Palestine and continue to grow for a long time. This will be done first with British aid and later with the help of our own bayonets—shamefully called Haganah [defense]—. . . but by that time we will not be able to do without the bayonets. The means will have determined our goal. Jewish Palestine will no longer have anything of that Zion for which I once put myself on the line.[20]

After resigning from Keren Hayesod in October 1929, Kohn continued his activities with Brith Shalom for one more year. His gradual detachment from the association during that time had two dimensions: on the operational level, Kohn lost all faith in Brith Shalom's impact, resolve, and methods; and on the ideological level, he gradually distanced himself from the vision of a binational state. While the association strove for the establishment of such a state, Kohn already spoke merely of securing for the Jews in Palestine the status as a protected minority. Whereas Brith Shalom's primary strategy was advocacy and propaganda within the Zionist movement and Yishuv society, Kohn completely despaired of the possibility of convincing them of the viability of a binational Palestine or influencing Zionist policy, and he desired instead to convince the British directly. He hoped that they, in turn, would dictate the rules of the game to the Zionists. In spite of these differences, he still saw great significance in Brith Shalom's agitation within the Zionist movement.[21]

For half a year Kohn oscillated between feeling morally committed to implementing the founding ideas of Brith Shalom and his growing concern that the association was not fulfilling its mission and even acting against it in three ways: first, Brith Shalom was not authorized to speak in the name of Zionism, and thus it misled the Arabs; second, the association had become a propagandistic fig leaf for political Zionism, imparting a dovish appearance to the movement, regardless of its actions; and third, the association provoked great hostility within the Zionist movement, thus strengthening the hawkish opposing camp.[22] The association's meetings left Kohn feeling gloomy: "All the discussions float in a vacuum. . . . Brith Shalom—with well-meaning intentions but lacking courage and panicked about its own impact—conveys a tragicomic impression. Hugo attempts to unify ethics and Zionism and this must fail."[23]

By the summer of 1930, Kohn's break with Brith Shalom had become inevitable. His criticism grew more and more pointed. In July he charged Zionist policy with deception and Hugo Bergmann with self-deception.[24] "The worst," Kohn wrote in his diary, "is the dishonesty of the Brith Shalom people; they want to 'do something for' the Arabs, but if the government does something that even looks like complying with this demand, then they scream in unison with all the rest."[25]

Kohn's breaking point came with Brith Shalom's meeting on the evening of June 14, 1930. Again, he described his gloomy impression to Weltsch: "Yesterday evening there was a Brith Shalom meeting. It was lethal in all aspects. . . . I decided never to go there again."[26] Kohn grew convinced that Brith Shalom did not, and never would, fulfill what he perceived as its mission as an active opposition party within Zionism. Two months later he wrote a formal letter of resignation to the association:

I would like to ask you to register me henceforth not as a "member" of Brith Shalom, but merely as its "friend." I would like to explain the reason for this request only briefly: Now—when Zionism is coming ever closer to being Judaism's most aggressive and reactionary faction—only a unified and resolute group can oppose this development. A group that is just as serious in its belief in peace, human solidarity, and liberal humanism as other groups are regarding their platforms. A group of people who insist on the implementation of their platform and who will stand or fall on its basis. People who do not merely profess their faith in the platform. . . . Brith Shalom errs and misleads others as to the real problem. It wraps itself in a cloud of innocence, but from this cloud, there is no possibility of influence.[27]

A central element in Kohn's break with Zionism was the development of a critical distance between himself and Buber, who had been Kohn's mentor since his initial Zionist stirrings. At the time that he was breaking with Brith Shalom and Zionism, Kohn also concluded writing the first biography of Buber, which he had begun in early 1924.[28] One cannot overstate Buber's influence on the young Kohn and the bond the pupil had with his teacher. From the very beginning of their friendship and correspondence, Kohn challenged Buber but also continued to see him as a teacher. For example, Kohn's initial breakthrough works—"Spirit of the Orient" in 1913 and "Nationalism" in 1922—took their titles from recently published works by Buber, although the pupil was already offering riper thoughts than those of his revered master. Kohn seemed to almost hide behind Buber. This, however, began to change in the mid-1920s as Kohn, with Buber's cooperation, began writing Buber's biography.[29] Kohn grew increasingly frustrated with what he saw as Buber's inaction and infuriatingly abstract stands regarding Zionism's Arab Question. Despite his growing criticism, Kohn composed a sympathetic biography of Buber by using the formula "Buber: His Work and Times." He attributed almost every negative element in the biography to the spirit of the times, whereas his descriptions of Buber's personality derived from his deep identification with and appreciation of Buber.

The writing of this book, however, was also a way for Kohn to take leave of Buber as a teacher. In those years of crisis, it enabled—perhaps even forced—Kohn to do some soul-searching and critical thinking about Buber's path and his own, even without making this criticism explicit in the pages of the book. After concluding the biography, Kohn wrote in his diary: "Some people wonder why, in my book about Buber, I so often quote my own works, my own deeds, etc. After all, the book should at the same time be my intellectual autobiography and my confrontation—simultaneously testifying to the strong feeling that lends unity to all of my books, which, at first sight, seem so disparate in their topics. Simultaneously, it reflects the unity of my essence, the dissonances therein, and its path."[30] In a letter to Weltsch, Kohn stated that the book "is truly more an autobiography than a biography of Buber. For it shows my path and ours, my youth and ours, from which I part ways in this book and which I have analyzed and criticized in the book. . . . I chose the legitimate form of a biography of another man, a great man, to be able to say things I couldn't have said on my own behalf."[31]

In the wake of the Arab riots, in an attempt to goad his mentor into even more radical and resolute action, Kohn confronted Buber with his far-reaching conclusions. Even though the theoretical gap between the two was not so significant, Buber thought of the 1929 events as tragedy and fate, while Kohn thought of them in terms of guilt and political accountability.[32] Kohn became increasingly critical of Buber's personality and conduct, and although he saw Buber as a great thinker, he also viewed him as a rather small man at a time of historical trial. "We do not need religion and ethics," Kohn snapped at Buber in one point, "but a clear, unambiguous program that we take seriously."[33] Kohn made small jabs in his letters to Buber. For example, he alluded to Buber's physical distance from Palestine and mentioned Buber's initial embrace of the Great War to draw a parallel to Buber's conduct in the current crisis. In turn, Buber found in Kohn's dramatic letters, which repeatedly dealt with the idea of a break with Zionism, a troubling degree of dogmatism.[34]

"Buber's conduct in this Zionist crisis is a major disappointment," Kohn wrote in his diary. "He doesn't take either himself or his teachings seriously. He labels that serious conduct as one-dimensional doctrinairism (is there, then, deliberate ambivalence in his teaching?) as he himself makes very dark compromises. This does not discredit his teaching; it only discredits him."[35] Kohn subtly embedded his escalating criticism of Buber in the biography, as he told Weltsch: "I've expressed excruciatingly harsh criticism in places where the regular reader could not detect my dispute with Buber."[36] After the biography was published, Kohn wrote to Buber:

> My book about you must be out by now. I clearly feel that it represents a turning point in my development, as it is a book that was not conceived or written as a confession and yet became one. . . . It is not an accident [that] I conclude your Zionist development with a Zionist creed that most people will no longer regard as Zionist . . . and now, in 1929, twenty years after 1909, your teachings—perhaps a practical, doctrinaire, consistent, Landauer-like conception of your teachings—have pointed the way to me that I am preparing to pursue.[37]

Kohn was convinced that the transformation he had undergone stemmed necessarily and coherently from Buber's teaching, a teaching that guided him "as a practical, doctrinaire, consistent" view. He believed that had Buber taken himself and his teaching seriously, he would have experienced a similar transformation. At the end of 1929, then, Kohn had reached the conclusion that Buber did not take his own humanist, Jewish, and Zionist views seriously and therefore did not act accordingly. This is the same accusation that Kohn directed at the Brith Shalom association a year later and was the very criticism he directed against himself.[38] The tension between Kohn and Buber never reached the level of open confrontation, and it seems that the two always retained a considerable amount of mutual respect. But their bond progressively weakened.

In addition to the ethical and ideological dimension of Kohn's break with Zionism there was also a purely personal one, following his failure to find an academic position. Having advanced greatly in the second half of the 1920s as a scholar of non-Western political modernities, Kohn increasingly wanted to be a university professor. He was pleased even with the position he had held since 1927 as adjunct lecturer (in Hebrew, of course) in political science at the Workmen's Seminary, but in 1929 he indicated in his diary that he yearned to do more: "Teaching, lecturing, conveying in a vivid manner the life of the mind and its struggles—that makes me happy. I certainly have a talent for it, and none of it is taken to good use (really, only in Siberia 1917-1919)."[39] In the spring of 1929, the Hebrew University of Jerusalem was about to establish the world's first academic chair in international peace. Kohn viewed himself as the most suitable person to fill the position, and he suggested as much to Magnes—a binationalist, a friend, and the chancellor of Hebrew University:

> In my opinion, it should be a chair for political science and political philosophy, held by a man who is a real pacifist and interested in and actively striving for international peace, at the same time especially devoted to the political dilemma of the Middle East. I do not think there are many serious candidates for this chair. This professor could have a very important task: giving our youth a really liberal and pacifist political education and combating the narrow outlook that we encounter so often in our midst. It would be a task that attracts and allures me. I should find here—after long years of thankless toil, but still at the zenith of my creative forces —as teacher and as author, my life task for which I believe myself qualified, by my general faculties, my inclinations and tendencies, my work and my training.[40]

Before the selection of the person to hold the chair, Magnes wrote to Buber —who, like him, worked for Kohn's appointment to the position—that many reservations, regarding Kohn's candidacy, "result[ed] from dissatisfaction with Dr. Kohn's political position."[41] In August 1929, two weeks after the outbreak of the riots, the university appointed someone else. Kohn's diary records his great frustration at the idea that his pacifism might have hindered his candidacy for the chair in international peace—an idea that struck him as utterly absurd. His

Figures 5.5 and 5.6 Hans Kohn at pacifist conferences in the late 1920s.
Courtesy of the Leo Baeck Institute, New York.

resolve not to let himself be crushed by the loss of what he had called his "life task" is remarkable. Soon after, he embraced the outcome and rationalized his loss, asserting that in the current conditions, the position "would have given me more suffering than joy. I would like at one time to be a teacher at a German or American university. There I could give full expression to my teaching abilities and I would have an incentive for scholarly work."[42] Kohn redoubled his academic efforts, remained prolific as ever, and even proposed the creation of a scholarly journal to be called *East and West: An Organ of Discussion of the Relations and the Interdependence of the Oriental and the Occidental Peoples.*[43] Under Magnes's mentorship, Kohn focused his attention on the US academic world. Planning his first visit to the United States, Kohn stressed both in his diary and to others that the journey was related to scholarly matters and would have no connection whatsoever to Zionist issues: "I do not wish to lecture before Zionist organizations. . . . I do not wish to come to America as a Zionist, I do not wish to be labeled or proclaimed as such, I do not wish to interfere in real Zionist politics but rather to come as a scholar, a lecturer in political science and Judaism."[44]

Kohn's commitment to pacifism animated his critical exploration of Zionism and was ultimately instrumental in his break with the movement. He became a pacifist in the wake of the Great War, and from 1925 on he served as the

Palestinian representative to War Resisters' International. As mentioned above, during the late 1920s he became one of the organization's central figures.[45] At its international conference in 1928, he delivered an influential address, titled "Aktiver Pazifismus" (Active pacifism), in which he stressed that the hardest tasks for the world's pacifists were in new nation-states, such as the successor states to the Austro-Hungarian Empire.[46] Those nations, he claimed, were previously strongholds of antimilitarism and now saw militarism as the highest expression of national sovereignty. His address connected this observation to Kohn's Zionist activity:

> In a state of multiple nationalities, the problem of pacifism in the context of domestic policy is presently more urgent and difficult than the problem of pacifism in the context of foreign policy. . . . For the Czechs need an army not for war against external enemies but rather to suppress the Germans at home. At present such a problem exists in each multinational state. . . . The quantitative concept of [a national] majority must cease to be a power and political concept bestowing exclusive rights (*Vorrechte*). A similar problem exists in Palestine. I do not regret this. Pacifist convictions are worth something only if upheld when one's own interests are at stake. For this offers us not only the possibility of espousing theoretical principles, an easy thing, but also the possibility of living out these principles.[47]

Kohn's pacifist theory of nationalism at the time contains what Rogers Brubaker identified as one of the myths in the study of nationalism, "the myth of resolvability" of national conflicts—that is, "the belief that the right 'grand architecture' . . . can satisfy nationalist demands, quench nationalist passions and thereby resolve national conflicts." Brubaker calls this a myth, insisting that "nationalist conflicts are in principle, by their very nature, irresolvable."[48] For Kohn, the Arab riots of 1929 were a test not only of Jewish and moral values but also, and equally, of pacifist principles. "Now we must put ourselves to the test," he wrote to Buber, "for otherwise, what is the worth of our pacifism, anti-imperialism, and socialism?"[49] After the riots, Kohn attributed greater importance to the conduct of his fellow pacifists in the Zionist movement and focused his gaze primarily on Magnes and Albert Einstein. Occasionally he praised them, but at other times he expressed doubt as to whether they would withstand the trial of insisting upon their pacifism even when it clashed with their Zionism, and often he expressed despair regarding their conduct.[50] For example, Kohn raged in his diary that Einstein had "published in the *Manchester Guardian* a scandalous article of deceitful Zionist phraseology of the most common kind, and he stabs me in the back in such a manner, for he is a pacifist.

It is precisely things like that that drive me crazy."[51] At the end of the Palestine chapter of his life, after he had already turned his back on Zionism, Kohn wrote that "the pacifists' struggle must primarily be against nationalism. The goal: absolute cosmopolitanism. Then, only then, will disarmament be possible. Setting of goals: (a) in the short term: the individual must not volunteer to participate in war or in the preparation for war ([with the pretense of] the defense of his own people); (b) in the long term: ending the era in which the highest duty was the individual's loyalty to the nation and educating men toward loyalty to humanity, a world state (*Erdstaat*) (protect humanity from the nation)."[52]

Transition: Out of Palestine

Four and a half years elapsed between Kohn's resignation from Keren Hayesod in the fall of 1929 and the spring of 1934, when he left Palestine and settled in the United States with his family. These were for the most part hard years, marked by isolation, loss, confusion, and mounting concerns. After all, Kohn did love the land, his Jerusalem milieu (which included, for example, the preeminent Hebrew writer Shmuel Yosef Agnon), and ultimately also the idealist people of the Yishuv, but he was finished with all of it. In late September 1931, ten years after the death of Kohn's mother and only days before his first visit to America, Kohn's father died: "My father died . . . a traveling salesman in his seventy-sixth year in a provincial railroad station, ready after a day's good work to board the train for home."[53] His father may have not been at home, but he was homeward bound. In contrast, Kohn was as homeless in midlife as anyone could ever be.[54] When he left Zionism, he lost much more than his livelihood: His social and intellectual life had been rooted in the Zionist movement. Most painfully, he also lost a dream, an aspiration, and a polity of his own in which he fought for his political values—whether social justice, anti-imperialism, or pacifism. All this was gone, and he faced the challenge of how to remain political after the loss of the polity. He was about forty, with a wife and son to support and without a real job or a clear vision of the future. The Central European newspapers scaled down his work as a Middle East correspondent even before Adolf Hitler became the German chancellor. Kohn experienced the Nazi rise to power—as we shall see—as devastating not because of the professional blow it dealt him, but because of what it meant to him as a Jew, a European, a human being. Professionally, however, he was in a very tough spot. He kept on publishing extensively, but he failed to secure a proper academic position.

Until he succeeded in finding one, Kohn felt trapped in Palestine and complained about the tremendous emotional stress he was experiencing: "I cannot stay in the country. I become too nervous because politics disturbs all the time. Time and again, I wish to end the story—and cannot."[55] His critique of Zionism grew harsher and harsher. "Zionism," he wrote in the summer of 1932, "is completely and openly an oppressive, antisocial, freedom-suppressing movement. . . . In this regard, the good will of a few [or] the subjective dignity that others may have, Hugo Bergmann for example, does not change a thing."[56] Though always composed in his publications about Zionism in Palestine, he grew increasingly discomposed in his diaries and much of his personal correspondence in those years. They were filled with sarcastic references to the pro-Zionist lobbies as the "Elders of Zion" and filled with crude, hurtful comparisons between Zionists and German fascists.

Only a few years previously, in his *Political Idea of Judaism*, Kohn had celebrated the universal dimensions of Jewish nationalism and messianism through a highly selective reading of Jewish sources, but he had reversed his opinion. Using a similarly selective and essentializing approach, he now depicted Judaism as the archetype of ethnic exclusionary tribalism.[57] Following a Passover seder in 1933 at Bergmann's home, Kohn noted that "the text of the *Haggadah*, and basically all Jewish prayer, is awfully nationalistic: constant appeal to God on behalf of the nation, as currently done by German nationalists (if God is on our side, who would stand against us?!). A hatred of the enemy: Jewish religion is the primary example of a fanatical religious nationalism, sanctioned by God (Jewish messianism as a model of sort for [the nationalism of Fyodor] Dostoevsky). Christianity, as a fundamentally universalist religion, is superior to Judaism. The dangerous nexus of religion and nationalism as cornerstone of reactionary [politics and thought]."[58] Bergmann, who understood well what his friend was going through, urged him not to just judge the Jewish idea of election the ethnic hierarchies of the *Kuzari*—which is not hard to do—but rather carry this problematic legacy as his Jewish yoke, and struggle to make it his own. Bergmann wrote Kohn cordially: "In the last year or two we have drifted apart. And as much as I regret this, I cannot change it, and neither can you— even though often it is not because of your views, but because of the manner in which you express them in smaller circles. There is no one who could not understand, on the personal level, your hatred and resentment of Jewish Palestine —you've been wronged too much and you were so deeply bound to the whole thing, and ultimately yours is nothing but a disillusioned love."[59]

The tension must have been exceptionally challenging for Kohn as long as he stayed in his Jerusalem milieu. So Kohn traveled extensively for long periods —in the Middle East, Europe, Soviet Russia, and the United States. In those years he was able to interact with (and be impressed by) the Arab nationalist historians George Antonius and Ameen Rihani and the future prime minister of Iraq, Mohammed Fadhel Jamali.[60] In the winter and spring of 1931, Kohn was based in Egypt. In the summer of that year, he was in Soviet Russia as a correspondent of the *Frankfurter Zeitung*, writing essays that would add up to his *Nationalism in the Soviet Union*. In the early fall, he made his first exploratory trip to the United States. The American-born Magnes assisted and advised the uninitiated Kohn, and the Institute of International Education facilitated the trip. There was nothing too glamorous about the visit, which was a lecture tour primarily through midwestern colleges. Though Kohn was unmistakably eager to find in America the future he no longer could see in Palestine, he had to admit in a letter to Bergmann: "I don't love the USA; I don't love the [American] type of person. And I would not like to live here. Jerusalem is preferable for me."[61] Yet, judging by his diaries and correspondence from 1932, a year that he spent primarily in Jerusalem, that city was probably not preferable.

In March 1932 the American Institute of International Education invited Kohn to have a second teaching tour in the United States. This fateful tour in the fall of 1933 was a mixed bag. Kohn thoroughly enjoyed the six weeks he spent in New York at the New School for Social Research, where he made several significant and beneficial connections: he bonded with the historian Koppel Pinson, gave a talk at the Council on Foreign Relations, and established a connection with the nationalism scholar Carlton J. H. Hayes. Kohn and Hayes would eventually be remembered as the twin founding fathers of the academic study of nationalism. However, Hayes, a professor at Columbia University, was already an established authority in the field, having written two important books on nationalism and created a very influential graduate seminar on the topic. Kohn eagerly shared with Hayes his ambitious plans for a three-volume critical study: the first volume would explore the idea of nationalism from antiquity to the French Revolution; the second would offer a comparative study of various national movements in the age of nationalism, 1789-1900; and the final volume would address the twentieth-century challenges of nationalism. The second half of Kohn's American tour—five weeks of lecturing at adult education institutions in Des Moines, Iowa—was very different in nature.

Meanwhile Kohn was pursuing several prospective academic jobs. With recommendations from Arnold Toynbee, he unsuccessfully applied to a political science position at the London School of Economics.[62] Even more exciting was a position in the political science department at Yale University. He was invited to Yale by the geopolitical strategist Nicholas J. Spykman in late September, visited the campus a month later, and some two weeks after that was devastated by the negative response: "A letter from Spykman that nothing will materialize at Yale. A blissful hope crashed. Could have been a beginning of a new life. Fourteen days in a beautiful dream. How terrible that for me everything fails."[63]

But when one door shut, another opened. On November 10, 1933, just a week after receiving the letter from Yale, Kohn visited Smith College, whose president, William Allan Neilson, invited him to come after having attended two of Kohn's classes at the New School in October. A day after his talk at Smith, Neilson told Kohn of his intent to recruit him as a professor of modern European history. Ten days later, Kohn received and accepted the formal offer.[64] On May 15, 1934, he finished work on *Western Civilization in the Near East*, his final book on the Middle East, which he dedicated to Magnes "in grateful memory of the years in Jerusalem."[65] The very next day, Kohn left Palestine for good, never to set foot on its soil again.[66] Not only Kohn's life, but also the focus of his research, turned westward.

AN
AFFIRMING
FLAME,
1933–71

PART THREE

"THE TOTALITARIAN CRISIS" AND "THE LAST BEST HOPE"

Catastrophic Americanization and Breakthrough

I have dedicated my life to the study of nationalism— that great historical force, which stormed through the nineteenth century and shaped it. We now witness its spread across the entire globe, exaggerated into totalitarian claims.
Hans Kohn to Jakob Wilhelm Hauer, May 9, 1933[1]

Fascism appears, not (as most Marxists believe) as the last stage of decaying capitalism but as the last and therefore most violent, most triumphant, most exaggerated stage of Nationalism.
Hans Kohn, "The Twilight of Nationalism?"[2]

"Strange That I Should Call America Home"

Kohn's years at Smith College (1934–49)—his first fifteen years in the United States—were filled with contradictions. During this time he put down roots and found security after the long period of unnerving homelessness. It was a period of growth after the political and academic impasse he had experienced in Palestine. Now in this New England setting, he told Judah Magnes, "Everything seems to have an atmosphere of non-reality about it, like a tender dream. It is, after Central Europe or Palestine, like a peaceful oasis in a storm-tossed ocean."[3] In his newfound environment of tranquility, however, Kohn went through years of deep personal midlife crisis, exacerbated by a world historical crisis that struck him in an unimaginable way. During this complicated period, Kohn largely redefined himself and his theory of nationalism and repositioned himself as a scholar and public intellectual in America. Understanding this crucial yet messy time in Kohn's life necessitates some untangling of interwoven biographical developments: Nazism's initial impact on him; then the effect of the Holocaust; his evolving American circles; and, finally, the emergence of his academic agenda and theory of nationalism.

Kohn's move to the United States coincided with an ideological conversion that can be understood only against the backdrop of his painful break with Zionism, on the one hand, and the rise of Nazism, on the other hand. Here, "conversion" connotes a conversion from as much as a conversion to. Hardly ever a simple break, an ideological conversion usually has elements of critical continuity. Often it indicates a change between diametrically opposed responses but retains the old framing question and thought patterns. Even the commitment to refute a previous position constitutes a continued engagement. As an erstwhile Zionist and socialist, or as a former pacifist, Kohn occasionally insisted —convincingly or not—that he remained true to the original question at the heart of the pertinent ideology more than those who remained Zionists, social-

previous page:
Figure 6.1 "Hans Kohn distills the essence of nationalism."
Wood engraving by Frances O'Brien, published under this title
in the *Saturday Review of Literature*, June 10, 1944.
Collection of the University of Arizona Museum of Art, Tucson.

ists, or pacifists. Kohn's worldview was naturally altered by his emigration to the United States, but even his decision to accept Smith College's offer and move to America indicated a considerable ideological change for a person whose anti-Americanism in the 1920s had been remarkably harsh.

In his earlier academic writing, Kohn's anti-Americanism had remained relatively subtle.[4] In Hebrew articles published in Palestine in *Hapo'el Hatza'ir* in the 1920s, however, his indictment was much harsher. After the election of a Conservative government in Britain in late 1924, Kohn feared the emergence of "the great union of the English-speaking nations, the center of gravity of which would be in the Pacific and Atlantic." Such a union would herald "a new stage in the war of the colonial empires of Europe against the independence aspirations of the peoples of Asia and Africa." It would bring about a setback in "the approach of colonial states to other races" and create a pattern in which the rights and aspirations of subject nations would be overrun by Anglo-American neo-imperialism. This would follow the notorious pattern of "the American military dictatorship that rules Haiti—itself a member of the League of Nations," or of "British advances on Egypt, independent since 1922."[5]

"The small Central American republics have become vassals of the United States," Kohn stated as a matter of course in an essay that depicted the United States as a capitalistic dystopia, drunk with power. "Nowhere in the world is capitalism as strong and firm as in America. . . . Nowhere on earth is intellectual and political freedom as curtailed as in America. Nowhere does the most superficial of all mediocrity rule as in America." American democracy, he insisted, was a sham: Democrats and Republicans were equally "representatives of big capitalism. Nowhere on earth does money rule in such a horrible and unrestricted manner as in America, in the absence of any time-honored tradition to keep it in check."[6] Indeed, in the 1920s, Kohn saw America as a modern-day Sodom and Gomorrah, and reeking of self-righteous doublespeak to boot. "Nowhere in the world," he asserted, "does one so willingly embrace the old slogan of equal rights," but "there is no other place in the world where people disregard the slogan to the extent they do in America."[7] His view of American Jewry was equally unflattering and remained unfavorable after his first visit to the United States. Given his distaste for American life, it is little wonder that he called for "the de-Americanization of American Jewry."[8]

It should also not be surprising that he confided to Martin Buber in February 1934 that he felt it was "strange that I should call America home." Yet when Kohn and his family arrived in Northampton, Massachusetts, later that year, he exclaimed in his diary: "In the new homeland, then!"[9] Trying to persuade Robert Weltsch to move to America (rather than to Palestine), Kohn explained his reevaluation of the United States:

> The United States certainly commits much injustice . . . and will continue to commit it; but the wrong done to the Indians is old and it is over; one hopes for progress. The 20th century has to be better than the 18th. And today, despite all the injustice in the United States, there is no country where one tries as much, and on liberal grounds, to correct and improve. . . . There is hope here that another ideology would once prove victorious over the ideology Italy currently applies in Ethiopia. [In] Palestine there is no hope. The ideology there is of conquest and "civilizing mission," and [hence] the battleground there will only grow fiercer.[10]

This reevaluation was informed, then, by his Palestinian experience, on the one hand, and by historical events in Europe, on the other hand. In tandem, the two transformed Kohn's scholarly and political commitments.

Hitler's Germany and Kohn's Liberal Turn

Whereas most of Kohn's lectures during his first American visit, in 1931, dealt with either Arab or Jewish politics, the lectures of his second visit, in 1933, addressed the rise of fascism and communism and the relationship of nationalism to that rise.[11] Indeed, his talk at Smith that succeeded in getting him a position there addressed the problems of nationalism in Central Europe, not a field in which had he established himself as a leading scholar. This new focus was tied to the impact of Adolf Hitler's rise to power in Germany in January 1933 and to Kohn's liberal turn.

In previous chapters I have established that Kohn's initial explorations of nationalism were openly antiliberal; that his politicization during the Great War was not liberal either; and that his writings immediately after that war were marked by revolutionary, religious socialist, and social anarchist thought. More often than not, his crusade against the nation-state model in the 1920s was waged against self-proclaimed Western liberals, whose policies of self-determination he found to be self-congratulatory and even dishonest. To be sure, Kohn saw old school militarist conservatives as a constant threat, but in the 1920s, these were seen as relic of the nineteenth century. In the wake of the Great War, he thought that the graver threat came from the practices of imperialism and aggressive nationalism that were now thinly veiled by the liberal slogans of self-determination, popular sovereignty, the League of Nations, and the Mandatory system.[12]

This may explain why so many of the Central European intellectuals who fascinated Kohn before his emigration to the United States or took special interest in him were conservative revolutionaries and *Völkists* of one stripe or another. In this regard, he was not alone: Buber, Weltsch, Gershom Scholem, and many of their milieu had similar connections. As noted above, Kohn was interested in —and more than once expressed his admiration for—Hans Zehrer's conservative revolutionary monthly, *Die Tat*. And during the 1920s, Kohn was close to the Indologist and theologian Jakob Wilhelm Hauer. Kohn hosted Hauer in Jerusalem and introduced him to his friends; he read Hauer's magazine *Kommende Geimeinde* and found in it "many similarities to Buber's positions and mine."[13] Most important was Kohn's attachment to German geopolitics and especially to Karl Haushofer, who at that moment was alarmingly close to Rudolf Hess and Hitler. As noted above in the discussion of Haushofer's introduction to Kohn's *Geschichte der nationalen Bewegung im Orient* (History of nationalism in the East), Kohn was always uneasy with the *deutschnational* perspective of these Central European intellectuals, yet he felt that they asked the right questions, boldly, and quite often with a remarkably broad global perspective. Furthermore, he found the geopolitical lens valuable, precisely because it was so absent in his own idealist and metaphysical Jewish circles. He took pride in his essay "The Realm of Islam as Bridge," written from a "pure geopolitical perspective, with interesting assumptions and angles."[14] So, when in Germany, Kohn would visit them, and when he was struggling with Zionism's "dishonesty," the friendly letters from Hauer and Haushofer cheered him up.[15]

But Kohn's slow journey to his break with Zionism marked the beginning of his much broader liberal turn. The shortcomings of Wilsonian liberalism called not for a revolution from left or right but rather for "radical liberalism." Kohn was inspired, for example, by a "very good" lecture by Norman Angell: "Matches my ideas; a truly rational, a critically thinking enlightener (*begriffs-kritischer Aufklärer*). The school of Mill's *On Liberty*. A radical liberal, exactly what is needed today." A couple of days later, along similar lines, he noted in his diary: "The nineteenth century believed man to be guided by reason; the twentieth century discovered the subconscious, irrational drives. All the more necessary is it for those to be governed by reason."[16] Brith Shalom, he claimed in 1928, was to serve as "a bridge between Zionism and the spiritual liberal movement of progressive humanity"; Zionism, he noted also on his way out, should have been the movement "within which we could realize our most fundamental humane convictions: our pacifism, liberalism, and humanism."[17] In short, Kohn may have entered Zionism as an antiliberal, but he left it as an outspoken liberal.

By the summer of 1932 Kohn had grown increasingly preoccupied with the failure of German democracy. He had heard from Weltsch how his son was bullied on the streets of Berlin for his Jewishness.[18] "What a horrible nation the Germans are," Kohn noted in June. "They are isolated not only politically, but also intellectually (geistig). The way they dress up militarism philosophically and theologically, the way they applaud all the darkest drives and find them aesthetic. Their pensiveness (Tiefsinn) renders them dangerous. So 'different,' and in this regard partly akin to the Jews."[19]

In early July, Kohn wrote the essay "Über einige Gesichtspunkte des politischen Judenproblems in Deutschland und Europa" (On several aspects of the political Jewish problem in Germany and Europe) for a "Jewish issue" of the Europäische Revue. Though by the 1920s he had already identified more with liberalism, this essay was his first unequivocally and systematically liberal credo. It may have been his final break with Zionism, the severity of affairs in Germany, the fact that he was writing for a non-Jewish public, or all of the above, but Kohn's writing had a new clarity. The essay opened with a recalibrated definition of the Jewish mission, a mission not so much of internationalism or humanization as of diversity. The Jewish legacy was both of integration and of resisting complete assimilation. The Jew becomes an insider while maintaining his difference.[20]

Antisemitism is the rejection of that inner diversity, and as such it is a constant hallmark of Jewish history. Yet German antisemitism is uniquely fierce and volatile. Kohn speculated that this may have been an outcome of a certain similarity hidden beneath the overt contrast between the two nations. One such fraught similarity between Jews and Germans is messianism. Jewish messianism (with its balance between tribalist and universalist dimensions) was the archetype of all Western messianisms. Since "a German national messianism is on the rise," Kohn assumes that a clash of messianisms is taking place. This German national messianism envisions a new world order, and liberalism emerges as its imagined foe; it falsely sees liberalism "as a 'Western' or 'Jewish' commodity," alien and non-German. But the time of liberalism was precisely "the period in European thought in which Europe attained full self-awareness and attained world mastery."[21] Here Kohn presents an early analysis of Nazis and the conservative revolution, not only as an antiliberal and anti-Western rebellion, but as an escape into irrationalism: "The new German nationalism is an expression of the decline of the nineteenth century, of the skepticism toward the sprit. One flees into forcefulness (Lebensmächtigkeit), in the impulsive, in self-referential will to power, from ethos and logos [Aristotle's elements of rhetoric] into the bios [biopolitics]; in [new German nationalism's] free intoxicating surge of force, unshackled from the control of reason and spirit. . . . Spirit and reason appear to have failed, and so one relies on the creative forces of irrationalism."[22]

Finally, after considering the uniqueness of both the Jew and the German, Kohn returns to his familiar prescription of multiethnic and multireligious federations: "The nation-state of the nineteenth century believed in the necessity of uniformity of all its inhabitants, the citizens of a single undivided state should be of one type (*Art*) and one spirit." That paradigm, however, has failed, and proved itself to have neither realistic and practical nor ethical merit. "It is precisely German history," Kohn stated, while relying on the work of right-wing geopoliticians, "that corresponds to an extensive interlaced federated state." This great federation, Kohn suggested, could secure its bright future precisely through inner diversity: "Only a German empire that grants a living space (*Lebensraum*) to minorities of religion and race and unites them with the German [element] in fertile symbiosis could take up global prestige and influence. Only such a Germany could become the heart of Europe." This great future German federation could, in its own way, grow in a manner comparable to the British commonwealth: "Great Britain knew how to bring together elements of such different and opposite race, background, predisposition, and intellectuality . . . into fertile symbiosis and crafted from it the force and mission behind its empire. . . . But the empire demands . . . no assimilation, no relinquishing of difference."[23] And with this, Kohn returned to the question of the Jews in future Germany: Germany's ability to contain difference, its treatment of the Jews, is a touchstone of its future.

At least equally important were the parts of this essay that the publisher cut out.[24] These passages laid the cornerstone for Kohn's later advocacy of a so-called German *Sonderweg*—that is, the claim regarding a unique German path in history, divorced from the Western model, and in Kohn's view a revolt against it. German Protestant antisemitism, he stressed, differed from all forms of antisemitism: "German Protestant antisemitism . . . grows into a theological absoluteness, to a grandiose demonical possession, it turns Judaism into anti-Germanism, into the Antichrist, to the anti par excellence (*zum Antischlechthin*)."[25] Germany, then, disengaged itself from the rest of Europe and the West at precisely the moment when much of the non-European world had Westernized.

After the Nazi rise to power, Kohn kept a close watch on events in Germany. His sense of where things were heading was based in part on letters (which usually arrived twice a week) from Weltsch, who lived in Berlin and served as editor of the Zionist newspaper *Jüdische Rundschau*. When Nazi state policy against the Jews began with the nationwide boycott of Jewish businesses on April 1, 1933, followed shortly by the Civil Service Law that dismissed Jews from the German civil service, Weltsch published an editorial titled "Wear the Yellow Badge with Pride," which established his position as one of the most important Jewish leaders in Nazi Germany.[26] April 1933 also brought Kohn to an unambiguous evaluation of the events. "News from Germany. Really bad," he wrote in his diary. "Above all barbarism of moral degradation. Real sadism (as it was once in the army) now in the concentration camps, etc. Nationalism advances triumphantly on all fronts. Yet the Zionists don't even note the parallels (boycott of Arabs by the Jews in Palestine for 'national' reasons, emphasis on 'blood and soil' as decisive factors) . . . without seeing that for Jews salvation is only in internationalism."[27] The Nazi state's persecution of the Jews forced Kohn to confront "Aryan" colleagues who now sympathized with their new regime, and that confrontation, in turn, proved formative for Kohn as it compelled him to unequivocally commit to liberalism.

For the political theorist Hannah Arendt, the personal shock she felt after the Nazis' ascension to power resulted primarily from the Nazification of her non-Jewish friends and colleagues who followed the party line. "The personal problem," Arendt explained, "was not what our enemies [the Nazis] did but what our friends did. In the wave of coordination (*Gleichschaltung*), which was relatively voluntary—in any case, not yet under the pressure of terror—it was as if an empty space formed around one. I lived in an intellectual milieu, but I also knew other people. And among intellectuals *Gleichschaltung* was the rule, so to speak. But not among the others. And I never forgot that. I left Germany dominated by the idea . . . . : I shall never again get involved in any kind of intellectual business. I want nothing to do with the lot. . . . I thought that [their conduct] had to do with this profession, with being an intellectual."[28] Though he did not live in Germany, Kohn's experience of 1933 was strikingly similar to Arendt's. Especially in the first months of Hitler's rule, Kohn viewed the betrayal of German colleagues as related in essence to what he saw as the betrayal by his Zionist colleagues in Palestine. In Germany and Palestine intellectuals acted in ways that Kohn's friend, Julien Benda, outlined in his 1927 *La Trahison des Clercs* (The treason of the intellectuals)—they betrayed their calling. The calling of the intellectuals—not unlike that of the Hebrew Prophets—was to resist the masses, governed by their tribal passions and partisan interests, and to do so by representing that which is beyond the tribal: "They preached, in the name of humanity or justice, the adoption of an abstract principle superior to and directly opposed to these passions." But now, they too succumbed to the political passions of the masses and put themselves at their service.[29]

Professor Richard Hartmann, a leading German Arabist who would serve as advisor to the Mullah Training School the SS set up in Dresden during World War II, was very supportive of Kohn in the 1920s. In early 1933, when Kohn was planning to create a new journal, *East and West*, he naturally invited Hartmann to serve on its editorial board. Hartmann enthusiastically accepted the invitation in February, only to reverse his decision on April 4, in the wake of the Nazi boycott of Jewish businesses. The journal, Hartmann wrongly assumed, would be affiliated with Hebrew University, and "as a German in these circumstances," he could not be associated with that; after the Jewish "atrocity propaganda" and "smear campaign" against Hitler's Germany, "certain consequences are inevitable."[30]

Kohn's response to Hartmann was loud and clear. To assess recent developments one does not need "atrocity propaganda"—listening to statements of the new German leaders and reading the public Nazi platform and articles in the official Nazi press are enough to establish that indeed "an official procedure takes place to remove persons of Jewish origin from their positions, and that—even if there were no atrocity [propaganda] and even if the life of each German person were secured—the Jews there [in Germany] would still have had to contend with intentional humiliation and discrimination." Moreover, it was in precisely such situations that scholarship had a unique supranational role that should never be betrayed: "the privilege and duty to labor in the service of science and truth undeterred by national and racial hatreds." Kohn concluded with a jab: "You know that *scientifically* I hold your contributions in the highest regards, and therefore would gladly welcome them."[31]

Theologian Jakob Hauer genuinely liked Kohn, Buber, Scholem, and other spiritual Zionists and saw them as potential partners. It may thus be surprising that a few months after the Nazis came to power, Hauer founded the völkisch neopagan *Deutsche Glaubensbewegung* (German faith movement). In April 1933, however, Hauer was not yet Nazified, and whereas Hartmann was quick to sever ties with his Jewish colleague, Hauer wished to co-opt Kohn precisely because he was a Jew. On the first day of the Nazi boycott, Hauer, in a friendly letter to Kohn, praised him as a man of analytic objectivity whose voice was needed and urged him to write an article for the *Kommende Gemeinde*, Hauer's magazine, about Jews in Hitler's Germany. Hauer acknowledged in the vaguest of terms that "the situation is very difficult," adding "though of course the [Jewish] propaganda abroad distorted everything terribly." Kohn reciprocated

Hauer's warmth yet was quick to set the record straight: "atrocity propaganda" or not, the simple fact of the disastrous new policy was plainly clear. He was evidently not eager to speak out in Hauer's forum, probably fearing that his words would be distorted to present the appearance of dialogue where there actually was none. Only the unique German conditions, Kohn stressed, could turn a tiny Jewish minority into such a central issue. What Hauer's letter called "the Jewish Question" was first a German one, and ultimately a human one: it was not really about the Jews but "about the ultimate judgment of the meaning of humanity, of nation, of religion, and of history."[32]

In his response, Hauer was cordial as ever, but tone deaf. He kept on insisting on "elucidating" the Jewish Question in the *Kommende Gemeinde*. Hauer must have had a vision of the spectrum of the debate: on the one hand, he asked Kohn to direct him to such Zionist speakers who actually "wish to see the Jews strictly separated from other nations," and, on the other, he instructed Kohn to leave any critical pokes at the new German government out of anything he wrote ("I myself will take care of the critique"). "The issue," he told Kohn, "must be designed so that it could offer some practical suggestions to the men who are now responsible for the solution of the Jewish Question." Under the impression that Buber would contribute an article to the issue, Hauer told Kohn how Buber had "delivered a talk in our seminar week and left a deep impression as he confronted National Socialists who were charitable (*weitherzig*) enough to listen to a Jew." Ultimately, Hauer already thought of Jews as a problem Germany had to solve, albeit through dialogue. Kohn certainly noticed that—with Hauer's vision of set points and counterpoints between Jews and Nazis—this had ceased to be a two-sided conversation.[33]

Kohn's response commended Hauer's courage for even addressing the Jewish Question in such a manner in Hitler's Germany: "Though the situation in Germany concerns the Jews on a practical level, on the moral plane this is a German question, to be solved by the Germans.... The Jewish Question seems to me to be a touchstone, not of what befalls the Jews, but of the spirit in which the question of race is addressed today in Germany." In addressing "the racial arrogance, the color bar, that Germans raise against blacks, Asians, semites," Kohn focused primarily on the inevitable global backlash this would necessitate:

> All this is not a criticism of the Germans. I know that similar phenomena occur also in other nations. They even can be found among the Jews.... In recent years I have harshly turned against all appearances within the Jewish nation of overreaching nationalism and national arrogance (like here in Palestine against the Asian na-

tives), against all overlooking of the growing unity of humanity and the duties that this entails for all nations. Germans would need to do this today in the German nation. . . . As you can see, I have written to you in cordial openness, which I owe to you and to the Germans.[34]

Kohn felt the depressing impact of Nazism well beyond the Third Reich's borders. In the Swiss *Neue Zürcher Zeitung* offices discussing Kohn's continued employment with the Swiss literary critic Eduard Korrodi (notorious for his 1936 exchange with Thomas Mann), Kohn found the latter "really hostile. Apparently under Nazi influence, nowadays he likes neither Jews nor leftists."[35] Through his former colleagues, Kohn witnessed in 1933 the appeal of the new Germany and its national messianism. Only a few of them, like the pacifist Carl von Ossietzky, would speak truth to power and pay the ultimate price. Many, willingly or reluctantly, aligned themselves with the new state and conformed to its mind-set.

After his break with Zionism, Kohn's distinction between cultural and political nationalism—which had become so crucial to him at the end of the Great War—no longer seemed the decisive distinction among twentieth-century nationalisms. "Zionism," he now wrote unequivocally, "is the Jewish national movement that aims at the reestablishment of Palestine as a Jewish nation-state."[36] Nor was Zionism the exception: for Kohn, nationalism everywhere was now simply state nationalism. This quiet acknowledgment expressed the extent of his ideological transformation. Still committed, even more urgently so, to the goal of taming the beast of nationalism, from now on he would distinguish among different state-nationalisms. German nationalism, especially after the rise of Hitler, marked for him what was clearly the most malignant type of state nationalism—in spite of the fact that (or maybe because) some of German nationalism's earliest proponents saw themselves as universalists, or as non-State nationalists. British nationalism, since the time of John Stuart Mill, spoke clearly in terms of state and territory, but from the perspective of 1933 and afterward, it seemed to have proven itself to be the kind of nationalism tamed by a supranational horizon and—most importantly—a nationalism open to internal diversity of origins and creeds. It was in this context that Kohn's distinction between civic and ethnic nationalism—which had its roots in the 1910s and 1920s—would emerge as the core of his scholarship.

In his 1932 essay "On Several Aspects of the Political Jewish Problem in Germany and Europe," Kohn had already identified Nazism as an antiliberal rebellion and as an appalling example of conservative thought. A few months after Hitler was sworn in as German chancellor, Kohn sketched an outline for a book about the deterioration in conservative philosophy across Europe, from Edmund Burke through Charles Maurras and to Oswald Spengler and Carl Schmitt. All these thinkers, he noted, were "united in opposition to the legacy of the French Revolution, [and its fundamental values of] liberty, equality, and fraternity." Furthermore, he added, their rebellion, especially that of the latter thinkers, was "in essence also . . . against early Christianity and its secularized forms: [the] French Revolution, the nineteenth century, or Bolshevism. At heart: [it was] an infernal and pessimistic revolt against God. History becomes meaningless."[37] Zionism, he believed, had failed completely; the heart of Europe was infested with fascism; and having accepted the position at Smith College, he was on his way across the ocean to build a new life in the new world. As of the 1930s liberalism was Kohn's bitter hope, and hope, as Seamus Heaney has noted, "is not optimism, which expects things to turn out well, but something rooted in the conviction that there is good worth working for."[38]

New American Circles

However, these were not easy times in the New World. Kohn immigrated to America during the Great Depression and became an American citizen during World War II. With astonishing energy, he stormed into American academic life: continuously publishing (while shifting to a new scholarly focus), constantly broadening his social and intellectual circles, and persistently deepening his inquiry into nationalism and its centrality for the present and the future. This indefatigable drive, as Kohn's correspondence and diaries attest, was linked to his unrelenting existential sense of being "unfulfilled," unable to make up for "lost years," constantly preoccupied with missed opportunities, and resenting his aging.[39] Struggles aside, Kohn seem to have felt at home in his new setting and in America more broadly—especially compared to the Palestinian and European environments he had left behind.

He simultaneously created social and intellectual ties in a variety of American academic circles.[40] One circle revolved around the Institute of International Education, which had brought Kohn to the United States in the first place (during his first visit he had befriended its assistant director, the legendary broadcast journalist Edward R. Murrow). Following his second visit to the United States, Kohn had kept in contact with Morse A. Cartwright, director of the American Association for Adult Education (Kohn would become the association's president in 1948, having been its vice president in 1938 and 1943).[41] Through the association Kohn also met the African American philosopher Alain

Locke, known as the father of the Harlem Renaissance, who would become the association's president in 1946. An important New York circle that Kohn entered soon after moving to the United States revolved around the New School for Social Research, where Kohn's teaching career began in 1933 and would last well into the 1960s. His New School friends included the school's administrator, Edith Jonas; assistant director, Clara W. Mayer; and the exiled political scientist Max Ascoli and the philosopher Morris Raphael Cohen. Most important of this group was the historian Koppel Pinson. Pinson, whose doctoral dissertation advisor at Columbia University was the nationalism scholar Carlton J. H. Hayes, would remain one of Kohn's closest friends. It was probably through Pinson that Kohn was invited to contribute to the *Encyclopaedia of the Social Sciences* and participate in the Conference on Jewish Relations, whose academic journal, *Jewish Social Studies*, he would cofound.[42] Another intellectual circle that played a central role in Kohn's early ears in the United States consisted of American Asianists interested in his work on oriental political modernities: these included the novelist Pearl S. Buck; members of the Asia Institute (Kohn would become a member of its governing council); Richard J. Walsh, an editor at John Day Company; the Chinese writer Lin Yutang; the leading Chinese scholar Hu Shih; and the philosopher William Ernest Hocking.

Having taught summer semesters at Harvard University starting in 1936, Kohn was quick to build networks there, too. His Harvard circle included William Yandell Elliott, an eminent professor of history and political science; Fritz T. Epstein, an émigré historian of Russia who joined Harvard's faculty in 1937; and Carl Joachim Friedrich, an émigré political theorist. Kohn occasionally met with the Harvard history professors Sidney Bradshaw Fay and Crane Brinton. At Harvard in 1937 Kohn got to meet and converse with the former German chancellor, Heinrich Brüning, now exiled and serving as professor of political science.[43]

Though Kohn would usually spend at least a day a week either in New York City or at Harvard, his social and intellectual life centered around Smith College and its neighboring academic institutions (Amherst College, Mount Holyoke College, Massachusetts State College, and a bit further afield Wesleyan and Williams Colleges). "Our socializing here has a similar character as in Palestine," Kohn told Hugo Bergmann: "small circles, constantly joined by welcome visitors from the outside." The academic community in and around Smith College, he added, consisted of "extremely interesting, stimulating people, representatives of many nations and language groups, almost all extremely well traveled and well read. The best part here, is of course, the president [William

Allan Neilson], an extraordinary man, a liberal, but remarkably efficient at the same time. There is cosmopolitanism here that makes its superiority to the seclusion of European universities really stand out. And the land offers, especially in the intellectual field, a great many opportunities and the immigrant rises here quickly in this young country."[44] The Kohns, as Hans's diaries show, were very social indeed, having not only students but also friends and colleagues to their home multiple times a week. In addition to Neilson, Kohn's significant local connections and friends included the Gestalt psychologists Fritz Heider and especially Kurt Koffka, the historian Merle Curti, the economist William A. Orton, and the exiled writer Giuseppe Antonio Borgese (Thomas Mann's future son-in-law). His exchanges with the exiled political scientist, Karl Löwenstein, now teaching at Amherst College, grew in intensity. Kohn's diaries from the time occasionally mentioned a certain "Neilson Klub"—a social circle around Smith's president, in which Kohn and other professors discussed current affairs or presented their works in progress (as Kohn did when he began studying early English nationalism).[45] Many members of this circle (like Löwenstein or Borgese) were engaged in a non-Marxist critical interpretation of fascism. The Kohns' home was frequented also by members of a younger cohort: the future foreign policy expert Dorothy Fosdick; Jane Dahlman, who would become the wife of Harold L. Ickes, future secretary of the interior; and Leonora Davison Cohen, an instructor of French who happened to also be the daughter of Kohn's New York colleague, the philosopher Morris Raphael Cohen.

Kohn had found his calling in teaching during his Russian captivity, and he was finally given the opportunity to do what he loved. An extremely committed and popular lecturer, he taught by far the most highly enrolled history courses at Smith. He hosted an open house "one afternoon and one evening in the week" for the discussion of "personal and world problems with my students."[46] Though occasionally exhausted by the many courses and public lectures he gave (he regularly delivered lectures for adult education), Kohn consistently found teaching gratifying and energizing: "It's exhausting because I do it so gladly and with full commitment—and the students appreciate it too."[47] His more famous students from those early years included Betty Friedan (then Bettye Naomi Goldstein); her politics differed from Kohn's quite significantly, yet she later reminisced fondly on "how, in the heady intellectual excitement of my days at Smith, we would linger outside Hans Kohn's history class . . . arguing about communism, fascism, democracy, war and peace, capitalism and workers' exploitation, and the future."[48] Smith alumna Dorothy Fosdick, who took his Harvard summer graduate seminar, became his colleague and friend in the 1930s, shortly before becoming a member of the State Department's Policy Planning Staff. In his memoirs, Kohn singled out two other students in his Harvard seminars who became "important teachers and scholars": the conservative intellectual, poet, and historian Peter Viereck and the nationalism scholar Karl Deutsch, a young émigré from Bohemia, who arrived at Harvard in the wake of the Munich Agreement.

At Smith, the New School for Social Research, and the Harvard Summer School, Kohn taught intellectual and political European history, as well as courses on the history of imperialism and nationalism. Notably, Jewish and Middle Eastern topics, which had dominated his curriculum vitae prior to his arrival in the United States, were virtually absent from his course offerings. Kohn did not stop publishing on those topics—indeed, he made a concerted effort to have more of his earlier German-language work translated into English—but they were increasingly marginalized, making room for his new academic agenda.

Kohn's political and academic agenda in the United States was by no means a simple continuation or application of the work he had done in the 1920s. As someone who analyzed the racial dimensions of late imperialism, wrote about and against the politics of blood, and broke from Zionism precisely because of its ethnocentricity, Kohn could have been expected to find racism the touchstone of American life—like the Arab Question was for Zionism. Furthermore, focusing on America's race problem would have made sense, as it would have shown the vital significance of Kohn's European, Jewish, and Middle Eastern knowledge to Americans. However, Kohn would remain uncommitted to the struggle for the rights of African Americans during the crucial years of the civil rights movement (indeed, throughout the Cold War). Yet in his first couple of years in the United States, he was drawn to a critical exploration of American racism. He wrote the entry on racial conflict for the 1934 *Encyclopaedia of the Social Sciences*. It was a long essay, global in scope, addressing the social and intellectual roots of the ideas of racial superiority on the one hand and of equality and fraternity on the other hand. One of the striking passages in that essay rejected the apologetic presentation of lynching as isolated exceptional cases disrupting the prevailing American order. On the contrary, Kohn argued, lynching creates America's racial order: it is "the basis of unequal treatment before the law meted [out] to the different races. . . . Racial inequality is thus conducive not only to the destruction of democracy and liberty but also to the undermining of justice and law."[49] In the fall of 1935, when the African American leader W. E. B. Du Bois invited him to contribute to his planned *Encyclopedia of the Negro*, Kohn enthusiastically accepted, adding: "I am very much interested in racial

Figure 6.2 Jetty Kohn, probably in the 1930s. Courtesy of the Leo Baeck Institute, New York.

problems and in the problems of 'backward' or 'colonial' peoples. I shall be glad to contribute some articles on the general problems or racial conflicts and racial theories or on the political and racial problems of 'backward peoples' in the age of modern imperialism."[50] In 1936 Kohn's positions on "minority problems and tactics" deeply impressed Alain Locke, who wrote to Du Bois that Kohn had "come to conclusions practically identical with your much criticized recent platform. I thought this was very interesting, especially since he did not know of your conclusions, which I told him about afterwards. His basis was a generalization of the Jewish experience as well as of the Soviet program for minorities."[51] However, Locke did not seem to connect Kohn's ideas with Du Bois's cultural nationalism, which would have made much more sense; instead, he linked Kohn's thinking with Du Bois's economic secession agenda. Locke would include Kohn's encyclopedic essay on racial conflicts in his anthology *When Peoples Meet: A Study in Race and Culture Contacts*. In 1937 Kohn applied to the Rosenwald Fund for assistance with his project of founding a high-quality "Negro quarterly," but that periodical never became a reality.[52] And in the same year, Kohn published a statement about race in America, which, though in the third person, was undoubtedly personal:

> To the student of social problems who comes to America from abroad, the Negro problem appears by far the sorest spot in the moral and political texture of Amer-

Figure 6.3 Hans Kohn after the last lecture of his series on modern nationalism, 1939. Courtesy of the Leo Baeck Institute, New York.

ican culture. Many white persons live in abject poverty, but they have a definite hope that they or their children may rise to better standards of life. There seems no hope for the Negro. Even education does not help, for the economic world offers him no opportunity for higher and better remunerated positions.

The visitor from abroad notes with astonishment and disgust, even in New England cities of old and great wealth, the incredibly dilapidated houses and squalid environments in which the Negro lives, the complete absence of Negro clerks or office workers in banks and stores, the lack of any decent places of amusement for the educated Negro youth.[53]

"Ultimately," he stated two years later, "the Negro problem in the United States, like most of our other problems, can be solved in only one way: by making of democracy a reality, a course of action, instead of an aspiration to which we merely give lip-service."[54] Yet given the European crisis of the 1930s, and its global as well as personal dimensions, Kohn would unmistakably focus his attention on other questions. He still believed that America's future depended on "making of democracy a reality . . . instead of an aspiration," but the vital arena for him—as his publications from this point on clearly indicate—was no longer race relations but international relations.

The Betrayal of Europe as a Personal Tragedy

The persecution of Jews in Nazi Germany, which Kohn followed closely, was just one aspect of a much wider European transformation in the 1930s. Democratization was pushed back by reactionary counterforces. Fascist Italy and Nazi Germany took advantage of the feeble international system and exposed the intrinsic frailty—both internal and external—of Western liberal democracies. Kohn had warned for well over a decade about the ultimate consequences of Europe's dismemberment into nation-states or, more accurately, into "nationalizing states."[55] In the absence of fundamental organizing principles in international affairs, the renewal of all-out war between these nation-states was only a matter of time. It was in the absence of such organizing principles, Kohn claimed, that Anglo-French appeasement came about; the League of Nations failed to prevent Japan's invasion of Manchuria (in September 1931); Fascist Italy invaded Ethiopia (October 1935); Nazi Germany remilitarized the Rhineland (March 1936); fascists intervened in Spain (July 1936); and Nazi Germany annexed Austria in the *Anschluss* (March 1938).[56] "The fight," Kohn pleaded in an assembly at Smith, "is not just a Central European fight: it is a fight for democracy, and a fight for something more than that—for whether there is to be established a new world order, where it will not be strength, nor force, nor threats which will dominate, but a new respect for the will of man."[57]

The existing world order—which amounted to chaos, in Kohn's view—eventually produced Czechoslovakia's abandonment by the British and French in the Munich Agreement of September 1938. In March, Weltsch, writing from Hitler's Berlin, had already predicted to Kohn bitterly that after the Anschluss, "Czechoslovakia's fate is sealed." Kohn's 1938 diary documents his misery: listening to Hitler's speeches on the radio, he believed that Europe was doomed, and he was "devastated by the news of 'democracy' betraying itself." "Democratic forces capitulated in Munich!" and as a result, "the world seems bleak (*trostlos*)." He was physically exhausted and sickened by global political developments and their implications for his siblings and close friends in Central Europe. Kohn wrote in his diary of Prague acquaintances (Rudi Thomas, editor of the German-language *Prager Tagblatt*, and his wife, Grete) who had committed suicide. He commented on his "helplessness facing fascist barbarity." At the annual meeting of the American Association of University Professors, he stated that "one of the saddest moments of my life was the moment when [British Prime Minister Neville] Chamberlain was acclaimed, in the autumn, as the man who had brought peace to the world, at a time when thousands were dying in Spain and China, when thousands of refugees were being torn from their homelands."[58] After the Anschluss, Kohn spent many long hours writing affidavits and filing paperwork in an attempt to rescue family members and friends. In May Weltsch's letters described an immediate threat: "What goes on in Vienna, and the inability to help, is inconceivable"; "I hope I do not have to stay much longer in Germany"; "If a war breaks out, all the Jews in Germany are lost, like the Armenians in Turkey"; "I will terminate my position here as soon as possible. . . . One can feel that now everything is being liquidated. I really want to move [my son] to the USA and would be very grateful if you could assist." By the end of the year, Weltsch had escaped to Jerusalem, and his son, Ruben, was on his way to America, where he would live in Kohn's home and study at the nearby Amherst College.[59]

"Hitler in Prague!!! What a calamity! (*Welch Un-Heil!*)," Kohn wrote in his diary in March 1939.[60] After Germany violated the terms of the Munich Agreement, set up a satellite Slovak state, and occupied the Czech lands, Kohn's friends and relatives in Prague found themselves living under the swastika banner. Even after the Nazi occupation of the Czech lands (the Protectorate of Bohemia and Moravia), the international community did not offer much more than condemnations. Worse still, the United States—Kohn's new home—remained neutral as World War II broke out, dismissing the conflict as a European war in which the United States had no role. Kohn wrote in his diary: "News of definite Nazi-Soviet agreement shatters international picture of politics. Colossal Soviet blunder. Even greater blunder of small states in Europe maintaining 'neutrality.' . . . The international outlook is dark, my heart aches, and the Americans are unbearable in their self-righteousness—their responsibility is terrible—the reckoning will come—it will destroy all of us."[61] In the next months and years, Kohn worked tirelessly to rescue his Prague relatives from Europe.[62] He successfully assisted in the immigration of two of his siblings and their families to the United States, but his brother Fritz; Fritz's wife, Grete; and one of their two children remained in occupied Prague. They were interned in the Theresienstadt concentration camp in 1942; in February 1944, Fritz and Grete managed to send a letter from the camp, through a Swiss middleman (Fritz Ullmann), to Leo Hermann that finally reached Hans Kohn's family:

Many thanks, again, to you and Leo Hermann for the letter and parcel. All that we miss is a note from or about Hans and his family. We are well. I work in the office,

Grete in the children's home. Ever since our [son] Michael passed away in August 1942, after a long illness, we feel doubly lonely, and all the more so when we receive no news from Leo [the other son, who had been evacuated to the United Kingdom]. Labor constitutes our sole distraction. We hope to hear again from you soon. Please report on friends and relatives. Again, many thanks for everything, and our very best regards, Fritz and Grete Kohn.[63]

The letter from Theresienstadt took half a year to reach the Swiss intermediary. A laconic sentence in a letter from Kohn to Pinson at the end of the war removes any doubt as to their fate: "Fritz and Grete are dead. They were transported to a Polish extermination camp from Theresienstadt in the fall of 1944—the last transports! . . . Leo is in the Czech Army with the Americans . . . soon to be demobilized and to settle in Prague."[64] In his publications, Kohn's language was typically abstract, calculated, dispassionate, as if addressing matters of principle in the utmost objectivity. The concealed personal dimension—which may have been too great for words—was, however, central to his life, and it strongly influenced his intellectual pursuits and political commitments in the 1930s and 1940s. His unspoken European trauma cast a shadow over his great American achievements.

Democratic World Order and the Alternative

The betrayal of Europe, then, was both a personal tragedy and an intellectual challenge for Kohn, and it reframed his academic and political agenda in the mid-1930s and increasingly into the 1940s. What, ultimately, is fascism? What does it want? What brought it about? What explains its survival, global spread, and success? How can it be stopped and ultimately eradicated? To combat fascism, there was a need to better understand it, and Kohn willingly participated in this task, which eventually brought about his refined theory of nationalism. In the mid-1930s he arrived at an early and hesitant piece of totalitarianism theory, pointing to the common denominator of the Soviet and fascist regimes. In his essay "Communist and Fascist Dictatorship: A Comparative Study," he found "the two types of dictatorship" to be "similar (and different from all other forms of dictatorship) in claiming absoluteness for their philosophy and in their effort to indoctrinate the masses and the youth with the new way of life. . . . Both types of dictatorship are ruthless and without regard for the happiness and freedom of the present individual. His concrete rights here and now must yield to the abstract claims of a future society."[65]

Kohn's attitude toward the Soviet Union was still conflicted, and he qualified this comparison with fascism, stressing Soviet superiority thanks to its su-pranational horizon. For him it was more important to theorize fascism and its relation to nationalism and the nation-state. Fascism, he wrote, is always char-acterized by "glorification of the nation-state and of the natural inequality of men." Furthermore, it "represents a form of nationalism in which the claims and happiness of the individual are entirely subordinated to national prosperity and even more to national aspirations for greatness."[66] This anti-individualism is the hallmark of totalitarianism that distinguishes it from liberal nationalism (in an attempt to juxtapose the two, Kohn established the interconnectedness of capitalism, individualism, and liberal nationalism).

Prominent among Kohn's early American publications was a series of his his-torical explorations of current affairs issued by Harvard University Press: *Force or Reason: Issues of the Twentieth Century* (published in February 1937), *Rev-olutions and Dictatorships: Essays in Contemporary History* (May 1939), *Not by Arms Alone: Essays on Our Time* (1940), and *World Order in Historical Per-spective* (1942). Kohn's diary indicates that his plans for those books were more ambitious than the actual published works, which still had something of the character of a popular encyclopedia and consisted largely of recently published work.[67] The volumes were centered on several presentist arguments with an overt political agenda, and collectively they constituted a battle cry of demo-cratic liberalism against fascism and the aggressive principles it sought to foist on the stronghold of the West. But Kohn championed a liberal West at a time when the West seemed to follow other principles. He theorized fascism as a counterrevolutionary force, rejecting the "liberal tradition of the great Western Revolutions."[68] Indeed, this was a rejection of what Kohn would soon call "the world revolution."[69] When a colleague commented that Kohn depicted an ide-alized and false image of the liberal "old order," Kohn protested and stressed that "liberal . . . values represent an appeal to the best in man; they are regulative principles, never realized, often falsified, nevertheless ever-present."[70] Kohn stood up against Anglo-French appeasement and later against American isola-tionism and advocated a fight for the moral principles of the West, for "there is no third possibility."[71] He regarded appeasement and isolationism as the great-est threats; they corroded the tenets of Western civilization in its stronghold and were, as he often repeated, de facto collaboration with the fascists.

Kohn found a calling in clarifying to the liberal democracies the depth and essence of the crisis they were in and their own tradition and destiny. He stressed repeatedly that his books were an attempt to reexamine the present crisis in its historical context, in search of a clearer understanding of the liberal West and its adversaries. These works had a striking similarity to Buber's 1909 address, "Meaning of Judaism" (later published as "Judaism and the Jews"), which had a great impact on Kohn and his Prague friends.[72] In all of the works, the heart of the problem and its solution lay in the exposure and embrace of a forgotten, yet real, essence and past. For Kohn, Europe of the 1930s and 1940s represented not the West but rather an eclipse of Western consciousness. Under the surface —he believed and urged his readers to believe—the essence of the liberal West awaited, but the West must first know itself and embrace its destiny to regenerate and defeat its enemies.

Force or Reason was the first book Kohn wrote in English (rather than translated into that language) and his first to be published in four editions. This book developed arguments Kohn presented in his 1932 essay "On Several Aspects of the Political Jewish Problem in Germany and Europe," in which he viewed fascism as a revolt against liberalism and the legacy of the Enlightenment. This was also the first book in which Kohn unequivocally wore his liberalism on his sleeve. Carlton Hayes reviewed it very favorably yet suggested that Kohn, whom he labeled "an incorrigible liberal," might be overlooking "a distressingly close connection between the historic 'Enlightenment' he thoroughly admires, and present ills which he properly abominates."[73]

Based on lectures that Kohn delivered at the Harvard Summer School in July 1936, Force or Reason suggested that there were three fundamental elements of fascism, which corresponded to the book's three essays. The first of these analyzes the antiliberal "Cult of Force" and its intellectual and philosophical roots, especially in Germany. The second, "The Dethronement of Reason," deals with irrationalism and reads as Kohn's final break with schools of thought that so deeply shaped his youth. The third discusses the varying European reactions to "the crisis of imperialism"—that is, reactions to the awakening of colonized populations. While liberal-minded Westerners embrace this crisis as leading to a more egalitarian world order of international cooperation, fascists "proclaim the necessity of a united fight of the whole white race in order to maintain its world dominion."[74] In other publication from this time, Kohn was even more clear about his juxtaposition between the old "liberal" imperialism and the new totalitarian imperialism.[75]

In Force or Reason Kohn attributed great importance to the Nazi legal thinker Carl Schmitt. A cornerstone of the first essay in the book was Schmitt's definition of "politics as based upon the inescapable antagonism between friend and enemy as ethics are based upon the antagonism between good and bad." Under such an assumption, Kohn pointed out, in all political conflicts "existence itself is at stake," and "war and extermination are always postulated as a guiding and real possibility." This, Kohn insists, is not just a deviation from but a rebellion against Western liberal concepts of law and politics as they have evolved since antiquity: "There is certainly a primitive instinct in man to regard an adversary or anyone in the way of our desires, [as] an implacable foe who has to be exterminated. Civilization and statesmanship consisted until recently in finding the ways and the means to overcome the primitive instinct by law, by compromise, by every effort at a peaceful settlement." Schmitt exemplifies a totalitarian worldview in which "force has come to be regarded as a great master-builder. Patience and compromise are laughed at. People do not try to convince their adversaries, to solve patiently difficult problems. They 'liquidate' their enemies." Kohn succinctly summarized the struggle with this cult of force: "Right and law protect the weaker; force opens the way for the stronger and the more powerful."[76]

Kohn's 1937 essay "The Twilight of Nationalism?" offered a distinctively liberal, non-Marxist, interpretation of fascism: "Today fascism appears, not (as most Marxists believe) as the last stage of decaying capitalism but as the last and therefore most violent, most triumphant, most exaggerated stage of nationalism." Unlike us, he added, fascism "believes nationalism eternal, history a struggle of races or nations, the inequality of races and men permanent and beneficial, and an international peaceful order a heinous dream." In that essay, Kohn accordingly rejected the claim that the Spanish Civil War was a struggle between two supranational ideas—communism and fascism—and saw it rather as a fight between two types of nationalism: "a nationalism which regards itself as part of a forward movement toward diminished nationalism, and a nationalism which considers itself and its foundation upon the past as eternal."[77]

Whereas *Force or Reason* was initially intended to counter Western defeatism and instill in American readers faith in their liberal values, the preface to the book's third printing—written immediately after the Munich Agreement—was somber, casting the agreement as "the most humiliating defeat which liberalism and the hope for rational order has suffered."[78] Twenty years after its defeat in the Great War, Germany had emerged as victor in not only the realm of aggressive politics but also in that of ideas. Anglo-French appeasement was the betrayal of these ideas by Western actors. The League of Nations was not defeated by the aggressors but by its ostensible defenders. A year and a half after the first edition of the book was published, liberalism's prospects seemed much slimmer to its author.

On the day Nazis entered his hometown of Prague, Kohn concluded his second American book, *Revolutions and Dictatorships*, most of whose essays had recently appeared elsewhere. The chapters addressed a variety of topics, including Zionism, nationalism and messianism, Soviet Russia, and the Middle East.[79] Many of the chapters present a somewhat modified version of Kohn's familiar historical vision of nationalism maturing beyond state nationalism and toward greater international codependence, pointing to an eventual—perhaps utopian—panhuman federation along the lines of Immanuel Kant's *Erdstaat*.[80] Indeed, the book's dedication page quotes Kant's plea (in his *Idea for a Universal History with a Cosmopolitan Purpose*) for "the establishment of a universal republic administering right according to law." Fascism, according to Kohn's diagnosis, is the reaction to that ultimately unstoppable world revolution. Kohn offered a few pioneering liberal (or at least non-Marxist) attempts at theorizing fascism. For example, he pointed to its Jacobin roots, the blending of romanticism and irrationalism with Prussian militarism, and its fixation on a heroic distant past. Kohn referred to his sense of a German "special path" (which he had already mentioned in 1932, in "Über einige Gesichtspunkte des politischen Judenproblems in Deutschland und Europa") and insisted that "National Socialism has its roots undoubtedly in the social structure and the intellectual traditions of Germany."[81]

Although Kohn had been a socialist—occasionally a radical one—throughout the 1920s, he now linked capitalism, individualism, and liberal nationalism together and praised these in a manner he could have not have imagined a decade earlier.[82] More than just altering his positions, at this point Kohn began presenting seemingly simple, sometimes simplistic, conceptions of issues he had seen in a highly ambivalent manner in the past. In *Revolutions and Dictatorships*, for example, Kohn dismissed all romantic or illiberal thought and was indifferent about the shortcomings of the Paris Peace Conference of 1919 and their deeper significance.[83]

The book's most important section is the chapter titled "The Totalitarian Crisis." The international crisis of the 1930s, Kohn asserted, had two causes. The first was a "German bid for world hegemony," which Kohn did not find it necessary to elaborate on, for "liberalism was stopped in one European country only—in Germany." He did, however expound at great length on the second cause, "the international anarchy of sovereign states."[84] The peace treaties following World War I and the principles of the League of Nations charted innovative new horizons for international relations, beyond separate treaties and realpolitik diplomacy. Tragically, however, the Western states failed to remain united behind this vision and started to work against one another, returning to old diplomacy and emptying the treaties of their revolutionary intent and content. Because of "a feeling of bitter disillusionment, . . . for which they alone were responsible," Westerners themselves lost confidence in the applicability of international law, collective security, and liberal principles in the realm of diplomacy: "The watchwords glorified in 1917–1918, the defense of universal rights and moral issues, were ridiculed; nothing seemed to count but the defense of national self-interest. Later on the same people asked whether they were 'expected to fight' for the Ethiopians, the Chinese, or the Czechs. They did not understand that their own fate and that of Western civilization was being decided on these distant battlefields, that to stand up for the Manchurians or the Ethiopians would have meant not to fight at all, but to eliminate the risk of war."[85]

Even greater than the threat to peace and democracy from fascists, Kohn insisted, was the threat from the alienation of Western statesmen from the core values of liberal democracy. There was also danger in the rise of so-called liberals, who repeatedly sided with the aggressor and diplomatically betrayed its victims in the name of the principle of self-determination. Fearing change and revolution, these Western conservatives deluded themselves that fascism did not differ substantially from nineteenth-century imperialism. Thus had come about the crisis of the 1930s. As Kohn saw it, "today the great task before the democratic countries is the same as that which faced them in 1919, the firm establishment of an international order" and of what he called democratic diplomacy, for a true democracy has a diplomatic dimension, manifesting its values and defending it on the international arena.[86]

"Democracy cannot exist any longer as a framework for a national order based upon individual liberty and equality and the protection of law," he cautioned, "but . . . must be supplemented by an international framework, as first designed in the Covenant of the League of Nations." The old slogan—to make the world safe for democracy—was still valid, but no armament would save "liberal civilization" from the fascist threat. "There is," Kohn maintained, "no security outside cooperation on the basis of firm adherence to international law." The nations were not yet ready for close cooperation, but this was the price that must be paid for peace: "We must secure peace for all, to secure peace for ourselves. . . . In this effort to establish peace on firm foundations and to save Western civilization, the United States cannot exclude itself."[87]

A separate issue that Kohn wove into the chapter was the Jews' place in this historic drama. Nazi antisemitism, he claimed as early as 1932, had evolved from Germany's distinctive antisemitic tradition, and now he wrote that "in Germany alone the natural feeling of strangeness towards minorities became a systematic philosophy of antisemitism. Thus Hitler found in Germany a fertile soil for the propagation of his antisemitic gospel."[88] This antisemitism, and its appeal in Germany and beyond, served the Nazis well in their struggle against liberal democracy.

In his discussion of Central European Jews in the liberal age, Kohn depicted Jewish assimilation as a matter of course as unproblematic: "Assimilation was the natural, progressive outcome of liberalism; it would have continued if not hindered by a conscious and artificial policy of dissimilation." Kohn's understanding of assimilation was never simplistic—it had not been in Prague or in Jerusalem—yet his celebrating it here as natural and progressive (and rejecting the opposition to it as unnatural and reactionary) marks a considerable change in his Jewish outlook. The fate of the Jews in Germany, as in any place and at any time, depended on liberalism: "Where the principle of liberty is sacrificed to conformity, the Jews must suffer. The war of extermination which the National Socialists wage against the Jews is a war against liberalism and against Christianity. . . . The National Socialist war against the Jews is a war against the equality of all men, against the dignity of the individual, against human brotherhood."[89]

It should be noted, however, that since his break with Zionism, Kohn had increasingly identified racism and tribal ethno-nationalism with "primitive Judaism," and to associate "the vision of universal brotherhood and peace" with prophetic Judaism and, especially, Christianity. His occasional references to the ostensible superiority of Christianity could have had a certain critical edge in earlier years, when he wrote to fellow Jews, yet in his writings for an overwhelmingly Christian American readership, his statements become awkwardly conformist. Thus, Kohn had no qualms about stating, "It is an historical irony that Hitler today is leading the German people back to the attitude of primitive Judaism."[90]

The book's postscript was written in March 1939, just after the Nazi occupation of Kohn's homeland. Bitterly he wrote an indictment against those he deemed "the liberal apologists for National Socialism," who demolished the world order and sacrificed the liberty of seven million Czechs in the name of the self-determination for three million Germans: "How long will this go on? . . . The answer does not lie with the fascist dictators. It lies with the democratic nations. Their understanding, resoluteness, and will power, or lack of it, will decide the future of democracy and the survival of human civilization."[91]

In February 1940, half a year after the beginning of World War II and long before the United States entered the war, Kohn published a sort of manifesto—

the essay "The World Must Federate! Isolation versus Cooperation," which appeared first as an article in *Asia* magazine and then was reprinted as a booklet.[92] Based on "The Totalitarian Crisis" and its interpretation of the international system as chaotic, this new essay was foremost a plea against American isolationism: "The policy of the United States," Kohn charged, "was that of other states: to help indirectly the aggressors against their victims."[93] His key argument was this: since "Fascism is essentially an exaggerated form of nationalism," it "cannot be answered by more nationalism. It can be answered only by bold steps towards international cooperation." With considerable wishful thinking, Kohn then pointed to "the Franco-British defensive alliance" as a first step toward a "system of collective security" and eventually "a system of federal union." He believed that voluntary federal union should be open to all states, and that beyond the member states' commitment to observe peaceful relations and defend fellow members of the union, the federation "must be built upon the principle of the equality of all individuals within the states, and of all states and peoples within the federation." As such, the federation is vital to both democratization and decolonization: "A federation alone can prepare the foundations for the emancipation of weaker and backward peoples and can protect them against exploitation."[94] Kohn's federalization agenda was apparently quite well known, prompting the anarchist economist Leopold Kohr—who advocated a diametrically opposed platform—to publish his essay "Disunion Now: A Plea for a Society Based upon Small Autonomous Units" under the pseudonym "Hans Kohr," hoping readers would mistake him for Kohn.[95]

Kohn's process of Americanization took place in the crucible of his anti-isolationist activities, as he demanded that the United States take up the banner of international democratic liberalism in response to the European crisis. Through this activity he defined his American outlook and agenda and found some of his closest American associates. He was already positioning himself as a bridging figure—an insider in relation to German and European culture and history who wrote about and explained to Americans the European cultural and historical roots of fascism. During World War II, and especially after America's entry into the war, his authority both as a man who truly understood nationalism and as a Central European who profoundly understood the Germans became a precious asset. As the dean of the University of Wisconsin–Madison Law School, Lloyd K. Garrison, wrote to Kohn: "You have the advantage over me for you know the German mind and the European mind and I don't." Americans thus praised his work as the "unique product of a mind steeped in the cultural tradition of Europe."[96] In the late 1930s, Kohn worked with numerous anti-isolationist intellectuals, such as the historian James T. Shotwell, a member of Wilson's Inquiry—the president's group of academic advisors to the peace conference—who shared Kohn's internationalism; and Bishop Henry W. Hobson, a member of the interventionist Fight for Freedom Committee. In a letter to Henry Pitney van Dusen, an internationalist ecumenical theologian, Kohn —a very committed member of the Fight for Freedom Committee—stressed that although the committee's publications would "have no 'practical' result," they would have "a very important moral effect in preparing the mind of the people and of youth here, a most needed work." Kohn also prided himself on his local branch's enlisting of former First Lady Grace Coolidge.[97]

The most colorful anti-isolationist organization that Kohn participated in must have been the Committee of the City of Man, also known as the Committee of Europe or the Committee of the Fifteen (though it had seventeen members).[98] Many of the people in this group were already acquainted with Kohn from one setting or another. The driving force behind its genesis was Borgese, the Italian literary critic and journalist who had been Kohn's colleague at Smith. Other émigré intellectuals in the committee included Thomas Mann, the uncrowned leader of the German intellectuals in exile (and Borgese's father-in-law); the Austrian author Hermann Broch; and Oscar Jaszi, a former Hungarian politician who had worked as a scholar in the United States since 1925.[99] Participants from the United States included the Christian theologian Reinhold Niebuhr; the Harvard political scientist William Yandell Elliott, at the time one of President Franklin D. Roosevelt's close advisors; Lewis Mumford, the scholar of urban life; Neilson, Smith's president; and several other scholars and journalists, such as Herbert Agar, Frank Aydelotte, and Dorothy Canfield Fisher.

During the bleak weekend of the evacuation of Dunkirk that marked the imminent fall of France and the rest of Europe, members of this anti-isolationist group gathered in Atlantic City on the gray and rainy May 26, 1940, to compose *The City of Man: A Declaration on World Democracy*, a manifesto geared to guide the path of the United States now that Europe's fate had been sealed. In his recollections from the meeting, Lewis Mumford remembered Kohn as "a heavy-set man, with a kindly pasty face, an earnest pessimistic air" who "talked volubly, but with great dialectic skill, real insight, well-supported arguments, and unshakable moral conviction. Kohn despaired of the international situation. Some of his comments on our political unreadiness were penetrating. He believes that [the noninterventionist historian] Charles Beard's attempt to justify his isolationism by debunking the valid reasons for participating in the First

World War had done much to undermine our will to resist the present Nazi assault on all democratic institutions."[100]

Thomas Mann's letters and diary entries from Atlantic City captured that same apocalyptic mood. "The disaster can clearly no longer be stopped," he wrote on May 23. "Sick with horror. . . . The sole hope of clueless French writers is America—which will prove as paralyzed and as oblivious as the West[ern] European states. An unprecedented affliction is looming, and even harder to endure would be the unparalleled triumph of the basest of all." On May 25 he wrote: "All this, after all, is only the culmination of the sufferings of seven years, which were filled with foreknowledge and despair at others' lack of knowledge and refusal to know. . . . [O]nly a miracle can prevent it from becoming a reality."[101]

"The entire Old World," the committee lamented in *The City of Man*, "where our forefathers lie and whence all life and light came to us, sinks in a catastrophe unequaled in the record[s] of man." The members of the group were alarmed that Americans had failed to grasp the full significance of Europe's demise, the true nature of the totalitarian threat, and the new responsibility that the war in Europe bestowed on the United States. They believed that America was mired in internal conflict and degenerate defeatism, which prevented it from realizing its duty to enter the war—indeed, from realizing that "the peace [the fascists] promise would be more terrifying than the war they wage."[102] The mood at the meeting was decidedly gloomy.

The declaration that ultimately emerged from this meeting, however, was as optimistic as it was ambitious. The authors assumed that US entry into the war was both inevitable and imminent: "War, declared or undeclared, actual or virtual, has chosen us."[103] Moreover, the declaration went beyond other pleas for US intervention in the European war, calling on America to prepare for its inevitable goal of constructing a new postwar order. The United States, the writers claimed, had no choice but boldly to assume global leadership and create a universal state. They also drafted a spiritual program, designed to guide the United States in this new global order: the declaration conceptualized isolationism as an age of calamitous innocence to be overcome. Innocence in this context, it should be noted, "took a counterintuitive meaning," no longer "signifying clear conscience or guiltlessness" but ignorant guilt. In this, *The City of Man* was an early participant in the theological critique of "American innocence," which Jason Stevens has identified as key motif in his "spiritual history of America's Cold War."[104] Much like Eric Voegelin, Kohn and his coauthors of *The City of Man* theorized totalitarianism as a political and secular religion, "a new—and perverted—religion, substitute for the lost creed of traditional beliefs." Since totalitarianism was a political religion, democracy too, *The City of Man* proclaimed, had to become a political religion if it were to prevail: "A constitutional reform of democracy cannot be founded but on the spirit of a new religion."[105]

The City of Man was in many ways a continuation of Kohn's plea in "The World Must Federate" for a democratic world federalization in response to what he and his colleagues saw as the nadir of isolationism. Just like Kohn, the committee was inspired by Kant's vision of a global state, imagining "the unity of man under one law and one government . . . the Universal State, and State of States." "Peace," they insisted emphatically, "is indivisible."[106] But there were some noteworthy new elements in their proposed federation, the clearest of which was America's role in it. According to *The City of Man*, the United States was the clear leader for the authors' utopian vision. In a narrative soon to become one of the core elements of Cold War ideology, the authors proclaimed it was the inevitable destiny of the United States to lead the world into a future of order and peace, eliminating the totalitarian threat along the way. This leadership, however, would ostensibly be far removed from arrogance and imperialism and would constitute a form of service to the entire globe. Leadership, they wrote, "implies some sort of imperium. But there is a difference between imperialism and imperium." Whereas imperialism is self-appointed, the imperium they envisioned is

> chosen by the objective circumstances of history for a privilege which is a service, for a right which is a duty. This is, indeed, the substance of a chosen people: power in the frame of service. . . . "Rome did not spread upon the world; the world spread upon the Romans." This was the destiny of other nations and cultures, in ancient and in modern ages as well. This—to the largest extent of world-leadership for world-communion in the comradeship of man—is the destiny of America, as manifest as it was unwanted, since the English speaking nations were "left to fight alone," and all the world must sink unless we take the helm.[107]

To secure international order and stability, the manifesto's authors believed that the United States was destined to lead the education of those nations that they likened to "children who must grow up," or to direct the treatment or confinement of those nations they saw as "sick," "maniac" or "criminal." With this statement, *The City of Man* reached its climax. Engaged in the fight for its own spiritual survival against totalitarianism, the United States was revealed also as the power responsible for the freedom of the entire world. It was the heir to all of civilization, its citizens the new chosen people. Most importantly, it was to be the leading polity and a determined force. As the authors concluded, "the healing of the world requires a firm hand. . . . American leadership is world-trusteeship; the *Pax Americana* a preamble to the *Pax Humana*."[108] With this promise of a *pax humana* the manifesto foresaw much more than the changing of the world's leaders—it foresaw the changing of the world order. The manifesto reflected the final transformation in the thought of former pacifists such as Kohn and Niebuhr, who, in the face of Nazi aggression, abandoned their earlier convictions and embraced the use of force as part of America's responsibility. This about-face, I would argue, was actually quite coherent with Kohn's long-standing notion that the path to a more peaceful world order necessarily goes through compromised national sovereignty, as he had written in 1935: "The only hope lies in going to the fundamentals of the universal situation and getting ready to pay the price that all nations without exception will have to pay if they sincerely believe in peace and cooperation as more essential than their own sovereignty or the standard of power and life they enjoy by virtue of temporary advantages."[109]

The manifesto sets a unique challenge to the historian and even more to the biographer, for it is impossible to know which of its cosignatories wrote which passage. Parts of the declaration seem to bear Kohn's fingerprints (like the use of the term "the Nation of Man," which is probably translated from the work of the anarchist Zionist thinker A. D. Gordon), while other parts seem quite foreign to his writings thus far. The manifesto was more Christian in language than anything Kohn published before or after. It assumed Christian supersession and likened the imagined postwar world order to the progression from the Old Testament (of isolationism) to the New Testament (of universality). Beyond this advocacy of a democratizing American global hegemony, *The City of Man* differed from Kohn's previous statements in its surprisingly conservative impulse, which presumably originated with Borgese. Since 1933 Kohn had been interested in writing about the decline of conservative thought from Burke to Hitler, but *The City of Man* called for a democratic rejuvenation of conservative values, indeed a conservative democratization.[110] Accordingly, the manifesto's indictment of communism and its unqualified equation to Nazism went well beyond anything Kohn had written thus far. And its recurring attacks on liberalism—referring to "corrupted liberalism," "disintegrated liberalism," and "the anarchy of laissez-faire liberalism"[111]—conflicted with Kohn's ultimately liberal commitments. One of Kohn's friends, the political thinker Carl J. Friedrich, rightly assumed that these expressions should not be attributed to Kohn.[112] Yet while the early 1930s generated a liberal turn in Kohn's thought and writing, in the 1940s his thinking began to move again, and he opened up to elements of conservative thought. "The older I grow," he would say in 1944, "the more conservative I grow."[113] The positions of the declaration that did not quite match Kohn's in 1940 at least anticipate some of his later ideological developments. A few years later, after the United States had entered the war, Kohn and three other authors of *The City of Man*—Aydelotte, Johnson, and Neilson—signed a declaration by the Commission to Study the Organization of Peace titled "United Nations Urged to Safeguard Human Rights." The commission, whose chairperson was the anti-isolationist Shotwell, was no longer a marginal group out of touch with real politics, as when some of its members had authored *The City of Man*. Indeed, a recent study found it "perhaps the most important of the private organizations that helped shape the State Department's postwar plan."[114]

Kohn published two additional books with Harvard University Press during the war: *Not by Arms Alone: Essays on Our Time* (1940) and *World Order in Historical Perspective* (1942). Consisting largely on recently published essays, these volumes further developed, yet failed to significantly transcend, Kohn's recent works analyzing fascism, democracy, nationalism, and international relations. Noteworthy in *Not by Arms Alone* was an essay titled "The Legacy of the Habsburgs" (the volume was originally conceived of as a monograph on nationalism and democracy in Central Europe). The essay explicitly linked the late-Habsburg plans for multinational federalization to the challenges of world order after the war's end: "Austria's fate and her end have become symbolic of Europe's destiny," for "the urgent problem before Central Europe in the period between the two wars of 1914 and 1939 was the same as the Austrian problem had been at the beginning of the twentieth century, and will be the same after the present war—the problem of federation of equal peoples, not in submission and uniformity, but in freedom and tolerance. In her best moments Old Austria had shown in a very imperfect form, as an embryonic promise, the possibility of such a federation without brutality or domination, without exclusiveness or exclusivism."[115]

Friedrich, who was born in Germany, could not go along with the tendency of Kohn, his former Austrian friend, to attribute Nazism to Germany and progressive federalization to Austria: "Like so many others who would like to forget that Hitler was born and raised in Austria, you state that 'National Socialism is undoubtedly a specific German movement.' Hitler's whole testimony in *Mein Kampf* specifically denies this, and I think it stands to reason that racial intolerance so characteristic of the Nazis is, in fact, a specific product of the clash of nationalities in Old Austria. Indeed, the cultural ideas of Nazi philosophy were forged by and in the Hapsburg realm . . . long before the World War, when no-body in Germany was dreaming of these terrible creeds."[116]

Kohn experienced the years prior to America's entry into the war against Nazi Germany as a trial of faith, which he withstood. Tellingly, it was Kohn who, on December 9, 1941—two days after the attack on Pearl Harbor and America's entry into the war—addressed the entire Smith College community in a special assembly. "Two days ago something happened to each one of us," he said. "Apathy [and] confusion . . . have been dispelled. We see more clearly and feel more clearly where our duty lies and where we stand." He urged his listeners to understand the broadest significance of the events: "We must always see that the whole of mankind is caught up in this tremendous crisis. It may be a crisis to death; but it may also be a crisis to rebirth. . . . There is no historical necessity that it must be one or the other: it depends on us, now. What we must do is to see it as a whole crisis—not only, or mainly, as a question of our survival, but much more, as the survival of civilization, of the peace of mankind, of human destiny."[117]

World Order in Historical Perspective was the first book Kohn published after the United States entered the war, and it marks the beginning of a new stage in his relationship to the United States. One can distinguish between four stages in that relationship: in the 1920s he was still distinctly anti-American; in the mid 1930s he was already writing as a self-critical new American, preoccupied with America's race problem; and as an anti-isolationist in the late 1930s he switched to an idealizing tone with a critical edge, in which he wrote about the American mission and values, primarily to juxtapose them to the less flattering American policies and realities. With America's entry into the war, however, even this critical edge was lost, and many of Kohn's statements began to read as self-congratulatory Americanism. With unprecedented, arguably postcatastrophic, conformity Kohn identified the present United States with the West:

> German totalitarianism and American democracy tend to represent, in the most outspoken form, the totalitarian and democratic trends. . . . All the great currents of Western liberal development of the seventeenth and eighteenth centuries were able to ripen to fruition under the especially favorable circumstances of the English colonies in North America and in the wake of their revolutionary moment. Here, more than anywhere else, emerged the Western man. Not as a race, because he was a mixture of all races, but as a social and intellectual type, professing a deep faith in man and his potentialities, and trying to build a civilization on the basis of rationalism, optimism and individualism. The American society more than

any other is a product of the eighteenth century, of the faith in freedom and in ultimate harmony; a typical middle-class society with its ultimately pacifist ideal.[118]

In early 1943 the US Office of War Information (OWI) cabled Kohn a request to serve as a regional specialist in the office's overseas information branch.[119] Though his paper trail does not indicate whether Kohn accepted the invitation, the OWI was correct to reach out to him, as he would have undoubtedly been overjoyed to participate in America's war effort in such a capacity. Some two years later, when defeated Germany was occupied, Kohn's diary mentions OWI's intent to translate his work into German.[120] His dedication to and identification with the United States from that moment on is remarkable in the broader context of his life. Never before had Kohn identified with any of the polities in which he lived: his affection for the Habsburg monarchy (or, as he would call it, Austria) was largely after the fact; with the Zionist Yishuv he mainly struggled, and Czechoslovakia he never cared for or accepted.

Kohn's juxtaposition of German and American nationalisms in the first chapter of *World Order* (titled "Democracy: The Way of Man") would ripen some twenty years later in his monographs *American Nationalism* (1957) and *The Mind of Germany* (1960). During the twelve years of the Third Reich, Kohn was instructively selective in his discussion of Nazism's intellectual foundations: he was almost surprisingly harsh with one of his acquaintances, the social-democrat sociologist Ferdinand Tönnies (creator of the influential distinction between *Gemeinschaft* [community] and *Gesellschaft* [society]), but he was remarkably silent about two other acquaintances, the famously Nazified Haushofer and Hauer.[121]

The ten years between the late 1930s and late 1940s, were bitter ones for Kohn, though they were also years of academic breakthrough. A severe midlife crisis is evident in his diary, where he wrote melancholy meditations on the passing of time. They reveal his unrelenting sense of achieving nothing of merit, of being too late and too old. In addition to long quotes from Rainer Maria Rilke, T. S. Eliot, and W. H. Auden, Kohn wrote about his crisis in the first person singular: "New Year [1938]: with it always the sense of a life unlived, unknown"; "Melancholy. Insomnia" (November 4, 1943); and "life escapes—soon beyond all possibilities—and one carries on—full of regrets" (September 7, 1944). At the end of 1945, he wrote: "Old age approaching—where was life? Worthwhile?" A year later he was feeling no better: "Finis 1946: what a poor year—in a poor life. How did my life run out and away?" Kohn sounded much the same on New Year's Day of 1948: "My last year? Or how many more? I feel ready and very list-

Figure 6.4 Hans Kohn and students, undated.
Courtesy of the Leo Baeck Institute, New York.

less—and yet sometimes I feel young. . . . A life lost, my young years badly used: to be 20 with the mind of 50!"[122] In his diary from those years of crisis Kohn meticulously documented both his weight and his affair with his young assistant, Laura Wells Oppenheimer, with whom he fell desperately in love and by whom he was then humiliatingly rejected ("It will take a very long time to get over it, if ever").[123] Though he wrote surprisingly candidly in his diary about Laura and affairs with other women, he wrote very little about the personal side of the Holocaust—about Fritz, the one brother he could not bring to the United States.

The Idea of Nationalism: The West and the Rest?
Through those horrible years—starting gradually in 1936 (the year Kohn identified as the real beginning of the war), and working with full steam as of 1942 —he wrote the one masterpiece for which he is still remembered, *The Idea of Nationalism: A Study of Its Origins and Background.* This book, a thorough yet engagingly written history of the idea of nationalism from antiquity to the eve

of the French Revolution, was a tour de force different than anything previously written on nationalism. The leading works on the subject at the time were Hayes's 1926 *Essays on Nationalism* and 1931 *Historical Evolution of Modern Nationalism*. Kohn's audacious new book—which, like the works by Hayes, was published by Macmillan—offered unprecedented research, breadth, and rigor: almost 600 pages of deftly argued and deeply researched engaging historical analysis, followed by an additional 150 pages of eye-opening notes on sources in Hebrew, Greek, Latin, French, German, Italian, Dutch, Polish, Czech, and other languages.

The 1940s, Craig Calhoun has rightly noted, "must have been an extraordinary time to write about nationalism. They were perhaps a still more extraordinary time to take up the challenge of showing that nationalism and liberal democracy were compatible, and indeed that enlightened nationalism was inseparable from liberalism."[124] In a time when vilifying nationalism seemed almost unavoidable, Kohn did the opposite. For better or worse, the insistence that nationalism could be benign, which stood out from the scholarship of the time, emerges as a key component of his legacy: as he did in the wake of World War I, so during World War II Kohn insisted that nationalism was also a force for good, and would continue to make that argument until the end of his life.

The book, planned in 1933 if not earlier, naturally reflected much of Kohn's previous work and insights, and many of the chapters of the book relied on his earlier writings.[125] However, the book's overall argument relied even more substantially on several of his essays from the second half of the 1930s. Kohn had long identified fascism as a historically conditioned distortion of nationalism, and as early as 1937, in "The Twilight of Nationalism?," he came to distinguish between two types of nationalism. His short "Roots of Modern Nationalism" from 1938, "The Nature of Nationalism" from 1939, and "Coalesce or Collide" from 1940 developed this distinction much further.[126]

Kohn established the modernity of nationalism, defining it as contingent on ideas of popular sovereignty, secularization, and the rise of the third estate. Thus, he began *The Idea of Nationalism* by proclaiming that "nationalism as we know it is not older than the second half of the eighteenth century" and that anything prior to it was merely "ethnographic material." Modern nationalism, however, was based on ancient concepts of nationhood, going back to Judea and Hellas (such as the concept of a chosen people). In antiquity both Jewish and Greek national concepts had already transcended, through a historical process, their original tribal basis; in the Greek case, this maturation was remarkably an outcome of the conquests of Alexander the Great (especially noteworthy in the context of Kohn's version of a looming American century). Though many European nationalists claimed to trace their national identities back to the Middle Ages, Kohn insisted that in that period nationalism "did not form any essential part of the communal world." Modern nationalism, he claimed, originated in Western Europe, first in seventeenth-century England, and about a hundred years later in the French Revolution, from where it spread in multiple ways to other European lands.[127] Nationalism developed in different nations at different times and in different fashions: in Western Europe, "where the third estate became powerful," it grew as a political phenomenon, but in Central and Eastern Europe, where the third estate was still weak, "nationalism found its expression predominantly in the cultural field." Civic Western nationalism, Kohn claimed, found its perfect expression on American soil: "for the first time a nation had arisen on the basis of these truths held 'to be self-evident, that all men are created equal, that they are endowed by their Creator with certain unalienable Rights, that among these are Life, Liberty, and the Pursuit of Happiness.'" Further, while Western nationalism carried notions of individual rights and cosmopolitanism, "nationalism in Germany and Italy, born under the influence of and in the struggle against, France, necessarily tended for its own self-preservation and development to emphasize elements diametrically contrary to the very essence of French nationalism. This nationalism thus became not only anti-French, but [also] a revolt against rationalism and cosmopolitan tendencies."[128]

Even at this early stage, however, Kohn qualified and allowed complexity in what soon would be known as the Kohn Dichotomy. No geographic determinism was at play in the divergence between the types of nationalism; rather, the impact of historical forces manifested themselves differently in different places and times. In "Coalesce or Collide," he had already elaborated on the liberal nature of the German *Vormärz* (the period between 1815 or 1830 and 1848); the Western pattern of Czech, Indian, and Turkish nationalism; and the Western originators of much of the anti-Western nationalism (including Burke, Arthur de Gobineau, Houston Stewart Chamberlain, and Charles Maurras. "The present great conflict of nations," Kohn concluded in that essay, "is the struggle between the two opposed patterns of reacting to the meeting of cultures—the rational and liberal pattern of cooperation, and the irrational pattern which, spell-bound by the past, stresses isolationism and peculiarities above the growing oneness and common destiny of contemporary mankind."[129]

The book's success was richly deserved, yet—given Kohn's career to date and the book's focus on the world before the nineteenth century—its almost immediate celebration as an important and timely standard work (arguably a masterpiece) was something of a surprise.[130] Regrettably, such a pleasant surprise never occurred again in Kohn's career. Kohn conceived of *The Idea of Nationalism* as the first of two or three volumes. While this first book analyzed only the roots of modern nationalism, the history of the idea of nationalism from antiquity until the eve of the French Revolution, the next volume, tentatively titled *The Age of Nationalism: A Study in the Growth and Fulfillment of an Idea*, was meant to analyze nationalism's full bloom in the years between the French Revolution and 1900, its global expansion, and its transformation of the world. In that new age, nationalism "dominated the impulses and attitudes of the masses, and at the same time served as the justification for the authority of the state and the legitimation of its use of force, both against its own citizens and against other states." And once nationalism reigns supreme, "humanity seems a distant idea, a pale theory or a poetic dream, through which the red blood of life does not pulsate."[131] A few years later, Kohn received grants to help him complete the second volume, but he ultimately failed to do so. He would publish multiple monographs on aspects of the planed project, but not the comprehensive comparative study he had envisioned as the sequel to *The Idea of Nationalism*.[132]

The book's opening and closing pages linked nationalism's historical development to the present and the future. Its preface referred to the book's publication in the midst of war—not just of World War II, but of what he called the Thirty Years' War of the twentieth century, "a war which is the consequence and climax of the age of nationalism and which can be seen as a struggle for its meaning." He emphasized nationalism's destructive and redemptive potential for the world, stating in the first sentence of the preface that "the Age of Nationalism represents the first period of universal history." Nationalism may appear to dissect the world along ethnic lines, but coming about precisely "under the conditions of a shrinking world," the universal spread of nationalism would ultimately lead to "higher forms of integration." Through the Western idea of nationalism, in the end all people will share "the faith in the oneness of humanity and the ultimate value of the individual."[133]

Almost seamlessly integrating his older and more recent works, *The Idea of Nationalism* enabled Kohn to present at length his theory of nationalism. His readers would learn much about the vital importance to their lives of the idea of nationalism. Furthermore, Kohn charted a rigorously comparative methodological agenda for leading studies of nationalism. For about a generation, he would remain the leading scholar of nationalism, and his *Idea of Nationalism*, the gold standard. That work, however, was often quite narrowly read, and it was remembered almost exclusively for the Kohn dichotomy, a term Kohn never used. The classic quotation from the book, thus, addressed the clear juxtaposition between the civic nationalism of the West and the ethnic nationalism of the East:

> In the West nations grew up as unions of citizens, by the will of individuals who expressed it [nationalism] in contracts, covenants, or plebiscites. Thus they integrated around a political idea, looking towards the common future which would spring from their common efforts. A nascent German nationalism, unable to find the rallying point in society or in a free and rational order, found it in nature or in the past, not in a political act but in a given national fact, the folk community, formed by the ties of a hoary past and later of prehistoric, biological factors. This natural foundation was not simply accepted as a fact, but raised to the dignity of an ideal or of a mystery. The political integration around a rational goal was replaced by a mystical integration around the irrational, precivilized folk concept.[134]

Western civic nationalism, Kohn stated, "was basically a rational universal concept of political liberty and the rights of man." Non-Western ethnic nationalism, he added disapprovingly, "was basically founded on history, on monuments and graveyards, even harking back to the mysteries of ancient times and of tribal solidarity." Kohn's advocacy of the Western model is important also in the biographical context, for it seems to indicate a complete inversion of his earlier concepts: his earliest Zionism was thought of as orientalization, and tellingly that was also the stage in which his own nationalism was a cultural one, still focused on the allure of blood and ancient history. If his prewar Zionism marks Kohn's "oriental phase," his scholarship and politics in the 1920s and early 1930s seem to mark a "bridging phase," in which he saw the modernizing East as endlessly more promising than the nationalism of the West and attributed to the East the potential to develop into polities superior to the Western nation-state. The mid- to late 1930s, however, mark Kohn's "occidental phase," which framed his scholarship and politics henceforth. Now Western nationalism, rather than the Eastern one, was the norm, civic rather than ethnic, political, rather than cultural. This inversion, in turn, shows the effect that his evolving political agenda and his morphing theories of nationalism had on each other.[135] Many later detractors would criticize this as a "Manichean view" of nationalism, insisting "that the distinction between civic and ethnic nationhood and nationalism is both normatively and analytically problematic."[136] Yet there was more to *The Idea of Nationalism* than the dichotomy: the book's eloquent insistence that nationalism is neither natural nor self-evident but a historically conditioned ideological construct, or "a state of mind," was not trivial—especially in academic works. Even more important was Kohn's acceptance of nationalism as "an integral part of the story of liberty." *The Idea of Nationalism* "rightly shows nationalism at work in the seventeenth- and eighteenth-century foundations of Western modernity, indeed democracy." It showed "how nationalism could be, at least sometimes, internationalist and even universalist." Kohn, then, did not see in fascism nationalism's true face but rather a degeneration—a temporary one, he hoped—of the idea of nationalism. Calhoun praised Kohn for taking this stand in 1944, when it would have been much safer to reject nationalism altogether as inherently irrational (as Hayes did at the time), or as "a malady, an infection" (as Ellie Kedourie later would write). Partha Chatterjee was much less impressed by what he saw as Kohn's "liberal rationalist dilemma in talking about nationalist thought" and viewed it as self-interested and willful blindness and a cop-out.[137]

Because *The Idea of Nationalism* presented a detailed view of Kohn's theory of nationalism, the book shows the extent of his ideological conversion and intellectual unfolding since the 1920s. This development in his thought over the previous twenty years first manifested itself in his reactions to current affairs and then altered the type of questions that nationalism raised for him (such as how to explain the Great War, fascism, and so on). Finally, his evolving worldview yielded different answers to those questions—that is, a different understanding of nationalism's essence and meaning. In the Great War Kohn was committed to taming the beast of nationalism, but he had come to find tradition, specifically Western political tradition, crucial to the restraint of nationalism. Nationalism, he now argued, becomes malignant only when it strays from that Western tradition, as in the case of fascism. In the 1920s, Kohn had felt that the right path to keep nationalism in check was by relying almost entirely on the prospects of internationalism and the eventual development of "higher forms of integration." By the 1940s, however, he found benign nationalism checked not only from above, by a supranational horizon, but also from below, by adherence to the "rights of man," "the ultimate value of the individual," and the pursuit of "deeper liberty." One may rightly ask "whose liberty?" but the preponderance of liberty and the integration of nationalism into the story of the advancement of liberty are markers of Kohn's new worldview and political allegiances. During the dark hours of World War II, he reminded Americans and others that "the good, liberal version of nationalism was not irrevocably lost" and that it could still "be recovered, claimed by Western Europe and the US, and even potentially spread throughout the world as part of the West's gift to humankind."[138] But as Calhoun aptly pointed out, Kohn's work might have encouraged the "overconfidence of mid-twentieth-century liberalism." After all, Kohn's theory of nationalism could very easily encourage "self-declared civic nationalists, liberal, and cosmopolitans to be too complacent, seeing central evils of the modern world produced at a safe distance by ethnic nationalists from whom they are surely deeply different."[139] So it is quite telling that the legacy of slavery and racism in America—which in his first years in the United States Kohn declared "the sorest spot in the moral and political texture of American culture"—became marginal in, almost absent from, *The Idea of Nationalism* and his contemporaneous publications and certainly did not challenge his championing of Western nationalism in general and of American nationalism in particular.

Midcentury Resolutions

The success of *The Idea of Nationalism* certainly opened many doors to Kohn, but in some regards it may have also set the bar a bit too high for him. The first page of the book's introduction promised the publication of a second volume: *The Age of Nationalism: A Study in the Growth and Fulfillment of an Idea*. As mentioned above, in 1945 Kohn received grants for the completion of the project and began to plan the research, but he was then silent for two years. In early March 1948 he began writing, but the manuscript was not completed, and the project seems to have been abandoned.[140]

Instead, the next book he published was *Prophets and Peoples: Studies in Nineteenth Century Nationalism*. Based on five lectures delivered in the summer of 1945, the slim and elegantly written volume offered an introduction to the significance of nineteenth-century European nationalism and the variety within it, through short studies of five respective "national prophets": John Stuart Mill (England), Jules Michelet (France), Giuseppe Mazzini (Italy), Heinrich von Treitschke (Germany), and Fyodor Dostoevsky (Russia). Each "was recognized and acclaimed in his own time as a national spokesman," and each "made a highly significant contribution to the understanding of nationalism and helped shape the age of nationalism." Kohn's eloquent juxtaposition of Eastern and Western nationalisms foreshadows his growing apprehension of the Soviet Union. Likening Western political ideas to a fruit tree, Kohn demonstrated that "while the seeds of [liberty and the rule of law] spread from [seventeenth-century England] to America and Western Europe, in Russia the fragile roots of lawful life and traditional freedom . . . withered away. Thus, the gulf between Russia and Europe created by the Mongol rule remained."[141] T. S. Eliot, who found Kohn "a brilliant talker as well as a charming person and a man about whom I should like to know more," read the book with great admiration.[142] But though reviews were positive overall, the book did not generate as much interest as the previous volume had, nor did it sell nearly as well, in spite of its absorbing subject matter and engaging prose.

Kohn had undergone multiple ideological conversions in more than a dozen turbulent years, but the US entry into World War II seems to mark a consolidation of Kohn's political and academic agenda. At its core, this profound change in Kohn's worldview, sensibilities, and agenda was the transition from his earlier rejection of the Western liberal concept of progress—based on the insincerity, willful blindness, and half-measures of interwar western democracies—as faulty, to supporting imperfect progress. America seemed the last best hope. By 1942, the considerable doubts he had originally had about aspects of American democracy—racism first among them—seem to have been forgotten or repressed. Kohn's clearly articulated links between his concept of nationalism, his understanding of the United States, and his Jewish outlook attest to a sense of ideological confidence absent in the previous decades of his life. During the next decades, the changes in his worldview, political agenda, and theory of nationalism would be much subtler. Age may have had something to do with this—he was, after all, in his early fifties—but historical forces were even more determinative. His initial response to the totalitarian crisis was a growing adherence to what he thought of as the Western legacy of enlightenment and its concept of progress. In the 1930s he, a new American, feared that his fellow Americans were oblivious to their own values, the totalitarian assault on those values, and their global mission as Americans and as Westerners. However, once America entered the war and in 1942 signed "The Declaration of the United Nations," Kohn found the country's conduct had become largely congruent with his vision. Occasionally—as in "This Century of Betrayal: Can America Lead a New Struggle for Independence?," an essay he published in *Commentary* in 1946— Kohn would reiterate his old imperative to Westerners in general, and Americans in particular, to reclaim their ostensible forgotten core values, yet much of Kohn's critical edge was now lost, although arguably his utopian vision remained.[143]

Kohn was thinking, lecturing, and writing about the postwar world order even before the United States entered the war. In 1940 he had already envisioned a postwar global federalization ("The World Must Federate"), and *The City of Man* merged that vision with the principle of American leadership, "healing of the world" with "a firm hand."[144] His 1942 book *World Order in Historical Per-*

spective continued along the same path, as did his 1943 published lecture "Patterns of the Coming Peace."[145] Without ever turning his back on growing global federalization, Kohn's new emphasis was more down to earth: "The three strongest powers [have to] remain united as the indispensable nucleus of the United Nations"; they must avoid "premature armistice" and make sure they "defeat and disarm Germany and Japan completely."[146]

As the war's end drew near, Kohn's added interest in the treatment of occupied Germany became evident. He was very skeptical of the Germans and the prospects of their reeducation, and he advocated complete German disarmament. This was also the thrust of his lecture on a suggested postwar American policy for handling Germany. He resented any attempts to distinguish between Nazis and Germans, insisting that "our enemy is not Hitler and National Socialism alone but the German people." Rather than hope to reeducate the Germans, the victors should reeducate themselves and learn from their recent past the absolute necessity for unity among the victors, which would now be facilitated through the work of the United Nations.[147]

Kohn's goal of a far-reaching international union led by the United States was doubly evident in the postwar years: he was affiliated with American and British Commonwealth Association, collaborated with the Committee to Frame a World Constitution, and was a member of the Citizens Conference on International Economic Union and the board of directors of Federal Union, Inc.[148] But although he was overjoyed by the establishment of the United Nations and saw it as all that the League of Nations had failed to be, he hoped foremost for a deepening international collaboration, especially with the Soviet Union, precisely because he saw it as a potential major threat. He expected the United States to be more committed to building trust and unity among the victors, including the Soviet Union. He was thus doubly shocked by the atomic bombing of Hiroshima and Nagasaki—by its inhumanity, of course, and by the deep sense that the atomic bomb had been used to intimidate the Soviet Union. On August 8, 1945, he wrote: "Stories of bomb used by us! Russian stab in the back for Japan! What a world!" Some weeks later, on September 25, his concern grew clearer: "Upset by Russian danger in reluctance of Western nations to follow road of union which alone can upset totalitarian plans. Again like with Germany! In a certain way it is good that Soviets are open and brusque in aggressiveness as Hitler." Indeed, with an eye on the Soviet Union as a likely, even natural, aggressor, Kohn feared that heavy-handed American moves would encourage the Soviets to reprise the role Nazi Germany had played in the 1930s. "Heavy threat to world and to civilization by Russian weighs upon me," he wrote in his diary. "German game completely repeated—we like Britain after 1918 abandoning victory and creating the opportunity for ruthless Russian self-assertion."[149]

The consolidation of Kohn's political and academic agenda in the mid-1940s created a new position for him from which to address Jewish questions, and he became more vocal about American Jewish affairs. The notoriety of his *Idea of Nationalism* must have generated greater Jewish interest in his work, but in addition he seems to have felt a greater urgency to speak out about what he saw as the mission of American Jews. By World War II, Kohn had come to believe that Jewish life always and everywhere was dependent on liberal democracy, held together by liberal civic nationalism:

> This is after all the essential war aim of the democratic world. The tribal nationalism, preached not only by Hitler, will be resolved, if democracy will be victorious, in a new humanism with a universal basis. What can be done in the meantime, are temporary palliatives, "designed to facilitate the transition to the more generous cosmopolitan and democratic society of the future." Only within such a society can the Jewish problem find a solution; this is as true as the fact that only within such a society can all other problems of group antagonism and conflict find their solution; in the present world crisis all these problems are most intimately interlinked. . . . The strength of democracy in America and elsewhere will determine the future of antisemitism and of the Jews.[150]

His keynote speech at the celebration of the thirtieth anniversary of the *Menorah Journal* in November 1944 tied the war and looming Allied victory with a Jewish one, not only because of the shared enemy—Nazi Germany—but, more importantly, because a victory for American or Western values was the only guarantee to a flourishing Jewish life: "We shall survive," he told the audience, adding "by 'we' I mean this American way of life, of tolerance, reason, progress, respect, amalgamation, cooperation, emancipation, which is the only way among which we Jews can live."[151] In January 1945, during the last months of the war against Nazi Germany, Kohn participated in the first annual conference of the anti-Zionist American Council on Judaism, at which he claimed—much as Hannah Arendt did in "Zionism Reconsidered,"[152] written in those very months—that

> the Jewish nationalist philosophy has developed entirely under German influence, the German romantic nationalism with the emphasis on blood, race and descent as the most determining factor in human life, its historicizing attempt to connect with a legendary past 2,000 or so years ago, its emphasis on folk as a mythical

body, the source of civilization. In that, this romantic nationalism is dramatically opposed to the liberal concepts of the West, especially [the] U.S.A. according to which men of all kinds of decent, 'blood,' past belong to the nation to which they wish to owe loyalty, and to the civilization in midst of which they grow up.[153]

More significant than his preaching to a rather marginal anti-Zionist choir, however, were Kohn's attempts to keep the American Jewish Committee from becoming pro-Zionist in the wake of the Holocaust. On August 5, 1946, Kohn "had luncheon with American Jewish Committee officials (Dr. [Max] Gottschalk, Dr. [John] Slawson) and I told them what I think of their Zionist front attitude." The next day, he "wrote in the morning a very long memo on the partition of Palestine with practical contributions [and] suggestions for American Jewish Committee."[154] But however valid Kohn's arguments against Palestine's partition into two nation-states may have been, Palestine was drifting quite rapidly in that direction. A year and a half later, in November 1947, the United Nations—the new organization so dear to Kohn's heart—adopted Resolution 181, calling for exactly that path.[155] And a half-year later, much to Kohn's chagrin, the Jewish nation-state, the State of Israel, proclaimed its independence. Even the opening sentence of the Israeli Declaration of Independence, claiming national historical rights, was diametrically opposed to Kohn's concept of nations: "The Land of Israel, Palestine, was the birthplace of the Jewish people. Here their spiritual, religious and political identity was shaped." Another key passage justified the establishment of the new Jewish state as "the natural right of the Jewish people to be masters of their own fate, like all other nations, in their own sovereign State." Kohn, who obviously lamented that state's establishment, also rejected the ostensibly universal concept of nations and national rights to political sovereignty that establishment was allegedly based on. Kohn soon thereafter wrote a "long letter to [Judah L.] Magnes on [the] Arab Jewish problem."[156] The death of Magnes five months later, on October 27, 1948, severed one more tie between Kohn and the Zionism he had left behind. In his obituary of Magnes, Kohn proclaimed that his passing was a loss of historic proportions, as there could be "no replacement" for a leader of his unique stature, background, and credentials.[157] Kohn may have believed what he thought, yet it is remarkable that a movement he saw as "lost" almost twenty years ago, is seen by him again and again as more and more "lost."

Speaking in late 1948 at an event of the American Council on Judaism, Kohn presented American and Jewish values not only as kindred but also as interwoven since the beginning of American history, and he "urged American Jews toward still greater identification with American culture." His main point, however, was that American Jews—and not the newly established State of Israel—were, or at least should be, the natural leaders and representatives of the Jewish people:

> As the United States is assuming today leadership within the lands of Western civilization . . . thus, in a parallel way and for the very same reason (the weakening of Europe) the Jews in America assume, through their achievements in American cultural life and through the example of their integration, a new and more responsible role. . . . Never before have so many Jews in Europe looked full of expectation to the New World. A strengthened Jewish community in America will be able to help many thousands of new immigrants to come to these shores, to integrate them fully as citizens in the American nation and civilization, and thus to continue and promote a tradition which was the foundation of American greatness and its glory in the eyes of all men.[158]

In May 1949, two days after the United Nations admitted the State of Israel as a member nation, Kohn packed up all the Zionist documents he had been collecting over the years: rare materials from Bar Kochba, unique documents of his Zionist activity as a prisoner of war, protocols of the Brith Shalom Association, and his extensive personal correspondence with Martin Buber and others. He sent the materials to the library of Hebrew Union College, the reform Jewish seminary. In his revealing letter to the college's president, Kohn explained why he had donated the collection to that institution and not to the Central Archives for the History of the Jewish People in Jerusalem (where Magnes's papers are kept) or to the National Library of Israel (to which most of his Zionist colleagues donated their papers). Kohn wanted the documents to be "accessible in a library which is connected with the problems of Jewish history and of the Jewish ethos, and yet will undoubtedly maintain the standards of the American liberal tradition." A historian himself, Kohn had remarkable hopes for the documents' study by future historians: "[The donated materials] may, for future interested historian[s] of the problems facing Zionism in the 1920s and 1930s, throw some light on Zionist mentality and conflicts. . . . Who knows whether after some decades, some young Jews, doubtful about the values of nationalism and of statehood, might not find comfort in the doubts and struggles of a past generation, even in its (perhaps temporary) defeat."[159]

NATIONALISM IN THE AMERICAN CENTURY

As long as the North Atlantic peoples exert the Western virtues of political restraint and public morality, they can hope to turn the destructive and inflammatory passions of twentieth century nationalism and socialism ... into constructive and civilized channels.

Hans Kohn, *Is the Liberal West in Decline?*[1]

The existence of nation-states ... has made the universal organization of the present time possible. ... The modern nation-state emerged in the great Western revolutions of the seventeenth and eighteenth centuries ... [By now] the peoples of all continents had chosen ... the nation-state as their basic form of organization. ... The rapid spread of this trend ... was a sign of the progressing Westernization of the earth.

Hans Kohn, *Prelude to Nation-States*[2]

Kohn's Cold War Idealism

In 1949, looking for "a new environment and new challenges," Kohn left Smith College and moved to the City College of New York, where he would teach until his mandatory retirement in 1962.[3] At his retirement he had spent only about thirteen years at City College, and thus his pension was insufficient. Consequently, in his seventies Kohn had to find various short-term teaching positions and constantly move with his wife from one place to another. He taught at Wesleyan University, in Connecticut (in 1963–64); the University of Texas in Austin (1964); the University of Pennsylvania (1965); the University of Heidelberg (1965); the University of Denver (1966); the University of Notre Dame (1967); the University of Texas again (1967–1968); the Free University of Berlin (1968–69); and finally, again, the University of Pennsylvania (1970). This was only one manifestation of what could be seen as Kohn's nonarrival.

In the final two decades of his career, Kohn published a book a year on average. Naturally, not all were equally innovative or noteworthy; some were little more than informative brochures, classroom textbooks, or compilations of previously published work. Almost half were published in Van Nostrand's Anvil Books series (under the general editorship of his friend and colleague Louis Leo Snyder, a City College professor and an early scholar of nationalism). The important publications of the 1950s and 1960s include *Pan-Slavism* (1953), *American Nationalism* (1957), *The Mind of Germany: The Education of a Nation* (1960), *Prelude to Nation-States* (1967), and two rather slim synthesizing volumes that summarized his theory of nationalism: *Nationalism: Its Meaning and History* (1955) and *The Age of Nationalism: The First Era of Global History* (1962).

"After I moved to New York," he noted, "some of my 'extracurricular' interests were centered less on the past than on the present and future."[4] Put more bluntly, Kohn's move from Smith to City College coincided with a modification of his political engagements and affinity with the state. He sought and received support from state agencies that recognized him as a scholar who effectively produced and transmitted politically useful scholarship. His anti-isolationist ac-

previous page:

Figure 7.1 Hans Kohn's passport photo, 1954.
Courtesy of the Leo Baeck Institute, New York.

tivities in the 1930s were still quite far from the views of those at the centers of power—perhaps because he used lofty, prophetic, utopian, and moralistic language. After the war, however, he continuously engaged concrete and contemporaneous questions of US foreign policy, and during most summers he worked in Europe for the State Department and its affiliated organizations. In the late 1940s and early 1950s, Kohn was very comfortable in the ideological landscape of Cold War America. He expressed his positions, for example, in discussions with friends from Palestine like Judah L. Magnes. Kohn dismissed Magnes's concern regarding "the American [anticommunist] witch-hunts," which Kohn seemed almost to justify as "very feeble efforts at self-protection against fanatical, subversive elements." Furthermore, Kohn stood firmly behind the US foreign policy of his day, defining the Truman Doctrine and the Marshall Plan as the only way to prevent a third world war and insisting that such a policy in the 1930s would have averted World War II. He saw the new American and British leaders as "intelligent and responsible men who understand the totalitarian game" better than their predecessors had.[5]

In the spring of 1949 Kohn completed *The Twentieth Century: A Mid-Way Account of the Western World*. To a large extent, this book was a Cold War adaptation of much of his writing of the previous decade. Yet as its ambitious title indicates, the book also made bold claims regarding the next half-century, which Kohn envisioned as an age of the triumph and hegemony of the liberal West. As Donald Puchala noted, Kohn identified "universalizing Liberalism as the goal of Western hegemony." Thus Puchala viewed "Francis Fukuyama's (1992) *The End of History and the Last Man* [as] the sequel to Hans Kohn's (1949) *The Twentieth Century: A Mid-Way Account of the Western World*."[6] Kohn's mid-century book's discussion of American leadership embraced quite literally what John Fousek identified as American "nationalist globalism."[7] Kohn wrote:

> Americans have learned in the last twenty years . . . to understand that their frontier is on the Rhine, as they learned in 1940; and in Manchuria, as they learned in 1941; and in the Eastern Mediterranean, as they learned in 1947. They are beginning to think in world-wide terms, to consider their responsibilities in an interdependent world society. . . . The new attitude does not imply a wish for American hegemony nor for the imposition of the American way of life on others. . . . The nations on the two shores of the Atlantic belong together in a close community of strategic interests, of moral ideas and political traditions. This belonging together cannot express itself through American leadership, but only in a union of the free, in an equal partnership for a common task.[8]

Not all of America's "equal partners," however, found Kohn's American mission attractive. The British historian E. H. Carr—who cautioned the British against increasingly relying on the United States—was not impressed with Kohn's book, nor with the views it conveyed. Kohn "believes in the American mission to save Europe," Carr wrote. "This attitude has its dangers." Kohn's "American illusion," he argued, aspires to rehabilitate Europe through a restoration and improvement of the best of its nineteenth-century liberal traditions. For Carr, however, "the moral and intellectual task which faces Europe to-day is not to surmount the horror and the decline of the last 40 years in the sense of returning to the ideals of a serener past, but to discover new ideals and new forms of political, social and economic life in place of those whose bankruptcy the last half-century seems to have conclusively demonstrated."[9] Kohn, in Carr's view, was an anachronism.

Ideologically and conceptually, the story of Kohn's final decades is one of increasingly waning certainties. This chapter begins with a look at a decade in which he was as vocal and ideologically confident as ever and ends with a discussion of his last decade—one in which he grew increasingly confused and disillusioned. Few, however, even registered the septuagenarian's dashed hopes.

Already after the catastrophe of World War I, Kohn was certain that the world was moving away from the age of nationalism and into an age of its transcendence. The ravages of World War II, including Auschwitz and Hiroshima; the collapse of the strongholds of old colonialism; the emerging bipolar world order—all seemed to point to an age that necessitated a higher degree of international cooperation and, hence, moved away from isolationism to international federalization at the price of compromising national sovereignty. This was the familiar vision of transcending the nation-state that had been a constant component of his worldview since World War I. Indeed, what Jewish theology refers to as the birth pangs of the messianic era was a recurring pattern in Kohn's thought throughout his life, when he believed the world—or at least the Western world, or Europe—to have come to the brink of self-destruction and to have learned from the experience to tame its nationalism. The crises—of 1918, the 1930s, and World War II—were real and indeed only grew worse. What Kohn imagined as emerging out of the ashes was not just what Henry Luce called an American Century;[10] it was not about changing the world leader, but about changing the world order. Following the demise of Old Europe, Kohn's new century had to be less centralized and to have much greater cooperation. It was in this context that Kohn would come to relegitimize the nation-state, which he now saw as a hallmark of Westernization or modernization, creating an increasingly open and collaborative world of nation-states.[11]

Modernization and Democratic
Nationalism and Internationalism

The idea of universally applicable Western progress, which Kohn now framed in terms of development and modernization theories, is the key to understanding the Cold War relevance of Kohn's scholarship and his political agenda. Western civic nationalism—which he saw as inevitably leading to its own transcendence into "higher forms of integration"—was characteristic of modernization, and to Kohn the United States was "the most 'modern' and most 'western' nation."[12] Eastern ethnic nationalism, in contrast, was a failed modernization, essentially counterrevolutionary.[13] Some of Kohn's works on Arab nationalism written before his move to the United States already contained many elements of modernization theory in the vision of a singular path of progressive change: some national movements were further along that path than others, and the failed development of some nations was the outcome of a rebellion against the Western modernizing path. Indeed, Nils Gilman's study of modernization theory named Kohn as "the first social scientist to equate modernization with nation building." Yet Gilman also wrote about the historical context of modernization theory: "The ideal terminus of development was an abstract version of what postwar American liberals wished their country to be."[14]

Modernization theory lent Kohn's work even greater credibility and urgency as of the mid-1950s, once the developing world became the Cold War's key arena and the issue of nation building grew fundamental. This, of course, is a part of the language of a global Cold War, and Kohn was speaking it well. "The United States and the Soviet Union were imperial in their reach," Jane Burbank and Frederick Cooper remind us, "but they insisted to themselves and others that they were not like previous empires. The American ideal drew on the fiction of an expanding world of nation-states, open to commerce, receptive to American culture, and united in opposition to the rival bloc. The Soviet version posited the myth of fraternal socialist states allied in the march toward . . . the end of capitalism. . . . Both visions built on—and in different ways encouraged—the dissolution of the colonial empires."[15] Kohn's work in the 1950s was framed by this American Cold War ideal and by its concept of political progress, but theories of development, progress, and modernization also rendered his claims for the supreme modernity of American nationalism tautological: if modernity is defined according to the American model, obviously no country would be as modern as America. With time, as historical developments seemed to have cast greater doubts on its premises, this master narrative of progress may have become Kohn's cross to bear. He could not renounce it without challenging his life's work, nor could he continue proclaiming it without losing his critical edge, intellectual rigor, and ability to convince others. Indeed, it rendered Kohn at times alarmingly apologetic of Western colonialism and may have desensitized him to the plight and struggle of African Americans.[16] For him, although America was imperfect, it was the rightful leader of a world revolution of modernization and individual liberty. Following a classic argument of Cold War liberals, Kohn claimed that focusing on America's imperfection distorts the bigger picture and is systematically manipulated by America's adversaries, who are also the opponents of its Western values. All this just enhanced the preponderance of world order in his writing and activism, which, in turn, locked his gaze on the global horizon and allowed him to overlook unbearable phenomena around him. "To see what is in front of one's nose," George Orwell famously wrote, "needs a constant struggle."[17] Too often Kohn's Cold War idealism permitted him to abandon that vital struggle.

German Reorientation and Western Integration

Understanding Nazism as a German revolt against the West left a deep mark on Kohn's theory of nationalism and his political agenda. In the early years of the Cold War, however, his views of Germany and its potential underwent a major transformation, which largely mirrored the abrupt transition of Germany from a suspect former enemy of the United States to its ally (in the form of West Germany). In the second half of the 1940s, Kohn's thoughts on Germany and the Germans still resembled those of Henry Morgenthau Jr.: German aggression was to be taken for granted. All ideas of Germany's democratization, Westernization, or reeducation still seemed illusory—or, at the very least, a distraction from the vital policy goal of Germany's weakening and complete disarmament. "It is not the task of the victor nations . . . to educate them [the Germans]. . . . The task . . . is to make further German aggression impossible, nothing more and nothing less," Kohn stated in 1945. Eventual German democratization "does not depend upon the Germans. It is idle to plan their re-education." Kohn radically changed his opinion, however, and around the 1950s he emerged as one of the most committed American academic agents of Germany's reeducation in the service of Cold War America. In fact, in the late 1950s Willy Bretscher, the editor-in-chief of the *Neue Zürcher Zeitung*, claimed to "know of no other representative of American academic life travelling abroad who has tried harder to spread a sense of awareness of the common bonds between the nations composing the Atlantic Community."[18]

Kohn had grown so committed to a Westernized Germany that he was one of the experts who published a statement strongly objecting to the 1957 proposal of the great historian and diplomat George Kennan—who called Kohn "my good friend"—for a reunited, demilitarized, and neutral Germany.[19] Even the title of Kohn's important 1960 book on German nationalism (*The Mind of Germany: The Education of a Nation*) attests to how far he had come from his initial skepticism regarding Germany's democratization. The book's concluding paragraphs celebrated West Germany's transformation in no uncertain terms:

> The new Germany, after 1945, was made possible by a new development of even wider scope and importance, the trend toward closer co-operation among the western European and north Atlantic nations. . . . German reintegration into the West for the sake of strengthening democracy and of weakening the appeal of military glory and imperial grandeur in Germany and elsewhere must proceed in closest co-operation with the English-speaking countries and with the neighboring small Germanic democracies. . . . Out of this catastrophe one great gain has come, a democratic Germany which is finally taking its due place in modern western life.[20]

Beginning in the later 1940s Kohn spent most summers in central Europe —primarily in West Germany—speaking to university professors and students and in America Houses.[21] These "houses" were institutions of the US Information Agency in Germany and Austria that, in the early 1950s, provided the local populations an opportunity to learn about and discuss American culture and politics. His visits to Germany in the early 1950s, for example, included joint three-day seminars with his friend the political scientist Waldemar Gurian, which were hailed by representatives of the Office of the US High Commissioner for Germany as "fruitful," and "extremely successful." A report on the two scholars' 1952 seminar mentioned that in it "America was presented as an integral part of that European and Western civilization which Moscow completely rejects and wishes to destroy."[22] Kohn's German hosts ranged ideologically from the Institute for Social Research, founded by Theodor Adorno and Max Horkheimer in 1958, to the Ostdeutsche Akademie Lüneburg (Academy for the Study of East German Culture), founded by the völkist Max Hildebert Boehm in 1956. Kohn's lectures were broadcast on the US-funded radio station RIAS (the German acronym for the Broadcasting Service in the American Sector).[23] It was a mutually beneficial engagement, and the initiatives clearly came from both directions—from the various sponsoring bodies as well as from Kohn.

"No political or economic solution of the German problem, and thereby of the European problems," Kohn observed, "will be possible without a reorientation of German thinking on German history and on Germany's relationship to the West."[24] He also described the purpose of his visits as "arousing a better understanding for the United States among European intellectuals who are, on the whole, rather critical of the United States, not only of its policies, but above all of its intellectual and moral quality."[25] Kohn's 1952 definition of Germany's challenges to Shepard Stone, director of international affairs at the Ford Foundation, also made a case for his own merits as an expert on nationalism. In West Germany, Kohn explained, there is no danger "of growing communism or of alliance with Russia against the West," but there is a real danger of a growing and "hardening German nationalism," accompanied by its dangerous myths. Many Germans thus do not recognize "that only America now has the cultural vitality needed for a revival of the West." In this regard Kohn "consider[ed] the work of the America-Houses—in addition to *Die Neue Zeitung, Der Monat*, and similar publications—as our most important element in trying to influence German opinion."[26]

Kohn was a founding member of the anticommunist Americans for Intellectual Freedom, in March 1949, and many of his subsequent European engagements were facilitated and coordinated by the affiliated Congress for Cultural Freedom (CCF), which we now know was funded by the CIA.[27] In a letter to Nicolas Nabokov, secretary general of the CCF, Kohn spelled out much of his own ideological and academic agenda: "There has grown up a dangerous mythology around the concepts capitalism, imperialism, nationalism, and it seems to me one of the most important tasks today [is] to attack this mythology, to clarify the issues, and to show that it depends on the concrete historical situation, and not on some abstract deduction whether nationalism, capitalism or imperialism—which are different in each individual case—are [conducive] to, or destructive of, human liberty, individual wellbeing and intellectual productivity."[28] Writing to Melvin Lasky—cofounder of the CCF and editor of its German-language *Der Monat* and its English-language *Encounter*—Kohn mentioned his wish to discuss American ideas of liberty and equality, as opposed to the different meanings these ideas had in German history.[29] Kohn's letters reiterate why he, a historian, would have such a vital role in the task of Germany's democratic reorientation. It thus comes as no surprise that Kohn's participation in this effort took place in what Astrid Eckert aptly called "the Transnational Beginnings of West German *Zeitgeschichte* in the 1950s"—that is, the beginnings of the study of German contemporary history in West Germany with a focus on a historical interpretation of National Socialism. In addition to publishing articles on the subject, Kohn intervened in its historiography, most prominently in a volume he edited in 1954 (*German History: Some New German Views*) and in his 1960 monograph, *The Mind of Germany: The Education of a Nation*.[30]

During the Cold War, Central European émigrés participated in what Volker Berghahn has called America's intellectual cold wars in Europe.[31] Their background became a true asset, as fellow Americans recognized their vital understanding of "the German mind and the European mind."[32] In the United States they became what Jeremi Suri called "Social Outsiders, Cold War Insiders."[33] Having explained Germany to the Americans during World War II, Kohn was now sent to explain America to the Germans. But his task was actually even broader. He was sent to Central Europe to lecture as an American about the tenets of Western civilization, the German break from them in the nineteenth and early twentieth centuries, and West Germany's need to realign with the new or North Atlantic West. In Germany, however, Kohn was—to quote Alfons Söllner's work on the political scientists returning from exile—one of the "virtuosi of cultural translation, acrobats in the fusion of entire value horizons, the political poles of which were formed by Germany and America."[34]

Thus, what seemed most important to Kohn in the mid-1950s was "not so much to combat Communism but to strengthen the West. . . . The community of the West must be more than an alliance, though less than a federation, it must be above all a community conscious of cultural and spiritual ties."[35] For Kohn, the questions of Germany and of Western integration were interrelated. The concern about Germany's integration into the West is indicative of Kohn's interest in and commitment to the North Atlantic community. "The integration of Europe" alone, he sensed, "may not be enough today."[36] No later than World War II, he had come to focus on the American-led liberal West, seeking a better understanding of its core values and mission. His Westernizing mission became increasingly overt and intense in the historical context of the bipolar struggle "for the Soul of Mankind."[37] Kohn became somewhat of a Cold War mandarin, singing the praise of a new transatlantic West, which allegedly overcame colonialist traditions and practices. He was well ahead of the curve in 1952 when he called for the establishment of academic centers for North Atlantic area studies, or what is now known as transatlantic studies:

> It is surprising that the one area not yet studied in any systematic way is the North Atlantic Area. . . . [After all] the North Atlantic area, its political integration and its economic and military problems have been and will be our main concern. . . . The term "North Atlantic Community" has entered the official vocabulary, here and

abroad. The roots of a common history and civilization of this community—within the broader context of Western civilization—go back to the second half of the seventeenth century. The eighteenth century was an age of closest intellectual and social intercourse between Britain, North America and north-western Europe.[38]

A Cold War Liberal and the Austrian School

Kohn's well-documented ties to the Austrian school of economics seem not to fit well with other aspects of his worldview. A socialist in the 1920s, Kohn took a liberal turn in the 1930s and became a supporter of the welfare state, which the Austrian school abhorred. His was a reform liberalism, or New Deal liberalism—not classical laissez faire liberalism. In the early 1940s, Kohn coauthored *The City of Man* as an attack on "the anarchy of laissez-faire liberalism."[39] The mutual interest between Kohn and the Austrian school, however, began during World War II and was based on quite a few significant shared sensibilities and positions: the totalitarian theory—that is, the understanding of fascism and communism as twin phenomena; the notion of a distinctively Western and universally valid concept of liberty; the celebration of the nineteenth century as an age of unprecedentedly great promise; the view—which Kohn would soon abandon —that Germany had to be militarily and economically disarmed; and most importantly, the advocacy of internationalism of one sort or another. This affinity signifies both Kohn's new ideological position in the early Cold War years, with his openness to libertarians and conservatives, and the fluidity of ideological categories in that period.

The final chapter of Hayek's *Road to Serfdom*—the canonical text of neoliberalism—opened with a proclamation that could have come from Kohn instead: the greatest calamity to befall the world following the abandonment of nineteenth-century liberalism was in international relations. The modern sequence of wars and revolutions could be stopped in only one of two ways: either by international law, curtailing the innate aggression of nation-states; or, better still, through multinational federation, which Hayek stressed was the proclaimed goal of all the key liberal thinkers of the nineteenth century, and was ridiculed as utopian only starting in the calamitous twentieth century. Kohn was also impressed by the link the Austrian school made between economic system and world order. According to them it was protectionism and economic nationalism that begot wars, and their alternative of a free market economy had to have a globally pacifying effect.

Thus, although Kohn may have been a New Deal liberal, he wrote very favorable reviews of Hayek's *The Road to Serfdom*, von Mises's *Omnipotent Gov-*

ernment, and Wilhelm Röpke's *The Social Crisis of Our Time*, and he insisted that all three authors were true liberals rather than libertarians, let alone conservatives.[40] As of 1949 Kohn was a member of the Mont Pèlerin Society (MPS), Hayek's brainchild, which has often been described as the birthplace of neoliberalism. A recent volume about the MPS depicted it as "the central thought collective that has consciously developed the neoliberal identity for more than sixty years. We will consider any person or group that bears any links to the society since 1947 as falling within the purview of the neoliberal thought collective."[41]

Though he seemed to have been one of the people on the margins of the MPS, who did not fit into it quite as neatly as others (his position was similar to that of Karl Popper and Karl Polanyi), Kohn was in ongoing contact with many of its pivotal members, such as Albert Hunold and Röpke, and was frequently included as an author in their affiliated publications. Given his marginality in MPS and the limited echoes of the Austrian school's thought in Kohn's writing, his and the society's intersection could easily be ignored as a curious anecdote. Yet recent work by Jan-Werner Müller suggests that this intersection is indicative of the ideologically diffused character of Cold War liberalism. Discussing decidedly different Cold War intellectuals, Müller investigated the affinity between Cold War liberalism, libertarianism, and even Cold War conservatism: "What, if anything, made it [Cold War liberalism] different from 'neoliberalism' or Ordoliberalismus—that is, the strand of liberal thought associated with the Mont Pèlerin Society, and the German 'Freiburg School'?" Indeed, "was [Cold War liberalism] simply conservatism by another name?"[42] Müller's response was largely in the affirmative. True, Kohn differed greatly from the intellectuals discussed by Müller (Isaiah Berlin, Raymond Aron, and Karl Popper). Kohn certainly does not fit Judith Shklar's concept of the "liberalism of fear,"[43] which Müller attributed to his protagonists. Whereas Berlin and Aron allegedly "did not stress progress in a major way,"[44] this concept constituted the very backbone of Kohn's oeuvre. All these qualifications aside, Müller's perspective does offer a key to understanding the Cold War affinity between Kohn and both libertarians and conservatives.

The Legacies of Russian Imperialism and American Liberty

In the 1950s Kohn published multiple monographs on nationalism in different regions, including *Making of the Modern French Mind* (1955) and *Nationalism and Liberty: The Swiss Example* (1956). However, of these works the two with the greatest historiographic impact must be *Pan-Slavism: Its History and Ideology* (1953) and *American Nationalism: An Interpretative Essay* (1957).

After all, these were also significant commentaries on the Cold War, pointing to the long history of the political ideas that guided the belligerents. The ideas of both parties allegedly go centuries back in time and were still formative in the Cold War, whether contemporaries were aware of that or not. Hannah Arendt's *Origins of Totalitarianism* impressed Kohn particularly with its evaluation of pan-Germanism and pan-Slavism as representing "a type of tribal nationalism unknown in the West." The eighth chapter of Arendt's book, "Continental Imperialism" (which relied on Kohn's (1948) "The Permanent Mission: An Essay on Russia") pointed out even before Kohn did that Bolshevism may owe to pan-Slavism "more . . . than to any other ideology or political movement."[45] This observation became central to his writing in *Pan-Slavism* and afterward. It provided Kohn—whose disapproval of the Soviet Union so far had little to do with nationalism—with an effective way to apply his theory of nationalism in the struggle against the Soviet Union.

Pan-Slavism—one of Kohn's finest works—is a fascinating book in many regards. In it, Kohn returned to the Slav-German strife that had formed the background of his Prague youth (Kohn's story of pan-Slavism begins in Prague, among western Slavs, and under German influence); it is also interesting to the biographer because it was Kohn's first Cold War work on Soviet history, which he depicted favorably (if not admiringly) until the mid-1930s. While he grew critical of totalitarianism, he quickly minimized his critique—especially during the latter half of World War II, as Soviets and Americans fought shoulder to shoulder against Nazi Germany and its allies. In those years, as shown in the previous chapter, Kohn presented Marxism as akin to liberalism and claimed that the Soviet Union has "lost the spirit of aggressive extremism and has never developed the military and economic power for large-scale aggression. It is not communism, but the fear of communism that represents a threat for the survival of democracy."[46] Furthermore, in spite of all of its shortcomings, the Soviet Union "has followed throughout a foreign policy based upon peace and an internal policy based upon the complete equality of all races . . . and the equalization of the standards of life. . . . The peace of 1919 was vitiated by the absence of Russia from the peace table; the peace after the Second World War can be assured by the inclusion of the Soviet Union as a United Nation."[47] Whatever Kohn actually believed in the years 1941–45, after World War II his advocacy of greater American-Soviet cooperation was founded on a pessimistic evaluation of the Soviet Union as a dictatorial aggressor, whose aggression could be held at bay only through international organizations. Uncoordinated or aggressive Western policy toward it would only render the Soviet Union more dangerous.

In a 1952 letter to Gurian, Kohn addressed this change in his understanding of the Soviet Union and acknowledged that his 1931 book on the country had been rendered obsolete.[48] *Pan-Slavism*, which he published through Gurian's initiative, was to be a corrective.

The Soviet Union was a major challenge for Kohn. Its normative approach toward nationalism—subordinating nationalism to higher panhuman ideals—was virtually identical to Kohn's in the 1950s. He also agreed with the anticolonialism proclaimed by the Soviet Union. The new key, which Kohn now used very effectively, was to point to the disparity between political creed and actual policy and link this policy to unacknowledged continued political legacies. The Cold War dimension of *Pan-Slavism*—explicit at least in the book's final third, yet evident throughout—complicates Kohn's federalization imperative: like the national idea, the federative or fraternal idea can degenerate and be manipulated to establish the hegemony of an imperial nation (in the case of the Soviet Union, Russia) over subject (Slavic) nations. This, Kohn claimed, was a key ideological component of Soviet dominance over Eastern Europe: "The non-Russian peoples, Slavs as well as non-Slavs, do not sufficiently appreciate being constantly reminded of the deep gratitude which they owe to the 'Great Russian people,' of the immutable dependence upon the leadership of the Russian people. It is not impossible that this enforced conformity and loyalty may prove a weakening factor in the vast Moscow Empire and may help to restore there one day the principles of liberty, equality and diversity, on which the Pan-Slav movement insisted in 1848."[49]

In this regard, Kohn's scholarly intervention is reminiscent of Benedict Anderson's classic *Imagined Communities*, published some thirty years later. Whereas Anderson began his exploration of nationalism with reflections on the Cambodian-Vietnamese war of his day, Kohn reflected on other national conflicts within the Soviet block of his day. Six years after the publication of *Pan-Slavism*, Kohn reiterated his points regarding the "fundamental tensions in communist doctrine and practice" as far as nationalism is concerned in his introduction to a documentary volume on "The Soviet-Yugoslav Controversy, 1948-58." What had separated the two socialist states for the previous ten years, Kohn argued, were "not minor doctrinal differences but nationalist considerations."[50] The critical reader may ask: did not the same hegemonic pattern prevail in the Western bloc as well? As early as 1940, in *The City of Man*, Kohn called for an American-led international collaboration and, ultimately, for federation. What, one may ask, is the difference? Kohn's oeuvre always included both rigorous studies that analyzed their subjects critically on their terms (such as self-determination and Zionist ideology in the 1920s) and idealizing works that—even if beautifully crafted—are not convincing because they shy away from challenging the ideology's terms or because they conflate creed and practice (for example, his earliest works on Jewish thought and his first books on the Soviet Union). In the 1950s the critical *Pan-Slavism* and the idealizing *American Nationalism* represented these two types of his works.

Kohn's *American Nationalism*—based on his lectures at Northwestern University in 1956—developed ideas he had already expressed in the 1940s, especially in his *Idea of Nationalism. American Nationalism* distinguished US nationalism from all others, arguing that the former "was not founded on the common attributes of nationhood—language, cultural tradition, historical territory or common descent—but on an idea, which singled out the new nation among the nations of the earth." That idea, embodied in the US Constitution, was "the English tradition of liberty," transformed through the American Revolution and the Enlightenment into "a universal message" of benefit to the entire world.[51] This work integrated American nationalism into Kohn's dichotomy of civic Western nationalism versus its ethnic Eastern counterpart and to its assumptions based on modernization theory (finding the United States to be "the most 'modern; and most 'western' nation").[52] Kohn's monograph was influenced by the pioneering work of his friend Merle Curti (especially his 1955 *Probing Our Past*) and by Frederick Jackson Turner's omnipresent frontier thesis. Like Turner, Kohn argued that the frontier served as yet another ideological unifier for the United States. By moving west across the continent, expansion provided a sense of stability not attainable by Britain or other nations: "The United States has been from its beginning, and is today, the frontier land of both the English tradition of liberty and modern Western civilization."[53] However, this view was related to the later American concept of democratic expansion into the world at large under Presidents Woodrow Wilson and Theodore Roosevelt. It is striking how little attention Kohn—who previously had been sensitive to these questions—devoted here to the legacy of black slavery and the virtual annihilation of Native Americans. He acknowledges "the problem of the Negro population and its status" briefly and marginally in the course of some three pages, almost rushing to put a lid on the subject with a quote from William Faulkner promising that the equality of the African American "is [an] inevitable, and irresistible force."[54] One cannot escape the suspicion that Kohn, who had warned everyone else against "self-centered nationalism," had become rather self-centered in evaluating his own.[55] This kind of "affirmative," "useful" historiography did not appeal to Max Savelle, a scholar of American colonial history: "The fact appears to be that Kohn is an American nationalist as well as a historian of American nationalism. . . . But when he shifts from a critical historical examination of what was to what is needed, when he directs the intent of his essay toward influencing the course of events, he ceases to be a historian and becomes a pleader of a cause. At this point, his book ceases to be history and becomes a nationalist tract."[56]

Kohn's critical work regarding the political legacy underlying the Soviet Empire (*Pan-Slavism*) and his idealizing work on the ideological roots of Cold War America (*American Nationalism*) certainly rendered his scholarship topical. At the very same time, however, it allowed more and more scholars, both at home and abroad, to attribute Cold War conformity to Kohn.[57]

Postcolonial Nation Building as Western Revolution

Kohn had long been committed to struggling against what he saw as a Soviet abuse of the ideas of anti-imperialism and nationalism and to exposing the Soviet Union as a continental colonial power. Following the lead of his 1953 *Pan-Slavism*, Kohn's 1956 "Some Reflection on Colonialism" begins with an impressive all-out refutation of Soviet anti-imperialist posturing and a less convincing claim that postcolonial transformations were the product of liberal and Westernizing colonialism. Written two years after Nehru's Five Principles of Peaceful Coexistence (the basis of the nonaligned movement), Kohn's essay asserted that the Soviets wrongly see all noncommunists as necessarily pro-Western. The United States should not repeat their mistake: "Americans are shocked at their neutralism [nonalignment], because, according to American folklore, one has only to remove 'foreign' rule in order that the 'liberated' peoples will become 'democrats' and above all friendly to the United States. The sooner we outgrow this cliché, the better it will be for our relations with the non-committed areas of the world and for our understanding of the forces and drives behind anti-colonialism. . . . It is Western unity and strength which saves the neutralists; it is not the friendliness of the neutralists which will save the West."[58]

A year later, Kohn's booklet *Is the Liberal West in Decline?* also addressed these questions at length, linking them to the Suez Crisis that Kohn saw as the greatest trial of the North Atlantic Treaty Organization (NATO)—a trial that partially failed—not only because it exposed a rift between the United States on the one hand and Britain and France on the other hand, but also because the latter exposed the West as continuing to use old colonial strategies and immoral tactics. However, Kohn found hope in America's conduct in the crisis. "The Israeli-Franco-British invasion of Egypt," he claimed, "aroused protest . . .

throughout the West," and "by disassociating itself from the invasion of Egypt, the United States has not only joined the large majority of mankind but has restored the moral position and influence of the West in Asia and Africa and thereby strengthened the North Atlantic Community and the United Nations." Kohn's resounding conclusion, then, was that "as long as the North Atlantic peoples exert the Western virtues of political restraint and public morality, they can hope to turn the destructive and inflammatory passions of twentieth century nationalism and socialism . . . into constructive and civilized channels."[59] It made no sense, he said, to hope to add the entire Third World to NATO. Kohn ultimately rejected the bipolar view of the world: the demise of fascism did not make all nations friends of the United States, and similarly "the disappearance of communism will not make all peoples like Western democracy." There is no reason to fear nonalignment, nor to object it: "the people have a right to be different, neither communist nor democratic, neither in the Russian nor the American camp."[60]

Kohn's 1958 essay "The United Nations and National Self-Determination" boldly merged his assault on what he saw as Soviet anticolonialist posturing with his vision of America's mission in the Third World. "The future historian," he speculated, "may regard as the greatest 'revolution' of the twentieth century not Lenin's overthrow of the short-lived free regime in Russia in November, 1917, but the less conspicuous . . . and, yet, more far-reaching process which brought Europe's four hundred years old dominion of the globe to an end." For Kohn, the United Nations (UN) embodied this revolution. Whereas the League of Nations "took the continuation of the existing power-system for granted," the UN knowingly challenges it. The UN revolution, he believed, ultimately serves the democratic liberal West: "The participation of the new Asian and African nations in the United Nations has certainly created difficulties for the Western nations, but seen in a long-range perspective, it is working out to the West's advantage. The spirit and the procedure of the United Nations has been shaped by Western democratic traditions."[61] The connection in Kohn's mind between self-determination and American values was so central that he viewed Third World nationalism as "Americanization" (comparable to his view in the early 1930s of "the Europeanization of the Orient"):[62] the striving "of underprivileged groups and peoples everywhere towards a fuller share of the social and cultural goods, and their hopes and determinations to attain it," he claimed, are "part of the Americanization of the World." This was true even of Third World nationalists that tended toward socialism. But whereas Americans' recognition of self-determination seemed to him a core value, Soviets' recognition of it was merely a matter of propaganda and tactics: "Communist practice could not, nor did it ever, recognize self-determination, whether for individuals or for groups." Indeed, Kohn defined "Communism as an ideology in the service of Russian and Chinese nationalism." American foreign policy in the Third World, he concluded, should not be "determined by reaction to Soviet threat," but rather "a policy of positive sympathy—a policy in agreement with the message which the United States and Western civilization have carried." Only such a policy will "in the long run defeat the threat of communist totalitarianism."[63]

NATO at the Crossroads: The Foreign Policy Research Institute and the Bruges Conference

One of the more significant friendships in Kohn's later years was with the Austrian-born Robert Strausz-Hupé, a conservative political scientist and diplomat. His service as foreign policy advisor to Senator Barry Goldwater during his 1964 campaign for the presidency and to President Richard Nixon in 1968 gives a sense of Strausz-Hupé's political worldview, and how it differed from Kohn's liberalism. Kohn always abhorred Nixon, to say nothing of Goldwater. Yet, as in the case of Kohn's affinity with the Austrian school, his relationship with Strausz-Hupé was more than a matter of personal friendship. Shared sensibilities were evident already in Kohn's laudatory review of Strausz-Hupé's 1952 *Zone of Indifference* (later retitled *The Estrangement of Western Man*), which highlighted opinions the two men shared: the North Atlantic West, both believed, needed to be united, for it is modernity, whereas "fascism, communism, and in many ways Asian nationalism are counter-movements of pre-modern, authoritarian collectivistic forces against modern civilization, in whose worldwide triumph the nineteenth century believed."[64]

As so often in his career, Kohn's affiliations defied simple ideological categorizations and expose options that may no longer seem possible, such as the vision of conservative democratization in the 1940 *City of Man*, the libertarian advocacy of international federalization of the Austrian school, and the conservative anticolonial critique of Strausz-Hupé's circle.

In 1954, Strausz-Hupé invited Kohn to become an associate of the Foreign Policy Research Institute (FPRI) of the University of Pennsylvania that the former was then establishing. Kohn wrote that "his brilliant mind and his facility of expression attracted me and we became close friends, although . . . our tastes differed in many ways."[65] During the institute's early years, it enjoyed the participation of the likes of William Y. Elliot and Henry Kissinger. Howard Wiarda has recently depicted the FPRI as "one of the leading think tanks in the

United States, and certainly one of the three or four best and most influential in the foreign policy field" and hailed Strausz-Hupé as "one of the great intellectual forces in both the field of international relations and in terms of his impact on American geopolitical thinking."[66] The historical context of the FPRI and Kohn's participation in it was the second phase of the Cold War in the mid-1950s, when "both America and Russia shifted their focus from Europe to the newly emerging nations of the world."[67] This was the age of the early formulation of nonalignment, which Kohn refused to see as a threat. Long gone was Kohn's optimistic expectation of a simple and truly global democratic integration. Now even Western integration could not be taken for granted. In view of the growing divides between Western powers, especially alarming to Kohn during the Suez Crisis, he scaled down his political expectations for greater North Atlantic integration.

"Two greater and more consequential transformations are making history in the second half of the twentieth century," Strausz-Hupé proclaimed: "the unification of the North Atlantic Community and the self-assertion of the long-dormant non-Western world. . . . The voluntary devolution of empire is a novel phenomenon; so is the virtually automatic graduation into the United [Nations] —on the basis of full equality—of peoples that only yesterday were classed as 'backward' or 'primitive' . . . the rise of the new states in Asia and Africa poses most serious problems both for the non-Western and the Western world."[68] Rather than seeing the West as losing its privileged colonial standing in the world, Kohn and Strausz-Hupé believed they were witnessing the coming of a new West that had transcended its colonial and imperial legacy and indeed had undertaken its own "voluntary devolution." This new West was no longer European but North Atlantic.

According to Kohn, "Strausz-Hupé and I took a keen interest in the North Atlantic Community; we were instrumental in arranging the Conference on the Community which met at Bruges, Belgium, in September, 1957. The Conference laid its emphasis, not on the military and anticommunist aspects of the North Atlantic Treaty Organization, but on the enduring spiritual and ethical values of modern Western civilization, on the values of an open, free, non-militaristic society that offers its heritage of freedom to all mankind."[69] This preponderant imperative of greater Western—indeed, North Atlantic—unity and sense of purpose is what brought together the liberal Kohn and the conservative Strausz-Hupé and rendered many of their contributions to the FPRI's periodical, Orbis, almost identical in tone. Kohn's most important role in the FPRI was in planning and putting together the Bruges conference, in reaction to what

Strausz-Hupé called "the crisis of NATO which . . . erupted in the spectacular disagreement over Middle Eastern policy." The conference became a forum for Kohn to promote his vision of a new West, which allegedly overcame colonialist traditions and practices.[70]

In May 1955 he sent a letter to prospective participants, inviting them to "a conference for strengthening NATO"—which, he stressed, "has saved the liberal traditions of Western Europe." Facing Soviet aggression, it had served its role to perfection, but now, in a post-Stalinist world, it was time for "Western nations . . . to transform an emergency military alliance into a cooperative or fraternal association of nations basing their life on common traditions of individual liberty, parliamentary institutions, tolerance and freedom of thought."[71] Kohn explicitly identified NATO with Western civilization and its historic dimension. "I believe," he wrote, "that modern Western Civilization is a distinct, vigorous and developing high civilization which originated on the shores of the North Atlantic in the seventeenth and eighteenth centuries. . . . It is a civilization which NATO seeks to defend and to develop. We should regard the nations of this civilization as a unit for our study of history. Very little has been done in that field yet."[72]

Shortly thereafter, Kohn wrote a revealing internal document for the FPRI titled "Concerning the NATO Conference." Even though he obviously equated NATO with Western civilization, Kohn stressed there that "the name should not be NATO Conference and military, political and economic questions should not be discussed. A possible name is Conference on the North Atlantic Community." The focus of the conference should be "the moral and intellectual matrix out of which the North Atlantic community can grow." The urgency of the conference for him stemmed from his conceptualization of the Cold War as the struggle against an effort "to destroy or undermine Western Civilization and strength."[73]

Kohn planned the forthcoming conference with Henry Kissinger, then a faculty member at Harvard University, and the FPRI. "The conference," Kohn wrote, "should in no way be connected with official personalities, with the NATO *qua* NATO." He and Kissinger envisioned four panels whose topics summarized well the organizers' intents. The subjects were the democratic North Atlantic West vis-à-vis totalitarianism—both fascist and communist; the past and traditions of the North Atlantic West; unity and differences within the North Atlantic West; and the North Atlantic West vis-à-vis the Third World and decolonialization.[74] This final point was especially crucial for Kohn, who constantly seemed to be defending the new West from the well-known critique of the old West as an agent of empire. The timing of the conference was essential, for the mid-1950s were crucial years in the Cold War's extension into the Third World.

The published summary of the conference stated the resulting decision to create "an Atlantic Institute" that would have the following aims: "To promote and develop: (1) A sense of community among the Atlantic peoples and all others who share their basic ideals; (2) The revitalization of Western cultural and spiritual values and of the social institutions of the Atlantic Community; (3) The harmonization of the long-term interests of the Atlantic Community with those of developing countries; (4) A point of focus for the Atlantic Community's cultural response to the challenge of Communism and other forms of totalitarianism; (5) The discovery and development of Atlantic leadership adequate to these tasks."[75] The future Atlantic Institute's second goal was most typical of Kohn's pattern of thought throughout his many ideological recalibrations: the belief in the power of political ideas and the notion that they can either degenerate or be revitalized. Indeed, the same pattern framed Kohn's own reflections on the conference. Using the global Cold War's language of modernization, he presented decolonization not only as the Westernization, or Americanization, of Asian and African nations but as their "rejuvenation" and "reinvigoration." The proposal to create the Atlantic Institute was approved by the NATO Parliamentarians Conference in June 1959, and the institute was finally established in January 1961. Valerie Aubourg has compared it with the Bilderberg Group, claiming that both nongovernmental atlanticist organizations were elite-oriented and constituted "a conscious effort to mold an Atlantic elite."[76]

Fitting his centrality in the conference, Kohn delivered its closing address. At least one of the key participants in the conference—the conservative Swiss journalist Ernst Bieri—was also a member of the Mont Pèlerin Society. His reflections on the "Atlantic dialogue in Bruges" also addressed European and Western integration. For him part of the significance of this conference was its transcendence of the national: "By considering Europe as part of the Atlantic Community . . . and by defining the global conflict as the clash between two civilizations, the Bruges conference contributed to a clearer understanding . . . : not nations confront each other [but rather civilizations]." Just like Kohn, Bieri identified the key Western challenge as "the fact that the enemies of liberal civilization exploit the latter's imperfections, which are discussed openly and often vehemently, as powerful weapon for gradually undermining confidence in this civilization; and totalitarianism often receives aid and comfort from those in the West who regard their society with cynical nihilism." Bieri then alluded to the rather dubious conference resolution, according to which "it must be shown how the failings of Atlantic civilizations are not the result of the application of its principles, but rather the result of turning away from them."[77] Western values, it seemed, were a priori good and just. Yet another speaker, Robert Schuman, the architect of the European integration project, spoke in a manner reminiscent of Hannah Arendt ("Among intellectuals *Gleichschaltung* was the rule, so to speak")[78] when he observed "that intellectuals, more than the masses, share a responsibility for weakening our defenses in the face of an opponent who is cynical enough to cloak his true intentions."[79]

The Idea of Progress and the Skeptics

The core of Kohn's worldview and of his studies of nationalism throughout the second half of his life was the belief in progress, Western in origin and globally applicable. Complementing Kohn's narrative of progress, however, was his diagnosis of backwardness or the totalitarian perversion of the originally progressive idea. On the concept of progress he differed dramatically from prominent thinkers of a similar background. Walter Benjamin's "Angel of History" ironically presented the concept of progress as a matter of perspective. From the perspective of its victims, "what we call progress" can be seen as "one single catastrophe which keeps piling wreckage upon wreckage."[80] Horkheimer and Adorno's *Dialectic of Enlightenment* could not have been further removed from Kohn's understanding of the Enlightenment's project of modernity. Indeed, Horkheimer's 1947 *Eclipse of Reason* carries a strong warning, similar to Benjamin's, against the "idolization of progress."[81] In contrast, though Kohn had friends in the Frankfurt school, he felt compelled to systematically oppose counternarratives of crisis or decline, especially the crisis or decline of the West. Thus, the most important element in Kohn's essay "Historian's Creed for Our Time" was his dislike in the existentialist moment of the fashionable concept of "crisis." His preferred way to deny the magnitude of the contemporaneous crisis was an escape of sorts into the long "historical perspective."[82] A concept that Kohn disliked even more than "crisis" was "the decline of the West." Both were linked to the historisophical question of progress, which, in turn was linked to his understanding of the West. In 1957 Kohn collected five of his relevant essays from the 1950s into the surprisingly coherent volume *Is the Liberal West in Decline?* The idea of progress, this volume claimed, may fall victim to the "self-doubt of modern Western civilization." In the book he established that "the faith in progress—absolutized and vulgarized in communism—has lately given way to another mythical interpretation of history, which regards at least modern history not as a story of progress and salvation but as the story of decay and doom." This perspective, Kohn insisted, was at least as naïve: the West is being transformed, but this is not a decline. The West itself is new and revolutionary. Its counterrevolutionary opponents wished to return to the Middle Ages. Indeed, the links between this "self-doubt of modern Western civilization," and the fascist and communist counternarratives seemed obvious to Kohn:

> The contemporary crisis is not so much a crisis within Western civilization as an attack upon it from without. The attack has come, in our time, from Germany and Russia. These are peripheral areas that never really were full partners in their political and social structure of the modern Western way of life, never assimilated fully the ideas and institutions that define it. Liberty understood as the inborn rights of the individual against authority, tolerance based upon the recognition of diversity—the open society; parliamentary government; freedom of inquiry—all these things were never firmly founded in Germany or Russia, Italy or Spain.[83]

Inevitably, Kohn was apprehensive about the manner in which Arnold Toynbee, a friend of Kohn since the 1920s, presented Western civilization as only one of many civilizations humanity has known—neither the first nor the last, neither the worst nor the best, just a passing historical construct. Instead, Kohn insisted that "modern western civilization has set new and to me higher standards of respect for the individual, of social responsibility, of critical inquiry, than any preceding civilization." The modern Western intellectual on the whole "does not overestimate, he rather underestimates his civilization. And Mr. Toynbee does too." Kohn insisted that the West was the young and revolutionary force, and the Eastern bloc—in spite of its proclamations to the contrary—is the counterrevolutionary continuation of the old authoritarian political order: "Modern Western civilization is not 'old,' it is 'young,' barely three centuries in existence even on the shores of the North Atlantic. Communism and fascism . . . are a rejection of it. . . . they were a 'return' to the Middle Ages."[84]

A critical review of Kohn's book in the *Times Literary Supplement*, and Kohn's response to it, give a sense of Kohn's position in the intellectual and political debates of the late 1950s: "Kohn, in a small and challenging volume entitled *Is the Liberal West in Decline?* takes Professor Toynbee severely to task for having given aid and comfort to those who answer the question in the affirmative."[85] Kohn, the review continued, found Toynbee's relativization of Western civilization a self-destructive self-criticism. In the 1930s Kohn's idealization of the liberal West met with usually friendly and civil criticism. A couple of decades later—in the wake of McCarthyism, at a moment Irving Howe so aptly described as "this age of conformity"[86]—Kohn appeared to more and more peo-

Figure 7.2 Hans Kohn in 1959.
Courtesy of the Leo Baeck Institute,
New York.

ple as a member of a conformist choir of Cold War orthodoxy, and the criticism grew less civil. The review asserted that "among the enemies of traditional Western society today are a naked and unashamed pragmatism which subordinated the pursuit of knowledge to missionary purposes, and a deep-seated insistence on conformity which—sometimes crudely, sometimes by subtler and more devious methods—outlaws the dissenter. . . . We live in an age when historians . . . should not perhaps be too easily condemned for indulging in self-criticism." The self-critical dissenter was Toynbee, and Kohn was seen as one of the conformist voices who censured that "precious self-critical voice."[87] "Kohn's philosophy of life," Aira Kemiläinen rightly stated, "appear clearly in his books. The essence of Western civilization," she continued, "is identical with the ideals of the author himself."[88]

The critical assessments of Kohn grew unforgiving in the 1960s. A review by Werner Dannhauser in *Commentary* of Kohn's 1963 *Reflections on Modern History* was as harsh as it was insightful. Dannhauser—a student of Leo Strauss—took Kohn to task for his allegedly shallow and overstated concept of progress, which not only informed Kohn's theory of nationalism but also, to put it bluntly, rendered him both insincere and quite boring. There is a profound crisis in the twentieth century, Dannhauser insisted, and it is a crisis everyone realizes. Yet Kohn, committed to the master narrative of progress, "comes close to denying that there is such a crisis. Kohn repeatedly rejects all discussion of the contemporary crisis as empty fashion." Therefore, "the typical essay," Dannhauser claimed sarcastically, "has an upbeat ending." According to him, Kohn writes as "a man deeply committed to modern Western civilization, understood as the consummation of ancient Western civilization, as a comprehensive 'intellectual and moral attitude.' The greatest enthusiasm is reserved for the Enlightenment; Professor Kohn is unstinting in praise of liberalism, individualism, cosmopolitanism, toleration, and the idea of One World." The review seems to attribute Kohn willful ignorance: "He fails to see the Enlightenment's decisive break with antiquity. For him there is a majestic mainstream, which includes Athens, Jerusalem, and all good things. Unfortunately this is insufficient. . . . Previously, all might be reconciled by a notion of progress, but it is no longer obvious to us that there is such a thing." Dannhauser, and probably also others of his generation (he was thirty-five when he wrote the review), saw Kohn as a man guided by the principles of moderation, which may be a moral virtue, "but it may be an intellectual vice."[89]

Containment of Uncertainty: Disillusioned Love Again

The unspeakable catastrophes of World War II, the collapse of the historic strongholds of old colonialism, and the emerging bipolar world order all seemed to Kohn to point to an age that necessitated a higher degree of international cooperation. The creation of the United Nations and arguably even NATO spoke to this historical trend and seemed to Kohn as boldly moving toward his old vision—spelled out clearly throughout the 1940s—of democratic federalization. The near future, he believed, would be an age of reduced, and hopefully sublimated, nationalism. The United States, he thought, was destined to lead this global transformation through its democratic model as *primus inter pares*. Thus, in the early years of the Cold War, and definitely throughout the presidency of Harry S. Truman, Kohn was very comfortable in the ideological landscape of Cold War America. Like the worldviews of many Americans, his increasingly revolved around a heightened sense of the tremendous threat of Soviet aggression. The threat seemed great, but equally great were the prospects of reduced nationalism and greater international cooperation, and since the task appeared clearer than before, there was reason for optimism. Kohn's *Pan-Slavism* and his observations on the nature of American foreign policy at the time resembled—indeed, belonged to—the orthodox school of Cold War studies: they focused on traditional Russian imperialism and claimed that American foreign policy "differed markedly from that of the Soviet Union. Guided by the principles of collective security, American leaders looked to the newborn United Nations to resolve future international conflicts."[90]

As the Cold War grew global and focused increasingly on nation building in the Third World, Kohn's nationalism theory became more important than ever. Yet these were also the years in which his hopes for the American Century were dashed repeatedly by American policies that systematically contradicted his values. As a result, though many of his Cold War publications may give the impression of simple conformity, closer inspection presents the 1950s and 1960s as a time for Kohn of diminishing optimism and waning certainties, in which he scaled his hope for truly global integration down to Western (North Atlantic) integration and modified his expectations for and understanding of the postcolonial world. Kohn's disappointment with, and increasing estrangement from, the foreign policy of both the United States and its allies was easy to overlook, as it was expressed primarily in minor publications, correspondence, and personal conversations.

Kohn's son remembered how "during the Korean War, in September 1950— after the Inchon Landing but before any American crossed the 38th parallel into north Korea," his father invited him to accompany him on a visit to Pearl Buck at her home in Bucks County, Pennsylvania: "One of the things that my father said was 'I certainly hope that the Americans are going to use good judgment and good sense and not cross over into North Korea, since there is no question in my mind that the Chinese are going to come in if we do that, and from their standpoint—they have to come in.' . . . That so stuck on [with] me, because then in a very short period of time—a few months—it was exactly what happened."[91]

In June 1951, Kohn published an essay in a collection titled *Atom Bombs Are Not Enough*. His essay, "American Foreign Policy in an Age of Fear," used remarkably hard language to characterize the Soviet threat. "Stalinism is as great a threat as Hitlerism," he claimed, and in some regards, the "fusion of world-revolutionary communism with Russia's powerful imperialism seems to present a greater threat to peace and democracy than did Hitlerism a decade ago." On the whole, he praised the new American foreign policy, represented by the Truman Doctrine, the Marshall Plan, and NATO's intervention in Korea. Yet he warned in the strongest terms against shortsighted politics caused by fear, epitomized by the attempt by NATO forces to push North Koreans beyond the 38th parallel. "Nothing," he wrote, "would expose the West more to the horrors of Stalinism than an involvement in the endless vastness of Asia. We face in Asia a complex of deep-seated, genuine, social and national revolutions, which Communism did not create but which it is eager to exploit. Communist propaganda tries to present the United States in Asia as an arch-imperialist, who does not care for the lives or well-being of Asiatics. It must be our most serious endeavor to dispel this wrongful propaganda and to win the Asians—from Egypt to Korea —to an understanding of our real intentions."[92] The Korean War led Kohn to take ever more public positions on matters of American foreign policy. "The expulsion of the aggressors from South Korea," he promised the readers of the

Washington Post, "will strengthen the faith in the principles of the United Nations and will consolidate the common front of freedom against aggression."[93] Yet he warned that the United States "cannot allow the Communists to 'liberate' non-Communist territory, be it West Berlin or South Korea. . . . But neither can the Communists allow us to 'democratize' Communist-held territory."[94] A wise, farsighted American foreign policy, he insisted, would take into account not only Asian nationalism but also Chinese interests and sensibilities.

Many of Kohn's positions in the Truman years resembled those of his friend, Walter Lippmann, one of the leading political commentators of the day, who "argued that America's statesmen, by assaulting Russia's vital interests in Eastern Europe, furnished the Soviet Union with a reason for seeking iron rule over countries on its borders."[95] In June 1945 Kohn and Lippmann exchanged opinions on how to achieve the right relationship between the United States and its Western allies, the British and French Empires. "We shall fail," Lippmann told Kohn, "if we continue to give the impression that from Malta to Singapore and Hong Kong our partnership with the British means underwriting their actions. . . . I quite agree with you on the need of a firm alliance with England and France and the Western powers, but . . . it is necessary for us somehow to influence British policy." Kohn still warned against the idea of rearming West Germany (which he still saw as "unwilling or undemocratic") and urged Americans to focus on "the consolidation of the democracies of the North Atlantic area in an ever closer union." "In such a union," he continued, "the United States must be most considerate and scrupulous not to arouse the impression of imposing its leadership; it should co-operate, in a spirit of equality and full partnership."[96]

Kohn's North Atlantic focus would only grow stronger in the next decade. By the mid-1950s a second phase of the Cold War had begun, which was focused no longer on Europe but on the emerging nations of the world in the wake of decolonization. "The fiction that an inclusive 'nation' existed within the mostly haphazardly drawn borders created by the colonial powers," Odd Arne Westad commented, "led to untold misery for those who did not recognize themselves as part of that entity. . . . The need to create an effective and integrationist state —which in some cases substituted for the non-existing 'nation'—led many Third World leaders to exacerbate preexisting ethnic tension instead of relieving it."[97] It was in this stage of the global Cold War—as it shifted from bipolar to pericentric and its arenas returned to aspiring nation-states—that Kohn's credentials as an authority on nationalism became doubly valuable. Much of his work at this stage, roughly the final fifteen years of his life, would center on postcolonial nations and on the North Atlantic community.

Kohn participated in the discussion of the impact of Cold War blocs (known as Blockism) on nations and nationalism at the conference "Nationalism and Mankind" in September 1961 in Italy, where participants from the First and the Third—but not the Second—Worlds presented their different understandings of nationalism and its role in the present. Kohn, Horkheimer, and thirteen other thinkers from multiple continents spoke at the conference.

Though he was the only true authority on nationalism in the conference, Kohn did not dominate the discussions. His major contribution to the conference was his introduction to the session on "Nationalism and Mankind in the United States." All documented responses to Kohn's words—which were as partisan and idealizing as his 1957 *American Nationalism*—were skeptical: Horkheimer saw the idea of mankind as nationalism's fig leaf everywhere. "What is true of the reality of the mankind idea in American history," he commented, "is no doubt true of other nations. The mankind idea can be clearly observed in the history of Germany . . . and many other countries both in and outside of Europe. Actually, nationalism satisfied the longing of the people for mankind." The Japanese political scientist and career diplomat Tatsuji Takeuchi expressed the "doubts in the minds of many people as to the sincerity of American statesmen and other political leaders in asserting their belief in democratic principles." The Indian political scientist Angadipuram Appadorai added that "some people cannot understand how the U.S. could support reactionary advancements in Asia, even taking into account the exigencies of the Cold War."[98] Kohn's responses are not documented, but the rest of what he said at this conference tells the familiar story of the ultimately liberalizing nature of the global progress of nationalism.

In the session on "Sociological Analysis of Nationalism, 'Blockism,' Mankind," other participants debated whether the historical development of blocs and nationalism was good or bad. In contrast, Kohn—whose view was already known—raised the discussion to a metahistorical level and seemed to revert momentarily to positions he had held in the 1940s: "There are really only two permanent things: one is man; the other, mankind. The nation is not permanent, it did not exist a few hundred years ago, and it is not likely to exist the form in which we know it, a few hundred years hence (if it will last that long). Bipolarization, of which much is made today, is passing, too. The trend today is toward pan-nationalism and pan-humanism. Mankind is on the march. If we do not see the distinction between the things that are on the way out and the new things that are coming in, then we lack historical perspective."[99]

In the session on "The United Nations and Mankind," Kohn stated that there was "no reason to be pessimistic about the future or mankind. Nationalism has been a tremendous factor in advancing civilization, not only in the United States but throughout the world. The progress made in the last half century has been very remarkable. Feudalism has been practically wiped out. Living standards have been improved in many countries. The advance of science and technology has brought about a great deal of international cooperation, not only among scientists and professionals, but among nations, not to forget artists and poets, architects, writers, and many others. Even under-developed countries, e.g. India, have made remarkable strides in economic and political development."[100] At this conference Kohn relied on the narrative of progress, and though he was optimistic, he was neither critically rigorous nor very original in his observations on nationalism.

. . .

The dawn of the American Century was the broader historical development Kohn had depicted in the prime of his academic authority, the early 1950s. But by the 1960s—facing more and more evidence to the contrary—it became harder and harder for him to defend his position. A good example for his change of heart is his "Nationalism and the Atlantic Community," published January 1965, right before the escalation of the Vietnam War. There, Kohn had to acknowledge the endurance and even intensification of nationalism (even of a shady kind) in the Cold War and in the Western world, which crushed his previous hopes for greater integration and cooperation. How did Kohn deal with that? Largely as he did throughout his life, with an escape into the broadest historical perspective. Kohn's belief in progress was an article of faith, and he could never openly proclaim—indeed, he often denied—that his certainties were waning. However, that fact is evident in his personal papers, hidden in the margins of his prolific body of works, and concealed behind his public guarded optimism.

Much of the news in the 1950s and 1960s seemed to contradict Kohn's advocacy—even belief in the inevitability—of Western integration. His 1963 "Future of Political Unity in Western Europe," for example, mourned the resurgence of old European nationalisms—particularly of French nationalism—that threatened to further divide the NATO member states. In this essay Kohn defined the recent Franco-German Élysée Treaty, which challenged the US role in Germany and Western Europe, as "a mistake," as a step away from "a multinational treaty that includes all the North Atlantic countries," which alone could defend "Western democratic values." He saw this as an alarming sign of the times: "World War II was followed by a period of political and economic weakness in

Figure 7.3 Hans Kohn in the late 1960s.
Courtesy of the Yad Tabenkin Archives.

Europe during which old-style nationalism appeared to wane. Recovery, which Western Europe owes to the United States, led, at least in France, to the resurgence of old nationalism, which turned against the United States, and to the revival of hegemonic aspirations." As a result, NATO—which had been "conceived . . . also to strengthen democracy, freedom, and welfare within Western civilization"—was noticeably weakened. The principal culpability, Kohn claimed, lay with "President [Charles] de Gaulle of France who does not believe in a united Europe or in an Atlantic community or in the United Nations. He is unable to understand that neither the United States nor Great Britain is as passionately nationalistic as he is."[101]

The more Western integration seemed to slip away, the less interested Kohn was in truly global democratic integration in the form of a world federation. What is needed, he wrote in 1957, is not the "unity of the world . . . but the unity of the nations of modern Western civilization, their outgrowing of nationalism and parochial loyalties into loyalty to their common civilization which is for them the spiritual source of their life. . . . Such a Western or Atlantic unity in diversity . . . is essential now when modern Western civilization has found itself under severe attack from non-Western civilizations or from anti-western movements like fascism and communism."[102]

Kohn envisioned the American Century as a postcolonial world revolution, inspired by American values, in which the United States would naturally stand as the primary ally of postcolonial nationalism everywhere. He abhorred the crossing by NATO forces of the 38th parallel into North Korea, which he felt allowed America's enemies to present it as an archimperialist power. Those responsible for American foreign policy in the 1960s clearly did not heed Kohn's warnings. Thus, he was evidently resorting to sarcasm when he proclaimed in his 1964 memoirs that "today it is unthinkable that the foremost democratic nation [the United States] would invade smaller neighboring countries because they were regarded as a threat to American security. . . . It would be equally out of the question for the United States to unleash a preventive war, even on a limited scale."[103] Indeed, in a speech at an event paying tribute to Kohn after his death, Wallace Sokolsky mentioned how "discouraged [Kohn was] in recent years by the prolongation of the War in Vietnam."[104] Hugo Bergmann commented more dramatically in his diary on "Hans Kohn's disappointment with president [Lyndon B.] Johnson and his politics. The American air force demanded the war against China. This shattered the ideals of Hans."[105]

In his final book, *Readings in American Nationalism*, which he coedited, Kohn—burdened by "the errors made in Vietnam"—wrote that he was witnessing "America's most serious crisis since the Civil War." Taking the 1961 farewell address of President Dwight D. Eisenhower on the military-industrial complex to heart, Kohn found that it was "not without significance that at a crucial time, when the incoming President [John F. Kennedy] had emphasized so strongly a non-existent missile-gap in the cold war with Russia and soon was to proclaim the race to the moon as part of this war, the outgoing president, a successful general, restated in a farewell address . . . [Lord] Acton's distrust of power. . . . In the two following administrations the evils, against which the outgoing president had warned, have grown." From that perspective, Kohn's evaluation of actual American nationalism differed dramatically from its idealized version in his 1957 *American Nationalism*. Now he exclaimed that "at the time of its rise, American nationalism was a colonial nationalism. . . . Especially in its relation to its redskinned and black-skinned fellow Americans, the United States has remained a colonial country deep into the twentieth century."[106] The septuagenarian's relatively quiet disillusionment with his last best hope was reminiscent of, and related to, his very public break with Zionism forty years earlier. Both are indicative not of a certain naïveté but of Kohn's ethical core. Whereas the first "disillusioned love"[107] forced Kohn, Sisyphus-like, to push his theory uphill, toward nationalism's end, the second gave him no such opportunity. Months after publishing his damning words on American nationalism, Kohn died, at the age of seventy-nine.

CODA

The Endurance of Kohn's Jewish Question

Who knows whether after some decades, some young Jews, doubtful about the values of nationalism and of statehood, might not find comfort in the doubts and struggles of a past generation, even in its (perhaps temporary) defeat.
Hans Kohn to Nelson Glueck, May 13, 1949[1]

[T]he Age of nationalism [is] an unfortunate age of which the State of Israel is an unfortunate creation.
Hans Kohn to Irving Engel, January 8, 1957[2]

Not a lot of people knew just how the Vietnam War had "shattered the ideals of Hans."[3] In the 1950s his public persona became increasingly that of an uncritical Cold War conformist, and the one realm in which he could convincingly see himself as an independent, nonconformist thinker, swimming against the tide, was Jewish politics. In 1908—at the beginning of the story told in this book—it was Zionism that made Kohn for the first time aware of and accountable to the power of nations and nationalism in his own life. Through Zionism, nationalism became his key to understanding the Jewish Question. Precisely because Kohn's lifelong struggle with nationalism seems to have long transcended its original Jewish dimension, this coda brings the book back to the ostensibly marginal Jewish Question in Kohn's final decades. In World War II (for example, in his speech at the thirtieth anniversary dinner of the *Menorah Journal*),[4] Kohn saw the flourishing of Jewish life anywhere as dependent only on what he saw as the Western values of a democratic open society committed to the rule of law. All Jewish distinctiveness aside, Kohn attempted throughout his life, including in the 1950s and 1960s, to analyze and judge Jewish politics with the same general conceptual tools that he used to frame his theory of nationalism and world order.

Ironically it was Kohn's charged relation to Zionism and the State of Israel that occasionally forced Kohn to diverge from the American Cold War consensus. The Jewish nation-state was established in the spring of 1948. He had fought tirelessly against the founding of such a state since his Zionist days, but it was the home of many of his old friends and relatives, including almost the entire family of his wife, Yetty. Furthermore, the Jewish nation-state he so categorically objected to had been established based on a resolution of the United Nations, the organization that embodied for him many of the correct principles for a future world order. And the State of Israel not only enjoyed the overwhelming support of American Jewry, but within a few years it also became a very close ally of the United States—Kohn's new home and the country he saw as the leader of the free world. Kohn's decision about how to treat the State of Israel could not have been simple.

previous page:

Figure 8.1 Hans Kohn (*right*) and Robert Weltsch, 1960s.
Courtesy of the Leo Baeck Institute, New York.

Two days after the United Nations admitted the State of Israel as a member nation—as mentioned at the end of chapter 6—Kohn symbolically disposed of his Zionist library and the valuable papers he had collected during his Zionist years, donating them to the Hebrew Union College. "Who knows," he wrote the college's president, "whether after some decades, some young Jews, doubtful about the values of nationalism and of statehood, might not find comfort in the doubts and struggles of a past generation, even in its (perhaps temporary) defeat."[5] But in spite of this symbolic gesture, Zionism did not cease to consume and bother Kohn. He never hesitated to speak his mind boldly on the matter in his publications and his public lectures and even in the classroom.[6]

The natural forum for Kohn's anti-Israel views was in overtly anti-Zionist bodies. In World War II Kohn became affiliated with the anti-Zionist American Council for Judaism, lending it his intellectual prestige. The council was created by leaders of American Reform Judaism whose opposition to Zionism was grounded in Reform Judaism's traditional disavowal of Jewish nationhood in the modern age. In January 1945, in his address at the council's first annual conference (which was later published as *The Struggle for Integration*), Sidney Wallach read an excerpt from his correspondence with Kohn, "perhaps the world's greatest authority on Nationalism." In the immediate wake of the Holocaust, Kohn did not hesitate to assure Wallach that "the Jewish nationalist philosophy . . . has developed *entirely* under . . . the influence of German romantic nationalism with its emphasis on 'blood,' race, descent as the most determining factor in human life, its historizing attempt to connect with a legendary past 2,000 or so years ago . . . , its emphasis on folk [*Volk*] as a mystical body, the source of civilization. In that this romantic nationalism is dramatically opposed to the liberal concepts of the West, especially u.s.a., according to which men of all kinds of descent, 'blood,' past belong to the nation to which they wish to owe loyalty and to the civilization in the midst of which they grow up."[7] One of Kohn's Israeli detractors told of an episode from those years that demonstrates Kohn's prominence as an anti-Zionist voice in American Jewry:

One night . . . following the un resolution in favor of [Palestine's] partition, a protest meeting convened in reform Temple Emanu-El, which at the time was vehemently anti-Zionist. I was told of it the next day by a young lad . . . [a Jewish veteran who] went there out of wonder and curiosity. The keynote speaker was Hans Kohn. . . . The lad . . . was too young to have encountered that type of Jew. After the assembly he followed Kohn until he exited, and when Kohn entered a backstreet (intending to intimidate him) he stood in front of him and asked "who are you, dirty bastard? Whom do you serve?" The professor actually conducted himself with the proper dignity, answering "I am a human and an American."—"with such a thick German accent?" asked the lad who only recently encountered Germans on their land. . . . The professor walked away frightened.[8]

Kohn was close to William Zuckerman, a Jewish anti-Israeli journalist and founding editor of the *Jewish Newsletter*, which Kohn praised as "notable for its insight and courageous stands. . . . [I]n an age of self-centered nationalism and conformity, it raised a lonely nonconformist voice and spoke out of an aroused conscience, but not to espouse any ethnic or religious vital interests."[9] Kohn's personal papers contain his extensive correspondence with people who identified him as anti-Zionist, or at least a harsh critic of the State of Israel. Most of the letters were were from people who shared his views and wished to praise him, but some were from irate colleagues who were surprised to discover this anti-Israel facet of his worldview.[10]

But Kohn's public stands against Israel were more interesting when he attempted to influence general American Jewish bodies, neither Zionist nor anti-Zionist. The prime example was the American Jewish Committee (AJC), in which Kohn was active in the 1940s and 1950s—serving as chair of its Subcommittee on Human Rights and a member of its Executive Board—until he resigned in 1958 in protest what he perceived as the organization's capitulating to Israeli state interests. It seems that Kohn's main interest in AJC in the first place was as a potential mouthpiece for what he understood as the values and true interests of American Jewry—an agenda markedly different from, if not opposed to, that of the Israeli state. Kohn seems to have taken his first step against Zionist lobbies in July 1946, when he signed a petition that originated in the AJC opposing the Zionist call on the US Congress to condition the American loan to Britain on British practices toward Zionists in Palestine.[11] On the eve of the establishment of the State of Israel and following a meeting of the AJC's executive committee, Kohn wrote to its vice president, John Slawson, stating how impressed he had been by "the level of the discussion and by the general understanding of the moral and political complexities in the Palestinian situation." Kohn was heartened by the organization's commitment to "a reconciliation with the Arabs," its "spirit of fairness," and the advancement of "points of view rarely heard in Jewish meetings at present." Kohn's letter assumed "the excellent equipment and leadership and extreme ruthlessness of the Zionist armed forces," and he added that the Zionists might indeed "succeed in expelling or annihilating most of the Palestinian Arabs." Even in this early stage of the war, when most of the future refugees were still in their homes, Kohn saw the Zionist forces as perpetrators of unspeakable massacres. In reference to the infamous Nazi massacre of a Czech village, Kohn mentioned to Slawson how "the Zionists expel Arabs from Tiberias and Haifa, conquer and destroy Arab villages, and create 'Lidices.'" Kohn thus found it vital that American Jewish leaders remain true to their core liberal values and distance themselves from such Zionist practices. He wished that the AJC would take "a position different from that of the overwhelming majority of American Jews." He hoped that its members would constitute the "small sane minority" that could separate itself clearly from the mainstream "in times of nationalist mass emotion," adding that "too few Germans did it in Germany." Kohn also hoped that the AJC would publish its "resolution on the necessity for Arab-Jewish cooperation." He continued:

> American policy, by its support of a Jewish state and its bungling in the face of reality—therein following the example of the British—has unfortunately contributed to this tragic situation. It will be in the interests of the United States and of world peace, of Judaism and of the Palestinian Jewish settlement, if the AJC will help to elaborate a different policy. Though it may arouse at present violent opposition among the majority of the Jewish masses in America, they will, in the not distant future, recognize that such a policy was the only one which could safeguard the security of Palestinian Jewry and the position of Judaism in America.[12]

But Slawson and the AJC failed to take up the mission Kohn had in mind for them, and his diary records his having written them "about their Zionist Fellow-Travelling." In the letter to Slawson mentioned there, Kohn expressed his dismay with the AJC's public statements and pointed him to Hannah Arendt's recent binationalist Commentary piece, "To Save the Jewish Homeland."[13] Kohn's letter then returned to his views of the role the AJC should—and should not—play in this fateful hour. "The tragedy in the present Jewish situation," he claimed, was not so much "the pseudo-messianic intoxication which has apparently seized the whole of Jewry," but the absence of any "large and responsible Jewish circles who [would even attempt to] resist" it:

> [The AJC] cannot write about the Egyptian measures in the very same way in which the Zionist press in America writes about it [sic], especially if one has not protested strongly about the seizure of Jaffa and numerous Arab villages by Zionist forces. . . . The AJC should not simply repeat the Zionist position. . . . [I] hope that the way may be found for Israel to avoid the perdition in which the Israelis are leading it, and that the AJC may help in finding the way, which must lead away from the state of Israel to a bold facing of reality, political and spiritual.[14]

Writing to James Marshall in early 1950 about a draft of an AJC statement critical of Israeli conduct, Kohn spoke "an 'unholy' alliance of the United States and the Soviet forces," which had created the State of Israel through the UN partition resolution of November 1947. In the war that ensued, Israelis "not only defended themselves" but conquered vast additional territories. By insisting on keeping "everything which they conquered by the sword," Israelis, Kohn pronounced, "go much farther than the Germans did in 1871 or intended to go, in case of victory, in 1917 or 1940." Time and again, Kohn sought to divide the AJC from the Jewish state through crude comparisons to German history:

> The world will judge the Jewish State by what it does to the Arabs. . . . The world looks aghast at the military conquests and the proclamation of the right of the sword by a people of whom they were told that it was not a horde of primitive conquerors. We have produced in Palestine a group of Zionist Realpolitikers who, like their German counterparts, mistake the passing factuality of a transitory situation for the ultimate expression of the march of the world spirit of history. It is difficult to describe how great the revulsion against Israel has become lately among many non-Jewish academic people. An immense fund of good will has been lost by the wanton spirit of the new Maccabees.[15]

All of Kohn's pleas were in vain, for in August 1950 AJC's president, Jacob Blaustein, had a constructive exchange of views with the Israeli head of state that became known as the Ben-Gurion Blaustein Agreement, which clarified Israel's relationship to the rest of the Jewish world, and to American Jewry in particular. Israel, Ben-Gurion assured Blaustein, has "no desire and no intention to interfere in any way with the internal affairs of Jewish communities abroad." In turn, Blaustein asserted, and Ben-Gurion had to agree, that "to American Jews, America is home," not exile. Blaustein was correct to conclude that this exchange of views would "lay the foundation for even closer cooperation" between American Jewry, especially the AJC, and the State of Israel.[16] Kohn remained in the AJC until March 1957. Then, following the Suez Crisis, he wanted it to act in support of Arab refugees. Once the AJC leaders politely rejected his proposal, claiming that the time was not ripe for it, he resigned from all his AJC positions.[17] Writing to the chairman of AJC's New York chapter a month later, Kohn proclaimed once more that he hoped "the AJC, in the traditions of Americanism and of liberal non-nationalist Judaism, will continue—and do it more publicly—to criticize the State of Israel for its attitude to Palestinian refugees, [who are] not allowed to return to their homes, and its discriminatory treatment applied to non-Jews in the State. I pray that the AJC may be successful in these activities, for the honor of Judaism and in the ultimate interests of the State of Israel itself. All forms of discrimination, exercised against minorities or refugee groups, have a repercussion on the position of Jews and on American principles everywhere."[18]

Kohn based his case on universal principles of struggle against "all forms of discrimination, exercised against minorities." His sensibility, however, was particularly Jewish, or that of an erstwhile Zionist. As noted above—unlike many people of his generation, background, and worldview—Kohn played no role in, and made no public statement in support of, the major and most crucial American arena for struggle against discrimination at the time—namely, the African American civil rights movement. This is doubly surprising given his 1937 characterization of racism as "by far the sorest spot in the moral and political texture of American culture."[19] Similarly, Kohn, a comparative scholar of nationalism, did not publicly address contemporaneous refugee problems that were vaster than those of the Palestinian Arabs (such as those in India, Pakistan, and Korea, to say nothing of the Soviet bloc). This observation is not intended to diminish the significance or magnitude of the Palestinian refugee problem, nor to challenge its moral implications. It does, however, draw attention to Kohn's continued preoccupation with Zionism, and to the manner in which his tense relationship to it jeopardized the coherence of his worldview and agenda. In an age in which America—especially American Jewry—drew ever closer to the Jewish state, Kohn found himself swimming against the tide.

When the State of Israel was established, Kohn felt very strongly that American Jewry should not play second fiddle but rather confront Israel and be very vocal about its liberal alternative to Jewish statehood. In the 1930s Kohn had seen the United States as destined to lead the Western world yet (for some reason) shying away from this responsibility. His vision of the Jewish world seems to have been somewhat similar, especially after 1948: By its traditions, values, and sheer numbers and power, American Jewry was destined to lead the Jewish world and to do so according to its own values—accentuating how they differed from Israeli values. Yet Kohn felt that American Jewry (for some reason) shied away from taking that position. In 1958 he lamented that "Jewish life in the United States suffers from spiritual atrophy at the very same time when American Jews are gaining rapidly in economic wealth and political influence."[20]

Arab lobbies and other opponents of Zionism and the State of Israel were quick to find in Kohn a guide for and a propaganda asset in their struggle (and they continue to use his work in this way in the twenty-first century). For example, in August 1946 Habib Ibrahim Katibah, an editor at the Institute of

Arab-American Affairs, referred the readers of the *New York Herald Tribune* to Kohn's *Nationalism and Imperialism in the Hither East*, which ostensibly refuted a "vicious double attack on the Arabs" and allegedly proved that "in Egypt, Syria, Iraq, Palestine and even in Saudi Arabia much is being done by Arab rulers and leaders to raise the living standard of the common people."[21] Kohn's credentials on migration being primarily those of an Arabist maintained ties with and his reputation among American scholars of the Middle East and of the East in general. In the late 1940s, for example, Kohn was elected to the Governing Council of the Institute of Arabic Studies, part of New York's Asia Institute.[22] Through this network, Kohn established lasting relationships with Arab diplomats. The honorary president of Institute of Arabic Studies was the Egyptian ambassador to the United States, Mahmoud Hassan Pasha. In the late 1950s Kohn had cordial relations with George Tomeh, the consul general of the United Arab Republic (Syria and Egypt) in New York, and with representatives of the Algerian Front for National Liberation such as Abdelkader Chanderli.[23]

In a letter in late 1952 to Eleanor Roosevelt—former first lady and at that time delegate to the UN General Assembly and representative to the UN Commission on Human Rights—Kohn criticized *inter alia* what he saw as a pro-Zionist policy of the Eisenhower administration:

> Having lived in the Islamic Middle East for many years . . . I think that France should declare that within a very foreseeable future Tunisian and Moroccan self-government will be established. But the main fault there is not of the French government, but of the French settlers in North Africa. They are afraid of losing their vested interests there. The danger to native populations does not come primarily from "imperialism" which may have a great humanizing [*sic*] and civilizing mission, but from white settlers or immigrants who like in Tunisia, Algeria *or Palestine* wish to take over the whole or parts of the native economy. . . . [A]s you see from my remarks about France *and Palestine*, I have full understanding for the aspirations of the Arabs and Asians.[24]

Thus, even when addressing broad foreign policy questions about places from Algeria to Korea, Kohn rarely failed to define Israel as a colonial regime and American alliance with it as a moral and strategic mistake. He stressed his fear that "our support of Zionist conquest of Palestine . . . turns the Arabs against us."[25] Kohn emerged as an advocate of a closer American alliance with the Arab world, especially with the pan-Arabism of Gamal Abdel Nasser. Kohn expressed his concern about America's alliance with Israel turning the Arab world into an enemy of the United States in frequent letters to the *New York*

Times. For example, in late 1951 he praised the newpaper's discussion of the Palestinian refugee problem as "especially welcome because of its emphasis on our responsibility, due to the fact that we were the first nation to recognize Israel and have always supported her as one of the democratic nations of the Middle East. An active contribution toward the solution of this long-overdue problem would not only be welcome for humanitarian but also for political reasons because it would tend to decrease the bitter tension prevailing in the Middle East today, making difficult the cooperation of all the Middle Eastern nations for common defense."[26] Another of his letters, from the summer of 1958, challenged American alliances in the Middle East, presenting Nasser as the West's natural ally. "Public opinion in the free world," Kohn wrote, "seems haunted by false fears" of Nasser, the Arabs, and their ostensible affinity to the Soviet bloc. Yet the "unrest in the Middle East is not due to communism or Nasser. It started in 1919. It has fed upon the hostility shown to Arab self-government by outside forces which divided the Arab lands against the wishes of the inhabitants. . . . If Arab lands are not invaded," he claimed, "oil will flow with speed and efficiency. The Arabs depend on it as much as the West does, if not more." He continued: "The West and the Arabs are mutually interdependent. As a result of their modern history the Arabs are suspicious of the West, as our people were suspicious of 'imperialism' for a long time after 1776. Some Westerners who speak as if 'natives' understood only force and who look down on 'native' abilities for running their own affairs, not only misjudge the situation but enhance fears and suspicions, not only in the Middle East. A wise Western policy could and would moderate and ultimately allay these fears and suspicions."[27]

Little wonder, then, that Tahseen Basheer—a member of the Permanent Mission of the United Arab Republic to the United Nations and who identified himself as one of Kohn's former students—praised this letter, especially given Kohn's Jewishness. Kohn's endorsement of pan-Arabism "lives up to the old tradition of Arab-Jewish harmony that typified for many generations the relationship between these Semitic people[s]." At the close of Basheer's letter was a sentence that must have pleased Kohn: "The Jewish people in the West could by [an] understanding of this dilemma of the Middle East bring more light and justice to that area."[28] At this time Kohn became quite popular among anti-Zionists and anti-Israelis alike, including officials of Arab states. A Dane named Alfred Nielsen told Kohn that a copy of his "Zion and the Jewish National Idea" "was sent to me by the Syrian-Egyptian Embassy in Copenhagen together with common propaganda literature." Nielsen, who was taken with Kohn's work, asked his permission to translate it into Danish with the intent of "counteracting the general Zionist propaganda and trying to make Danish readers see the Palestine problem with your eyes."[29]

The most baffling aspect of Kohn's anti-Israeli activity was his continued attachment to Israeli binationalists. What did Kohn's casual endorsements of Ahad Ha'am's spiritual Zionism and of the statements by the binationalist Ihud Association even mean at that late stage? He had passed two points of no return since his days as a binational Zionist in the 1920s: the first was his slow but irrevocable break with Zionism (including spiritual and binational Zionism) in the wake of the 1929 Arab riots; and the second, and more important, point was the establishment of the State of Israel. The Jewish nation-state had become a fact. These watersheds rendered Kohn's endorsements of another Zionism purely theoretical and politically irrelevant. On the personal level, Kohn's continued interest in friends who remained in Jerusalem and proponents of binational Zionism is clear. But at the same time, this idea of another Zionism served him as an effective way to condemn the young state and its policies. In this Kohn anticipated an anti-Israeli pattern that remains common in the twenty-first century —but, unlike many other critics of Israel, Kohn had been scarred by many years of uphill struggles to transform Zionism (indeed, Kohn himself was used as an embodiment of an alternative, better Zionism in similarly motivated works).

Kohn's personal bond with Zionist friends after his move to the United States differed from case to case. His friendships with Martin Buber and Hugo Bergmann initially lost much of their importance but never completely died out. In the late 1930s and 1940s Kohn was eager to use his new position to assist his friends in all possible ways (indeed, he urged them to join him in the United States). In his old age, his relations with both Buber and Bergmann warmed up again. The ideological divide between him and them, which had once meant the world, suddenly seemed inconsequential. "Looking back at our political endeavors 30 or 35 years ago," Bergmann wrote Kohn, waxing philosophical, "nothing is left but a big question mark. . . .We live in a world that is in such an instable balance that we cannot know . . . what other things we should expect before we have finished our current wanderings on earth. And that's why it is good to remember the good and the loved, and what we have experienced in our lives until now, among which I count my relationship to you."[30] Kohn's friendship with Judah Magnes—which had soured in Kohn's final Zionist years —healed more quickly, largely thanks to Magnes's great assistance in securing Kohn's first academic position in the United States, but this friendship was also cut short tragically on Magnes's passing in late 1948. Kohn was one of the four speakers at Magnes's memorial service on December 16, 1948. He compared

Magnes to Ahad Ha'am and defined his passing not only as a personal blow to his friends but also as a monumental blow for Zionism.[31] In the years 1953-55 Kohn, worked with Arendt, Georg Landauer, and Robert Weltsch on a commemorative volume in Magnes's honor, which ultimately was not published.[32] Kohn's friendship with Weltsch—who had become an Israeli citizen and a correspondent for *Ha'aretz* in London—was different. Weltsch probably remained Kohn's closest friend, and the intensive correspondence between the two (they often wrote each other twice a week) constantly addressed Zionism and Israel. Perhaps because Weltsch remained in the Zionist fold, his criticism of Israel and Zionism was almost always harsher and even less forgiving than Kohn's. For years Weltsch wrote "Israel" only between quotation marks, and he was also much more pessimistic regarding Israel's future.

These friends and others kept Kohn informed about binationalist activity and writings in Israel. His marginalia on Hebrew binationalist publications that he kept in his personal papers attest that he read them regularly. And Kohn and his like-minded friends sent letters to editors in support of the Ihud Association's appeals to alleviate the Palestinian refugee problem: "We believe that the United Nations, the United States Government and individually very many American citizens of Jewish and other faiths who have always been eager to help refugees, Jewish and non-Jewish alike, should back up the proposal. In a difficult and tragic situation every proposal inspired by a spirit of humanitarianism and international responsibility deserves the closest sympathetic attention."[33] Two years later Kohn published in the *Menorah Journal* his most comprehensive essay on Jewish politics since his Americanization some twenty-five years earlier, called "Zion and the Jewish National Idea." In this essay he proclaimed that "ultimately the Jewish problem is but part of the human problem. . . . Modern Jewish life with its great promise of creativeness in freedom is based on Enlightenment and Emancipation everywhere. . . . For wherever Enlightenment and Emancipation are rejected or scorned, they will be endangered, morally or physically more than others."[34] This claim resembles ideas that Kohn had been expressing since World War II. It is remarkable, however, that—although he had broken with Zionism thirty years before—to convey his ideas effectively, he felt compelled to anchor them in the work of Ahad Ha'am and other alternative Zionist thinkers. Kohn apparently still needed Zionism and the State of Israel to formulate his Jewish outlook through negation.

He had never returned to Palestine after 1934 or visited the State of Israel, but he had no qualms about depicting critically and unequivocally the ostensibly faulty nature of Israeli society and young Israelis. "Many of the young Israeli generation," he proclaimed, "not only look down on the native Arabs; they have turned also, with pride in their own valor and in bitter disgust, from the two thousand years of the diaspora, from the life of their fathers and grandfathers, which they reject." There was a fundamental Israeli "opposition to the spiritual foundations of prophetic Judaism and Jewish life in the diaspora." Kohn caricatured not only Israeli Negation of the Diaspora, but also Israeli militarism. He presented as infantile Israeli "pride in their own valor," in being "more valiant," and "more tough-minded," and in their victory. Kohn was dismissive of that victory, and rejected even the Israeli designation of the 1948 war as the War of Liberation: "The question, from whom was the land 'liberated' is difficult to answer. From the British . . .? From its native inhabitants?" And thus the Israeli victory was in his view no "miracle," and ultimately not a victory at all: "In the long run the foundation of a nation-state on military victory and its continuing temper usually defeats its own purpose. Militarism rapidly changes the whole character of the nation which succumbs to its temptation."[35]

In spite of his steadfast position and of never having visited Israel (though his wife and son did so in the fall of 1949), Kohn maintained contacts not only with his Israeli relatives and binationalist friends but also with broader circles of German-speaking Israelis from Central Europe (known as *Yekkes*). Kohn did not become a persona non grata in those circles—maybe because of his continued friendship with Bergmann, Buber, Weltsch, and others. This may reflect the political marginality of some Yekkes. Many of them expressed their harsh criticism of their new home to Kohn, who ostensibly predicted Israel's many problems. The *Mitteilungsblatt*—a Yekke publication that Kohn read regularly —reported occasionally on his achievements, invited him to contribute articles, and even celebrated his seventieth birthday with multiple essays, including one from Weltsch. On that birthday, Kohn received in addition to letters from his old friends a letter from the *Mitteilungsblatt*: "Warmest congratulations, both on my behalf as well as on that of the editorial staff of the *Mitteilungsblatt*. I probably do not need to stress how strong the spiritual bond is that connects us with you across all distances. Even when the paths of life diverge, there remains the common tradition of humanistic thinking which especially you have expressed in all your doing and particularly in all your scientific work. . . . Be assured that your voice had its impact on us and will be heard."[36]

This may give the impression that Kohn's Israeli friends lived in an inner exile of sorts, while Kohn ultimately found a modern Jewish equilibrium in liberal America. But that was not the case. It is precisely the overt disquiet and bold dissent of his Israeli friends that indicate a critical sense of belonging absent from Kohn's programmatic ruminations. In a letter to his son and daughter-in-law in early 1953, Kohn very atypically saw fit to proclaim his Jewish American creed: "It speaks very well for Immanuel's future that he received so many offers from the leading 'Christian' law firms. . . . You see again how exaggerated the widespread belief is that a gulf separates Jews and Christians in this or in any modern civilized country." Kohn went on to list the various prestigious schools that had admitted his son, only highlighting that he did not take this acceptance of Jews for granted. "There are certainly Christians in this country who do not wish to intermarry or to mix with Jews," he admitted. "If some Christians . . . don't wish to enter with me into *connubium* and *commercium*, I accept it and I am certainly not unhappy about it." He told his son, "I can only advise you from a long experience, not to worry about it." Kohn then described Jewishness as devoid of any intrinsic value, as something merely to be tolerated: "There is no reason to be proud of being a Jew or a Christian or a Turk. Nor is there a reason to be unhappy or depressed by it. That is something with which one is born, which one has to accept and to make the best out of it. . . . Even if as a Jew one does not like Judaism or many thin[g]s about Jews . . . there is no use in allowing one's dislikes to upset us instead of control[l]ing them. . . . Like in everything else, there is in Judaism the good and the bad mingled." And while Kohn presented Jewish American life in this letter as blissfully harmonious, to him Israel embodied a Jewish tragic spiritual decline, indeed a perversion of Judaism:

> But it is not so long ago that among the Jews another type predominated and was highly regarded, a type concerned with learning for its own sake, dedicated to books and not to money, humble and unoffensive, abhor[ring] violence and brutality living in poverty and modesty. The tragedy in Palestine is that this type of Jew, whom they call there contemptuously Ghetto Jews, has disappeared and that there a generation is growing up which is not humble but domineering, given to violence, brutal, preferring power to the matters of the spirit. My objection to Palestine was that I regard life and youth there as a perversion of Judaism, much nearer to the bad features of American Jewry than to the good features of Eastern European Ghetto life.[37]

This need to deny, using convoluted explanations, even the possibility of marginalization or exclusion of Jews in the United States seems to manifest a certain lack of confidence on Kohn's part. The unusual letter may have been in response to the trial of Julius and Ethel Rosenberg. "The arrest, trial, and execution of this Jewish couple," wrote Hasia Diner, "could not have come at a worse time for American Jews, particularly for those most prone to worrying about their status. The fact that at the height of American anti-Communism, the two people executed by the United States government happened to be Jewish sent a shudder of fear through a community with a profound historical memory of being scapegoated."[38] Kohn undoubtedly loved America and identified with its values, but the question of whether he felt at home there may have a more complicated answer.

Kohn passed away in February 1971, at the end of a decade with no permanent home of his own, a decade of involuntary wandering. True to the extraterritorial motif in his life—but counter to the traditional Jewish prohibition—Kohn had his body cremated and his ashes strewn.[39] In Israel, Shlomo Grodzensky saw it fit to publish a spiteful column in *Davar* with the title "Upon Closure of the Hans Kohn File." With noticeable satisfaction he recounted how for years he had followed the orbit of "that character, Hans Kohn." Grodzensky saw Kohn as a spineless opportunist, "a man of fashion, and as the fashions changed, he too changed along with them." Nor did he see Kohn as a true scholar or creative thinker, but rather as a man of "compilatory scholastics, in which Jews have always excelled." Grodzensky was especially annoyed by what he saw as Kohn's transformation from a nonconformist critic within Zionism to an archconformist in the United States: "He is one of those Jews who are intrepid in their treatment of Jews, but meek and mild with the non-Jews." Grodzensky also accused Kohn of "defecting to the United States under false pretenses, masquerading as a German academic émigré." Finally, he ridiculed Kohn's autobiography as "a truly farcical book."[40]

Israeli President Zalman Shazar, who learned of Kohn's passing only from Grodzensky's article, was put off by it. "The news of the decease of Hans Kohn has reached me," he wrote to Weltsch. "May his memory be blessed! I have not known to whom to express my condolences, and in my heart I direct them to you. This man, with all the wandering of his mind, deserves a different appreciation from that he received in our press."[41] "Woe to the cruel hand who wrote such words," responded Bergmann to "Grodzensky's blind hatred." In a response in *Davar*, Bergmann charted Kohn's path as an erstwhile Zionist and as a historian, and his tragic path as a man who felt that Zionist policy toward the Arabs has pushed him out of the movement. "I do not second his opinions," wrote Bergmann. However, one should not forget that

> Hans Kohn was not the only one who felt that way. I could mention here Leon Roth (1896-1963), who, as a Hebrew writer and an authority in Jewish thought, was

much more rooted here among us, and who left us—"defected Zionism and the Land" in Grodzensky's words—and many others who, revolted by the path Zionism takes, grew estranged from it. Again: I have no intention of backing the positions of my friend, Hans Kohn, but I will defend his memory and image among us. Finally, there is a lesson to be learned from the tragic path of this thinker. Instead of defaming our opponents, we have to learn from them.[42]

AFTERWORD

Hugo Bergmann's public defense of Hans Kohn was remarkably guarded given their long friendship. Bergmann considered Kohn to be a friend, but also an ideological opponent and a tragic figure. Why "tragic" Bergmann did not explain, but many *Davar* readers must have assumed the tragedy to be linked to Kohn's break from Zionism. Yet Bergmann insisted that "there is a lesson to be learned from" him.[1] But what lesson?

Had this book been written in the early or mid-1990s, when the Oslo Accords between Israel and the Palestine Liberation Organization were in effect, Kohn may have appeared to be an unlikely visionary of a Zionism ultimately transformed through recognition of the national demands, rights, and self-determination of the Palestinian Arabs. Had this book been written on the heels of the Maastricht Treaty and during the rise of the European Union, Kohn might have seemed to be a visionary of international integration in Europe and beyond, under Western leadership. Had this book been written after the publication and phenomenal reception of Francis Fukuyama's *The End of History and the Last Man*, Kohn—with his concept of universalizing liberalism as the goal of Western hegemony—would have been seen as the author of the prequel, published more than forty years earlier. Had this book been written during the boom in nationalism studies during the 1990s, Kohn would have stood as a harbinger of the notion that nationalism and national sentiments are modern constructs. At that point, the view of nations as imagined and invented artifice so permeated the academy that it became virtually self-evident. Kohn's anticipation of those notions was grounded in his internationalist and transnationalist sensibilities, and in his belief that nationalism could and should be transcended —indeed, had already been transcended. This view anticipated the postnationalist expectations of the late Cold War and the period immediately after it in the West.

But this book was written a generation later, and now Kohn's legacy resonates quite differently. The book was written some fifteen years after the collapse of the Oslo peace process and its replacement, on the Israeli side, by unilateralism, an increasing denial of the national root of the conflict, and ultimately a growing denial of Palestinian peoplehood. This book was written not in the days of the Maastricht Treaty but against the backdrop of the European debt crisis and the European migrant crisis, and in the immediate aftermath of the Brexit vote. Both nationalism and American power look very different in the twenty-first century. Kohn's advocacy of what he saw as a natural American alliance with postcolonial Arab nationalists—an alliance that he believed was linked to the spread of democracy in the Arab world under American stewardship—appears tragically differently in the wake of America's long wars in Afghanistan and Iraq. Kohn believed in American power, but he would undoubtedly have seen America's wars in the twenty-first century as following old colonial practices, which he believed America had already overcome.

What only twenty years ago might have seemed to be Kohn's prescience is now exposed, yet again, as illusory. Kohn, readers may conclude, got almost everything wrong: Israel seems to maintain its power and policies, independent of the fate and aspirations of the Palestinians; American power works in ways that Kohn would have deemed colonialist; greater international integration may be giving way to a return to old nationalism; nationalism in the West is no more civic than its Eastern counterpart, as manifested in the English nationalist dimensions of Brexit and the nativism underlying Donald Trump's path to the White House; and finally, whereas Kohn challenged ethnicity, blood, and soil as myths, many contemporary scholars challenge his concept of civic nationalism as a myth, implying again the greater authenticity of kin and soil.[2]

Thus, at this point in history, I could not have written a hagiography even if I wanted to, nor could I have presented Kohn as a prescient or omniscient scholar. Kohn was no Cassandra. He was not always blessed with the gift of foresight, nor was he cursed by the deep skepticism of his contemporaries. As a matter of fact, many listened to him even when he was wrong. The beauty, importance, and critical edge of Kohn's work; his life and times; and his struggle with nationalism defy any serious efforts to mystify him and his positions.

However, Kohn undoubtedly taught later generations how to think about nationalism. "A ghost is stalking studies of nationalism!" proclaimed André Liebich as late as 2006. "It is the ghost of Hans Kohn. And the chains it is rattling are those of Kohn's paradigm or dichotomy, the thesis that there are two types of nationalism, which Kohn calls 'Western' and 'non-Western', radically unlike each other."[3] While certainly credited—arguably, overcredited—for making the distinction between civic and ethnic nationalisms, Kohn rarely received due credit for his early and forceful claim to nationalism's constructedness ("a state of mind")[4] and modernity (not earlier than the seventeenth century). Later detractors notwithstanding, Kohn largely defined the governing paradigms of nationalism studies long after his death. Nationalism studies emerged as a field more than a decade later, with the publication of immensely popular works by such authors as Benedict Anderson, Ernest Gellner, and Eric Hobsbawm, and all three of those authors shared, updated, and popularized Kohn's understanding of nationalism as a modern construction. Furthermore, all have tellingly named Kohn and Carleton J. H. Hayes the twin founding fathers of the academic study of nationalism.[5]

Yet the new cohort of scholars already saw Kohn's work as obsolete. In his recent autobiography, the late Benedict Anderson—without naming Kohn—captured three flaws in Kohn's work that he wished to correct in *Imagined Communities*. The first was geographical: taking a Eurocentric view and seeing nationalism as originating with Europeans or European colonists. The second was ideological: the subordination of all previous theories of nationalism to either the Marxist creed or the liberal one. The third flaw was methodological: previous studies offered histories of the idea of nationalism but never a cultural and social history of nationalism.[6] Further criticism of Kohn came from scholars like Anthony Smith, who challenged both the modernist school and the distinction between civic and ethnic nationalism.[7] The Subaltern Studies Group, especially Partha Chatterjee, has been remarkably insightful in exposing the liberal thought patterns that shaped and confined Kohn's understanding of nationalism. Many of the vital aspects of later studies of nationalism—like the analysis of its gendered nature—were simply beyond Kohn's scope.

In addition to poor timing—by the time that nationalism studies came into its own, Kohn was already dead and his major work dated—there was another reason why Kohn is not celebrated as the great analytical demystifier of nation and nationalism. Kohn consistently pulled apart the political myths of various ideologies and polities. Yet whenever he encountered and exposed a malignant political myth, he felt the need to create a countermyth. This is an unmistakable and unjustifiable pattern of thought, one that failed Kohn time and again. This tendency was apparent in the Bar Kochba years before World War I (blood and soil as countermyths), during that war (the myth of depoliticized nationalism), between the world wars ("the political idea of Judaism"),[8] during World War II (the promise in *The City of Man* to counter the fascist political religion by recreating democracy as a counter political religion), and finally during the Cold War (the myth of an anti-imperial liberal empire). These were all futile attempts. Kohn's unpersuasive, half-baked countermyths rarely mobilized his contemporaries or convinced later readers, and all too often they diminished his theoretical rigor beyond repair. This Achilles heel of countermyth served me as a reminder to avoid any attempts to turn Kohn into a myth, and certainly into a mythically prescient thinker who had all of the right answers.

No stranger to disillusionments and defeats, Kohn wrote in his memoir: "I was always impressed by Lucanus' report to Cato's words 'The victorious cause pleased the Gods, but the defeated cause pleased Cato.' Even the gods apparently have often changed their minds in history, and what was heralded as the victorious cause has become sooner or later . . . the cause of the vanquished."[9] Much of what we learn from Kohn's biography can be gleaned from his bold answers to the pressing political crises of his times and his participation in struggles, often for "the cause of the vanquished"—indeed, for causes that nowadays may seem unimaginable, such as Bar Kochba's antiliberal spiritual Zionism in prewar Prague, Brith Shalom's binational struggle in Palestine in the 1920s against the creation of a Jewish state; and the advocacy in 1940 in *The City of Man* of an American-led democratic world federation.

When Kohn concluded his biography of Martin Buber, his great teacher, in 1930 he realized that though his book "was not conceived or written as a confession," it somehow "became one." The format of a biography, Kohn realized in hindsight, enabled him "to say things I couldn't have said on my own behalf." Writing that biography during his break with Zionism forced Kohn to think critically not only about Buber's path, but also about his own. "It is truly," he told Robert Weltsch, "more an autobiography than a biography of Buber. For it shows my path and ours, my youth and ours, from which I part ways in this book and which I have analyzed and criticized in the book."[10] As the biographer's biographer, I had to wonder if something comparable happened in my own biographical endeavor. True, Kohn was never my teacher or friend—he was not even my contemporary—yet witnessing the way the twentieth century repeatedly shattered his worldview and forced him to retheorize nationalism furnished me with a greater understanding of how encounters with history change our worldviews (mine included) even when sensibilities and thought patterns persist. Writing about Kohn forced me to think anew about the ideologies of my place and time, both as an Israeli and as someone who grew up during the Cold War. At some level, it seems, all writing is autobiographical. Furthermore, even if many of Kohn's formulas have not stood the test of time, the questions he raised persist. His Sisyphean struggle with nationalism is now ours.

Notes

Abbreviations

CAHJP	Central Archives for the History of the Jewish People
CZA	Central Zionist Archives
HKC-Klau	Hans Kohn Collection, Klau Library, Hebrew Union College
HKC-LBI	Hans Kohn Collection, Leo Baeck Institute Archives
HKRWC	Hans Kohn-Robert Weltsch Correspondence, Leo Baeck Institute Archives
HBA	Shmuel Hugo Bergman Archive, Archives Department, National Library of Israel
LBI	Leo Baeck Institute Archives
MBA	Martin Buber Archive, Archives Department, National Library of Israel
RWC	Robert Weltsch Collection, Leo Baeck Institute Archives

Introduction

1. Hans Kohn, *Nationalismus: Über die Bedeutung des Nationalismus im Judentum und in der Gegenwart* (Nationalism: on the significance of nationalism in Judaism and in the present) (Vienna: R. Löwit, 1922), 123–4. The English translation is from Hans Kohn, "Nationalism," in *The Jew: Essays from Martin Buber's Journal Der Jude, 1916–1928*, edited by Arthur Allen Cohen and translated by Joachim Neugroschel (Birmingham: University of Alabama Press, 1980), 28.

2. Hans Kohn, *Living in a World Revolution: My Encounters with History* (New York: Trident, 1964), 21.

3. Hans Kohn, *World Order in Historical Perspective* (Cambridge, MA: Harvard University Press, 1942), 93. See also Kohn, *The Idea of Nationalism: A Study in Its Origins and Background* (New York: The Macmillan Company, 1944), 10. Carlton J. H. Hayes shared Kohn's understanding of nationalism as both a modern phenomenon and a constructed one; indeed, though Hayes's major works on nationalism were published more than a decade before Kohn's, the two men are correctly remembered as "the twin founding fathers" of nationalism studies. Both Benedict Anderson and Eric Hobsbawm attributed the phrase ("the twin founding fathers") to Aira Kemiläinen. While certainly holding that "the investigation of nationalism . . . began with Hayes' and Kohn's works," she apparently did not use the phrase. See Benedict Anderson, *Imagined Communities: Reflections on the Origin and Spread of Nationalism* (London: Verso, 1983), 4; Eric J. Hobsbawm, *Nations and nationalism since 1780: Programme, Myth, Reality* (Cambridge: Cambridge University Press, 1990), 3; Aira Kemiläinen, *Nationalism: Problems Concerning the Word, the Concept, and Classification* (Jyväskylä, Finland: Jyväskylän Kasvatusopillinen Korkeakoulu, 1964), 8.

4. Umut Özkirimli, *Theories of Nationalism: A Critical Introduction*, 2nd ed. (Basingstoke, England: Palgrave Macmillan, 2010), 37.

5. Kohn, *Living in a World Revolution*, 53.

6. Kemiläinen, *Nationalism*, 8; see also 60. Max Lerner stated: "The great center of research in the history of nationalism is likely to be wherever Professor Kohn is" ("Nationalism: The Root and the Flower," *Saturday Review of Literature*, June 10, 1944, 5).

7. David Sorkin, "The Genesis of the Ideology of Emancipation: 1806–1840," *Leo Baeck Institute Yearbook* 32 (1987): 11. Kohn would tell Mordecai Kaplan that he came "from an assimilationist background" (Mordecai M. Kaplan, *Communings of the Spirit: The Journals of Mordecai M. Kaplan* [Detroit, MI: Wayne State University Press, 2001], 465). See also David Sorkin, "The Impact of Emancipation on German Jewry," in *Assimilation and Community: The Jews in Nineteenth-Century Europe*, edited by Jonathan Frankel and Steven J. Zipperstein (London: Cambridge University Press, 1991), 177–98.

8. Kohn, *Living in a World Revolution*, 89.

9. Erez Manela, *The Wilsonian Moment: Self-Determination and the International Origins of Anticolonial Nationalism* (New York: Oxford University Press, 2007).

10. Minorities and majorities, Kohn insisted, are "primarily political and not numerical concepts" ("Minorities," in *Encyclopaedia Britannica*, 15th ed. [Chicago: Encyclopedia Britannica, 1947], 564).

11. Hans Kohn, *Revolutions and Dictatorships: Essays in Contemporary History* (Cambridge, MA: Harvard University Press: 1939), 331.

12. Hans Kohn, *American Nationalism: An Interpretative Essay* (New York: Macmillan, 1957), 227.

13. The brief exception may have been the early 1920s, when, influenced by Soviet policy and theory, Kohn rejected all national movements as "the religion of the bourgeoisie" (Hans Kohn to Robert Weltsch, November 6, 1922, HKC-LBI, 13/19).

14. Kohn, *The Idea of Nationalism*, 576.

15. Partha Chatterjee, *Nationalist Thought and the Colonial World: A Derivative Discourse?* (Minneapolis: University of Minnesota Press, 1986), 2.

16. Umut Özkirimli has recently promised to pursue this approach in the forthcoming third edition of his *Theories of Nationalism* (see his lecture, "Nationalism Studies as Invented Tradition: Moving Beyond Anachronous Debate," University College Dublin, June 9, 2015, accessed September 3, 2016, https://youtube/W2cPc8cG004).

17. T. S. Eliot to Edward Mead Earle, October 14, 1948 HKC-LBI, box 8, folder 4 (see also Eliot to Hans Kohn, November 8, 1948, HKC-LBI, box 8, folder 4); Gershom Scholem, *Briefe I, 1914–1947*, edited by Itta Shedletzky (Munich: Beck, 1994), 292.

18. Stanley Moses, e-mail message to the author, July 12, 2016.

19. Lewis Mumford, *My Work and Days: A Personal Chronicle* (New York: Harcourt, 1979), 391–92.

20. Kohn, *Living in a World Revolution*, 44.

21. Immanuel "Ike" Kohn, interview with the author, Manhattan, November 13, 2007.

22. Hans Kohn diary, January 7, 1927, HKC-LBI, box 18, folder 2.

23. Arnold Toynbee to Hans Kohn, May 14, 1964, HKC-LBI, box 13, folder 17.

24. Hans Kohn, "Aktiver Pazifismus," *Neue Wege* 23, no. 2 (1929): 89–90. All translations are my own, unless otherwise indicated.

25. Hans Kohn, "Race Conflict," in *Encyclopedia of the Social Sciences*, edited by Edwin R. A. Seligman and Alvin Saunders Johnson (New York: Macmillan, 1934), 13:40.

26. Karen Brutents, "Apologiia kolonializma, ili 'teoriia natsionalizma' Gansa Kona [The apology of colonialism, or Hans Kohn's "theory of nationalism"]," *Voprosy Filosofii* 7, no. 2, (1958): 90. Brutents's career is discussed in Odd Arne Westad, *The Global Cold War: Third World Interventions and the Making of Our Times* (Cambridge: Cambridge University Press, 2005).

27. Y[uri Fedorovich] Karyakin and E[vgenii Grigorevich] Plimak wrote: "Kohn smelled what wonderful prospects were offered him by anticommunism" (*Hans Kohn Analyses the "Russian Mind"* [Moscow: Progress, 1966], 13). They also repeated Brutents's argument: "Kohn's theory is not original. It was born when the West was colonizing the East" (ibid., 15).

28. Tom Nairn, "Demonising Nationalism," *London Review of Books*, February 25, 1993, 4 and 5.

29. Zionists, however, labeled Kohn a "bleeding heart" and "righteous" in 1921 (Siegmund Kaznelson, "Jüdisches und arabisches Selbstbestimmungsrecht," *Der Jude* 5, no. 11 [1920–21]: 671), then attacked him as a "traitor" around 1929 (Shmuel Samburski to Leo Hermann [1929?], CZA, Leo Hermann Collection, A 145, 153), and finally—after Kohn's public break with the movement—depicted him as a spineless opportunist (Shlomo Grodzensky, "Im Sgirat Tiko shel Hans Kohn," *Davar*, April 15, 1971).

30. Sidney Wallach, *The Struggle for Integration* (Philadelphia: American Council for Judaism: 1945), unnumbered page.

31. Tahseen M. Basheer, "To Stabilize the Mideast; Recognition of Aspirations of Arab Peoples for Betterment Urged," *New York Times*, August 1, 1958.

32. Jacqueline Rose, *The Question of Zion* (Princeton, NJ: Princeton University Press, 2007), 84 (see also 69, 74, 76).

33. Judith Butler, *Parting Ways: Jewishness and the Critique of Zionism* (New York: Columbia University Press, 2012), 25.

34. Alain Locke to W. E. B. Du Bois, March 6, 1936, in *The Correspondence of W. E. B. Du Bois*, edited by Herbert Aptheker (Amherst: University of Massachusetts Press, 1997), 2:83.

1. A Turning Inward: Kohn's Youth in Multinational Late Habsburg Prague

1. John Stuart Mill, *Considerations on Representative Government*, 2nd ed. (London: Parker, Son, and Bourn, 1861), 298–99.

2. Gustav Landauer, "Sind das Ketzergedanken?" in *Vom Judentum: Ein Sammelbuch*, edited by Hans Kohn (Leipzig: Kurt Wolff, 1913), 256–57. The English translation is from "Jewishness Is an Inalienable Spiritual Sensibility (1913)," translated by Jakob Hessing, in *The Jew in the Modern World: A Documentary History*, 2nd ed., edited by. Paul R. Mendes-Flohr, and Jehuda Reinharz (New York: Oxford University Press, 1995), 277.

3. Hans Kohn, *Living in a World Revolution: My Encounters with History* (New York:

Trident Press, 1964), 47-48. After moving to the Land of Israel in 1920, Hugo Bergmann changed the spelling of his family name to Bergman and published his writings under the name of Samuel (or sometimes Schmuel or Shmu'el) Hugo Bergman.

4. Kohn, *Living in a World Revolution*, 56 (see also 50); and *Martin Buber: Sein Werk und seine Zeit: Ein Versuch über Religion und Politik* (Hellerau, Germany: J. Hegner, 1930), 50-51.

5. In their understanding of their nationalism as spiritual (rather than material) and internal (rather than external) and in their resistance to normalization, the prewar Prague Zionists made distinctions that were remarkably similar to those used eighty years later by Partha Chatterjee to distinguish between Eastern and Western nationalism ("Whose Imagined Community?" *Millennium* 20, no. 3 (1991): 521-26).

6. Hans Kohn to Robert Weltsch, July 14, 1919 (transcript), RWC (AR 7185), Box 5, folder 10.

7. Kohn, *Living in a World Revolution*, 31 and 22.

8. Ibid., 19.

9. Some important English-language works include Kateřina Čapková, *Czechs, Germans, Jews? National Identity and the Jews of Bohemia* (New York: Berghahn, 2012); Wilma Iggers, *The Jews of Bohemia and Moravia: A Historical Reader* (Detroit, MI: Wayne State University Press, 1992); Hillel J. Kieval, *The Making of Czech Jewry: National Conflict and Jewish Society in Bohemia, 1870-1918* (New York: Oxford University Press, 1988), and *Languages of Community: The Jewish Experience in the Czech Lands* (Berkeley: University of California Press, 2000); Society for the History of Czechoslovak Jews, ed., *The Jews of Czechoslovakia: Historical Studies and Surveys*, vol. 1 (Philadelphia: Jewish Publication Society of America, 1968).

10. Following Carl Schorske's lead, the term "postliberal" has become essential in cultural histories of Austria around the beginning of the twentieth century. See, for example, Steven Beller, *Rethinking Vienna 1900* (New York: Berghahn, 2001); Mary Gluck, *Georg Lukács and His Generation, 1900-1918* (Cambridge, MA: Harvard University Press, 1985); David S. Luft, *Eros and Inwardness in Vienna: Weininger, Musil, Doderer* (Chicago: University of Chicago Press, 2003; Carl E. Schorske, *Fin-de-Siècle Vienna: Politics and Culture* (New York: Knopf, 1979); Scott Spector, *Prague Territories: National Conflict and Cultural Innovation in Franz Kafka's Fin de Siècle* (Berkeley: University of California Press, 2002); Michael P. Steinberg, *Austria as Theater and Ideology: The Meaning of the Salzburg Festival* (Ithaca, NY: Cornell University Press, 2000). In the Jewish European context, the term "postliberal" also signifies a generational shift in the expectations for Jewish integration away from the hope for a harmonious integration facilitated by greater civil equality for Jews.

11. Kohn, *Living in a World Revolution*, 8.

12. Ibid. Classic studies include Gary B. Cohen, *The Politics of Ethnic Survival: Germans in Prague, 1861-1914*, 2nd ed. (West Lafayette, IN: Purdue University Press, 2006); Pieter M. Judson, *Exclusive Revolutionaries: Liberal Politics, Social Experience, and National Identity in the Austrian Empire 1848-1914* (Ann Arbor: University of Michigan Press, 1996); Jeremy King, *Budweisers into Czechs and Germans: A Local History of Bohemian Politics, 1848-1948* (Princeton, NJ: Princeton University Press, 2002); Mikuláš Teich, *Bohemia in History* (Cam-

bridge: Cambridge University Press, 1998); Elizabeth Wiskemann, *Czechs and Germans: A Study of the Struggles in the Historic Provinces of Bohemia and Moravia* (New York: Oxford University Press, 1938).

13. Rogers Brubaker, *Ethnicity without Groups* (Cambridge, MA: Harvard University Press, 2006), 2. According to Brubaker, "By invoking groups, they [the entrepreneurs] seek to evoke them [groups] . . . reifying groups is precisely what ethnopolitical entrepreneurs are in the business of doing. When they are successful, the political fiction of the unified group can be momentarily yet powerfully realized in practice" (ibid., 10).

14. Pieter M. Judson, *Guardians of the Nation: Activists on the Language Frontiers of Imperial Austria* (Cambridge, MA: Harvard University Press, 2006).

15. Kohn, *Living in a World Revolution*, 9-10.

16. Ibid., 3. For examples of newer scholarship on Habsburg political identities, see Laurence Cole and Daniel Unowsky, eds. *The Limits of Loyalty: Imperial Symbolism, Popular Allegiances, and State Patriotism in the Late Habsburg Monarchy* (New York: Berghahn, 2007); Pieter M. Judson and Marsha L. Rozenblit, eds. *Constructing Nationalities in East Central Europe* (New York: Berghahn, 2005); Fredrik Lindström, *Empire and Identity: Biographies of the Austrian State Problem in the Late Habsburg Empire* (West Lafayette, IN: Purdue University Press, 2008). See also Dominique K. Reill, *Nationalists Who Feared the Nation: Adriatic Multi-Nationalism in Habsburg Dalmatia, Trieste, and Venice* (Stanford, CA: Stanford University Press, 2012).

17. Kohn, *Living in a World Revolution*, 10.

18. Ibid., 18.

19. Adolf Fischhof, "Austria and the Guarantee of Its Existence," in *Modernism: The Creation of Nation States*, edited by Ahmet Ersoy, Maciej Górny, and Vangelis Kechriotis (Budapest: Central European Press, 2010), 34-42.

20. Karl Renner, "State and Nation," in *Modernism*, edited by Ersoy, Górny, and Kechriotis, 104.

21. David Sorkin, "The Genesis of the Ideology of Emancipation: 1806-1840," *Leo Baeck Institute Yearbook* 32 (1987): 11-40.

22. Kieval, *Languages of Community*, 30. Two classic studies of the nationality status of Habsburg Jews are Kurt Stillschweig, "Die nationalitätenrechtliche Stellung der Juden im alten Österreich," *Monatsschrift für Geschichte und Wissenschaft des Judentums* 81, no. 4 (1937): 321-40; Gerald Stourzh, "Galten die Juden als Nationalität Altösterreichs? Ein Beitrag zur Geschichte des cisleithanischen Nationalitätenrechts," *Studia Judaica Austriaca* 10 (1984): 73-116.

23. Kieval, *The Making of Czech Jewry*, 4.

24. Tara Zahra, *Kidnapped Souls: National Indifference and the Battle for Children in the Bohemian Lands, 1900-1948* (Ithaca, NY: Cornell University Press, 2008). See also Čapková, *Czechs, Germans, Jews?*; Cole and Unowsky, *Limits of Loyalty*; Judson, *Exclusive Revolutionaries* and *Guardians of the Nation*; Judson and Rozenblit, *Constructing Nationalities in East Central Europe*; King, *Budweisers into Czechs and Germans*; Lindström, *Empire and Identity*; Marsha L. Rozenblit, *Reconstructing a National Identity: The Jews of Habsburg*

Austria during World War I (New York: Oxford University Press, 2001); Dimitry Shumsky, *Ben Prag Liyerushalayim: Tsiyonut Prag Ve-Ra'ayon Hamedinah Hadule'umit Beerets-Yiśra'el* (Jerusalem: Mekhon Leo Baeck, 2009).

25. Kohn, *Living in a World Revolution*, 67.

26. Ibid. See also ibid., 70 and 76; Cohen, *Politics of Ethnic Survival.*

27. Dimitry Shumsky, "Historiografiya, Leumiyut Veduleumiyut: Yahadut Tcheho-Germanit, Tsiyoney Prag Vemekorot Hagisha Haduleumit Shel Hugo Bergmann," *Zion* 69, no. 1 (2004): 62–63. See also Kohn, *Living in a World Revolution*, 35; Cohen, *Politics of Ethnic Survival*, 248.

28. *Meldungsbuch*, October 1910, HKC-LBI, box 25, folder 5. Kohn's military service journal, issued in Prague, May 9, 1925, in the same collection, registered Kohn as a Czech speaker. Tellingly, however, his diaries attest that when he read Czech poetry (for example, by Otokar Fischer) he did so in German translation (diary, March 20, 1937, same collection, box 19, folder 3).

29. Kohn, *Living in a World Revolution*, 10; see also 67.

30. Ibid., 37 and 39. Kohn's archives include many documents regarding his parents, yet none seems to indicate any Jewish communal engagement on their part (see HKC-LBI, box 24). Furthermore, in 1931 Kohn described his upbringing as remarkably un-Jewish: "Hans Kohn said that ... he had come from an assimilationist background. At every Christmas there was a Yule tree in his home and they sang Christmas songs" (Mordecai M. Kaplan, *Communings of the Spirit: The Journals of Mordecai M. Kaplan* [Detroit, MI: Wayne State University Press, 2001], 465–66).

31. Hans Kohn, "Before 1918 in the Historic Lands," in Society for the History of Czechoslovak Jews, *The Jews of Czechoslovakia*, 1:19.

32. For Kohn's transcripts, see *Meldungsbücher*, HKC-LBI, box 25, folder 5. Kohn described Buber's early Zionist work (around 1900) this way: "That nationalism of inwardness is a gratifying self-discovery and self-actualization" (*Martin Buber*, 50–51). There was a striking divergence between the neoromantic, idealist, irrationalist worldview that Kohn was attracted to and the philosophy of his professors, which he described thus: "They rejected all post-Kantian idealism . . . and all forms of mysticism. The true method of philosophy, for them, was that of the natural sciences" (*Living in a World Revolution*, 57–58).

33. Michael A. Meyer, "Liberal Judaism and Zionism in Germany," in *Zionism and Religion*, edited by Shmuel Almog, Jehuda Reinharz, and Anita Shapira (Hanover, NH: University Press of New England, 1998), 93–106.

34. Robert Weltsch, "Theodor Herzl und Wir," in *Vom Judentum: Ein Sammelbuch*, edited by Hans Kohn (Leipzig: Kurt Wolff, 1913), 157–58.

35. Martin Buber, "Judaism and the Jews," in Martin Buber, *On Judaism*, edited by Nahum N. Glatzer, translated by Eva Jospe (New York: Schocken, 1967), 12; Hans Kohn to Martin Buber, December 10, 1929, in Martin Buber, *The Letters of Martin Buber: A Life of Dialogue*, edited by Nahum N. Glatzer and Paul Mendes-Flohr and translated by Richard Winston, Clara Winston, and Harry Zohn (New York: Schocken, 1991), 372–73.

36. Hans Kohn, "Der Geist des Orients," in *Vom Judentum*, 9.

37. Kohn, *Living in a World Revolution*, 67. See also Kieval, *The Making of Czech Jewry*, 102; *Vom Judentum*.

38. Kohn, *Martin Buber*, 64.

39. Kohn, *Living in a World Revolution*, 65.

40. Whereas Michael Mack pointed to "inner anti-Semitism" in the philosophy of German idealism and to multiple Jewish responses to it (*German Idealism and the Jew: The Inner Anti-Semitism of Philosophy and German Jewish Responses* [Chicago: University of Chicago Press, 2003]), Manfred Voigts saw Fichte as a "prophet" of the Central European cultural Zionists ("Fichte as 'Jew-Hater' and Prophet of the Zionists," *Leo Baeck Institute Yearbook* 45 [2000]: 81–91; and *Wir sollen alle kleine Fichtes werden! Johann Gottlieb Fichte als Prophet der Kultur-Zionisten* [Berlin: Philo, 2003]).

41. Kohn, *Nationalismus*, 116. To be sure, Fichte, contrary to popular belief, did not advocate the creation of a unified German nation-state per se; he continued to see the state as a way to achieve the goal of national growth, and not as an end in itself. Furthermore, his addresses repeatedly stressed the distinction between nation and state. Yet even after all these qualifiers, Fichte established a link between the two. For example, his sixth address claimed that "the establishment of the perfect state" could be achieved only by "the nation that has first solved in actual practice the problem of educating perfect men" (Johann Gottlieb Fichte, *Addresses to the German Nation*, translated by Reginald Foy Jones and George Henry Turnbull [Chicago: Open Court, 1922], 102). See also Sven-Erik Rose, *Jewish Philosophical Politics in Germany, 1789-1848* (Waltham, MA: Brandeis University Press, 2014), especially chapter 1.

42. George L. Mosse, *German Jews beyond Judaism* (Bloomington: Indiana University Press, 1985), 44. See also Robert Weltsch, "Zum Fichte-Jubiläum," *Die Welt*, June 7, 1912.

43. Hans Kohn, "The Paradox of Fichte's Nationalism," *Journal of the History of Ideas* 10, no. 3 (1949): 336.

44. Quoted in Voigts, "Fichte as Jew-Hater and Prophet," 85–86.

45. Kohn, "Der Geist des Orients," 12. Kohn elaborated on the same points—the early transition from a diasporic Jewry lacking idealism to the participation of Jewish philosophers in the new kind of idealism all across Europe, in "Jüdische Philosophen," *Die Welt*, March 21, 1913. One of the contemporaneous Zionist books that impressed Kohn most was Daniel S. Pasmanik's *Die Seele Israels* (The soul of the Jews), which stated in a similar vein that the diasporic Jews of the present had "lost their idealism" (*Die Seele Israels: Zur Psychologie Des Diasporajudentums* [Cologne: Jüdischer Verlag, 1911], 74). For a recent discussion of Pasmanik, see Taro Tsurumi, "Jewish Liberal, Russian Conservative: Daniel Pasmanik between Zionism and the Anti-Bolshevik White Movement," *Jewish Social Studies* 21, no. 1 (2015), 151–80.

46. Hans Kohn to Martin Buber, June 7, 1912, MBA, Arc. Ms. Var. 376.2.

47. Hans Kohn to Martin Buber, April 1, 1913, MBA, Arc. Ms. Var. 376.21. Kohn had already stated this in his Bar Kochba lecture "Über den Begriff der 'Erneuerung' des Judentums und unsere Gegenwart," on June 15, 1912. See Kohn's 1912 notebook, HKC-LBI, box 1, folder 16.

48. Rudolf Eucken, *Christianity and the New Idealism: A Study in the Religious Philoso-*

phy of To-Day, translated by Lucy Judge Gibson and W. R. Boyce Gibson (London: Harper and Brothers, 1909).

49. Kohn, "Jüdische Philosophen." See also Hans Kohn, "Skizze zu einer Rede gehalten 2.2.1912," HKC-LBI box 1, folder 16; Kohn, "Der Zionismus und die Religion II," *Zionistische Briefe*, June 1912 (HKC-Klau, Bar Kochba box); Yotam Hotam, *Modern Gnosis and Zionism: The Crisis of Culture, Life Philosophy, and Jewish National Thought* (London: Routledge, 2013). For a recent major contribution to the field of the history of Lebensphilosophie, see Nitzan Lebovic, *The Philosophy of Life and Death: Ludwig Klages and the Rise of a Nazi Biopolitics* (New York: Palgrave Macmillan, 2013), especially chapter 1 (which addresses the connection between German idealism and Lebensphilosophie). On Lebensphilosophie as "New Idealism," see Fritz K. Ringer, *The Decline of the German Mandarins: The German Academic Community, 1890-1933* (Cambridge, MA: Harvard University Press, 1969), 195-97 and 301.

50. Before Kohn's days in the association, however, the spirit of heroism was there. See, for example, Julius Loewy, "Bethar—Basel," *Neue Wege* (a 1903 Bar Kochba publication), HKC-Klau, Bar Kochba box.

51. R[obert] W[eltsch]. "Bar Kochba Verein der jüdischen Hochschüler in Prag," in *Jüdisches Lexikon: ein enzyklopädisches Handbuch des jüdischen Wissens*, edited by Georg Herlitz and Bruno Kirschen (Berlin: Jüdischer Verlag, 1927), 1:725-26.

52. Kohn, *Martin Buber*, 314. Their understanding of the term "renaissance" was already broader than Buber's own 1903 definition:

We are speaking of the Jewish Renaissance. By this we understand the peculiar and basically inexplicable phenomenon of the progressive rejuvenation of the Jewish people in language, customs, and art. We justifiably call it "Renaissance" because it resembles—in the transfer of human fate to national fate—the great period that we call Renaissance above all others, because it is a rebirth, a renewal of the entire human being like this Renaissance, and not a return to old ideas and life forms, [it is] the path from semi-being to being, from vegetation to productivity, from the dialectical petrification of scholasticism to a warm, flowing feeling of life, from the constraints of narrow-minded communities to the freedom of the personality, the way from volcanic, formless cultural potential to a harmonious, beautifully formed cultural product. ("The Jewish Cultural Problem and Zionism," in Martin Buber, *The First Buber: Youthful Zionist Writings of Martin Buber*, edited by Gilya G. Schmidt [Syracuse, NY: Syracuse University Press, 1999], 176)

53. Asher D. Biemann, *Inventing New Beginnings: On the Idea of Renaissance in Modern Judaism* (Stanford, CA: Stanford University Press, 2009), 8. See also Kohn, *Martin Buber*, 314.

54. John Plamenatz, "Two Types of Nationalism," in *Nationalism: The Nature and Evolution of an Idea*, edited by Eugene Kamenka (Canberra: Australian National University Press, 1973), 23-36.

55. Inka Bertz, "Jüdische Renaissance," in *Handbuch der deutschen Reformbewegungen 1880-1933*, edited by Diethart Kerbs and Jürgen Reulecke (Wuppertal, Germany: P. Hammer, 1998), 551-64. See also Inka Bertz, "Jewish Renaissance—Jewish Modernism," in *Berlin*

Metropolis: Jews and the New Culture, 1890–1918, edited by Emily D. Bilsky (Berkeley: University of California Press, 1999), 165–87.

56. Franz Kafka, "Letter to His Father," in Franz Kafka, *Dearest Father: Stories and Other Writings*, translated by Ernst Kaiser and Eithne Wilkins (New York: Schocken, 1954), 171–72. Tellingly, Kafka's letter also describes his turning to Judaism as a young adult, just as Kohn and his young friends did.

57. Robert Weltsch, *An der Wende des Modernen Judentums: Betrachtungen aus fünf Jahrzehnten* (Tübingen, Germany: Mohr, 1972), 282.

58. David Rechter, "Autonomy and Its Discontents: The Austrian Jewish Congress Movement, 1917–1918," in *Literary Strategies: Jewish Texts and Contexts*, edited by Ezra Mendelsohn (New York: Oxford University Press, 1996), 162.

59. Kohn, *Living in a World Revolution*, 121.

60. Kieval, *The Making of Czech Jewry*, 106–7.

61. Hans Kohn to Martin Buber, September 22, 1911, MBA, Arc. Ms. Var. 376.1. Though the two men had met two years before, this is the earliest letter between them in all the pertinent archives, and its formal tone suggests this was indeed the first letter between Buber and his future biographer.

62. Kohn, "Der Geist des Orients," 17.

63. Hans Kohn, "Der Zionismus und die Religion [I]," *Zionistische Briefe*, May 1912. A longer extract is: "Der Zionismus wird endgueltig mit der Phrase brechen muessen die 'Religion sei Privatsache.' ... Der Zionismus muss den Kampf aufnehmen mit der heutigen juedischen traditionellen Religionsform, weil die heutige Form eben nur leere Form ist mit nichtigen Worten, deren schwere Folgen aber eine Immoralitaet ist, die von hier ausgehend, das ganze jüdische Leben der Gegenwart ergreift, und der aergste Gegner jeder Erneuerung ist."

64. Martin Buber, "Jewish Religiosity" (1923), in Martin Buber, *The Martin Buber Reader: Essential Writings*, edited by Asher D. Biemann (New York: Palgrave Macmillan, 2002), 115.

65. Zohar Maor, *Torat Sod Hadashah: Ruhaniyut, Yetsirah Ule'umiyut Behug Prag* (Jerusalem: Merkaz Zalman Shazar letoldot Yisrael, 2010).

66. This work seems to have been interrupted by the outbreak of the war and by Kohn's enlistment in the Austro-Hungarian army. For an early draft of Kohn's introduction to and selection of items for the anthology, see Notebook F (1912–14), 44–71, HKC-LBI, box 23, folder 1. Kohn's memoirs mention this unfinished project (*Living in a World Revolution*, 63–64). He also linked mysticism and the contemporaneous crisis of language (*Krisis der Sprache*) in one of his Bar Kochba talks ("Skizze zu einer Rede gehalten 2.2.1912," HKC-LBI box 1, folder 16).

67. Hans Kohn to Robert Weltsch, July 4, 1911, RWC box 1, folder 33. In the ecstatic mystic, the individual experiences a union with the divine. Jewish national redemption, similarly, relies on the chosen people's reconnection with their inner image of God and subsequent assumption of their role in universal redemption.

68. Shai Hurwitz, "Hahasiduth ve Hahaskala," *He'atid* 2 (1909): 94–99. On Shai Hurwitz (Saul Israel Hurwitz), see Stanley Nash, *In Search of Hebraism: Shai Hurwitz and His Polemics in the Hebrew Press* (Leiden, the Netherlands: E. J. Brill, 1980). I thank Noam Zadoff for this essential reference.

69. Hans Kohn, "Feuilleton: Sabbatai Zewi," *Selbstwehr*, July 21, 1911. Kohn returned in other early publications to the positive, vital qualities of Tsevi and Sabbatianism: the creative and unifying desire for redemption and a redeemer. See, for example, Kohn, "Feuilleton: Der Literat," *Selbstwehr*, September 20, 1912.

70. Kohn, "Über den Begriff der 'Erneuerung' des Judentums und unsere Gegenwart," 9. See also Martin Buber, "Der Mythos der Juden," in *Vom Judentum*, 31; Hugo Bergmann, "Die Heiligung des Namens," in ibid., 39; Elijahu Rappeport, "Jeschualegenden," in ibid., 44–48.

71. Kohn wrote: "Wir wollen die Revolutionierung der Judenheit . . . aus der eine neue Religion kommen muss" ("Der Geist des Orients," 17). He had conveyed the very same ideas, for example, in the final sentences of a letter to Robert Weltsch a year earlier (July 4, 1911, RWC, box 1, folder 33).

72. For one of the finest recent discussions of the relationship between religion and nationalism, see Rogers Brubaker, "Religion and Nationalism: Four Approaches," *Nations and Nationalism* 18, no. 1 (2011), 1–19.

73. Friedrich Nietzsche, *Kritische Studienausgabe*, vol. 10: *Nachlass 1882–1884*, edited by Giorgio Colli and Mazzino Montinari (Berlin: de Gruyter, 1999), 86.

74. Kohn, *Living in a World Revolution*, 199 and 206.

75. Henrik Ibsen, *Peer Gynt: A Dramatic Poem*, translated with an introduction by Peter Watts (London: Penguin, 1966), 23 and 201 (emphasis in the original).

76. Tellingly, Kohn was not alone in feeling these connections: his friend Bergmann named *Peer Gynt* as one of the major inspirations for Prague Zionism (Shmuel Hugo Bergmann, *Hogim Uma'aminim: Massot* [Tel Aviv: Agudat Hasofrim Ha'ivrim Leyad Devir, 1959] 196). Kohn was also familiar with Otto Weininger's discussion of Peer Gynt, as laid out in the latter's posthumous *On Last Things: A Translation of Weininger's* Über die letzten Dinge (*1904–1907*), translated by Steven A. M. Burns (Lewiston, NY: E. Mellen Press, 2001).

77. Michael Brenner, *The Renaissance of Jewish Culture in Weimar Germany* (New Haven, CT: Yale University Press, 1996).

78. Schmuel Hugo Bergmann to Franz Kafka, undated 1902–03, in Bergmann, *Tagebücher und Briefe*, edited by Miriam Sambursky (Königstein, Germany: Jüdischer Verlag bei Athenäum, 1985), 1:9.

79. Schmuel Hugo Bergmann to Carl Stumpf, undated (probably from 1914 before the outbreak of war), in ibid., 49. Remarkably, Bergmann also claimed there that many Jews had "lost their spiritual equilibrium" following emancipation: "Jews are not organically grown into the European culture; they have only appropriated its [European culture's] *results*, as in 1789 [the French Revolution] or 1848 [the Spring of Nations]," in which they started seeing themselves, and being seen by some of their neighbors, as a part of the people. (ibid., emphasis in the original).

80. Kenneth H. Wolf, "The Idea of Nationalism: The Intellectual Development and Historiographical Contribution of Hans Kohn" (PhD diss., University of Notre Dame 1972), 34.

81. Based on his prewar publications, one could assume that Robert Weltsch—who did attempt to write theoretically and comparatively on nationalism—not Kohn, would become

the nationalism scholar. Kohn donated an extensive archive of Bar Kochba publications and correspondence to the Hebrew Union College (see HKC-Klau, Bar Kochba box).

82. Boaz Neumann, *Land and Desire in Early Zionism* (Waltham, MA: Brandeis University Press, 2011).

83. See Spector, *Prague Territories*, 135-59, especially 158; Shumsky, *Ben Prag Liyerus-halayim*.

84. Statutes of the Bar Kochba Association, n.d., HKC-Klau, Bar Kochba box.

85. For the original, unedited text of the address, see Martin Buber, "Das Judentum und die Menschheit," April 3, 1910, 10, HKC-Klau, Bar Kochba box. For the edited English translation, see Buber, "Judaism and Mankind," in Buber, *On Judaism*, 29-30.

86. Activity report of Bar Kochba Association, winter semester 1909-10, HKC-Klau, Bar Kochba box. In the words of the report: "Ein reiner, ganzer, gefundener und glücklicher Jude wird, ein Mensch ohne Riss und Zwiespalt, dabei voll freudiger Zukunftsgewissheit" (ibid., 12).

87. For the original, unedited text of the address, see Martin Buber, "Die Erneuerung des Judentums," HKC-Klau, Bar Kochba box.

88. Kohn, "Über den Begriff der 'Erneuerung' des Judentums und unsere Gegenwart."

89. Prof. Dr. [Benzion] Mossinson, "Palästina in der jüdischen Geschichte und Literatur," *Zionistische Briefe*, November 1911, HKC-Klau, Bar Kochba box.

90. Buber, "Judaism and the Jews," 17 and 16.

91. Kohn, "Der Geist des Orients," 16-17.

92. It also echoes Buber's bold claim that the occidental is "a sensory-type man," while the oriental (including the Jew) is "a motor-type man" ("The Spirit of the Orient and Judaism," in Buber, *On Judaism*, 58; see also 57, 64, and 73). See also Martin Buber, "The Renewal of Judaism," in Buber, *On Judaism*, 34-55, especially 44-49.

93. Kohn, "Der Geist des Orients," 9 and 16. He expressed very similar statements in his review of Jakob Wassermann's *Der Literat oder Mythos und Persönlichkeit* ("Feuilleton: Der Literat").

94. The concept of East and West in Jewish history, of course, is a vast and multidimensional topic in itself. See. for example, Yitzhak Conforti, "East and West in Jewish Nationalism: Conflicting Types in the Zionist Vision?" *Nations and Nationalism* 16, no. 2 (2010): 201-19; Jonathan Frankel, introduction to *Assimilation and Community: The Jews in Nineteenth-Century Europe*, edited by Jonathan Frankel and Steven J. Zipperstein (Cambridge: Cambridge University Press, 1992), 1-37; Steven Lowenstein, "The Shifting Boundary between Eastern and Western Jewry," *Jewish Social Studies* 4, no. 1 (1997): 60-78; Guy Miron, "Between 'Center' and 'East': The Special Way of Jewish Emancipation in Hungary," *Jewish Studies at the CEU* 4 (2004-5): 111-38. Both Mathias Acher [Nathan Birnbaum] and Robert Weltsch took this East-West dichotomy into the Jewish world in their respective Bar Kochba talks in winter 1911, Acher on Eastern and Western Jewry and Weltsch on Zionism and the Western Jew. For more on these talks, see the activity report of the Bar Kochba Association, winter semester 1911-12, 5, HKC-Klau, Bar Kochba box.

95. Paul R. Mendes-Flohr, *Divided Passions: Jewish Intellectuals and the Experience of Modernity* (Detroit: Wayne State University Press, 1991), chapter 4.

96. Quoted in Maor, *Torat Sod Hadashah*, 150.

97. Hugo B[ergmann], "Über die Bedeutung des Hebräischen für die jüdische Jugend," *Zionistische Briefe*, December 1910, HKC-Klau, Bar Kochba box, 3–8.

98. Ibid., 4–5. See also the activity report of the Bar Kochba Association, winter semester 1910–11, HKC-Klau, Bar Kochba box, 1.

99. Siegmund Katznelson, "Weltanschauung und Partei," *Zionistische Briefe*, March 1911, HKC-Klau, Bar Kochba box.

100. Nathan Birnbaum, "Das Erwachen der jüdischen Seele," in *Vom Judentum*, 240.

101. Kohn, "Der Zionismus und die Religion II," 9.

102. Kohn, "Jüdische Philosophen."

103. Quoted in Voigts, "Fichte as Jew-Hater and Prophet," 85–86.

104. Hans Kohn to Martin Buber, January 31, 1913, MBA, Arc. Ms. Var. 376, 22. Kohn wrote: "*die Notwendigkeit, das metaphysische Bar Kochba gegenüber dem empirischen zu halten.*"

105. Quoted in Kohn, *Martin Buber*, 315.

106. Etan Bloom, *Arthur Ruppin and the Production of Pre-Israeli Culture* (Leiden, the Netherlands: Brill, 2011), and "What 'the Father' Had in Mind? Arthur Ruppin (1876–1943), Cultural Identity, Weltanschauung, and Action," *History of European Ideas* 33, no. 3 (2007): 330–49; John M. Efron, *Defenders of the Race: Jewish Doctors and Race Science in Fin-de-Siècle Europe* (New Haven, CT: Yale University Press, 1994); Rapael Falk, *Tsiyonut Veha-biyologyah Shel Hayehudim* (Tel Aviv: Resling, 2006); Mitchell B. Hart, *Social Science and the Politics of Modern Jewish Identity* (Stanford, CA: Stanford University Press, 2000), *The Healthy Jew: The Symbiosis of Judaism and Modern Medicine* (New York: Cambridge University Press, 2007), *Jewish Blood: Reality and Metaphor in History, Religion, and Culture* (London: Routledge, 2009), and *Jews and Race: Writings on Identity and Difference, 1880–1940* (Waltham, MA: Brandeis University Press, 2011), edited by Hart; Amos Morris-Reich, "Race, Ideas, and Ideals: A Comparison of Franz Boas and Hans F. K. Günther," *History of European Ideas* 32, no. 3 (2006): 313–32.

107. Gil Anidjar blurb on the back cover of Hart, *Jews and Race*.

108. Sievert P. Blom, *Martin Buber and the Spiritual Revolution of the Prague Bar Kochba: Nationalist Rhetoric and the Politics of Beauty* (PhD thesis, University of Oxford, 1996). See also Mark H. Gelber, *Melancholy Pride: Nation, Race, and Gender in the German Literature of Cultural Zionism* (Tübingen, Germany: M. Niemeyer, 2000), 125–60; George L. Mosse, "The Influence of the Völkisch Idea on German Jewry," in *Studies of the Leo Baeck Institute*, edited by Max Kreutzberger (New York: Frederik Unger, 1967), 81–115.

109. Franz Rosenzweig, *The Star of Redemption*, translated by Barbara E. Galli (Madison: University of Wisconsin Press, 2005), 317–18.

110. Mitchell B. Hart, "Jews and Race: An Introductory Essay," in *Jews and Race*, xxiv.

111. Hans Kohn, "Geleitwort," in *Vom Judentum*, vii.; Robert Weltsch, "Gelegentlich einer Rassentheorie," *Die Welt* 17, no. 12 (1913): 365–67.

112. Activity report of the Bar Kochba association, winter semester 1908–9, HKC-Klau, Bar Kochba box.

113. Hugo Salus, "Das Lied des Blutes," in Hugo Salus, *Glockenklang: Gedichte* (Munich: Langen, 1911), 50-51.

114. Martin Buber, "Der Sinn des Judentums," January 20, 1909, HKC-Klau, Bar Kochba box. Buber edited the address twice; its latest form is "Judaism and the Jews."

115. Buber, "Die Erneuerung des Judentums."

116. Willy Stein, "Wir und unsere Geschichte," *Zionistische Briefe*, February 1911, HKC-Klau, Bar Kochba box, 6.

117. Robert Weltsch, "Ein Brief an einen jüdischen Abiturienten," *Zionistische Briefe*, June 1912, 6, HKC-Klau, Bar Kochba box, 6-7.

118. "Stimmen des Blutes," *Zionistische Briefe*, June 1912, 13-14, HKC-Klau, Bar Kochba box.

119. Kohn, "Der Geist des Orients," 18.

120. Activity report of the Bar Kochba Association, winter semester 1910-11, 5, HKC-Klau, Bar Kochba box. Hermann's racialist language is documented in a letter to Zollschan quoted in Joachim Doron, "Rassenbewusstsein und naturwissenschaftliches Denken im deutschen Zionismus während der Wilhelminischen Ära," *Tel-Aviver Jahrbuch für Deutsche Geschichte* 9 (1980): 408.

121. Activity report of the Bar Kochba Association, winter semester 1909-10, HKC-Klau, Bar Kochba box, 8; activity report of the Bar Kochba Association, summer 1910, ibid., 11.

122. Oskar Epstein, "Was bedeutet die Rasse für uns? Nach Zollschan, Das Rassenproblem," *Zionistische Briefe*, February-March 1911, HKC-Klau, Bar Kochba box, 1-3. See also Snait Gissis and Eva Jablonka, eds. *Transformations of Lamarckism: From Subtle Fluids to Molecular Biology* (Cambridge, MA: MIT Press, 2011).

123. Robert Weltsch, "Concerning Racial Theory," in *Jews and Race*, 250 and 253.

124. Hans Kohn, "Bücher zur Geschichte und Literatur des Judentums," *Selbstwehr*, November 15, 1912, 9.

125. Kohn, "Geleitwort," vii.

126. Iris Bruce, *Kafka and Cultural Zionism: Dates in Palestine* (Madison: University of Wisconsin Press, 2007); Mark H. Gelber, *Melancholy Pride: Nation, Race, and Gender in the German Literature of Cultural Zionism* (Tübingen, Germany: M. Niemeyer, 2000); Mendes-Flohr, *Divided Passions*; Ritchie Robertson, *The "Jewish Question" in German Literature, 1749-1939: Emancipation and Its Discontents* (Oxford: Oxford University Press, 1999); Na'ama Rokem, *Prosaic Conditions: Heinrich Heine and the Spaces of Zionist Literature* (Evanston, IL: Northwestern University Press, 2013).

127. For an extensive collection of Bar Kochba publications and activity reports, see KHC-Klau, Bar Kochba box.

128. One such evening is mentioned in the activity report of Bar Kochba Association, winter semester 1910-11. The activity report for the winter semester 1911-12 mentions the festive Bar Kochba evening dedicated to "The Song of the Eastern European Jews" (for these reports and programs for such events from December 9, 1912, and January 21, 1914, for example, see KHC-Klau, Bar Kochba box.

129. Adolf Böhm, "Jüdische Romantik," in *Vom Judentum*, 150.

130. Siegmund Katznelson, "Die Assimilation," *Zionistische Briefe*, March 1912, 6–7; Robert Weltsch, "Theodor Herzl und wir," in *Vom Judentum*, 158; Ernst Klinger, "Kultur und Zivilisation," *Zionistische Briefe*, November 1912, HKC-Klau, Bar Kochba box.

131. Berthold Feiwel, "Die Einwirkung der neu-juedischen Bewegung auf das Judentum: Ein Vortrag," January 18, 1910, HKC-Klau, Bar Kochba box.

132. Stein, "Wir und unsere Geschichte." Stein was interested in the construction of Jewish knowledge. The activity report of Bar Kochba Association, winter semester 1909–10, mentions a double lecture he delivered on "Jüdische Altertumswissenschaft," stressing the need for a Jewish national perspective in a field dominated by Christian scholars, and a lecture he delivered on Hermann Cohen's understanding of Judaism (HKC-Klau, Bar Kochba box.). And he published "Wissenschaft des Judentums," *Zionistische Briefe*, November 1911, 2–5.

133. Hans Kohn, "Feuilleton. Chinesische Philosophen," *Selbstwehr*, October 18, 1912, 9. Kohn wrote: "Es ist ein Verhängnis, dass diese alte wahrhaftige Kultur . . . heute in Brüche zu gehen droht, dass Sie ihre Tradition und ihre Kontinuität abbrechen, um unvermeidlicherweise—wie die Juden vor hundert Jahren in die Rolle des Parvenus zu verfallen . . . dass sie ihre grossen Denker vergessen, um dafür Kanonen, Biergärten und 'allgemeine Bildung' sich anzueignen."

134. B[ergmann], "Über die Bedeutung des Hebräischen für die jüdische Jugend."

135. Moritz Goldstein, "Wir und Europa," in *Vom Judentum*, 204.

136. John E. Toews, "Refashioning the Masculine Subject in Early Modernism: Narratives of Self-Dissolution and Self-Construction in Psychoanalysis and Literature, 1900–1914," *Modernism/Modernity* 4, no. 1 (1997): 48–49. See also Felix W. Tweraser, "Leo Golowski as Minor Key in Schnitzler's 'Der Weg ins Freie': Musical Theory, Political Behaviour, and Ethical Action," *Austrian Studies* 17 (2009), 98–112.

137. Hans Kohn, "Der Weg ins Freie: Roman von Arthur Schnitzler," *Zionistische Briefe*, December 1910, 13–14, HKC-Klau, Bar Kochba box. Kohn's admiration of Schnitzler may have something to do with Buber's own interest in the author. See Gilya G. Schmidt, *Martin Buber's Formative Years: From German Culture to Jewish Renewal, 1897–1909* (Tuscaloosa: University of Alabama Press, 1995), 5–20.

138. Arthur Schnitzler, *The Road into the Open*, translated by Roger Byers (Berkeley: University of California Press, 1992), 183.

139. Jakob Wassermann, *Der Literat; oder, Mythos und Persönlichkeit* (Leipzig: Insel Verlag, 1910); Kohn, "Feuilleton: Der Literat." Kohn adopted and developed Wassermann's characterization of the Jew as oriental.

140. Jakob Wassermann, "Der Jude als Orientale," in *Vom Judentum*, 7.

141. Gershon Shaked, *Zehut: Sifruyot Yehudiyot Bileshonot La'az* (Haifa: Haifa University Press, 2006), 257–65.

142. Shmuel Hugo Bergmann, *Hogim Uma'aminim: Massot* (Tel Aviv: Agudat Hasofrim Ha'ivrim Leyad Devir, 1959), 196; activity report of of the Bar Kochba Association, winter semester 1910–11, HKC-Klau, Bar Kochba box.

143. Otto Weininger, *Sex and Character*, translated by Ladislaus Loeb (Bloomington: Indiana University Press, 2005), 290.

144. Mendes-Flohr, *Divided Passions*, 89 and 216. There were clear literary expressions of auto-antisemitism also in Schnitzler's *The Road into the Open*: "I'm Jewish. It's a national illness with us. Decent people try to turn it into anger or rage" (143).

145. Martin Buber, in *On Judaism*, 17.

146. Ibid., 18.

147. Ibid., 19.

148. Ibid., 21.

149. B[ergmann], "Über die Bedeutung des Hebräischen für die jüdische Jugend," 7–8. This article may be based on a similarly titled article published in 1904—that is, before Buber's first address. See also Shumsky, *Ben Prag Liyerushalayim*, 329.

150. Buber, 19.

151. Landauer, "Sind das Ketzergedanken?," 256–57. The English translation is partially based on "Jewishness Is an Inalienable Spiritual Sensibility (1913)," 277.

152. "Landauer disappointed me," wrote Kohn to Buber, without spelling out the nature of his disappointment (September 8, 1913, MBA, Arc. Ms. Var. 376, 300). But Kohn would later state that he and his Bar Kochba friends "owed it to Gustav Landauer . . . that our nationalism was tempered by an emphasis on mankind" (*Living in a World Revolution*, 69).

153. Shumsky, *Ben Prag Liyerushalayim*.

154. Kohn, "Geleitwort," ix; Adolf Böhm, "Wandlungen im Zionismus," in *Vom Judentum: Ein Sammelbuch*, edited by Hans Kohn (Leipzig: Kurt Wolff, 1913), 148. Yiddish—the other Jewish national language—also belongs to this discussion. But Bar Kochba's members' interest in Yiddish seemed limited to Jewish folklore and popular culture. Hebrew received greater intellectual and political reverence from them.

155. Eric J. Hobsbawm, "Ethnicity and Nationalism in Europe Today," in *Mapping the Nation*, edited by Gopal Balakrishnan (London: Verso, 1996), 255.

156. In addition to the articles by Willy Stein cited above, see his short "Unsere Geschichte" in *Vom Judentum*, 135–38.

157. Kohn, "Bücher zur Geschichte und Literatur des Judentums," 9.

158. Two major contributions to the interpretation of the Zionist fascination with Jesus appeared in recent years: Tsvi Sadan, *Basar Mibsarenu: Yeshua Minatsrat Bahagut Hatsiyonit* (Jerusalem: Carmel, 2008); Neta Stahl, *Other and Brother: Jesus in the 20th-Century Jewish Literary Landscape* (Oxford: Oxford University Press, 2013).

159. Kohn, *Living in a World Revolution*, 66–68.

160. Hans Kohn, *World Order in Historical Perspective* (Cambridge, MA: Harvard University Press, 1942), 93; and *The Idea of Nationalism: A Study in Its Origins and Background* (New York: Macmillan Company, 1944), 10.

161. Leora F. Batnitzky, *How Judaism Became a Religion: An Introduction to Modern Jewish Thought* (Princeton, NJ: Princeton University Press, 2011), especially chapters 2 and 4.

162. *Stenographisches Protokoll der Verhandlungen des XI. Zionisten-Kongresses in Wien vom 2. bis 9 September 1913* (Berlin: Jüdischer Verlag, 1914), 327 (emphasis in the original).

163. Martin Buber to Hans Kohn, September 26, 1913, HKC-Klau, Bar Kochba box.

2. "The Decisive Years": The Great War and the Waning of Imperial World Order

1. Charles Péguy, *Notre Jeunesse* (Paris: Cahiers de la quinzaine, 1910), 27.

2. Martin Buber, *The Letters of Martin Buber: A Life of Dialogue*, edited by Nahum N. Glatzer and Paul Mendes-Flohr and translated by Richard Winston, Clara Winston, and Harry Zohn (New York: Schocken, 1991), 160.

3. Hans Kohn, *Karl Kraus, Arthur Schnitzler, Otto Weininger: Aus dem jüdischen Wien der Jahrhundertwende* (Tübingen, Germany: J. C. B. Mohr,1962), 9.

4. Hans Kohn, war diary, September 22, 1914 (rewritten by Kohn in late April 1915), HKC-LBI, box 23, folder 2.

5. Hans Kohn, *Living in a World Revolution: My Encounters with History* (New York: Trident Press, 1964), 1.

6. Hans Kohn, "Ode an Mein Volk," July 28, 1914, HKC-LBI, box 2, folder 1.

7. Jeffrey Verhey's 1991 dissertation paved the way for current historians' thinking on this point. See his published revision: *The Spirit of 1914: Militarism, Myth, and Mobilization in Germany* (New York: Cambridge University Press, 2000). See also Niall Ferguson, *The Pity of War: Explaining World War I* (New York: Basic, 1999).

8. Kohn, war diary, September 23, 1914 (misdated as 1915 when Kohn rewrote the diary in late April 1915). It is noteworthy that Kohn would later deny this Jewish agenda and claim to have volunteered purely out of "traditional patriotism" (*Living in a World Revolution*, 85).

9. The pioneering work on the formation of the modern myth of the war experience is George L. Mosse, *Fallen Soldiers: Reshaping the Memory of the World Wars* (New York: Oxford University Press, 1990).

10. Alfred Kraus to Robert Weltsch, from the Serbian front, September 25, 1914, RWC, box 1, folder 58. A dozen members of Bar Kochba fell in World War I. See Felix Weltsch, ed., *Prag vyi-Yerushalayim: Sefer Lezikhron Le'o Hermann* (Jerusalem: ha-Lishkah ha-rashit shel Keren ha-yessod, 1954), 119.

11. On September 2, 1914, Kohn wrote in his war diary: "So far it has been a big disappointment. . . . I hoped to be trained within weeks and be sent to the front. Instead they played with us. I saw aimlessness, incompetence, confusion everywhere, and above all—whoever can shirk, shirks. And no one condemns it as wrongdoing. . . . [A]ll see it as obvious. . . . Poor Austria! Or have people everywhere lost their dignity?"

12. Martin Buber, *The Letters of Martin Buber: A Life of Dialogue*, edited by Nahum N. Glatzer and Paul Mendes-Flohr and translated by Richard Winston, Clara Winston, and Harry Zohn (New York: Schocken, 1991), 160. Writing Buber's biography fifteen years later, Kohn responded to Buber's words by stating that at the war's outbreak "Der Sinn des Evangeliums . . . wurde verdeutet und verlogen [the meaning of the gospel was . . . misinterpreted and falsified]" (*Martin Buber: Sein Werk und seine Zeit: Ein Versuch über Religion und Politik* [Hellerau, Germany: J. Hegner, 1930], 141-42.

13. "Nicht allein fürs Vaterland," undated poem found in Kohn's collected notes from his military service, HKC-LBI, box 21, folder 1. The opening sentence of this poem seems to relate to the recurring sentence "*Gut und Blut fürs Vaterland*" in the Austro-Hungarian anthem (which at the time was sung to the Haydn tune that serves as the current German anthem).

Ulrich Sieg (*Jüdische Intellektuelle Im Ersten Weltkrieg: Kriegserfahrungen, Weltanschauliche Debatten Und Kulturelle Neuentwürfe* [Berlin: Akademie-Verlag, 1999], 58) assumes that the poem is by Kohn, but the handwriting and archival location suggest that it was written (or copied) by Kohn's friend Mirjam Scheuer.

14. Martin Buber, *Vom Geist des Judentums: Reden und Geleitworte* (Leipzig: Kurt Wolff, 1916), 47 ("Das deutsche Volk ist berufen. . . . Orient und Okzident zu fruchtbarer Gegenseitigkeit zu verknüpfen, wie es vielleicht berufen ist, den Geist des Orients und den Geist des Okzidents in einer neuen Lehre zu verschmelzen"). See also Buber, "The Spirit of the Orient and Judaism," in Buber, *On Judaism*, edited by Nahum N. Glatzer, translated by Eva Jospe (New York: Schocken, 1967), 56–78.

15. Kohn, *Living in a World Revolution*, 87.

16. Mirjam Scheuer to Hans Kohn, October 28, 1914, HKC-LBI, box 21, folder 1.

17. Kohn, *Living in a World Revolution*, 87–88. The quotations are from Kohn, war diary, February 1, 1915 (rewritten in late April 1915). Kohn's notes in his war diary about his time in Salzburg primarily discuss concerts, family visits, cafés, and two women: Edit Böhm and Mizzi Möser (the latter seems to have been his love interest at the time).

18. Kohn sounds somewhat bored in his letters from the front to his family. On February 20 he wrote about boredom. Two days later, he mentioned that "the war as we see it, is not as dangerous as one thinks." And two days after that, he wrote, "Only when the Russian—whom we await every night—will show up, will it be gay (*bunt*)."

19. Kohn, *Living in a World Revolution*, 90.

20. Kohn's unit had left Salzburg only a month before March 20, 1915.

21. Kohn, war diary, March 26, 1915. See also Kohn, *Living in a World Revolution*, 89–90.

22. On this the plight of Galician Jews in the wake of the Russian occupation, see Carole Fink, *Defending the Rights of Others: The Great Powers, the Jews, and International Minority Protection, 1878–1938* (New York: Cambridge University Press, 2004), 76.

23. On POWs on the Eastern Front during World War I, see Alon Rachamimov, *POWs and the Great War: Captivity on the Eastern Front* (Oxford: Oxford University Press, 2002). On the Czech Company, see ibid., 115-17; Spencer C. Tucker, "Prisoners of War," in *World War I: Encyclopedia*, edited by Spencer C. Tucker (Santa Barbara, CA: ABC-CLIO, 2005): 3:321–23.

24. Rachamimov, *POWs and the Great War*. See also an innovative recent addition to the scholarship on Turkish prisoners: Yücel Yanikdağ, *Healing the Nation: Prisoners of War, Medicine and Nationalism in Turkey, 1914–1939* (Edinburgh: Edinburgh University Press, 2013).

25. Kohn, *Living in a World Revolution*, 89–90, 90–91.

26. Kohn, war diary, July 11, 1915.

27. On inner Jewish life in the POW camp, see ibid., September 9 (Rosh Hashanah) and October 13 and 17, 1915.

28. Ibid., July 11, 1915.

29. On malaria and other aspects of the living conditions in the Samarkand camp, see Hans Kohn to his parents, May 5, 1915, HKC-LBI, box 21, folder 10. See also Kohn, war diary, July 9, 11, and 26; August 7 and 13; September 26; October 3; and November 27, 1915.

30. Tucker, "Prisoners of War," 3:321–32.

31. Kohn, war diary, August 15, 1915.

32. Hans Kohn to his parents, September 15, 1915.

33. Kohn, war diary, October 13, 1915.

34. Hans Kohn to his parents, December 22, 1915. "The house of the dead" may be an allusion to Fyodor Dostoevsky's novel of that name.

35. Hans Kohn, "Neujahr: Eine Ansprache," *Vom Judentum* [handwritten newspaper], September 1, 1918, HKC-Klau, Bar Kochba box.

36. Ibid.; Kohn, war diary, October 14, 1915.

37. Kohn, *Living in a World Revolution*, 94–95, 130. See also Kohn, war diary, October 14 and 17, 1915.

38. On Russian colonialism in Turkestan in general and in Samarkand in particular, see Adeeb Khalid, *The Politics of Muslim Cultural Reform: Jadidism in Central Asia* (Berkeley: University of California Press, 1998), especially 45–79; Alexander Morrison, *Russian Rule in Samarkand, 1868–1910: A Comparison with British India* (Oxford: Oxford University Press, 2008); Jeff Sahadeo, *Russian Colonial Society in Tashkent: 1865–1923* (Bloomington: Indiana University Press, 2007). On Russian colonialism more broadly, see Nicholas B. Breyfogle, Abby M. Schrader, and Willard Sunderland, eds., *Peopling the Russian Periphery: Borderland Colonization in Eurasian History* (London: Routledge, 2008); Willard Sunderland, *Taming the Wild Field: Colonization and Empire on the Russian Steppe* (Ithaca, NY: Cornell University Press, 2004). See also Aleksandr Etkind, *Internal Colonization: Russia's Imperial Experience* (Cambridge: Polity Press, 2011).

39. On the failure of earlier escape attempts (and bickering about the cowardice of other POWs who were afraid to try to escape), see Kohn, war diary, January 4, 1916.

40. Kohn, *Living in a World Revolution*, 95–96; Hans Kohn to Robert Weltsch, August 26, 1917, RWC, box 5, folder 10: "I had to ride [on horseback] for ten days close to the Chinese border, part of the time on rarely used mules' roads. Five days uphill, in winter, on a draft horse with a wooden saddle, while feverish with 41 degrees [106 degrees Fahrenheit] with malaria.... These were truly wonderful views and enchanted sights. They were even prettier three months later, in the spring, after having recovered, going downhill upon an exquisite Cossack [cavalry] horse with a military saddle."

41. Hans Kohn letter to Robert Weltsch, August 26, 1917, RWC, box 5, folder 10. On these months, see also Kohn, *Living in a World Revolution*, 43, 92, and 96–97. During that time, Kohn devoted himself to learning, and most of his correspondence with his family revolves around the shipping of books for him to study. See, for example, Hans Kohn to his parents, April 24 (Easter), 1916.

42. Kohn, *Living in a World Revolution*, 97. For picturesque description of his eastbound journey, see Hans Kohn to Leo Hermann, June 19, 1916, and Hans Kohn to Robert Weltsch, June 27, 1916 (transcript), CZA, Leo Hermann Collection, A145/143; and Kohn to his parents, June 17 and 18, 1916.

43. See, for example, Kohn, war diary, November 22, 1916.

44. See, for example, the November 22, 1916, reading report in Kohn's war diary, HKC-LBI, box 23, folder 1.

45. Hans Kohn to Robert Weltsch, August 26, 1917, RWC, box 5, folder 10.

46. Hans Kohn to his parents, August 26, 1916. On his foul mood in captivity, see also Kohn, war diary, October 19, 1916. For further book orders to his parents, see, for example, Hans Kohn to his parents August 27, 28, and 29; and October 20, 1916.

47. Kohn, war diary, especially 1916-17.

48. Ibid., November 4, 1916.

49. Ibid.

50. Ibid.

51. Ibid., November 25, 1916.

52. Kohn's diary mingles both personal and historical reflections on the significance of the kaiser's passing: "Today came the news of the Emperor's death. The blow was more moving than it would have been at home. It doubled one's sense of exile and captivity. How unfamiliar must everything at home have become. Since time immemorial, no one can remember any other picture than that of Franz Joseph I in school, in barracks, in court. And on the coins. And the 18th August [the emperor's birthday was a national holiday]! How linked to Europe's fate was his legendary name. When he was young, he was surrounded by men who seemed to us to have come from ancient sagas. Now the times of those ancestors seem magical and unreal to the grandchildren and great-grandchildren. His life, from coronation to death, was riddled with unrest and turmoil. Now he has found peace. Time has such a sanctifying and transfiguring effect" (war diary, November 24, 1916).

53. Kohn, war diary, 1917. See Immanuel Kant, *Toward Perpetual Peace and Other Writings on Politics, Peace, and History: Rethinking the Western Tradition*, translated by David L. Colclasure (New Haven, CT: Yale University Press, 2006); Charles Irénée Castel de Saint-Pierre, *An Abridged Version of the Project for Perpetual Peace*, translated by Carmen Depasquale (Valletta, Malta: Midsea, 2009).

54. Kant, *Toward Perpetual Peace*, 74 and 82. Kant's universalist vision, which apparently appealed to Kohn, was clearly not a pluralistic one but rather was based on a demand for a high degree of political uniformity.

55. J. G. Fichte, "Review of Immanuel Kant, *Perpetual Peace: A Philosophical Sketch*," translated by Daniel Breazeale, *Philosophical Forum* 32, no. 4 (2001): 319.

56. Mark Mazower has recently offered a broad and thought-provoking exploration of this idea and its political manifestations. See his *Governing the World: The History of an Idea* (New York: Penguin, 2012).

57. For "Revolution," a poem he wrote celebrating the event, see Kohn, war diary, March 1917.

58. Jonathan F. Vance, "Education," in *Encyclopedia of Prisoners of War and Internment*, edited by Jonathan F. Vance (Santa Barbara, CA: ABC Clio, 2000), 79; Elizabeth D. Schafer, "Music," in ibid., 195.

59. Kohn, *Living in a World Revolution*, 150-51 and 98.

60. Martin Buber to Hans Kohn, September, September 20, 1914, in Buber, *The Letters of Martin Buber*, 160. An exhaustive source about Kohn's Zionist college is Hugo Knoepf-macher, "Some Recollections of My Encounter with Hans Kohn in Siberia, 1917-1919," LBI, Hugo Knoepfmacher Collection, AR 7172. A similar report by Knoepfmacher, in letter form, found in the same collection, is titled "The Jewish Prisoners of War in Siberia." His activities at the Zionist college are surprisingly well documented, yet the documents are split among multiple archives: The Bar Kochba box in HKC-Klau holds copies of the college's handwrit-ten newspaper, *Vom Judentum*. HKC-LBI, box 23, folder 2, contains Kohn's captivity diary, April-June 1917, which lists his activities, including the topics of his lectures in the camp (many of the lectures themselves are available in the college's newspaper). Indeed, in all of his letters from the time Kohn stressed that he was doing well and was in good spirits, and all he asked for were books on Judaism, especially new publications. See Kohn to his family, March 13, April 8 and 15, May 20, August 5, and October 7 and 20, 1917. See also Michael Berkowitz, *Western Jewry and the Zionist Project, 1914-1933* (Cambridge: Cambridge University Press, 1997), 16-17.

61. The letter to Bar Kochba is a part of Hans Kohn to Robert Weltsch, August 19, 1917, RWC, box 5, folder 10.

62. Hans Kohn, "Die Erneuerung des Herzens," *Vom Judentum* [handwritten news-paper], October 15, 1917, HKC-Klau, Bar Kochba box.

63. Erez Manela, *The Wilsonian Moment: Self-Determination and the International Ori-gins of Anticolonial Nationalism* (New York: Oxford University Press, 2007), 37 and 38.

64. Hans Kohn to Martin Buber, 21 November 1917, in Martin Buber, *Martin Buber, Brief-wechsel aus sieben Jahrzehnten*, edited by Grete Schaeder (Heidelberg, Germany: L. Schnei-der, 1972), 1:510-12.

65. Ibid., 1:512.

66. Hans Kohn, "Das kulturelle Problem des modernen Westjudentum," *Vom Juden-tum* [handwritten newspaper], reprinted in *Der Jude* 5 (1920-21): 291 and 292-93. In October Kohn published a shorter essay titled "Formal and Material Nationalism," which addressed similar questions and ended with prescriptions along the lines of diaspora nationalism: the creation, already in the Diaspora, of Jewish "professional organizations, financial aid insti-tutes, national loan funds, credit unions" but also of an educational system, cultural organiza-tions, sports institutions, and so on, to cover and shape all aspects of the Jew's life ("Formaler und Materialer Nationalismus," *Vom Judentum* [handwritten newspaper], October 1, 1918, HKC-Klau, Bar Kochba box. There he wrote that the Zionist *"Gegenwartsarbeit"* (work in the present—that is, in the Diaspora) was in preparation for the future, in Zion. This aspect is absent from Kohn's program for a nationalization of Jewish life in the Diaspora, which seems to have become a goal in itself.

67. Kohn, war diary, April 14, 1918.

68. Kohn, "Neujahr: Eine Ansprache." See also Kohn, *Living in a World Revolution*, 111-12.

69. On the broader political and military context of early civil war in Siberia, see Norman G. O. Pereira, *White Siberia: The Politics of Civil War* (Montreal: McGill-Queen's Univer-sity Press, 1996), especially 50-81.

70. Kohn, *Living in a World Revolution*, 112. The itinerary of the trip is documented in

Kohn's 1918 diary, HKC-LBI, box 23, folder 2. Entries mark the train's arrival in Novonikolaevsk on May 23, 1918, and notes "capture by the Czechs" on the next day. The journey is lucidly chronicled in Knoepfmacher, "Some Recollections of My Encounter with Hans Kohn in Siberia, 1917–1919," 5–6.

71. Kohn, *Living in a World Revolution*, 53; Knoepfmacher, "Some Recollections of My Encounter with Hans Kohn in Siberia, 1917–1919," 6–7; the final page of Kohn's address book, HKC-LBI, box 23, folder 4.

72. Hans Kohn, "Zum zweiten Jahr," *Vom Judentum* [handwritten newspaper], July 15, 1918, HKC-Klau, Bar Kochba box.

73. Kohn, "Neujahr: Eine Ansprache."

74. Yoel Zvi Schlesinger in an album for Kohn on his twenty-seventh birthday, HKC-LBI, box 23, folder 5.

75. Knoepfmacher, "The Jewish Prisoners of War in Siberia," 5.

76. Hans Kohn to Leo Hermann, December 9, 1918 (transcript), RWC, box 5, folder 10.

77. Kohn, war diary, January 25, 1919 (the final entry), HKC-LBI, box 23, folder 2. See also Knoepfmacher, "The Jewish Prisoners of War in Siberia," 1.

78. Kohn, *Living in a World Revolution*, 111–12; and "Krasnojarsk: Frühjahr 1919," HKC-LBI, box 23, folder 5; Knoepfmacher, "Some Recollections of My Encounter with Hans Kohn in Siberia, 1917–1919," 8 and 10. On the POWs' reactions to atrocities perpetrated by the Czech Legion, see Rachamimov, *POWs and the Great War*, 13.

79. Indeed, in his memoirs Kohn would state that "during no other period of our imprisonment were our activities so well organized or our intellectual life as rich" (*Living in a World Revolution*, 112).

80. Hans Kohn, second activity report [of the Zionist Association of POWs in Krasnoyarsk], early July 1919, RWC, box 4, folder 17. Kohn would soon renounce the Zionist cult of the farmers. The prisoners' certainty regarding their imminent departure to Palestine is expressed, for example, in Kohn's letter to The Zionist Association of POWs in Krasnoyarsk, July 6, 1919, RWC, box 5, folder 10.

81. In an undated letter to his brother, Fritz, in 1918 or 1919, Kohn confesses having "come closer to the so-called utopian socialism" (HKC-LBI, box 6, folder 2).

82. Hans Kohn to Robert Weltsch, June 16, 1919, RWC, box 5, folder 10.

83. Kohn, *Living in a World Revolution*, 105.

84. Hans Kohn, "Das Wesen des Nationalismus," based on a stenograph of a lecture delivered April 10, 1919 in Krasnoyarsk), is in Kohn, war diary, April 10, 1919.

85. Ibid., 10.

86. Ibid., 22–23.

87. Hans Kohn to Robert Weltsch, July 16, 1919, RWC, box 5, folder 10.

88. Knoepfmacher, "The Jewish Prisoners of War in Siberia," 2.

89. Hans Kohn to Robert Weltsch, July 14, 1919 (transcript), RWC, box 5, folder 10. Kohn published about a dozen articles in this periodical, including the insightful essays "Outcomes and Risks" and "Zionism and Territorialism" and articles on Herzl, Ahad Ha'am, and Leon Pinsker.

90. Kohn told his parents, "We are asked whether we will take the new Czechoslovak citizenship. As an indigenous Prague native (*Urprager*) I said yes, though I have no intention to return to Bohemia." He went on to describe his Zionist activity in Irkutsk and his constraints and plans (Kohn to his parents, May 28, 1919).

91. Farewell note from The Zionist Association of POWs in Krasnoyarsk to Hans Kohn, July 25, 1919, HKC-LBI, box 23, folder 7.

92. Hans Kohn to his mother, undated, HKC-LBI, box 21, folder 13. In other letters to his parents, Kohn elaborated on his Zionist activity in Irkutsk and his intent to emigrate to Palestine, rather than return to Prague (Kohn to his parents, September 4 and 24, 1919).

93. Kohn, *Living in a World Revolution*, 113–14; Hans Kohn, diary, January 18, 1929, HKC-LBI, box 18, folder 4 (this diary includes Kohn's Irkutsk reminiscences, written ten years later).

94. Hans Kohn to Robert Weltsch, July 14, 1919 (transcript).

95. Ibid.

96. Ibid.

97. Hans Kohn, "Perspektiven," *Der Jude* 4, no. 11 (1919): 488–92. Kohn was not the only Zionist to feel as he did. Buber's "Vor der Entscheidung" (Toward the decision) from March 1919 conveyed similar notions (for an English translation, see Martin Buber, *A Land of Two Peoples: Martin Buber on Jews and Arabs*, edited by Paul R. Mendes-Flohr [New York: Oxford University Press, 1983], 38–41). "This is not the day of our [national] self-determination," Buber claimed, "but only of newer and perhaps deeper [political and imperial] entanglement" (ibid., 40).

98. Kohn, "Perspektiven," 489.

99. Ibid., 490. Kohn also wrote: "Not only did [the war] inflict endless suffering upon the Jews; not only did it force them to combat one another; it was, in its essence diametrically opposed to all that Judaism has given the world" (ibid., 489). There was not a trace of his previous idealization of the war. In contrast to its romantic and dangerous appeal, Kohn now saw war as a wild force, entirely destructive and never even marginally creative.

100. Ibid., 490.

101. Ibid., 489, 490, and 492.

102. Ibid., 492. Kohn must have been aware of the centrality of this universal concept of Jewish messianism in Reform Judaism.

103. Kohn, "Der Zionismus und die Religion [I]." The full quote is: "Der Zionismus wird endgueltig mit der Phrase brechen muessen die 'Religion sei Privatsache.' . . . Der Zionismus muss den Kampf aufnehmen mit der heutigen juedischen traditionellen Religionsform, weil die heutige Form eben nur leere Form ist mit nichtigen Worten, deren schwere Folgen aber eine Immoralitaet ist, die von hier ausgehend, das ganze juedische Leben der Gegenwart ergreift, und der aergste Gegner jeder Erneuerung ist."

104. Kohn, "Perspektiven," 491–92. Kohn expressed these principles, and especially his rejection of the pursuit of a Jewish nation-state, in multiple texts. See, for example, Hans Kohn, "Briefe an Freunde," *Der Jude* 5, no. 11 (1920): 649–51.

105. Hans Kohn, "Perspektiven," 491.

106. Ibid., 492.

107. Hans Kohn to Robert Weltsch, October 19, 1919, RWC, box 5, folder 10. The first World Zionist Congress, held in Basel in 1897, ratified the core agenda of the Zionist movement in a brief document known as the Basel Platform.

108. Kohn, *Living in a World Revolution*, 94–95 and 130–31; war diary, October 14 and 17, 1915.

109. Ahad Ha'am, "Truth from the Land of Israel [1891]," translated by Alan Dowry, *Israel Studies* 5, no. 2 (2000): 157.

110. For an excerpt from Yitzhak Epstein's "Hidden Question," see *The Jew in the Modern World: A Documentary History*, 2nd ed., edited by Paul R. Mendes-Flohr, and Jehuda Reinharz (New York: Oxford University Press, 1995), 558–62.

111. Hans Kohn, "Zur Araberfrage," *Der Jude* 4, no 12 (1919–20): 567–69. An English translation was published as Kohn, "The Arab Question," in *The Jews of Bohemia and Moravia: A Historical Reader*, edited by Wilma Abeles Iggers and translated by Wilma Abeles Iggers, Káča Poláčková-Henley, and Kathrine Talbot (Detroit, MI: Wayne State University Press, 1992), 239–42. For information on the date when the essay was written, see Hans Kohn to Leo Hermann, May 27, 1921, HKC-LBI, box 8, folder 9.

112. On discussions of the Arab Question in *Der Jude*, see Eleonore Lappin, *Der Jude, 1916–1928: Jüdische Moderne zwischen Universalismus und Partikularismus* (Tübingen, Germany: Mohr Siebeck, 2000), 254–73.

113. See Paul R. Mendes-Flohr, *Divided Passions: Jewish Intellectuals and the Experience of Modernity* (Detroit: Wayne State University Press, 1991), 77–132. Also see Ivan Davidson Kalmar and Derek Jonathan Penslar, eds. *Orientalism and the Jews* (Waltham, MA: Brandeis University Press, 2005); Arieh Bruce Saposnik, "Europe and Its Orients in Zionist Culture before the First World War," *Historical Journal* 49, no. 4 (2006): 1105–23.

114. Even Martin Buber expressed this notion in his dovish April 1920 essay "At This Late Hour" (see Buber, *A Land of Two Peoples*, 42–47). Note that Buber, unlike Kohn, thought of Zionists as "intermediaries between Europe and Asia" (ibid., 64). Though trying to keep Zionism from becoming imperialism's lackey, Buber at the time still clung to the movement's civilizing mission.

115. Kohn, "The Arab Question," 239. In the 1920s Kohn would develop his geopolitical argumentation in this essay further. Kohn's reluctant adaptation of the claims that Palestine naturally belonged to Syria should be understood in the historical context of the time. See Benny Morris, *Righteous Victims: A History of the Zionist-Arab Conflict, 1881–1999* (New York: Vintage Books, 1999), 32–38 and 78.

116. Quoted in Buber, *A Land of Two Peoples*, 72–73.

117. Kohn, "The Arab Question," 239–40.

118. Ibid., 240–41. On voluntary segregation as the guiding principle of Kohn's binational Zionism, see Yfaat Weiss, "Central European Ethonationalism and Zionist Binationalism," *Jewish Social Studies* 11, no. 1 (2004): 93–117.

119. Kohn, "The Arab Question," 241. Before the collapse of the Austro-Hungarian Empire, Kohn imagined such a mechanism being established all over central, eastern, and

southern Europe. See, for example, Hans Kohn, "On the State of Affairs" in: Kohn, war diary, November 4, 1916, HKC-LBI, box 23, folder 32.

120. Kohn, "The Arab Question," 241-42.

121. Siegmund Kaznelson, "Jüdisches und arabisches Selbstbestimmungsrecht," *Der Jude* 6 no. 11 (1920-21): 643-45. For Kohn's response, see Hans Kohn, "[Umschau] Zur Araberfrage," *Der Jude* 6, no. 12 (1920-21): 737-38. For Kohn's strongest condemnation of the Jewish Legion as an embodiment of a different, misguided brand of Zionism, see Hans Kohn, "Legionen," *Freie Zionistische Blätter*, January 1921, 83-87; Hans Kohn to Leo Hermann, May 27, 1921, HKC-LBI, box 8, folder 9.

122. Kohn, *Living in a World Revolution*, 116. It is hard to determine the accuracy of Kohn's later accounts of his protracted stay in Irkutsk and the timing of his return home. A delayed return was quite typical for POWs and was affected primarily by the unimaginably complex transportation and financial arrangements necessary for the return of millions of prisoners. See Rachamimov, *POWs and the Great War*, 191-213.

123. Quoted in Hans Kohn, "This Century of Betrayal: Can America Lead a New Struggle for Independence?" *Commentary*, September 1, 1946, 202.

124. Hans Kohn, *Martin Buber: Sein Werk und seine Zeit: Ein Versuch über Religion und Politik* (Hellerau, Germany: J. Hegner, 1930), 139 and 143.

125. Hans Kohn to Robert Weltsch, August 26, 1917, RWC, box 5, folder 10.

126. Kohn, *Living in a World Revolution*, 116-18.

3. To Tame Empire, Nation, and Man: Political Agenda in the 1920s

1. Hans Kohn, "Perspektiven," *Der Jude* 4, no. 11 (1919): 492.

2. Hans Kohn to Robert Weltsch, November 6, 1922, HKC-LBI, 13/19.

3. Hans Kohn, "Aktiver Pazifismus," *Neue Wege* 23, no. 2 (1929): 84.

4. Hans Kohn, *Living in a World Revolution: My Encounters with History* (New York: Trident Press, 1964), 89.

5. Ibid., 119. Kohn, whose worldview and scholarship would be transformed by the Nazi accession to power in 1933, visited Berlin in 1920 shortly after his return from Russia. Berlin had just weathered the failed antidemocratic Kapp Putsch, and it seemed to Kohn "a place where the defeated authoritarian order had been replaced not by liberty but by license" (ibid., 120).

6. For a discussion of the nation-state character of Czechoslovakia, see Todd W. Huebner, "The Multinational 'Nation-State': The Origins and the Paradox of Czechoslovakia, 1914-1920" (PhD diss., Columbia University, 1993).

7. Hans Kohn, "Briefe an Freunde," *Der Jude* 5, no. 11 (1920): 645-57. Kohn published some letters to friends from that period as an essay of sorts, first in *Der Jude* and later in *Nationalismus: Über die Bedeutung des Nationalismus im Judentum und in der Gegenwart* (On the significance of nationalism in Judaism and in the present) (Wien: R. Löwit, 1922).

8. Kohn, "Briefe an Freunde," 645-47 and 649.

9. In his memoirs Kohn did not even mention the committee by name (*Living in a World Revolution*, 124 and 127). His committee activity is documented, for example, in his corre-

spondence with Leo Motzkin, who headed the committee, and David Simonsen, Copen-hagen's chief rabbi (CZA, A126/503, A126/670; Royal Library: National Library of Denmark and Copenhagen University Library, David Simonsen Archives, Correspondents—Comité des Délégations Juives).

10. On the committee, see David Engel, "Perceptions of Power: Poland and World Jewry," *Jahrbuch des Simon-Dubnow-Instituts* 1 (2002): 17–28; Nathan Feinberg, *La Question des Mi-norités à la Conférence de la Paix de 1919–1920 et l'Action Juive en Faveur de la Protection Internationale des Minorités* (Paris: Conseil pour les droit des minorités juives, 1929); Carole Fink, *Defending the Rights of Others: The Great Powers, the Jews, and International Minority Protection, 1878–1938* (New York: Cambridge University Press, 2004); Oscar I. Janowsky, *The Jews and Minority Rights (1898–1919)* (New York: Columbia University Press, 1933); Erwin Viefhaus, *Die Minderheitenfrage und die Entstehung der Minderheitenschutzverträge auf der Pariser Friedenskonferenz 1919: Eine Studie zur Geschichte des Nationalitätenproblems im 19. und 20. Jahrhundert* (Würzburg, Germany: Holzner, 1960).

11. Hans Kohn to Jetty Wahl, August 20, 1920, HKC-LBI, box 10, folder 1.

12. Fink, *Defending the Rights of Others*, 258, 268, 297–98, and 363; Margaret MacMillan, *Paris 1919: Six Months That Changed the World* (New York: Random House, 2002), 316–21. The selective recognition of minority rights parallels that of self-determination: "The ideal of self-determination, honored largely in the breach in the peace settlement as far as the world outside Europe was concerned, served to draw the battle lines between imperialism and its enemies in the succeeding decades" (Erez Manela, "Imagining Woodrow Wilson in Asia: Dreams of East-West Harmony and the Revolt against Empire in 1919," *American Historical Review* 111, no. 5 (2006): 1351.

13. Hans Kohn, "Perspektiven," *Der Jude* 4, no. 11 (1919): 490.

14. Kohn, *Living in a World Revolution*, 131.

15. Kohn seemed especially "impressed with the importance of the *hommes des lettres*, of the intellectual in French life; again and again they had spoken up as *la voix de la conscience du monde*, something unknown in Germany. They had made their voice heard during the Dreyfus affair, and they won the battle against blind chauvinism and emotional nationalism, against the entrenched forces of the army and the Church" (ibid, 125).

16. Ibid., 125 and 126.

17. For an excellent discussion of the prophets' place in the Jewish political tradition, see "Prophets," in *The Jewish Political Tradition*, edited by Michael Walzer, Menachem Lorber-baum, Noam J. Zohar, and Yair Loberbaum (New Haven, CT: Yale University Press, 2000), 1:199–243. On Ahad Ha'am's distinction between prophets and priests (in the Zionist contem-poraneous context), see Leora F. Batnitzky, *How Judaism Became a Religion: An Introduction to Modern Jewish Thought* (Princeton, NJ: Princeton University Press, 2011), 157–60.

18. Hans Kohn, "Der Augenblick," *Der Jude* 5, no. 8 (1920): 437–39.

19. Ibid., 439. The same message was conveyed in Martin Buber "In später Stunde," *Der Jude* 5, no. 1 (1920), 1–5.

20. Hans Kohn, "Briefe an Freunde," *Der Jude* 5 no. 11 (1920): 656.

21. Hans Kohn, "Vom Kongress," *Der Jude* 6, no. 1 (1921): 48 and 49. Kohn also expressed

this criticism in his letter to his friend Joseph "Pepi" Wien (Kohn, "Briefe an Freunde," 649-50). Kohn was registered with the Zionist Congress as a representative of Tzeirei Zion, though this group had already merged with Poalei Zion (*Stenographisches Protokoll der Ver-handlungen des XII. Zionisten-Kongresses in Karlsbad vom 1. bis 14. September 1921* [Berlin: Jüdischer Verlag, 1922], 8). For a different and much more positive view of the congress, see RW [Robert Weltsch], "Nach dem Kongress," *Jüdische Rundschau*, September 23, 1921.

22. Kohn, *Living in a World Revolution*, 127. See also Kohn, "Briefe an Freunde," 649-50. This enchantment may account for the postponement of his immigration to Palestine, which he had referred to as imminent during his years as a POW. "Now," he wrote, "I am surrounded and enchanted by the metropolis, and occasionally I think I could not [emigrate] to Palestine.... Palestine is not a wilderness, and yet it is the remotest of provinces." It is strik-ing that Kohn stressed there that those who immigrate to Palestine must have "a European consciousness" (ibid., 653).

23. Joseph B. Schechtman, *The Life and Times of Vladimar Jabotinsky* (Silver Spring, MD: Eshel, 1986), 375; Martin Gilbert, *Israel: A History* (London: Doubleday, 1998), 46.

24. Kohn, *Living in a World Revolution*, 132, 133, and 134. See also Kohn's correspondence with representatives of the Independent Labour Party and the Fabian Society, HKC-LBI, box 8, folder 6.

25. Hans Kohn, "Hafabianim," *Hapo'el Hatza'ir*, August 4, 1925. See also Hans Kohn, "Die Fabians," *Zeitschrift für Politik* 18 (1929): 663-75.

26. Kohn, *Living in a World Revolution*, 129.

27. Ibid., 130.

28. Ibid., 131.

29. See Adi Gordon, "Nothing but a Disillusioned Love: Hans Kohn's Break from the Zionist Movement," in *Against the Grain: Jewish Intellectuals in Hard Times*, edited by Ezra Mendelsohn, Stefani Hoffman, and Richard I. Cohen (New York: Berghahn, 2013), 117-42.

30. Kohn, "Briefe an Freunde," 657.

31. Hans Kohn on behalf of the Jüdische Gesellschaft für Internationale Verständigung, circular letter, December 5, 1921, HKC-Klau, folder Jüdische Gesellschaft für Internationale Verständigung.

32. In different ways, both essays diagnosed contemporaneous nationalism as a hazard-ous degeneration of its original ideal, which might morally threaten Zionism. Both essays are available in English: Hans Kohn, "Nationalism," in *The Jew: Essays from Martin Buber's Journal Der Jude, 1916-1928*, edited by Arthur Allen Cohen and translated by Joachim Neu-groschel (Birmingham: University of Alabama Press, 1980), 20-30; Martin Buber, *A Land of Two Peoples: Martin Buber on Jews and Arabs*, edited by Paul R. Mendes-Flohr (New York: Oxford University Press, 1983), 47-57.

33. Much of the correspondence of the Jüdische Gesellschaft für Internationale Verstän-digung is kept in HKC-Klau, folder Jüdische Gesellschaft für Internationale Verständigung. Kohn's hope was that with the society, intellectuals would achieve what the bureaucrats and diplomats of the Comité des Délégations Juives and the Paris Peace Conference had failed to do. See Paul R. Mendes-Flohr, "The Mandarins of Jerusalem," *Naharaim* 4, no. 2 (2011):

179; and *Divided Passions: Jewish Intellectuals and the Experience of Modernity* (Detroit: Wayne State University Press, 1991), 173-76.

34. Jeanne Morefield, *Empires without Imperialism: Anglo-American Decline and the Politics of Deflection* (New York: Oxford University Press, 2014), 114. See also ibid., 99-132; Lionel Curtis, *The Commonwealth of Nations: An Inquiry into the Nature of Citizenship in the British Empire, and into the Mutual Relations of the Several Communities Thereof* (London: Macmillan, 1916), and *The Problem of the Commonwealth* (Toronto: Macmillan, 1916); Jeanne Morefield, *Covenants without Swords: Idealist Liberalism and the Spirit of Empire* (Princeton, NJ: Princeton University. Press, 2005).

35. Erez Manela, *The Wilsonian Moment: Self-Determination and the International Origins of Anticolonial Nationalism* (New York: Oxford University Press, 2007), 225.

36. See Hugo Bergmann, "Die wahre Autonomie," *Der Jude* 8-9 (1918-19): 368-73; Buber, *A Land of Two Peoples*, 70-72.

37. Hans Kohn to Martin Buber, August 9, 1922, HKC-Klau, folder Jüdische Gesellschaft für Internationale Verständigung; Hans Kohn to Robert Weltsch, August 29, 1922, HKC-LBI, box 13, folder 19. Kohn went so far as to view the Zionist use of the term "Eretz Israel" (Land of Israel) as a provocation.

38. Hans Kohn diary, July 20, 1923, HKC-LBI, box 18, folder 2. See also entries for July 18-August 16, 1923. In a notebook from 1923 Kohn toyed with the idea of writing a book based on his impressions of Palestine, to be called "Problems of a New People." The penultimate chapter, "The Eternal Rhythm," was to combine the "escape into normalcy: Herzl's State," with the prophetic "escape into the desert: a plea to Judaism from the Orient" (HKC-LBI, box 25, folder 3).

39. Winston Churchill, "Palestine White Paper: June 3, 1922," in *Israel in the Middle East: Documents and Readings on Society, Politics, and Foreign Relations, Pre-1948 to the Present*, 2nd ed., edited by Itamar Rabinovich and Jehuda Reinharz (Waltham, MA: Brandeis University Press, 2008), 33-34.

40. Kohn's list of members included Arthur Ruppin, Hugo Bergmann, Yehoshua Radler-Feldmann (his pen name was Rabbi Binyamin—or, in Yiddish pronounciation, Reb Binyomin), Markus Reiner, and Robert Weltsch.

41. Hans Kohn, "Plan of Activity and Platform" (probably from April 1925), CZA, Moshe Jacob Ben-Gabriel (Eugen Hoeflich) Collection, A197/5. See also Hans Kohn to Eugen Höflich, April 5 and August 1, 1925, in the same collection. I thank Hanan Harif for generously sharing these documents with me.

42. Copy of Robert Weltsch to Arthur Ruppin, December 16, 1924, HKC-Klau, Brith Shalom box.

43. Arthur Ruppin, *Memoirs, Diaries, Letters*, edited by Alex Bein and translated by Karen Gershon (New York: Herzl, 1971), 219.

44. Quoted in Buber, *A Land of Two Peoples*, 73.

45. Hans Kohn to Martin Buber, September 1, 1925, MBA, Arc. Ms.Var. 350, Het, 376/145. Unfortunately, Kohn's 1925-26 journals are missing from his various archives.

46. Hans Kohn to Martin Buber, November 17, 1925, MBA, Arc. Ms.Var. 350, Het, 376/146.

In contrast to Kohn's initial optimism, he wrote in his diary some two years later: "Strange: Since arriving in Palestine, since … 1925, I have a sense of proximity to death (*Todesnähe*), almost every [waking] hour I must think of death" (January 7, 1927, HKC-LBI, box 18, folder 2).

47. Quoted in Aharon Kedar, "Brith Shalom," *Jerusalem Quarterly*, 18 (Winter 1981), 68.

48. Israel Zangwill, *Speeches, Articles and Letters of Israel Zangwill* (London: Soncino Press, 1937), 310 and 311.

49. Quoted in Buber, *A Land of Two Peoples*, 37.

50. R.[eb] B.[inyomin] [Yehoshua Radler-Feldmann], "Misaviv Lankuda," *She'ifoteinu* 1, no. 2 (1927): 21–23.

51. Kohn, *Living in a World Revolution*, 58.

52. Kohn, diary, February 4 and December 9, 1927, HKC-LBI, box 18, folder 2. In early December of that year, Scholem indicated that he did not seem equally fascinated with Kohn, writing to Adolf Oko of "that everlasting *Ober-Quatscher* [windbag] who is known by the name of Hans Kohn" (Gershom Scholem, *A Life in Letters, 1914–1982*, edited and translated by Anthony David Skinner [Cambridge, MA: Harvard University Press, 2002], 319). Nor was Scholem any more respectful in his first correspondence with Kohn in 1921 (ibid., 191–21).

53. The Palestine Land Development Company's monetary support is documented in Georg Landauer to Arthur Ruppin, August 4, 1927, HKC-Klau, Brith Shalom box; Kohn, diary, May 5, 1929, HKC-LBI, box 18, folder 4.

54. The association did not receive its name, Brith Shalom, until 1926, and it seems to have been Kohn who suggested that name (Hans Kohn to Arthur Ruppin, March 7, 1926, HKC-Klau, Brith Shalom box). Other suggested names were Shalom VeAvoda (Peace and labor), Bnei Shem (Sons of Shem—that is, semites), Bnei Kedem (Sons of the orient), Moledet (Homeland), Binyan (Construction), and Aguda Lehavana Hadadit (Society for mutual understanding).

55. Kedar, "Brith Shalom," 57.

56. Minutes of Brith Shalom meeting, November 3, 1925, HKC-Klau, Brith Shalom box.

57. "Pratekol Ha'asefa shenikre'a Alyedey Hava'ada Hamesaderet Lesehm Berur Hashe'ela Ha'ravit-Ivrit," 13th of Kislev, 5686 [November 30, 1925], 1 and 6, HKC-Klau, Brith Shalom box. The group, it seems, did not become a permanent official forum.

58. Ibid., 10.

59. Untitled minutes of meeting, July 7, 1926, 3 (see also 7), HKC-Klau, Brith Shalom box.

60. Arthur Ruppin, *Memoirs, Diaries, Letters* (New York: Herzl, 1972), 224.

61. Hans Kohn to Arthur Ruppin, December 6, 1925, HKC-Klau, Brith Shalom box.

62. Mordechai Avi-Sha'ul and Hans Kohn, "Outline to an Arab-Hebrew Understanding" [July 12, 1926, Rosh Chodesh Menachem Av 5686], HKC-Klau, Brith Shalom box.

63. The essay was published in various forms and languages. A short Hebrew version was published first in *Hapo'el Hatza'ir* on July 9, 1926, and later in the first volume of *She'ifoteinu* (1927). A longer version, in German, was published in Hans Kohn and Robert Weltsch, *Zionistische Politik: Eine Aufsatzreihe* (Mährisch-Ostrau, Czechoslovakia: Verlag Dr. R. Farber, 1927).

64. Hans Kohn, "Zur Araberfrage," *Der Jude* 4, no. 12 (1919): 567–69.

65. Hans Kohn, "Zur künftigen Gestaltung Palästinas," in *Zionistische Politik: Eine Aufsatzreihe*, edited by Hans Kohn and Robert Weltsch (Mährisch-Ostrau, Czechoslovakia: Verlag Dr. R. Färber, 1927), 281.

66. Ibid., 275.

67. Yfaat Weiss, "Central European Ethonationalism and Zionist Binationalism," *Jewish Social Studies* 11, no. 1 (2004): 93–117.

68. "Zionist maneuvers" is a quote from an article in the Arabic newspaper *Sowt-Ashaab*, January 28, 1928, HKC-Klau, Brith Shalom box. See also Kohn, diary, January 9, 1928, HKC-LBI, box 18, folder 2; minutes of the Committee for Organizing [Arab-Jewish] Lectures in Jerusalem, January 4, 1928, HKC-Klau, Brith Shalom box.

69. Minutes of Brith Shalom meeting at Kohn's home, June 16, 1928, HKC-Klau, Brith Shalom box. See also Hans Kohn to Robert Weltsch, 21 June 1928, HKC-Klau, Brith Shalom box.

70. Minutes of Brith Shalom meetings, March 20 and 24, 1928, HKC-Klau, Brith Shalom box. See also Hans Kohn and Joseph Lurie, "Outline of the Issue of Basic Rights in the Constitution and Parliamentary Representation," March 24, 1928, HKC-Klau, Brith Shalom box (another copy is in CZA, Arthur Ruppin Collection, A107/695).

71. Ruppin, *Memoirs, Diaries, Letters*, 237.

72. Hans Kohn to Arthur Ruppin, May 28, 1928, HKC-Klau, Brith Shalom box.

73. Ruppin, *Memoirs, Diaries, Letters*, 237; see also 236 and 238.

74. Ruppin, *Memoirs, Diaries, Letters*, 242; Brith Shalom, "Giluy Daat shel Brith Shalom," *Davar*, December 22, 1928. A few days later, on December 26, 1928, the right-wing newspaper *Do'ar Hayom* published "Al Noseh Matrid," a harsh attack against what it called the anti-Zionist Brith Shalom.

75. Kohn, diary, October 28, 1928, HKC-LBI, box 18, folder 2. See also the entries for February 15 and September 29, 1928.

4. Nation and State in Kohn's Scholarship and Jewish Thought

1. Hans Kohn to Robert Weltsch, December 21, 1925, RWC, box 7, folder 18.

2. *Hans Kohn, A History of Nationalism in the East*, translated by Margaret M. Green (New York: Harcourt, Brace, 1929), 431.

3. Friedrich W. Nietzsche, *Human, All Too Human: A Book for Free Spirits*, translated by Reginald John Hollingdale (Cambridge: Cambridge University Press, 1996), 175.

4. Leora F. Batnitzky, *How Judaism Became a Religion: An Introduction to Modern Jewish Thought* (Princeton, NJ: Princeton University Press, 2011), 112.

5. Gabriel Riesser, "The Paulus-Riesser Debate (1831)," translated by Mark Gelber and Paul R. Mendes-Flohr, in *The Jew in the Modern World: A Documentary History*, 2nd ed., edited by Paul R. Mendes-Flohr, and Jehuda Reinharz (New York: Oxford University Press, 1995), 144–45; Reform Rabbinical Conference at Brunswick, "The Question of Patriotism (June 1844)," in ibid., 177.

6. Samson Raphael Hirsch, "Religion Allied to Prgress (1854)," in in ibid., 201.

7. One of the people he invited in 1921 to contribute to a second volume was Gershom Scholem, who thought very poorly of the original *Vom Judentum* and declined to participate. Kohn would raise the idea of a second volume of *Vom Judentum* again in 1927–28, as a *Festschrift* to celebrate Buber's fiftieth birthday, and in the 1940s. On the efforts to publish a new *Vom Judentum* as a Buber festschrift in 1928, see Hans Kohn to Martin Buber, January 5, 1927, MBA 376/10; Hans Kohn to Martin Buber, August 26, and October 22, 1926, MBA 376/9; Hans Kohn to Martin Buber, January 26, 1927, MBA 376/10; Kohn, diary, February 4, 1927, HKC-LBI box 18, folder 2. Kohn was not alone in these endeavors; Hugo Bergmann's similar attempts are documented in his published correspondence (Schmuel Hugo Bergmann, *Tagebücher und Briefe* [Königstein, Germany: Jüdischer Verlag bei Athenäum, 1985], vols. 1–2).

8. Hans Kohn, *Nationalismus: Über die Bedeutung des Nationalismus im Judentum und in der Gegenwart* (Nationalism: on the significance of nationalism in Judaism and in the present) (Vienna: R. Löwit, 1922); Hans Kohn, *Die politische Idee des Judentums* (Munich: Meyer and Jessen, 1924), Hans Kohn and Robert Weltsch, *Zionistische Politik: Eine Aufsatzreihe* (Mährisch-Ostrau, Czechoslovakia: Verlag Dr. R. Färber, 1927); Hans Kohn, *L'humanisme juif: quinze essais sur le juif, le monde et Dieu* (Paris: Rieder, 1931).

9. See, for example, Hans Kohn, "Judenfrage" (Jewish Question; with Robert Weltsch), 3:421–6; "Nationalismus, jüdischer" (Jewish nationalism), 4.1: 423–28; "Antizionismus" (anti-Zionism), 1: 371–76; "Internationalismus der Juden" (the internationality of the Jews), 3: 26–28; "Kultur, Jüdische" (Jewish culture), 3:922–27; "Assimilation," 1:517–23; and "Renaissance Jüdische" (Jewish renaissance), 4.1:1418–19, all in *Jüdisches Lexikon: Ein enzyklopädisches Handbuch des jüdischen Wissens*, edited by Georg Herlitz and Bruno Kirschen (Berlin: Jüdischer Verlag, 1927–30).

10. Hans Kohn, *Prakim Letoldot Hara'ayon Hatzioni*, 2 vols. (Warsaw: Hava'ad Hapo'el shel "Berit Hano'ar" Umerkaz "Hehalutz" Ha'olami, 1929–30); Samuel Hugo Bergmann and Hans Kohn, *Lezikhro shel Gustav Landauer* (Tel-Aviv: Hapo'el Hatza'ir, 1929) and *Am-Adam: Divre Hamatzpun Ha'enoshi: Kovets Ne'umim Uma'amarim* (Tel-Aviv: Hotsa'at Moriyah, 1930); Hans Kohn, *Martin Buber, sein Werk und seine Zeit: Ein Versuch über Religion und Politik* (Hellerau, Germany: J. Hegner, 1930). Part of the biography's title (*Ein Versuch über Religion und Politik* [An essay on religion and politics]) was changed in a later edition to *Ein Beitrag zur Geistesgeschichte Mitteleuropas, 1880–1930* (A work on Central European intellectual history, 1880–1930).

11. Noam Pianko, *Zionism and the Roads Not Taken: Rawidowicz, Kaplan, Kohn* (Bloomington: Indiana University Press, 2010), 3 and 14. See also Rogers Brubaker, *Ethnicity without Groups* (Cambridge, MA: Harvard University Press, 2006), 144–45.

12. Kohn, *Nationalismus*, 8–9.

13. The essay first appeared as Hans Kohn, "Nationalismus," *Der Jude* 6, no. 11 (1921–22): 674–86. For an English translation of the essay, see Hans Kohn, "Nationalism," in *The Jew: Essays from Martin Buber's Journal Der Jude, 1916–1928*, edited by Arthur Allen Cohen and translated by Joachim Neugroschel (Birmingham: University of Alabama Press, 1980), 20–30.

14. Hans Kohn, "Das Wesen des Nationalismus," in Kohn, war diary, HKC-LBI, box

23, folder 2. Indeed, Kohn signed the 1922 essay with his name followed by "(1919-1922)." Whereas Kohn's essay distinguished between true, mature nationalism and the ideology of the nation-state, Buber distinguished among "a people," "a nation," and "nationalism": "a people," he explained, "is a phenomenon of life, a nation one of awareness, nationalism one of overemphasized awareness" (Martin Buber, *A Land of Two Peoples: Martin Buber on Jews and Arabs*, edited by Paul R. Mendes-Flohr [New York: Oxford University Press, 1983], 51 and 52). Unlike Kohn, Buber saw all nationalism as unhealthy but distinguished transient nationalism (which is hence "legitimate") and the enduring, "arbitrary," pathological one (ibid., 52-53). This was not the first time that Kohn had "hid" behind Buber, publishing an essay with a title identical to that of an essay his mentor had just released (the "Spirit of the Orient" is a case in point), which arguably indicates Kohn's lack of confidence. Oddly, Kohn did not address the very similar discussion in Franz Rosenzweig's 1921 *Star of Redemption* (translated by Barbara E. Galli (Madison: University of Wisconsin Press, 2005)). Kohn would do so only marginally in his biography of Buber. The state, according to Rosenzweig, "is the ever-changing form under which time moves to eternity step by step." The Jews, however, are in no need of that form of statehood: "The Jewish people is in itself already at the goal toward which the peoples of the world are just setting out" (ibid. 351-52). Buber introduced Kohn and Rosenzweig, who met occasionally. See also Kohn, *Martin Buber*, 350-58.

15. Simon Dubnow, "Fourth Letter: Autonomism, the Basis of the National Program," in *Nationalism and History: Essays on Old and New History*, edited by Koppel S. Pinson (Philadelphia: Jewish Publication Society of America, 1958), 140-41; Lord Acton, "Nationality [1862]," in *Mapping the Nation*, edited by Gopal Balakrishnan (London: Verso, 1996), 17-38. "The presence of different nations under the same sovereignty," Lord Acton wrote, "is similar in its effect to the independence of the Church in the State" (ibid., 30).

16. Hans Kohn, "Nationalism," 29.

17. Ibid., 27.

18. Hans Kohn to Hugo Bergmann, August 28, 1922, HKC-LBI, box 13, folder 19.

19. Hermann Cohen, *Religion of Reason: Out of the Sources of Judaism*, translated by Simon Kaplan (New York: Frederick Ungar, 1972); Hermann Cohen and Martin Buber, "A Debate on Zionism and Messianism," in *The Jew in the Modern World: A Documentary History*, 2nd ed., edited by Paul R. Mendes-Flohr, and Jehuda Reinharz (New York: Oxford University Press, 1995), 571-77.

20. "The Political Idea of Judaism: Interview for the Jewish Chronicle with Dr. Hans Kohn," *London Jewish Chronicle*, August 14, 1925.

21. Ibid. The comparison between Jews and Greeks dates back to Kohn's prewar Jewish thought (including his "Spirit of the Orient") and would reemerge briefly in his 1944 *Idea of Nationalism*.

22. Hans Kohn, *Die politische Idee des Judentums* (Munich: Meyer and Jessen, 1924), 18. For example: "The historical consciousness of the Jewish people instills unity in historical events. The concept of world history as a unified process has emerged with greater clarity ever since [the prophet] Amos. The human task—as morally acting agents of this development—has been evident ever since the Mosaic covenant, and the words of the prophets only

lend it a world-historical framework, and this unified history is completed by identifying its goal and destination: God. His path [history] is the path to Him" (ibid.).

23. Kohn, ibid., 54 and 51.

24. Kohn named Moses Hess, Karl Marx, Henri Bergson, Herman Cohen, Otto Weininger, Buber, and Gustav Landauer as modern Jewish thinkers whose work is centered in very different fashions on the same Jewish political idea.

25. Kohn, *Die politische Idee des Judentums*, 24. There Kohn wrote of the prophet: "Sie zerstören den Staat, der immer etwas Relatives ist, Notbehelf im Ausgleich menschlicher Triebe, indem sie ihn am Absoluten messen. Sie stehen wider das Volk, seinen Staat, seine Könige und Mächtigen [They destroy the state—which is always a relative thing, a temporary tool to balance human passions—by judging it in comparison to the absolute. They stand against the people, its government, its kings and men of power]."

26. Saadya Gaon, *The Book of Doctrines and Beliefs*, edited and translated by Alexander Altmann (Indianapolis: Hackett, 2002), 112.

27. Kohn, *Die politische Idee des Judentums*, 25 and 10-11. The English translation is from Hans Kohn, "The People of the Yoke," in *Rebirth: A Book of Modern Jewish Thought*, edited by Ludwig Lewisohn (New York: Harper and Brothers, 1935), 118.

28. "The spiritual process of Judaism," Buber told the members of Bar Kochba in 1910, "manifests itself in history as the striving after an ever more perfect realization of three interrelated ideas: the idea of unity, the idea of the deed, and the idea of the future" (Martin Buber, "Renewal of Judaism," in Buber, *On Judaism*, edited by Nahum N. Glatzer, translated by Eva Jospe [New York: Schocken, 1967], 40).

29. Indeed, when Kohn wrote his monumental *Idea of Nationalism*—the work most identified with this distinction—twenty years later, he would cite and develop long passages from the *Political Idea of Judaism*. However, he did not entirely disavow the formative roles of land and language, either in 1924 or in his later works (see Kohn, *Die politische Idee des Judentums*, 8-9).

30. Kohn, *Die politische Idee des Judentums*, 45; "The Political Idea of Judaism."

31. Hans Kohn to Robert Weltsch, December 21, 1925, RWC, box 7, folder 18.

32. Ibid.

33. Ibid.

34. Theodor Herzl, "A Solution of the Jewish Question (1896)," in *The Jew in the Modern World: A Documentary History*, 2nd ed., edited by Paul R. Mendes-Flohr, and Jehuda Reinharz (New York: Oxford University Press, 1995), 534.

35. Hans Kohn to Robert Weltsch, December 21, 1925, RWC, box 7, folder 18.

36. Kohn's binationalist texts in Kohn and Weltsch's *Zionistische Politik* included "Zur künftigen Gestaltung Palästinas" (The political future of Palestine) and "Die Legion" (The legion). Some of Kohn's other essays in this book—"Der Eintritt des Judentum in die europäische Welt" (Judism enters European Culture), "Moses Hess," "Ahad Ha'am," and "Liberales Judentum" (Liberal Judaism)"—would constitute the core of his *Prakim Letoldot Hara'ayon Hatzioni*. The American *Menorah Journal* would publish English translations of many of these essays in 1930.

37. Kohn, "Kultur, Jüdische," in *Jüdisches Lexikon*, 3:926 and 927.

38. Kohn, "Assimilation," 1:521.

39. Ibid., 1:519.

40. Hans Kohn and Robert Weltsch, "Judenfrage," 1:422.

41. Kohn, *Prakim Letoldot Hara'ayon Hatzioni*, 1:21. Kohn could not praise Herzl's emphasis on diplomacy, but he could at least agree with Herzl's notion of a model society.

42. Ibid., 1:14.

43. Ibid., 2: 6 and 9.

44. Ibid., 2:32–33.

45. Michael A. Meyer views Kohn's stand on this issue differently ("Liberal Judaism and Zionism in Germany," in *Zionism and Religion*, edited by Jehuda S. Almog, Jehuda Reinharz, and Anita Shapira [Hanover, NH: University Press of New England, 1998], 93–106).

46. Bergmann and Kohn, *Lezikhro shel Gustav Landauer* and *Am-Adam*. See also Kohn, diary, January 30, 1929, HKC-LBI, box 18, folder 4.

47. Kohn, *Prakim Letoldot Hara'ayon Hatzioni*, 1:16.

48. Ibid.

49. This intentional omission is discussed in Paul R. Mendes-Flohr, *Kidmah ve-naftuleha: ma'avakam shel intelektu'alim Yehudim 'im modernah* (Tel Aviv: Am Oved, 2010), 305.

50. Hans Kohn to Martin Buber, December 10, 1929, in Martin Buber, *Martin Buber, Briefwechsel aus sieben Jahrzehnten*, edited by Grete Schaeder (Heidelberg, Germany: L. Schneider, 1972), 2:357. The translation is based on Martin Buber, *The Letters of Martin Buber: A Life of Dialogue*, edited by Nahum N. Glatzer and Paul Mendes-Flohr and translated by Richard Winston, Clara Winston, and Harry Zohn (New York: Schocken, 1991), 372–73.

51. Hans Kohn to Robert Weltsch, May 3, 1930, HKRWC.

52. Hans Kohn, *L'humanisme juif: quinze essais sur le juif, le monde et Dieu* (Paris: Rieder, 1931).

53. Hans Kohn to Robert Weltsch, November 6, 1922, HKC-LBI, 13/19.

54. Hans Kohn, *Sinn und Schicksal der Revolution* (Vienna: E. P. Tal, 1923), 48 and 56. The book was quite well received and was even translated into Czech. *The Nation and Athenaeum*, a British weekly newspaper whose political line was close to that of the Labour Party, praised it as "brilliantly written and well worth attention" ("Revolutions," May 26, 1923, 276).

55. Kohn, *Sinn und Schicksal der Revolution*, 87.

56. Ibid., 90.

57. Ibid., 5; see also 12–14, and 16. Kohn's brief survey of recent Russian political history allowed him to voice other key impressions, familiar from his earlier work: his description of the Narodniks' romantic nationalism as cosmopolitan reapplies his earlier definition of Johann Gottlieb Fichte and his generation, which constituted for him a model for Zionism (ibid., 30).

58. Ibid., 11.

59. Ibid., 17 and 15. My translation changes the order of some words but remains true to the meaning.

60. Hans Kohn, *Toldot Hatnu'ah Hale'umit Ha'arvit* (Tel Aviv: Hotza'at "Hapo'el Ha-tza'ir," 1926). The Hebrew book is identical to chapter 9, "The New Arabia," in the larger German book (Hans Kohn, *Geschichte der nationalen Bewegung im Orient* (Berlin: K. Vowinckel, 1928), with just two exceptions: the German book contains occasional discussions of events that occurred after the Hebrew book's publication, and whereas the earlier book focused on the distinction between cultural and political Zionism, the chapter in the later book focused on various interpretations of the Balfour Declaration and the San Remo commitments.

61. Kohn, *Toldot Hatnu'ah Hale'umit Ha'arvit*, 4.

62. Even his depiction of Wahhabism as "aimed at reforming every department of Arabian life" is reminiscent of the Jewish renaissance's self-understanding as a *Lebensreformbewegung* (a movement of life reform; ibid., 14).

63. Ibid., 46. This pan-Arab vision, Aaron Berman suggests, was mediated through Ameen Rihani's work ("Ameen Rihani and Hans Kohn: The Construction of a Pan-Arab Nationalist Narrative in the United States," in *Ameen Rihani's Arab-American Legacy: From Romanticism to Postmodernism: Proceedings of the Second International Conference on Lebanese-American Literary Figures*, edited by Naji B. Oueijan and Roger Allen [Louaize, Lebanon: Notre Dame University Press, 2012], 155–76).

64. Kohn, *Toldot Hatnu'ah Hale'umit Ha'arvit*, 11.

65. Judy Tzu-Chun Wu, *Radicals on the Road: Internationalism, Orientalism, and Feminism during the Vietnam Era* (Ithaca, NY: Cornell University Press, 2013), 137–38.

66. Kohn, *Toldot Hatnu'ah Hale'umit Ha'arvit*, 16; see also 38–43. This movingly detailed discussion may very well have been intended to convince Zionists—according to Kohn's politics as of 1919—to view the guarantees of colonial empires with more than a grain of salt and to anchor Zionists' future in a friendly, mutually beneficial relationship with Arab nationalists.

67. Richard Hartmann, review of *Geschichte der nationalen Bewegung im Orient*, *Deutsche Literaturzeitung* 50, no. 6 (1929): 285.

68. William L. Langer, review of *A History of Nationalism in the East*, *Foreign Affairs*, January 1930, 316–17; *Times Literary Supplement*, September 26, 1929; Gerald Clair William Camden Wheeler, "The Changed East," *Times Literary Supplement*, September 26, 1929; Raymond Leslie Buell, review of *A History of Nationalism in the East*, *New York Herald Tribune*, January 12, 1930.

69. Kohn, *A History of Nationalism in the East*, 1, 5, and 431.

70. Ibid., 12, 432, and 10.

71. Vowinckel Verlag accepted the book for publication in the summer of 1927 (Kohn, diary, July 22 and 27, 1927, HKC-LBI, box 18, folder 2).

72. Gearóid Ó Tuathail, introduction to *The Geopolitics Reader*, edited by Gearóid Ó Tuathail, Simon Dalby, and Paul Routledge (New York: Routledge, 1998), 1 and 4. Indeed, in the Weimar Republic the entire political spectrum proudly engaged in geopolitics (see David T. Murphy, *The Heroic Earth: Geopolitical Thought in Weimar Germany, 1918-1933* [Kent, OH: Kent State University Press, 1997]).

73. See, for example, Karl Haushofer to Hans Kohn, May 30, 1928; January 6 and 14, 1930; and November 17, 1932, HKC-LBI, box 4, folder 1.

74. Karl Haushofer, "Zur Einführung," in Kohn, *Geschichte der nationalen Bewegung im Orient*, ix. Kohn was not the only spiritual Zionist befriended by Haushofer. The German corresponded with Ernst Simon in 1927 (see Hans-Adolf Jacobsen, *Karl Haushofer: Leben und Werk*, [Boppard am Rhein, Germany: Boldt, 1979], 2:78).

75. Karl Haushofer, "Zur Einführung," undated (probably early 1928) draft, HKC-LBI, 4/1. The Nazi slogan "*Volk ohne Raum*" comes from Hans Grimm's novel of that title (Munich: Langen,1926). The saying "[a land without a people for] a people without a land," often wrongly attributed to Israel Zangwill, originated with nineteenth-century Christian restorationists.

76. Kohn documented a visit to Grabowsky, whom he described as "a wise and clever man," for a discussion of politics and nationalism (diary, August 9, 1928, HKC-LBI, box 4, folder 1). Grabowsky was a Jewish convert to Protestantism; he and Kohn also corresponded in the early 1930s about the fate of German Jewry.

77. Kohn, diary, January 3, 1930, HKC-LBI, box 18, folder 4.

78. Hans Kohn to Martin Buber, April 3, 1930, MBA, 376/232.

79. Kohn, diary, March 7-10, April 20, and August 14, 1932, HKC-LBI, box 19, folder 1.

80. Heinrich Rogge, "Europas Nationalismus im Spiegel des Orients," *Der Ring*, February 3, 1929, 95 and 97. During the Nazi years, Rogge, an expert on international law, would be famous for his books *Nationale Friedenspolitik: Handbuch des Friedensproblems und seiner Wissenschaft auf der Grundlage Systematischer Völkerrechtspolitik* (Berlin: Junker, 1934) and *Hitlers Friedenspolitik und das Völkerrecht* (Berlin: Schlieffen Verlag, 1935).

81. Kohn, diary, March 14, 1929, HKC-LBI, box 18, folder 4.

82. Hans Kohn, *Nationalism and Imperialism in the Hither East*, translated by Margaret M. Green (London: G. Routledge and Sons, 1932), 4.

83. Ibid., 49: "In the wider sense, Czechoslovakia and Poland, where dominant nationality in the state uses the power of the State organization in order to exercise political and economic control over alien races within the national boundaries, are likewise imperialist."

84. Ibid., 52, 58–59, and 267. Though the last quotation refers specifically to missionaries, it is part of Kohn's broader thesis about the transformed interplay between East and West.

85. Kohn, *Nationalism and Imperialism in the Hither East*, 61.

86. Ibid., 49; see also 50-51. The assumption that all nationalism is state-nationalism made it necessary for Kohn to distinguish between civic and ethnic (state) nationalism.

87. Ibid., 65-66 and 269. Kohn's departure from the juxtaposition of political and cultural nationalism was not that simple and necessitates some further explanation. Kohn would continue to use the term "cultural nationalism" as analytically distinct from "political nationalism," but with a different meaning and evaluation. John Hutchinson, the great theoretician of cultural nationalism, has recently provided an overview of the concept with an extensive discussion of Kohn's evolving applications of it (see "Cultural Nationalism," in *The Wiley Blackwell Encyclopedia of Race, Ethnicity, and Nationalism*, edited by John Stone, Rutledge Dennis, Polly Rizova, Anthony D. Smith, and Xiaoshuo Hou [Chichester, UK: John Wiley and Sons, 2016], http://onlinelibrary.wiley.com/doi/10.1002/9781118663202.wberen400 /abstract.

88. Hans Kohn, *Orient and Occident* (New York: John Day, 1934), v and 105.

89. Aaron Berman, "Ameen Rihani and Hans Kohn: The Construction of a Pan-Arab Nationalist Narrative in the United States," in *Ameen Rihani's Arab-American Legacy*, 160; Ameen Rihani to Hans Kohn, July 25, 1932, HKC-LBI box 4, folder 1. In contrast, Nijmeh Hajjar has recently pointed to Kohn's influence on Rihani and suggested that it was Kohn who informed Rihani's pan-Arabism and not the other way around (*The Politics and Poetics of Ameen Rihani: The Humanist Ideology of an Arab-American Intellectual and Activist* [London: Tauris Academic Studies, 2010], 227). Kohn recorded his opinion of Rihani after a meeting with him "on the flaws of the Arabs. Smart, if somewhat Americanized" (diary, March 28, 1933, HKC-LBI, box 19, folder 1; see also the entries for March 29 and 30).

90. Umut Özkirimli, *Theories of Nationalism: A Critical Introduction*, 2nd ed. (Basingstoke, England: Palgrave Macmillan, 2010), 31.

91. Carlton J. H. Hayes, *Essays on Nationalism* (New York: Macmillan, 1926).

92. Terry Martin, "Affirmative Action Empire: The Soviet Union as the Highest Form of Imperialism," in *A State of Nations: Empire and Nation-Making in the Age of Lenin and Stalin*, edited by Ronald Grigor Suny and Terry Martin (Oxford: Oxford University Press, 2001), 67 and 76.

93. Hans Kohn, *Nationalism in the Soviet Union* (New York: AMS Press, 1966), 44, 35, and 48. One of the classic twenty-first century works on the topic of Soviet nationalities policy is Terry D. Martin, *The Affirmative Action Empire: Nations and Nationalism in the Soviet Union, 1923–1939* (Ithaca, NY: Cornell University Press, 2001).

94. Kohn, *Nationalism in the Soviet Union*, 45.

95. Ibid., 100.

96. Ibid., ix, viii, and xi.

97. Hans Kohn, *Western Civilization in the Near East*, translated by E. W. Dickes (New York: Columbia University Press, 1936), 227.

98. Elizabeth P. MacCallum, "Eyes on Asia Minor," *New Republic*, April 7, 1937, 272–73.

5. "A Disillusioned Love:" Break with Zionism

1. Hans Kohn, diary, August 29, 1932, HKC-LBI, box 19, folder 1. An earlier version of this chapter appeared as Adi Gordon, "Ein Zo Ela Ahava Nichzevet: Prishat Hans Kohn Me'hatnu'ah Hazionit," in *Brith Shalom Vehzionut Hadule'umit: Hashe'ela Ha'aravit Keshe'ela Yehudit*, edited by Adi Gordon (Jerusalem: Carmel, 2008). An English version of that text appeared as Adi Gordon, "Nothing but a Disillusioned Love: Hans Kohn's Break from the Zionist Movement," in *Against the Grain: Jewish Intellectuals in Hard Times*, edited by Ezra Mendelsohn, Stefani Hoffman, and Richard I. Cohen (New York: Berghahn, 2014), 117–42.

2. Hans Kohn to Robert Weltsch, July 2, 1936, HKRWC.

3. Hans Kohn to the Brith Shalom association, September 22, 1930, CZA, Brith Shalom Collection, A187-1a.

4. Hans Kohn, *Living in a World Revolution: My Encounters with History* (New York: Trident, 1964), 143 and 145.

5. Robert Weltsch interview by Hagit Lavsky and Israel Kolatt, July 9, 1979 (transcript),

Hebrew University of Jerusalem's Institute of Contemporary Jewry, Oral History Division, 183/15; Nathan Hofshi (formerly Frankel) interview by Ayala Dan-Kaspi, 1974, ibid., 114/37.

6. Hans Kohn, "Perspektiven," *Der Jude* 4, no. 11 (1919): 488–92.

7. Kohn, diary, January 2 and 7, 1927, HKC-LBI, box 18, folder 2. Kohn wrote: "Ahad Ha'am died. The great teacher of the Jews in the past generation. . . . It becomes increasingly clear to me that only he recognized the practical reality and the only possible meaning of Zionism" (ibid., January 2, 1927).

8. Kohn, diary, February 15, September 29, and October 28, 1928, HKC-LBI, box 18, folder 2. See also Hans Kohn to Robert Weltsch, May 8, 1930, RWC, AR7185, box 7, folder 18. This confrontation is documented also in a formal document of the Brith Shalom association (see "A [Correction of a] Report regarding a Debate between Dr. Arthur Ruppin, Dr. Hugo Bergmann, and Dr. Hans Kohn on Brith Shalom Issues," November 16, 1928, CZA, Brith Shalom Collection, A187-40.

9. Kohn, diary, June 8, 1928, HKC-LBI box 18, folder 2.

10. Hans Kohn to Robert Weltsch, June 12, 1928, RWC, box 7, folder 18.

11. Kohn, diary, August 26, 1929, HKC-LBI, box 18, folder 4.

12. Hans Kohn to Martin Buber, August 26, 1929, in Martin Buber, *The Letters of Martin Buber: A Life of Dialogue*, edited by Nahum N. Glatzer and Paul Mendes-Flohr and translated by Richard Winston, Clara Winston and Harry Zohn (New York: Schocken, 1991), 370.

13. Hans Kohn to Judah L. Magnes, September 2, 1929, CAHJP, P3/2665.

14. Kohn, diary, September 3, 1929, HKC-LBI, box 18, folder 4.

15. Ibid., September 4, 1929, HKC-LBI, box 18, folder 4.

16. Ibid., September 18, 1929, HKC-LBI, box 18, folder 4.

17. Robert Weltsch to Fritz Naphtali, October 24, 1929, CZA, Leo Hermann Collection, A 145/153.

18. Shmuel Sambursky to Leo Hermann, undated, CZA, Leo Hermann Collection, A 145, 153. Kohn was well aware of the plot, but since nothing was openly said, he could not do much more than complain, in a private letter to Leo Hermann, about the ugly atmosphere (see Hans Kohn to Leo Hermann, October 3, 1929, HKC-LBI, box 8, folder 9).

19. A copy of Hans Kohn to Arthur Hantke, October 22, 1929, is in CAHJP, P3/2399.

20. Hans Kohn to Berthold Feiwel, November 21, 1929, HKC-LBI, box 8, folder 9. English translation based on Martin Buber, *A Land of Two Peoples: Martin Buber on Jews and Arabs*, edited by Paul R. Mendes-Flohr (New York: Oxford University Press, 1983), 97–99.

21. Hans Kohn to Robert Weltsch, April 21, 1930, HKRWC. Kohn described his ideological progression during those years in another letter to Weltsch: "When I talked about binationalism, . . . the others still did not want to hear anything about it. And today, when I say that one can no longer talk about binationalism in its old sense, but only of a protected minority status, I am once again isolated, and the others say what I had said already in 1925" (Hans Kohn to Robert Weltsch, May 17, 1930, HKRWC).

22. Kohn, diary, November 15, 1929, and April 24, 1930, HKC-LBI, box 18, folder 4.

23. Ibid., November 21, 1929, HKC-LBI, box 18, folder 4.

24. Hans Kohn to Robert Weltsch, July 17, 1930, HKRWC.

25. Kohn, diary, June 12, 1930, HKC-LBI, box 18, folder 4.

26. Hans Kohn to Robert Weltsch, June 15, 1930, RWC, box 7, folder 18. See also Kohn, diary, June 14, 1930, HKC-LBI, box 18, folder 4.

27. Hans Kohn to the Brith Shalom association, September 22, 1930, CZA, Brith Shalom Collection, A187-1a. See also Kohn, diary, September 22, 1930, HKC-LBI, box 18, folder 4. Kohn wrote similarly to Magnes about his reasons for leaving Brith Shalom: "I do not think the B[rith] Sh[alom] [association] of much worth as long as those members who have any influence do not consider the principals of B. Sh. that they profess—binding for their public life. . . . The revisionists or the workers' party exercise some appeal because they stand and fall by their principles. The B. Sh. members do not" (Hans Kohn to Judah L. Magnes, October 2, 1930, CAHJP, P3/2665). Even after quitting Brith Shalom, however, Kohn continued to publish articles in its magazine, *She'ifoteinu*.

28. Hans Kohn to Martin Buber, March 8, 1924, in Buber, *The Letters of Martin Buber*, 310–11. The actual writing of the biography began only in 1927. Most of the correspondence between Buber and Kohn—beginning in 1911 and continuing into 1964—is at MBA, Arc. Ms. Var. 350, CHET, 376.

29. Much of their correspondence in the second half of the 1920s, most of which is in HKC-Klau, deals with the biography.

30. Kohn, diary, April 11, 1930, HKC-LBI, box 18, folder 4.

31. Hans Kohn to Robert Weltsch, May 3, 1930, HKRWC.

32. Hans Kohn to Martin Buber, September 2, 1929, in Martin Buber, *Martin Buber, Briefwechsel aus sieben Jahrzehnten*, edited by Grete Schaeder (Heidelberg, Germany: L. Schneider, 1972), 2:347–48.

33. Kohn wrote this ("Wir brauchen keine Religion u. Ethik, aber ein klares, eindeutiges Programm, das wir ernst nehmen") in the margin of a copy of an undated letter from Buber (probably from 1929 and probably to Robert Weltsch), which he sent back to Buber. See MBA, 376-I/15.

34. In a letter to his wife, Paula, on October 3, 1929, Buber compared Weltsch's "remarkable" conduct to that of Kohn, who, he argued, was "more doctrinaire, . . . tended to proclamations rather than seeking a real breakthrough in the labyrinth of facts" (Martin Buber, *Martin Buber, Briefwechsel aus sieben Jahrzehnten*, edited by Grete Schaeder [Heidelberg, Germany: L. Schneider, 1972], 2:318).

35. Kohn, diary, September 30, 1929, HKC-LBI, box 18, folder 4.

36. Hans Kohn to Robert Weltsch, May 3, 1930, HKRWC.

37. Hans Kohn to Martin Buber, December 10, 1929, in Buber, *Martin Buber, Briefwechsel aus sieben Jahrzehnten*, 2:357–60. The translation is based on Buber, *The Letters of Martin Buber*, 372–73.

38. In another letter to Weltsch, Kohn noted that only a year previously he had been "blind," but then he corrected himself immediately: "that is, I wasn't blind anymore. . . . But I did not have the courage to think things through; it was too convenient" (Hans Kohn to Robert Weltsch, July 20, [1930], HKRWC). In the turbulent months of the autumn of 1929, Kohn's relationship with Magnes deteriorated in a manner reminiscent of his relationship

with Buber (see, for example, Kohn diary, October 24, 1929, HKC-LBI, box 18, folder 4). But, in contrast to his relationship with Buber, Kohn seems to have been intimate enough with Magnes to criticize him directly (see Hans Kohn to Judah L. Magnes, November 29, 1929, CAHJ, P3/2665).

39. Kohn, diary, January 2, 1929, HKC-LBI, box 18, folder 4.

40. Hans Kohn to Judah L. Magnes, May 13, 1929, CAHJP, P3/2665.

41. Magnes wrote, "vieles davon auf Unzufriedenheit mit Dr. Kohns politischer Einstellung zurückzuführen ist" (Judah L. Magnes to Martin Buber, July 4, 1929, in Buber, *Martin Buber, Briefwechsel aus sieben Jahrzehnten*, 2:335). However, Norman Bentwich, who received the post, though less accomplished than Kohn, was also a binationalist (albeit a less radical one).

42. Kohn, diary, August 16, 1929, HKC-LBI, box 18, folder 4. For more on the chair in international peace and Bentwich's appointment to it, see Nachum T. Gross, "Social Sciences at the Hebrew University before 1948," in *Toldot hauniversitah haivrit biyerushalayim: Hitbasesut utsemihah*, edited by Hagit Lavsky (Jerusalem: Magnes, 2005), 505–8.

43. In some of his 1934 correspondence, Kohn used the letterhead of the planned publication, which indicated that Kohn's coeditor was to be the philosopher William Ernest Hocking and the publisher was to be the John Day Company.

44. Hans Kohn to John Haynes Holmes, January 28, 1930, CAHJP, P3/2400. See also Kohn, diary, January 7, 1930, HKC-LBI, box 18, folder 4.

45. Kohn was a member of the International Council of the War Resisters' International from 1926 to 1928 and again from 1931 to 1934. On his pacifist career, see Dieter Riesenberger, "Hans Kohn (1891–1971): Zionist und Pazifist," *Zeitschrift für Religions-u. Geistesgeschichte* 4, nos. 1–2 (1989): 166–74. See also Adi Gordon, "The Ideological Convert and the 'Mythology of Coherence': The Contradictory Hans Kohn and His Multiple Metamorphoses," *Leo Baeck Institute Yearbook* 55 (2010): 273–93. On the War Resisters' International in general and Kohn's role in it, see Devi Prasad, *War Is a Crime against Humanity: The Story of "War Resisters' International"* (London: War Resisters' International, 2005), especially 118–32.

46. A version of the address was published as Hans Kohn, "Aktiver Pazifismus," *Neue Wege* 23, no. 2 (1929): 82–94. Kurt Tucholsky, the Weimar master of political satire and one of the most vocal representatives of German pacifism, corresponded with Kohn regarding different pacifist concepts. Tucholsky flatly rejected Kohn's "active pacifism" (which, to him, did not seem active at all) on two levels: he said it was neither sufficiently sociopolitical nor adequately revolutionary (see Kurt Tucholsky to the War Resisters' International, May 21, 1929, and Hans Kohn to Kurt Tucholsky, June 22, 1929, HKC-LBI, box 14, folder 4). Kohn was closer to the German pacifist Carl von Ossietzky, who replaced Tucholsky as editor of the *Weltbühne* (see Kohn, diary, September 12 and 21, 1929, HKC-LBI, box 18, folder 4).

47. Kohn, "Aktiver Pazifismus," 84.

48. Rogers Brubaker, "Myths and Misconceptions in the Study of Nationalism," in *The State of the Nation: Ernest Gellner and the Theory of Nationalism*, edited by John A. Hall (Cambridge: Cambridge University Press, 1998), 273.

49. Hans Kohn to Martin Buber, September 2, 1929, in Buber, *Martin Buber, Briefwechsel aus sieben Jahrzehnten*, 2:437. For similar statements, see Hans Kohn to Judah L. Magnes, September 2, 1929, CAHJP, P3/2665. At the end of that letter, Kohn told Magnes that he "participated here [Zurich] in the meeting of the International Council of the War Resisters' International." There could be no clearer expression of the manner in which pacifism and Zionism merged in Kohn's world.

50. Kohn, diary, August 31 and September 2, 1929, HKC-LBI, box 18, folder 4.

51. Ibid., October 22, 1929, HKC-LBI, box 18, folder 4. Equally harsh remarks on both Einstein and Buber can be found in the entry for October 17, 1929.

52. Ibid., April 13, 1933, HKC-LBI, box 18, folder 4.

53. Kohn, *Living in a World Revolution*, 191–92.

54. At times Kohn seemed to have elevated homelessness to a Jewish imperative, a feature of cosmopolitan transcendence of state nationalism. For example, he wrote: "Jewish liberalism has . . . turned Judaism into the religion of citizens (just like Zionism turned Judaism into the religion of the citizens in the Jewish state). It is then like Zion, only with different aspirations. It drew no conclusions from its own feat (humanization), that Judaism is to be the vanguard, the church among the nations, that Jews should be an international community: some liberals did speak of it, but . . . remained Jewish citizens of their [respective] state, they never became homeless, and never did more . . . than reposition their domicile (to the United States, Paris, or Palestine), they may have changed their citizenship, but never transcended it into world citizenry (cosmopolitanism)" (Kohn, diary, December 31, 1932, HKC-LBI, box 19, folder 1). See also his entry eulogizing Rilke as "homeless and cosmopolitan" (Kohn, diary, January 7, 1927, HKC-LBI, box 18, folder 2).

55. Hans Kohn to Robert Weltsch, May 30, 1930, HKRWC.

56. Kohn, diary, August 29, 1932, HKC-LBI, box 19, folder 1.

57. Kohn wrote: "How wrong we were to think of universalism as Jewish. On the contrary: Judaism with its exclusive God, who commands them to conquer lands and eradicate their inhabitants, . . . always chauvinistic, it is a people that isolates itself out of a monstrous racial arrogance" (ibid., June 3, 1933, HKC-LBI, box 19, folder 1).

58. Ibid., April 10, 1933, HKC-LBI, box 19, folder 1.

59. Schmuel Hugo Bergmann, *Tagebücher und Briefe* (Königstein, Germany: Jüdischer Verlag bei Athenäum, 1985), 1:345.

60. Kohn, diary, April 2, July 7, and August 5, 1932, and March 28, 1933, HKC-LBI, box 19, folder 1. Another recurring name from Rihani's circle in Kohn's correspondence and diaries was that of George M. Haddad of Hebron and Beirut.

61. Hans Kohn to Hugo Bergmann, November 29, 1931, HBA, Arc. 4°1502/1561. Two years later, Kohn still felt this way: "I would have much preferred London over America!" (diary, September 13, 1933, HKC-LBI, box 19, folder 1).

62. Kohn, diary, October 18, 1933, HKC-LBI, box 19, folder 1.

63. Ibid., November 3, 1933, HKC-LBI, box 19, folder 1.

64. Ibid., November 10–11, 1933, HKC-LBI, box 19, folder 1; William A. Neilson to Hans Kohn, November 17, 1933, Neilson Presidential Collection, Smith College Archives, 15/28.

65. Hans Kohn, *Western Civilization in the Near East*, translated by E. W. Dickes (New York: Columbia University Press, 1936), v.

66. Kohn mentioned the symbolic timing in his letter to Magnes (Hans Kohn to Judah L. Magnes, September 6, 1935, CAHJP, P3/2665).

6. "The Totalitarian Crisis" and "the Last Best Hope": Catastrophic Americanization and Breakthrough

1. Hans Kohn to Jakob Wilhelm Hauer, 9 May 1933, HKC-LBI, 3/4.

2. Hans Kohn, "The Twilight of Nationalism?," *American Scholar* 6, no. 3 (1937): 268–69.

3. Hans Kohn to Judah L. Magnes, October 4, 1934, CAHJP, P3/2665.

4. For example, when discussing US oil interests in Mesopotamia, he was content to quote a Henry U. Höpli's reference to America's "open door policy" as "the theory under which the economically stronger is enabled to exploit the economically weaker." (Hans Kohn, *Western Civilization in the Near East*, translated by E. W. Dickes [New York: Columbia University Press, 1936], 179).

5. Hans Kohn, "Hapolitika shel Ha'imperia Habritit," *Hapo'el Hatza'ir*, December 12, 1924.

6. Hans Kohn, "Ma'atzamot," *Hapo'el Hatza'ir*, August 15, 1924.

7. Hans Kohn, "Neged Hazerem [I]," *Hapo'el Hatza'ir*, January 4, 1924.

8. Quoted in Brian Smollett, "The Rise and Fall of a Jewish Vision in the Life and Thought of Hans Kohn," in *Reappraisals and New Studies of the Modern Jewish Experience: Essays in Honor of Robert M. Seltzer*, edited by Brian Smollett and Christian Wiese (Leiden, the Netherlands: Brill, 2014), 275. Kohn was especially alarmed by what he saw as a lack of spiritual leadership among American Jews. Smollett is correct to identify Kohn's transition from advocating the de-Americanization of American Jews to advocating their Americanization, yet another of Kohn's ideological conversions (albeit a gradual one).

9. Hans Kohn to Martin Buber, February 13, 1934, MBA, Arc. Ms. Var. 350, CHET, 376/252; Kohn, diary, September 18, 1934, HKC-LBI, box 19, folder 2.

10. Hans Kohn to Robert Weltsch, February 7, 1936, HKRWC.

11. There was one exception: his talk at the Council on Foreign Relations addressed Arab nationalism. See correspondence between Kohn and the Institute of International Education, HKC-LBI, box 6, folder 1. These documents include even the syllabi of the lecture series.

12. Seeing the League of Nation as failed, Kohn longed throughout the 1920s, for the coming of a true League of Nations that would include all nations and grant them complete equality.

13. Kohn, diary, May 4, 1928, HKC-LBI box 18, folder 2. See also the discussion of Hauer in ibid., April 19, 1928; Jakob Wilhelm Hauer to Hans Kohn, March 27, 1929 (in which Hauer speaks ill of German pacifists), and December 9, 1929, HKC-LBI box 14, folder 4.

14. Kohn, diary, January 1, 1928, HKC-LBI box 18, folder 2; Hans Kohn, "Das islamische Gebiet als Brücke: Die verkehrsgeographischen Probleme der Orientpolitik," *Zeitschrift für Politik* 17, no. 3 (1928), 634–45.

15. Kohn, diary, August 5, 1929 (during the fifteenth World Zionist Congress), and October 27–28, 1930, November 23, 1932, HKC-LBI box 18, folder 3.

16. Ibid., August 20 and 24, 1928, HKC-LBI box 18, folder 2. The latter entry may be a quotation he admired from a lecture he heard, though he did not indicate this clearly.

17. Hans Kohn to Arthur Ruppin, May 9, 1928, CZA, Brith Shalom Collection, 107/695; Hans Kohn to Berthold Feiwel, November 21, 1929, HKC-LBI, box 8, folder 9.

18. Weltsch wrote, "Why do I even stay in Germany?" (Robert Weltsch to Hans Kohn, March 1, 1932, HKRWC).

19. Kohn, diary, June 8, 1932, HKC-LBI, box 19, folder 1.

20. Hans Kohn, "Über einige Gesichtspunkte des politischen Judenproblems in Deutschland und Europa," *Europäische Revue* 8 (August 1932): 479–89.

21. Ibid., 483. Liberalism, Kohn insisted, was not Jewish, but it did offer Jews "a familiar way to find meaning in history, in the pursuit of greater justice and peace" (ibid.).

22. Ibid., 484.

23. Ibid., 487.

24. The original twenty-one-page essay (referred to here as "Über einige Gesichtspunkte") is in HKC-LBI, box 2, folder 5.

25. Kohn, "Über einige Gesichtspunkte," 3 and 13, HKC-LBI, box 2, folder 5.

26. Robert Weltsch, "Wear the Yellow Badge with Pride (April 4, 1933)," in *The Jew in the Modern World: A Documentary History*, 2nd ed., edited by Paul R. Mendes-Flohr, and Jehuda Reinharz (New York: Oxford University Press, 1995), 640–41.

27. Kohn, diary, April 10, 1933, HKC-LBI, box 19, folder 1.

28. Hannah Arendt, "What Remains? The Language Remains: A Conversation with Günther Gaus," translated by Joan Stambaugh, in Hannah Arendt, *The Portable Hannah Arendt*, edited by Peter R. Baehr (New York: Penguin, 2000), 11.

29. Julien Benda, *The Treason of the Intellectuals*, translated by Richard Aldington (New Brunswick, NJ: Transaction, 2007), 44. See also Kohn, diary, June 3, 1933, HKC-LBI, box 19, folder 1.

30. Richard Hartmann to Hans Kohn, April 4, 1933, HKC-LBI, box 3, folder 4. See also Hartmann's letter to Kohn on February 8, 1933 (HKC-LBI, box 3, folder 4).

31. Hans Kohn to Richard Hartmann, April 20, 1933, HKC-LBI, box 3, folder 4.

32. Jakob Wilhelm Hauer to Hans Kohn, April 1, 1933; Kohn to Hauer, April 20[, 1933], HKC-LBI, box 3, folder 4.

33. Jakob Wilhelm Hauer to Hans Kohn, April 25, 1933, HKC-LBI, box 3, folder 4. Hauer may have been referring to the exchange between Buber and the Nazi theologian Gerhard Kittel described in: Martin Buber, "An Open Letter to Gerhard Kitter (1933)," and Gerhard Kittel, "Response to Martin Buber (1934)" in *The Third Reich Sourcebook*, edited by Anson Rabinbach and Sander L. Gilman (Berkeley: University of California Press, 2013), 200–203.

34. Hans Kohn to Jakob Wilhelm Hauer, May 9, 1933, HKC-LBI, box 4, folder 1.

35. Kohn, diary, August 11, 1933, HKC-LBI, box 19, folder 1.

36. Hans Kohn, "Zionism," in *Encyclopaedia of the Social Sciences*, edited by Edwin Robert Anderson Seligman and Alvin Saunders Johnson (New York: Macmillan, 1934),

15:528), reprinted in Hans Kohn, *Revolutions and Dictatorships: Essays in Contemporary History* (Cambridge, MA: Harvard University Press, 1939), 299.

37. Kohn, diary, August 8, 1933, HKC-LBI, box 19, folder 1.

38. Quoted in Katrina vanden Heuvel, *The Change I Believe In: Fighting for Progress in the Age of Obama* (New York: Nation, 2011), xii.

39. Kohn, diary, January 1, 1948, HKC-LBI, box 20, folder 3.

40. The mapping of Kohn's social life here relies largely on his diaries, which regularly documented his meetings and visits with other people (his diaries for the years 1934–43 are in HKC-LBI box 19, folders 2–6). Many of his relationships—such as those with Koppel Pinson, William Ernest Hocking, Merle Curti, and Carl Joachim Friedrich—are also documented in correspondences in their respective archives.

41. Malcolm S. Knowles, *A History of the Adult Education Movement in the United States* (Huntington, NY: Krieger, 1977), 199. The list of the association's presidents includes many of Kohn's acquaintances and colleagues, among them Charles A. Bird (president in 1935), William Allen Neilson (1937), and Alvin Johnson (1939).

42. Kohn's ties with Jewish American organizations included his relationship with Henry Hurwitz's *Menorah Journal*, to which he had contributed before moving to America. On Hurwitz and the *Menorah Journal*, see Daniel Greene, *The Jewish Origins of Cultural Pluralism: The Menorah Association and American Diversity* (Bloomington: Indiana University Press, 2011).

43. Kohn also had dinner with Brüning when the latter delivered a talk at Smith, titled "Constitutional Problems in Germany, 1930–1933." Kohn found many interesting elements both in their personal conversation and in the lecture, but ultimately he found Brüning "antisemitic, against Jewish bankers who [ostensibly] supported the Nazis and put them on the throne" (Kohn, diary, February 6, 1939, HKC-LBI box 19, folder 5).

44. Hans Kohn to Hugo Bergmann, February 14, 1935, HBA, Arc. 4° 1502/1561.

45. One diary entry lists the "Neilson Klub" members as including—beyond Neilson, Kohn, and Borgese—Koffka and William Francis Ganong (psychologists); Curti, Harold Underwood Faulkner, Sydney Raymond Packard, and Vincent M. Scramuzza (historians); Esther Lowenthal and William Aylott Orton (economists); Michel F. Cantarella and Arthur Wake Locke (musicologists); Walter Carl Barnes (in German studies); Ralph Harlow (in religious studies); and Otto Kraushaar (in philosophy) (Kohn, diary, January 9, 1937, HKC-LBI box 19, folder 3). Kohn presented his thoughts on the nationalism of John Milton and Oliver Cromwell to the group in early 1938.

46. Hans Kohn, *Living in a World Revolution: My Encounters with History* (New York: Trident, 1964), 160.

47. Kohn, diary, May 5, 1935, HKC-LBI box 19, folder 2.

48. Betty Friedan, *Life So Far: A Memoir* (New York: Simon and Schuster, 2000), 102.

49. Hans Kohn, "Race Conflict," in *Encyclopaedia of the Social Sciences*, 13:40.

50. Hans Kohn to W. E. B. Du Bois, October 9, 1935, W. E. B. Du Bois Papers, MS 312, Special Collections and University Archives, University of Massachusetts, Amherst, Libraries.

51. Alain Locke to W. E. B. Du Bois, March 6, 1936, in W. E. B. Du Bois, *The Correspondence of W. E. B. Du Bois*, edited by and Herbert Aptheker, paperback ed. with corrections (Amherst, MA: University of Massachusetts Press, 1997), 2:83.

52. Kohn, diary, February 2, 1937, HKC-LBI, box 19, folder 3.

53. Hans Kohn, "Negro Folk Education," *Journal for Adult Education* 9, no. 3 (1937): 312.

54. Hans Kohn, "Terra Incognita," *Journal for Adult Education* 11, no. 1 (1939): 80.

55. The term "nationalizing states" is borrowed from Rogers Brubaker, *Nationalism Reframed: Nationhood and the National Question in the New Europe* (Cambridge: Cambridge University Press, 1996), 63-65.

56. Kohn wrote in his diary: "Hitler in Vienna! How many mistakes enabled this!" (March 12, 1938, HKC-LBI, box 19, folder 4).

57. Quoted in "Chapel and Assembly Notes," *Smith Alumnae Quarterly*, May 1938, 266.

58. Robert Weltsch to Hans Kohn, March 24, 1938, HKRWC; Kohn, diary, September 16 and 29, October 2 and 12, and November 11, 1938, HKC LBI, box 19, folder 4; Hans Kohn, "The Choice before Us," in *Report of the American Association of University Professors' Twenty-Fifth Annual Meeting, 27–28 December 1938*, HKC-LBI, box 6, folder 3.

59. Robert Weltsch to Hans Kohn, May 13, 15, and 21, and June 8, 1938, HKRWC.

60. Kohn, diary, March 15, 1939, HKC-LBI, box 19, folder 5.

61. Ibid., August 23 and September 10, 1939, HKC-LBI, box 19, folder 5.

62. Much of this tragic correspondence is concentrated in HKC-LBI, box 12, folder 8. See additional letters and telegrams from Kohn on behalf of his siblings in the Office of the President William Allan Neilson Files, box 15, folder 28, Neilson Presidential Collection, Smith College Archives.

63. This short letter is included in Fritz Ullmann (sent from Geneva) to Leo Hermann (in Jerusalem), August 23, 1944, HKC-LBI, box 12, folder 9. See also Hermann to Ullmann (detailing the new developments in the life of Hans Kohn and his family so that Ullman could send them on to Fritz and Grete) Ullmann, October 5, 1944, HKC-LBI, box 12, folder 9.

64. Hans Kohn to Koppel Pinson, August 15, 1945, Koppel S. Pinson Collection, LBI. See also Pinson to Kohn, August 18, 1945, HKC-LBI, box 12, folder 8. Kohn kept in his personal papers (HKC-LBI, box 8, folder 10) a chilling twenty-three-page report by Hermann on his first post-Holocaust visit to the remains of Jewish Prague, September–October 1945; the report presents the fate of many murdered friends and relatives.

65. Hans Kohn, "Communist and Fascist Dictatorship: A Comparative Study," in *Dictatorship in the Modern World*, edited by Guy Stanton Ford (Minneapolis: University of Minnesota Press, 1935), 148.

66. Ibid., 151 and 153. Kohn's totalitarianism became more sweeping in the second edition of the book , which included an entirely different contribution by Kohn: "Now again Moscow and Berlin seemed united in a similar form of statehood, alike in a totalitarian control of all individual activities, in authoritarian leadership, in considering the state as the vested interest of one party, in abusive violence of language, in a fanatical and arrogant faith" ("Between Democracy and Fascism," in *Dictatorship in the Modern World*, edited by Guy Stanton Ford, 2nd ed. [Minneapolis: University of Minnesota Press, 1939], 83). And on November 17, 1939,

Kohn and Hayes spoke at a public meeting about totalitarianism, sponsored by the American Philosophical Society, and Kohn's talk clearly and without reservation equated Germans and Russians (see William L. Laurence, "Despots Pictured against the Ages," *New York Times*, November 18, 1939).

67. The original plans included a book on the deterioration of conservative thought, traced from Edmund Burke to Hitler, and another book on democracy and nationalism in Central Europe (Kohn, diary, August 8, 1933, HKC-LBI, box 19, folder 1).

68. Hans Kohn, *Revolutions and Dictatorships: Essays in Contemporary History* (Cambridge, MA: Harvard University Press: 1939), 340; see also 7. It is easy to see how this notion of a global and largely one-directional spread of Western ideas continued almost seamlessly from Kohn's late works on the Middle East, primarily his *Die Europäisierung des Orients* (Berlin: Schocken, 1934).

69. Kohn, *Revolutions and Dictatorships*, 137.

70. Hans Kohn, "Mr. Kohn Refutes a Point," *American Scholar* 9, no. 4 (1940): 506.

71. Hans Kohn, *World Order in Historical Perspective* (Cambridge, MA, Harvard University Press, 1942), xii.

72. Buber asked his audience: "Why do we call ourselves Jews? Because we are Jews? What does it mean: we are Jews? . . . Why do we call ourselves Jews? Only out of inherited custom—because our fathers did so? Or out of our own reality?" ("Judaism and the Jews," in Martin Buber, *On Judaism*, edited by and Nahum N. Glatzer, translated by Eva Jospe [New York: Schocken, 1967], 11).

73. Carlton J. H. Hayes, "A Popular Front against Unreason: Force or Reason, by Hans Kohn," *Saturday Review*, April 3, 1937, 13. Kohn's liberal commitment is evident even in the book's dedication to Smith's president, William Allan Neilson, "the example of a true liberal and a true humanitarian" (Hans Kohn, *Force or Reason: Issues of the Twentieth Century* [Cambridge, MA: Harvard University Press, 1937], unnumbered page).

74. Kohn, *Force or Reason*, 98.

75. Kohn, "Race Conflict." Kohn also referred to a "fundamental difference between the imperialism of the liberal powers and that of Fascist nations": the former "is based upon the fundamental assumption of the equality of all men and races," and so "liberal imperialism grows by necessity less and less oppressive" (*Revolutions and Dictatorships*, 378).

76. Kohn, *Force or Reason*, 19–21.

77. Hans Kohn, "The Twilight of Nationalism?" *American Scholar* 6, no. 3 (1937): 286 and 270.

78. Hans Kohn, *Force or Reason: Issues of the 20th Century*, 3rd ed. (Cambridge, MA: Harvard University Press, 1938), x.

79. The chapter on Zionism, originally published in the 1934 *Encyclopaedia of the Social Sciences*, opens with a straightforward definition of the movement as the aspiration for a Jewish nation-state in Palestine (Kohn, *Revolutions and Dictatorships*, 299). This indicated the complete break with Zionism of a man who for twenty years had struggled to create a Zionism that would mean something other than a Jewish nation-state in Palestine.

80. Ibid., 82, 225, and 241.

81. Ibid., unnumbered page, 209, 50, and 74. However, Kohn was no determinist: Germany did not have to become nor would it have to remain Nazi.

82. Ibid., 185.

83. Ibid., especially 200, 216, and 333. The Peace Conference's shortcomings, he now claimed, were not in its precepts but in their absence of seriousness of purpose and implementation.

84. Ibid., 333 and 337.

85. Ibid., 349.

86. Ibid., 362.

87. Ibid., 357, 362, 386, and 409.

88. Ibid., 391; see also 394.

89. Ibid., 396 and 397–98.

90. Ibid., 6 and 36–37. His Christian supersessionism, or replacement theology, would ironically also be manifested in *City of Man*, which he coauthored as a member of the Committee of Fifteen (Committee of Fifteen, *The City of Man: A Declaration on World Democracy* [New York: Viking, 1940])—a work that also celebrated Judeochristianity.

91. Kohn, *Revolutions and Dictatorships*, 417 and 420.

92. Hans Kohn, "The World Must Federate," *Asia*, February 1940, 63–66, reprinted as Kohn, *The World Must Federate! Isolation versus Cooperation* (New York: Press of the Woolly Whale, 1940).

93. Kohn, *The World Must Federate!*, 3–4. He further ridiculed these "ferocious isolationists," who looked the other way when Manchuria, Austria, Ethiopia, and Czechoslovakia were invaded, and who now "abandoned their isolationism and clamored for action against the Soviet Union" (ibid., 5).

94. Ibid., 15–16, 21–23, and 24–25.

95. Leopold Kohr, *The Breakdown of Nations* (London: Kegan Paul, 1957), xv–xvi; John McClaughry, "A Visionary of Disunion," *New York Times*, December 28, 1991.

96. Lloyd K. Garrison to Hans Kohn, May 31, 1940, HKC-LBI, box 9, folder 1; Paul Birdsall, "Beneath the War [a review of Kohn's *Not by Arms Alone*], *Saturday Review*, January 4, 1941, 19.

97. Hans Kohn to Henry Pitney Van Dusen, July 11, 1940, Fight for Freedom, Inc. Records (MC 025), box 13, folder 13. Manuscripts Division, Department of Rare Books and Special Collections, Princeton University Library. See also James T. Shotwell to Hans Kohn, March 23, 1939, HKC-LBI, box 9, folder 1 (Shotwell expressed the "hope that American public opinion will be informed by thinkers like yourself of the nature of the present situation"); Hans Kohn to Bishop Henry W. Hobson, December 12, 1941, HKC-LBI, box 9, folder 1; Hans Kohn to F. H. Peter Cusick, May 1, 1941, HKC-LBI, box 9, folder 1.

98. The committee members were Herbert Agar, Frank Aydelotte, G. A. Borgese, Hermann Broch, Van Wyck Brooks, Dorothy Canfield Fisher, Ada L. Comstock, William Yandell Elliott, Christian Gauss, Oscar Jaszi, Alvin Johnson, Hans Kohn, Thomas Mann, Lewis Mumford, William Allan Neilson, Reinhold Niebuhr, and Gaetano Salvemini. See Paul Michael Lützeler, "Visionaries in Exile: Broch's Cooperation with G. A. Borgese and

Hannah Arendt," in *Hermann Broch, Visionary in Exile: The Yale Symposium 2001*, edited by Paul Michael Lützeler (Rochester, NY: Camden House, 2003), 67-88; Adi Gordon and Udi Greenberg, "*The City of Man*, European Émigrés, and the Genesis of Postwar Conservative Thought," *Religions* 3, no. 4 (2012): 681-98.

99. Kohn had hosted Thomas Mann and his wife when the two visited Palestine in 1930 (Katia Mann to Hans Kohn, April 7, 1930, HKC-LBI, box 8, folder 7). According to Kohn's son, some of Kohn's fellow anti-isolationists from the late 1930s would remain his close friends for many years.

100. Lewis Mumford, *My Work and Days: A Personal Chronicle* (New York: Harcourt, 1979), 391-92. On the program of the Atlantic City event, see Giuseppe Antonio Borgese to Hans Kohn, May 3, 1940, HKC-LBI, box 9, folder 1. Notably, Beard would later publish a very positive review of Kohn's *Idea of Nationalism* (Charles A. Beard, "The Idea of Nationalism by Hans Kohn," *American Political Science Review* 38, no. 4 [1944]: 801-3).

101. Thomas Mann, *Tagebücher 1940-1943*, edited by Peter de Mendelssohn (Munich: S. Fischer, 1977), 81-82; Thomas Mann to Agnes E. Meyer, May 25, 1940, in Thomas Mann, *Letters of Thomas Mann, 1889-1955*, selected and translated by Richard Winston and Clara Winston (Berkeley: University of California Press, 1990), 262.

102. Committee of Fifteen, *The City of Man*, 11-12.

103. Ibid., 14.

104. Jason W. Stevens, *God-Fearing and Free: A Spiritual History of America's Cold War* (Cambridge, MA: Harvard University Press, 2010), 2-3 and 30.

105. Committee of Fifteen, *The City of Man*, 80. See also Eric Voegelin, *Die politischen Religionen* (Vienna: Bermann-Fischer, 1938); Hannah Arendt, "Reply to Eric Voegelin," in Hannah Arendt, *The Portable Hannah Arendt*, 162.

106. Committee of Fifteen, *The City of Man*, 23-24.

107. Ibid., 64-65. "Rome did not spread . . ." is a quote from Francis Bacon.

108. Ibid., 65-66.

109. Hans Kohn, "Blessed Are the Peacemakers," *New Republic*, July 17, 1935, 7.

110. Committee of Fifteen, *The City of Man*, 35, 58-60, 68, and 94. This argument was made in Gordon and Greenberg, "*The City of Man*, European Émigrés, and the Genesis of Postwar Conservative Thought."

111. Committee of Fifteen, *The City of Man*, 30, 31, and 51.

112. Carl J. Friedrich to Hans Kohn, January 20, 1941, Carl J. Friedrich Papers, Harvard University Archive, box 22, file Hans Kohn Correspondence.

113. Hans Kohn, "From the Address by Professor Hans Kohn of Smith College: at the Thirtieth-Year Dinner of the Menorah Journal: Hotel Commodore. New York City, November 29, 1944" (transcript), 13, Henry Hurwitz/Menorah Association Collection, MS-2, box 27, folder 4, American Jewish Archives, Cincinnati, Ohio, 50.

114. Trygve Throntveit, "A Strange Fate: Quincy Wright and the Trans-War Trajectory of Wilsonian Internationalism," *White House Studies* 10, no. 4 (2011): 361.

115. Hans Kohn, *Not by Arms Alone: Essays on Our Time* (Cambridge, MA: Harvard University Press, 1940), 56-57 and 64.

116. Carl J. Friedrich to Hans Kohn, January 20, 1941, Carl J. Friedrich Papers, Harvard University Archive, box 22, file Hans Kohn Correspondence.

117. Hans Kohn], "The Crisis and Its Implications: Hans Kohn at a Special Assembly at Smith College, December 9, 1941," box 15, folder 28, in William Allan Neilson Presidential Papers, Neilson Presidential Collection, Smith College Archives.

118. Kohn, *World Order in Historical Perspective*, 6–7.

119. Reuben H. Markham, cable to Hans Kohn, March 22, 1943, HKC-LBI, box 9, folder 1.

120. Kohn, diary, November 10, 1945 and "Letter from Macmillan also German OWI translation of the Idea," HKC-LBI, box 20, folder 1.

121. Kohn, *World Order in Historical Perspective*, 46; Ferdinand Tönnies to Hans Kohn, September 15, 1930, HKC-LBI, box 8, folder 7; Hans Kohn, "Book Review: Hupe's *Geopolitics* and Weigert's *German Geopolitics*," *Annals of the American Academy of Political and Social Science* 223 (September 1942), 207–8; Hans Kohn, "Book Review: *Generals and Geographers*," *Annals of the American Academy of Political and Social Science* 225 (January 1943): 230–31; Hans Kohn, "Story of Haushofer," *New York Times*, June 27, 1948.

122. Kohn's diaries for this period are in HKC-LBI, boxes 19 and 20.

123. Kohn, diary, September 28, 1943, HKC-LBI, box 19, folder 6.

124. Craig J. Calhoun, *Nations Matter: Culture, History, and the Cosmopolitan Dream* (London: Routledge, 2007), 119.

125. On October 27, 1933, Kohn spelled out to Hayes the outline of three books on nationalism (discussed in more detail below in the text): first, the idea of nationalism before the French Revolution; second, a comparative study of nationalisms in the age of nationalism, 1789–1900; and third, the problems of nationalism in the present and the future. For example, parts of chapter 4 ("Renaissance and Reformation: The Emergence of Nationalism") of *The Idea of Nationalism* were based on his 1940 essay "Genesis and Character of English Nationalism" (*Journal of the History of Ideas* 1, no. 1 [1940] 69–94); and more notably, parts of chapter 2 ("Israel and Hellas: From Tribalism to Universalism") relied on his earliest work, including *The Political Idea of Judaism* (1924), and even his "Spirit of the Orient" (1913). Kohn went so far as to proclaim in his preface to *The Idea of Nationalism* that his 1922 essay "Nationalismus" "contained already in outline some of the main conclusions of" the later book (*The Idea of Nationalism: A Study in Its Origins and Background* [New York: Macmillan Company, 1944], viii).

126. Kohn, *The Idea of Nationalism*, viii; "The Twilight of Nationalism?," 259–70; "The Roots of Modern Nationalism," *Bulletin of the International Committee of Historical Sciences* 10 (1938): 388–91; "The Nature of Nationalism," *American Political Science Review* 33, no. 6 (1939): 1001–21; and "Coalesce or Collide," *American Scholar* 9, no. 3 (1940): 261–73.

127. Kohn, *The Idea of Nationalism*, 3, 13, and 78. For a recent discussion of Kohn's argument regarding nationalism in the Middle Ages, see Patrick J. Geary, *The Myth of Nations: The Medieval Origins of Europe* (Princeton, NJ: Princeton University Press, 2001).

128. Kohn, *The Idea of Nationalism*, 4 and 291. For a more detailed exploration of Kohn's book, see Brian Matthew Smollett, "Reviving Enlightenment in the Age of Nationalism: The Historical and Political Thought of Hans Kohn in America" (PhD diss., City University of New York, 2014), 92–137.

129. Kohn, "Coalesce or Collide," 273.

130. The one recurrent criticism of the book is that it focuses on the history of the idea of nationalism, instead of presenting a social history of nationalism. For example, J. Salwyn Schapiro wrote that "Professor Kohn does not stress sufficiently the social and economic aspects of the growth of nationalism" ("The Modern Religion," *Menorah Journal* 32 [Autumn 1944]: 222).

131. Kohn, *The Idea of Nationalism*, 20 and 22.

132. The slim paperback that Kohn called *The Age of Nationalism: The First Era of Global History* (New York: Harper and Brothers, 1962) was certainly not the second volume that Kohn planned in the 1940s. Even into the mid-1950s, his correspondence indicates his commitment to finish the second volume. It was for this purpose, for example, that he was invited to spend the academic year 1955-56 at the Institute for Advanced Study in Princeton, New Jersey. See Hans Kohn to J. Robert Oppenheimer, March 14, 1955, HKC-LBI, box 7, folder 4; Hans Kohn to Brigham Day, October 21, 1957, HKC-LBI, box 7, folder 3.

133. Kohn, *The Idea of Nationalism*, viii, x, 20, 23, and 576.

134. Ibid., 351. For another formulation of the same principle, see ibid., 329.

135. Ibid., 574. The quotes are from Adi Gordon, "The Need for West: Hans Kohn and the North Atlantic Community," *Journal of Contemporary History* 46, no. 1 (2011): 35.

136. Rogers Brubaker, "Myths and Misconceptions in the Study of Nationalism," in *The State of the Nation: Ernest Gellner and the Theory of Nationalism*, edited by John A. Hall (Cambridge: Cambridge University Press, 1998), 274.

137. Calhoun, *Nations Matter*, 118-19 and 146; Ellie Kedourie, *The Chatham House Version and Other Middle-Eastern Studies* (London: Weidenfeld and Nicolson, 1970), 286; Partha Chatterjee, *Nationalist Thought and the Colonial World: A Derivative Discourse* (London: Zed, 1986), 2.

138. Kohn, *The Idea of Nationalism*, 20 and 576.

139. Calhoun, *Nations Matter*, 118 and 146. The usual critique leveled—with varying degrees of severity—at Kohn's work after his move to the United States was that it was unduly forgiving and uncritical of liberalism and of the excesses of Western nationalism and imperialism. See, for example, Louis Dolivet, "[Review of] *World Order*," *Free World*, September 1942, 381.

140. Kohn, diary, July 6 and September 6, 1945, March 8, 9, and 23, 1948, HKC-LBI box 20, folders 1-2.

141. Hans Kohn, *Prophets and Peoples: Studies in Nineteenth Century Nationalism* (New York: Collier-Macmillan, 1946), 2-3 and 133.

142. T. S. Eliot to Edward Mead Earle, October 14, 1948, and to Hans Kohn, November 8, 1948, HKC-LBI, box 8, folder 4.

143. Hans Kohn, "This Century of Betrayal: Can America Lead a New Struggle for Independence?" *Commentary*, September 1, 1946, 201-7.

144. Committee of Fifteen, *The City of Man*, 65.

145. Hans Kohn, "Patterns of the Coming Peace," in Hans Kohn, André Géraud, and Reginald George Trotter, *Patterns of the Coming Peace: Three Lectures Delivered on the*

Fenton Foundation (Buffalo: State University of New York at Buffalo, 1943), 5–14. See also his book review essay, Hans Kohn, "War Aims and Peace Patterns," *Saturday Review*, July 4, 1942, 9–10 and 26.

146. Kohn, "Patterns of the Coming Peace," 6 and 14.

147. Hans Kohn, "The Morgenthau Plan for Germany," *Saturday Review*, October 6, 1945, 11; and "Germany," in *America and the New World: The Merrick Lectures for 1945*, edited by Norman Angel (New York: Abingdon-Cokesbury, 1945), 29.

148. Kohn's correspondence with those organizations is in HKC-LBI, box 8, folder 1. Kohn advocated for the federal union as early as 1941: "On Lincoln's Birthday, Mr. Kohn spoke for the movement for Federal Union, saying that Lincoln fought first not for the abolishment of slavery, but for federal union. And our task now is threefold: (1) To win the war; (2) To win the peace; (3) To establish a better democratic order here and everywhere" ("Chapel Notes," *Smith Alumnae Quarterly*, May 1941, 166. On the Committee to Frame a World Constitution, see Or Rosenboim, *The Emergence of Globalism: Competing Visions of World Order in Britain and the United States (1939–1950)* (Princeton, NJ: Princeton University Press, forthcoming), chapter 6; Robert L. Tsai, *America's Forgotten Constitutions: Defiant Visions of Power and Community* (Cambridge, MA: Harvard University Press, 2014), chapter 6.

149. Kohn, diary, August 8 and September 25, 1945, and February 20, 1946, HKC-LBI, box 20, folder 1.

150. Hans Kohn, "Jews in a Gentile World," *Jewish Social Studies* 4, no. 3 (1942): 275–77.

151. Kohn, "From the Address by Professor Hans Kohn of Smith College," 27.

152. Hannah Arendt, "Zionism Reconsidered," *Menorah Journal* 33, no.2 (1945): 162–96.

153. Quoted in Jack Ross, *Rabbi Outcast: Elmer Berger and American Jewish Anti-Zionism* (Washington: Potomac, 2011), 68.

154. Kohn, diary, August 5–6, 1946, HKC-LBI, box 20, folder 1.

155. The degree of Kohn's support for the United Nations is documented in his memoirs: "The Western political tradition, the heritage of England and of the Enlightenment, of Locke and Kant, found its expression in the Preamble to the Charter of the United Nations and in the Universal Declaration of Human Rights" (Kohn, *Living in a World Revolution*, 178).

156. Kohn, diary, May 27, 1948, HKC-LBI, box 20, folder 3.

157. Quoted in Hans Kohn to Max Steinbock, October 27, 1948, HKC-LBI, Box 14, folder 10.

158. Quoted in "Dr. Kohn Pleads for Identity of Jews with U.S. Culture," *Council News* 2, no. 12 (1948): 1 and 8.

159. Hans Kohn to Nelson Glueck, May 13, 1949, HKC-LBI, box 14, folder 12.

7. Nationalism in the American Century

1. Hans Kohn, *Is the Liberal West in Decline?* (London: Pall Mall, 1957), 73.

2. Hans Kohn, *Prelude to Nation-States: The French and German Experience, 1789–1815* (Princeton, N J: Van Nostrand, 1967), 1–2.

3. Hans Kohn, *Living in a World Revolution: My Encounters with History* (New York: Trident, 1964), 179.

4. Ibid., 184.

5. Hans Kohn to Judah L. Magnes, February 24, 1948 (transcript), RWC, box 1, folder 48. Magnes's response (March 31, 1948) exemplifies the continued ideological gap between the two men: "When one hears that there is the possibility of war between the United States and Russia, the question that arises is, why? . . . Is the war to come because Russia has done in Rumania, Bulgaria, Hungary and Czechoslovakia what the United States is doing in Greece, Turkey and Italy"? (ibid.).

6. Donald J. Puchala, "World Hegemony and the United Nations," *International Studies Review* 7, no. 4 (2005): 579 and 581.

7. John Fousek, *To Lead the Free World: American Nationalism and the Cultural Roots of the Cold War* (Chapel Hill: University of North Carolina Press, 2000), 7-8.

8. Hans Kohn, *The Twentieth Century: A Mid-Way Account of the Western World* (New York: Macmillan, 1949), 217-18. Kohn expressed similar views in a lecture at Brooklyn College, where he spoke of America's role in revitalizing Western civilization across the Atlantic (quoted in "Ideals not Guns, Held Best Export," *New York Times*, November 16, 1950).

9. [E. H. Carr], "Eyes across the Sea," *Times Literary Supplement*, May 12, 1950, 287.

10. Henry R. Luce, "The American Century," *Life*, February 17, 1941, 61-65.

11. Kohn's reevaluation of the nation-state grew clearer in his later works (see, for example, the epigraph in this chapter from *Prelude to Nation-States*).

12. Hans Kohn, *American Nationalism: An Interpretive Essay* (New York: Macmillan, 1957), 227.

13. Rogers Brubaker sees this perception of "all of eastern Europe—and many other world regions—as a seething cauldron of ethnic and national conflict, on the verge of boiling over into violence," as one of the key "myths and misconceptions in the study of nationalism" ("Myths and Misconceptions in the Study of Nationalism," in *The State of the Nation: Ernest Gellner and the Theory of Nationalism*, edited by John Hall (Cambridge: Cambridge University Press, 1998), 273.

14. Nils Gilman, *Mandarins of the Future: Modernization Theory in Cold War America* (Baltimore, MD: Johns Hopkins University Press, 2003), 3 and 281. Most overt elements of modernization theory in Kohn's pre-American works are manifested in *Die Europäisierung des Orients* (Berlin: Schocken, 1934). Though the title literally means "the Europeanization of the East," the book appeared in the United States (as well as in England) as Hans Kohn, *Western Civilization in the Near East*, translated by E. W. Dickes (New York: Columbia University Press, 1936).

15. Jane Burbank and Frederick Cooper, *Empires in World History: Power and the Politics of Difference* (Princeton, NJ: Princeton University Press, 2010), 414.

16. As noted in a previous chapter, Kohn did not participate in the civil rights movement. And although he taught in West Harlem (in City College) for years and proclaimed in his memoir that "the survival of our civilization depends upon winning [the African American] struggle for equality," he seemed impervious to the irony of his use of the so-called Noble Savage trope just two sentences before, where he mused that "Negro children seemed closer to nature than white children, and young Negro men and women seemed taller, better built,

and more graceful than their white counterparts" (*Living in a World Revolution*, 180; see also 179).

17. George Orwell, *In Front of Your Nose, 1946-1950*, edited by Sonia Orwell and Ian Angus (Boston: D. R. Godine, 2000), 125.

18. Hans Kohn, "The Morgenthau Plan for Germany," *Saturday Review*, October 6, 1945,11; and "Germany," in *America and the New World: The Merrick Lectures for 1945*, edited by Norman Angel (New York: Abingdon-Cokesbury, 1945), 29; Willy Bretscher to Francis A. Young, March 1, 1959, HKC-LBI, box 7, folder 1.

19. George F. Kennan, *Memoirs 1950-1963* (Boston: Little, Brown, 1967), 2:250.

20. Hans Kohn, *The Mind of Germany: The Education of a Nation* (New York: Charles Scribner's Sons, 1960), 350 and 354.

21. The *Frankfurter Allgemeine Zeitung* noted that Kohn was "one of those who, by invitation of the America-Houses, visited Germany most frequently to lecture" (clipping from the *Frankfurter Allgemeine Zeitung*, July 4, 1957, HKC-LBI, box 7, folder 1).

22. [Hans Kohn and Waldemar Gurian], "Seminar on 'Weltpolitik 1952' by Prof. Kohn and Prof. Gurian," HKC-LBI, box 9, folder 3.

23. E. Lee Fairley to Hans Kohn, November 19, 1956; Theodor Adorno to Hans Kohn, November 6, 1957; Max Horkheimer to Hans Kohn, April 30, 1958, all in HKC-LBI, box 7, folder 1; Edmund Schechter to Hans Kohn, July 3, 1953, HKC-LBI, box 7, folder 1.

24. Hans Kohn, "Report on Germany (May 20-July 4, 1951)," HKC-LBI, box 9, folder 3.

25. Hans Kohn to Harold E. Howland, July 3, 1957, HKC-LBI, box 7, folder 1.

26. Hans Kohn to Shepard Stone, June 27, 1952, HKC-LBI, box 9, folder 3.

27. "200 Sponsors Join Culture Unit Foes," *New York Times*, March 25, 1949.

28. Hans Kohn to Nicolas Nabokov, February 8, 1955, HKC-LBI, box 7, folder 1.

29. Hans Kohn to Melvin J. Lasky, April 17, 1956, HKC-LBI, box 9, folder 3. See also Lasky to Kohn, July 13, 1951, HKC-LBI, box 7, folder 1.

30. Astrid M. Eckert, "The Transnational Beginnings of West German *Zeitgeschichte* in the 1950s," *Central European History* 40, no. 1 (2007): 63-87; Hans Kohn, ed., *German History: Some New German Views* (Boston: Beacon, 1954), and *The Mind of Germany*.

31. Volker R. Berghahn, *America and the Intellectual Cold Wars in Europe: Shepard Stone between Philanthropy, Academy, and Diplomacy* (Princeton, NJ: Princeton University Press, 2001).

32. Lloyd K. Garrison to Hans Kohn, May 31, 1940, HKC-LBI, box 9, folder 1.

33. Jeremi Suri, *Henry Kissinger and the American Century* (Cambridge, MA: Belknap Press of Harvard University Press, 2007), 11.

34. Alfons Söllner, "Normative Westernization? The Impact of Remigres on the Foundation of Political Thought in Post-War Germany," in *German Ideologies since 1945: Studies in the Political Thought and Culture of the Bonn Republic*, edited by Jan-Werner Müller (New York: Palgrave Macmillan, 2003), 57. Regarding Kohn's status as a social and cultural outsider in America, one of his former students claimed that Kohn "was always a stranger to the guts of the U.S. environment" (Stanley Moses, e-mail message to the author, July 14, 2016).

35. Hans Kohn to Shepard Stone, March 28, 1955, HKC-LBI, box 7, folder 1.

36. Hans Kohn, "Nationalism and the Integration of Europe," in *European Integration*, edited by C. Grove Haines (Baltimore, MD: Johns Hopkins University Press, 1957), 34.

37. Melvyn P Leffler, *For the Soul of Mankind: The United States, the Soviet Union, and the Cold War* (New York: Hill and Wang, 2007).

38. Hans Kohn, "Regional Study Urged: Systematic Inquiry into North Atlantic Area Is Favored," *New York Times*, April 23, 1952.

39. Committee of Fifteen, *The City of Man: A Declaration on World Democracy* (New York: Viking, 1940), 51.

40. Hans Kohn, "World Challenge," *Saturday Review*, October 21, 1944, 26–27; "Omnipotent Government: The Rise of the Total State and Total War, by Ludwig von Mises," *American Historical Review* 50, no. 3 (1945): 531–33; and "The Ideal State," *Saturday Review*, November 11, 1950, 12–13.

41. Philip Mirowski and Dieter Plehwe, *The Road from Mont Pèlerin: The Making of the Neoliberal Thought Collective* (Cambridge, MA: Harvard University Press, 2009), 4.

42. Jan-Werner Müller, "Fear and Freedom: On 'Cold War Liberalism,'" *European Journal of Political Theory* 7, no 1 (2008): 49.

43. Judith Shklar, "The Liberalism of Fear," in *Liberalism and the Moral Life*, edited by Nancy L. Rosenblum (Cambridge, MA: Harvard University Press, 1989), 21–38.

44. Müller, "Fear and Freedom," 57.

45. Hannah Arendt, *The Origins of Totalitarianism* (New York: Harcourt, Brace, 1951), 222. See also Hans Kohn, "The Permanent Mission: An Essay on Russia," *Review of Politics* 10, no. 3 (1948): 267–89.

46. Hans Kohn, *World Order in Historical Perspective* (Cambridge, MA: Harvard University Press, 1942), 4–5. See also ibid., 155, 160, and 166.

47. Kohn, *World Order in Historical Perspective*, 275–76. See also Hans Kohn, "Fundamentals of Peace," *American Scholar* 12, no. 4 (1943): 401–13; and "Patterns of the Coming Peace," *University of Buffalo Studies* 17, no. 1 (1943): 5–14.

48. Hans Kohn to Waldemar Gurian, October 15, 1952, Library of Congress, Waldemar Gurian Collection, Box 4, Folder 27.

49. Hans Kohn, *Pan-Slavism: Its History and Ideology* (Notre Dame: University of Notre Dame Press, 1953), 252. Kohn would continue to discuss Soviet imperialist practices for the remainder of his career. One of the final examples appeared posthumously: Hans Kohn, introduction to *Russian Imperialism from Ivan the Great to the Revolution*, edited by Taras Hunczak (New Brunswick, NJ: Rutgers University Press, 1974), 3–17.

50. Hans Kohn, introduction to *The Soviet-Yugoslav Controversy, 1948-1958: A Documentary Record*, edited by Robert Bass and Elisabeth Marbury (: Prospect Books, 1959), xi. See also Benedict Anderson, *Imagined Communities: Reflections on the Origin and Spread of Nationalism* (London: Verso, 1983), 1–2.

51. Kohn, *American Nationalism*, 8.

52. Ibid., 227.

53. Ibid., 22.

54. Ibid., 130.

55. Kohn, *Living in a World Revolution*, 181.

56. Max Savelle, "*American Nationalism: An Interpretative Essay* by Hans Kohn," *American Historical Review* 63, no. 3 (1958): 693. Kohn returned to American nationalism in the last year of his life, coediting a slim reader that was much more critical (Hans Kohn and Daniel Walden, eds., *Readings in American Nationalism* [New York: Van Nostrand Reinhold, 1970]).

57. Karen Brutents, "Apologiia kolonializma, ili 'teoriia natsionalizma' Gansa Kona," *Voprosy Filosofii* 7, no. 2 (1958): 90–101; Y[uri Fedorovich] Karyakin and E[vgenii Grigorevich] Plimak, *Hans Kohn Analyses the "Russian Mind"* (Moscow: Progress, 1966).

58. Hans Kohn, "Some Reflections on Colonialism," *Review of Politics* 18, no. 3 (1956): 268.

59. Kohn, *Is the Liberal West in Decline?*, 71–73.

60. Hans Kohn, "Tocqueville, Wilson and the Present World," *Orbis* 1, no. 1 (1957): 49.

61. Hans Kohn, "The United Nations and National Self-Determination," *Review of Politics* 20, no. 4 (1958): 526, 528, and 531.

62. Kohn, *Die Europäisierung des Orients*.

63. Kohn, "The United Nations and National Self-Determination," 539, and 545.

64. Hans Kohn, "Times of Troubles," *Saturday Review*, January 17, 1953, 16.

65. Kohn, *Living in a World Revolution*, 184.

66. Howard J. Wiarda, *Think Tanks and Foreign Policy: The Foreign Policy Research Institute and Presidential Politics* (Lanham, MD: Rowman and Littlefield, 2010), 13–14.

67. Francis G. Couvares, Martha Saxton, Gerald N. Grob, and George Athan Billias, "The Cold War and Beyond: Stability, Hegemony, Chaos?," in *Interpretations of American History*, edited by Francis G. Couvares, Martha Saxton, Gerald N. Grob, and George Athan Billias., 8th ed. (Boston: Bedford, 2009), 2:252. The seminal work on Third World interventions during this phase of the Cold War is Odd Arne Westad, *The Global Cold War: Third World Interventions and the Making of Our Times* (Cambridge: Cambridge University Press, 2007).

68. [Robert Strausz-Hupé], "Reflections on the Quarter," *Orbis* 1, no. 1 (1957): 5.

69. Kohn, *Living in a World Revolution*, 184.

70. [Strausz-Hupé], "Reflections on the Quarter," 4. Kohn summarized his concept of the North Atlantic community in his introduction to Istvan Szent-Miklosy, *The Atlantic Union Movement: Its Significance in World Politics* (New York: Fountainhead, 1965), xi–xiii.

71. [Transcript of Kohn's letter], *Occidente* 12 no. 3 (1956): 249. A draft of that letter, titled "NATO Letter (Documents Kohn D-7)," is in HKC-LBI, box 9, folder 4.

72. [Transcript of Kohn's letter], 250. See also Wilfried Mausbach, "Erdachte Welten: Deutschland und der Westen in den 1950er Jahren," in *Deutschland und die USA in der Internationalen Geschichte des 20. Jahrhunderts*, edited by Manfred Berg and Philipp Gassert, (Stuttgart, Germany: Steiner, 2004), 423–48, especially 436. Mausbach sees the FPRI's and Kohn's initiative as manifesting an understanding of NATO as Western civilization. This, Mausbach stresses, was but one key conceptualization of NATO at the time. The conservative intellectual Russel Kirk, for whom "the North Atlantic community" was just another term for Christian civilization, praised the conference ("Cultural Debris: Two Conferences

and the Future of Our Civilization," *Modern Age* 2, no. 2 [1958]: 164–69). Interestingly, the other conference Kirk's article covered was that of the Mont Pèlerin Society).

73. Hans Kohn, "Concerning the NATO Conference (Documents Kohn D-11)," August 12, 1955, HKC-LBI, box 9, folder 4. Kohn's shifting definitions of both the North Atlantic and the totalitarian paradigms is apparent in a later document. There he described the North Atlantic community not as an idea or a potential, but as a real self-conscious entity with a long history. World War II, he claimed, came about when "Communism and fascism, movements hostile to, and contemptuous of, modern Western civilization, gained strength and confidence from Western disunity and spiritual decay" (Foreign Policy Research Institute [Hans Kohn], "Proposal for a Conference on the North Atlantic Community" [summer 1956], HKC-LBI, box 9, folder 4.

74. Hans Kohn to Robert Strausz-Hupé, April 11, 1956, HKC-LBI, box 9, folder 4. The letter refers to a steering committee made up of Kohn, Kissinger, Strausz-Hupé, and Walden Moore (who had also been instrumental a few years earlier in the Declaration of Atlantic Unity group).

75. *Summary and Findings of the Conference on North Atlantic Community and Closing Speech of the Conference by Paul-Henri Spaak, Secretary-General of N.A.T.O.*, 4.

76. Hans Kohn, "The Atlantic Community and the World," *Orbis* 1, no. 4 (1958): 420; Valerie Aubourg, "Organizing Atlanticism: The Bilderberg Group and the Atlantic Institute, 1952–1963," *Intelligence and National Security* 18, no. 2 (2003): 100.

77. Ernst Bieri, "An Atlantic Dialogue in Bruges," *Orbis* 1, no. 4 (1958): 401 and 406.

78. Hannah Arendt, "What Remains? The Language Remains: A Conversation with Günther Gaus," in Hannah Arendt, *The Portable Hannah Arendt*, edited by Peter R. Baehr (New York: Penguin, 2000), 11.

79. Robert Schuman, "The Atlantic Community and Europe," *Orbis* 1, no. 4 (1958): 410. The conference looked favorably at a European integration but advocated more—namely, Atlanticism or North Atlantic integration (*Summary and Findings of the Donference on North Atlantic Community*, 11).

80. Walter Benjamin, "Theses on the Philosophy of History [1940]," in Walter Benjamin, *Illuminations*, edited by Hannah Arendt and translated by Harry Zohn (New York: Schocken, 1968), 257–58.

81. Max Horkheimer, *Eclipse of Reason* (New York: Bloomsbury, 2013), 108. See also Max Horkheimer and Theodor W. Adorno, *Dialectic of Enlightenment: Philosophical Fragments*, edited by Gunzelin Schmid Noerr and translated by Edmund Jephcott (Stanford, CA: Stanford University Press, 2007).

82. Hans Kohn, "A Historian's Creed for Our Time," *Bulletin of the American Association of University Professors* 39, no. 4 (1953–54): 613 and 614.

83. Kohn, *Is the Liberal West in Decline?*, 10 and 16.

84. Ibid., 35–36 and 41.

85. "Self-Criticism and the Historian," *Times Literary Supplement*, July 26, 1957, 45.

86. Irving Howe, "This Age of Conformity," *Partisan Review*, January–February 1954, 7–33.

87. "Self-Criticism and the Historian," 45.

88. Aira Kemiläinen, *Nationalism: Problems Concerning the Word, the Concept, and Classification* (Jyväskylä, Finland: Jyväskylän Kasvatusopillinen Korkeakoulu, 1964), 141.

89. Werner J. Dannhauser, "The Brink of Moderation: Reflections on Modern History by Hans Kohn," *Commentary*, May 1964, 93.

90. Couvares, Saxton, Grob, and Billias, "The Cold War and Beyond," 2:248.

91. Immanuel "Ike" Kohn, interview with the author, Manhattan, November 13, 2007.

92. Hans Kohn, "American Foreign Policy in an Age of Fear," in *Atom Bombs Are not Enough*, edited by Chester Bowles and Hans Kohn (New York: Citizens Conference on International Economic Union, 1951), 8 and 10.

93. Hans Kohn, "The Meaning of Korea," *Washington Post*, May 8, 1951.

94. Hans Kohn, "What Next in Korea?" *Christian Science Monitor*, March 10, 1951. See also Hans Kohn, "China and the Peace," *New York Times*, November 9, 1950; "Historian Decries Policy Blunders," *New York Times*, February 11, 1951; "A Time for Wisdom," *New York Herald Tribune*, February 17, 1951; Hans Kohn, "Lessons of Korean War," *New York Times*, May 9, 1951; Hans Kohn, "Truce Negotiations Questioned," *New York Times*, November 16, 1951; Hans Kohn, "The Korean War," *New York Herald Tribune*, November 25, 1951; Hans Kohn, "Deterring Aggression: Requirements for Leadership of Free World Considered," *New York Times*, January 6, 1952.

95. Couvares, Saxton, Grob, and Billias, "The Cold War and Beyond," 2:249.

96. Walter Lippmann, *Public Philosopher: Selected Letters of Walter Lippmann*, edited by John Morton Blum (New York: Ticknor and Fields, 1985), 466–67; Kohn, "American Foreign Policy in an Age of Fear," 10 and 11.

97. Westad, *The Global Cold War*, 94–95.

98. Quoted in Council for the Study of Mankind, "Report on the Conference on Nationalism and Mankind, September 17–23, Inclusive, 1961. Villa Serbelloni, Lake Como, Italy," 15–17.

99. Quoted in ibid., 13–14.

100. Quoted in ibid., 39B.

101. Hans Kohn, "The Future of Political Unity in Western Europe," *Annals of the American Academy of Political and Social Science* 348 (July 1963): 95.

102. Kohn, *Is the Liberal West in Decline?*, 42.

103. Kohn, *Living in a World Revolution*, 176.

104. Wallace Sokolsky, untitled speech, March 16, 1971, HKC-LBI, box 25, folder 16.

105. Schmuel Hugo Bergmann, *Tagebücher und Briefe* (Königstein, Germany: Jüdischer Verlag bei Athenäum, 1985), 2:497.

106. Hans Kohn and Daniel Walden, preface to *Readings in American Nationalism*, edited by Hans Kohn and Daniel Walden (New York: Van Nostrand Reinhold, 1970), iii; Hans Kohn and Daniel Walden, introduction to *Readings in American Nationalism*, 9 and 1.

107. Schmuel Hugo Bergmann, *Tagebücher und Briefe* (Königstein, Germany: Jüdischer Verlag bei Athenäum, 1985), 1:345.

8. Coda: The Endurance of Kohn's Jewish Question

1. Hans Kohn to Nelson Glueck, May 13, 1949, HKC-LBI, box 14, folder 12.

2. Hans Kohn to Irving M. Engel, January 8, 1957, HKC-LBI, box 8, folder 1.

3. Schmuel Hugo Bergmann, *Tagebücher und Briefe* (Königstein, Germany: Jüdischer Verlag bei Athenäum, 1985), 2:497.

4. Hans Kohn, "From the Address by Professor Hans Kohn of Smith College: at the Thirtieth-Year Dinner of the Menorah Journal: Hotel Commodore. New York City, November 29, 1944" (transcript), 13, Henry Hurwitz/Menorah Association Collection, MS-2, box 27, folder 4, American Jewish Archives, Cincinnati, Ohio, 27.

5. Hans Kohn to Nelson Glueck, May 13, 1949, HKC-LBI, box 14, folder 12.

6. One of Kohn's students mentions his prediction in class that the bipolar collision would take place in the Middle East (Betty Altschuler-Jones to Hans Kohn, August 6, 1958 [HKC-LBI, box 8, folder 5]). Stanley Moses, then a pro-Israeli student and later a professor of urban affairs, remembers angry fellow students who heard Kohn's untypically harsh proclamation in the wake of the Suez Crisis that "Israel is a whore" of the British and the French (phone conversation with the author, March 16, 2014).

7. Sidney Wallach, *The Struggle for Integration* (Philadelphia: American Council for Judaism, 1945), 7. Kohn's activity in the American Council for Judaism is documented, for example, in his diary (see December 9, 1948, November 14, 1951, HKC-LBI, box 20, folder 4).

8. Shlomo Grodzensky, "Im Sgirat Tiko shel Hans Kohn," *Davar*, April 15, 1971.

9. Hans Kohn, *Living in a World Revolution: My Encounters with History* (New York: Trident, 1964), 181.

10. See, for example, Reuben Fink to Hans Kohn, January 30 and February 14, 1956, and Kohn to Fink, February 5, 1956, HKC-LBI, box 8, folder 13; Lienhard Bergel to Hans Kohn, January 22, 1957, and to the editor of the *New York Times Magazine*, January 14, 1957, HKC-LBI, box 8, folder 5; Hans Kohn to Rabbi Phillip Sigal, November 25, 1960, HKC-LBI, box 8, folder 13; Betty Pudney to Hans Kohn, April 16, 1962, box 14, folder 13.

11. "Leaders Back Loan to Britain; Decry Using Hunger as Political Weapon and as Means to Punish Entire People," *New York Times*, July 11, 1946.

12. Hans Kohn to John Slawson, May 3, 1948, HKC-LBI, box 8, folder 11.

13. Kohn, diary, May 21, 1948, HKC-LBI, box 20, folder 3; Hannah Arendt, "To Save the Jewish Homeland: There Is Still Time," *Commentary*, May 1948, 398–406.

14. Hans Kohn to John Slawson, May 21, 1948, HKC-LBI, box 8, folder 11.

15. Hans Kohn to James Marshall, January 4, 1950, HKC-LBI, box 8, folder 11.

16. David Ben-Gurion and Jacob Blaustein, "An Exchange of Views (1950)," in *The Jew in the Modern World: A Documentary History*, 2nd ed., edited by Paul R. Mendes-Flohr, and Jehuda Reinharz (New York: Oxford University Press, 1995), 527.

17. Irving M. Engel to Hans Kohn, January 7, 1957; and Kohn to Engel, January 8, 1957; Kohn to Frank [family name unknown], January 15, 1957; Kohn to Louis Lempel, April 7, 1957, all HKC-LBI, box 8, folder 13.

18. Hans Kohn to Richard S. Zeisler, April 27, 1957, HKC-LBI, box 8, folder 13.

19. Hans Kohn, "Negro Folk Education," *Journal for Adult Education* 9, no. 3 (1937), 312.

Leading civil rights activists from a milieu similar to Kohn's include Will Maslow and Rabbi Joachim Prinz. Kohn taught in Harlem (in City College) from 1949 to 1961, yet his son speculated that "the African American issue was beyond his horizon: He just did not see it" (Immanuel "Ike" Kohn, interview with the author, Manhattan, November 13, 2007).

20. Hans Kohn, "Principles and Activities of the Menorah Collegium: A Program Suggested by Hans Kohn," [August 7, 1958], HKC-LBI, box 4, folder 5.

21. Quoted in Yetty Kohn to Hans Kohn, September 7, 1946, HKC-LBI, box 10, folder 5.

22. Arthur Upham Pope to Hans Kohn, July 25, 1947, HKC-LBI, box 8, folder 1.

23. George Tomeh to Hans Kohn, October 26, 1959, August 11, 1961, HKC-LBI, box 8, folder 5; Abdelkader Chanderli to Hans Kohn, November 17, 1958, HKC-LBI, box 9, folder 6.

24. Hans Kohn to Eleanor Roosevelt, December 8, 1952, HKC-LBI, box 9, folder 2. (Emphasis added.)

25. Ibid.

26. Hans Kohn, "Toward Diminishing Tensions," *New York Times*, December 26, 1951.

27. Hans Kohn, "To Deal with the Mid-East: Policy Recognizing Nationalism as Driving Force Asked," *New York Times*, July 20, 1958.

28. Tahseen M. Basheer, "To Stabilize the Mideast; Recognition of Aspirations of Arab Peoples for Betterment Urged," *New York Times*, August 1, 1958,

29. Alfred Nielsen to Hans Kohn, March 23, 1961, HKC-LBI, box 4, folder 5.

30. Hugo Bergmann to Hans Kohn, October 7, 1961, Shmuel Hugo Bergman Archive (Arc. 40 1502/1561 c), National Library of Israel. On the same date, Bergmann explained in his diary that he wanted to convey to Kohn the notion that ultimately "we don't know what we do with our political activity" (Bergmann, *Tagebücher und Briefe* [Königstein (Königstein, Germany: Jüdischer Verlag bei Athenäum, 1985], 2:386).

31. Hans Kohn, "Hans Kohn at the Judah L. Magnes Memorial Meeting, December 16, 1948," HKC-LBI, box 8, folder 12. See also Hans Kohn to [Max] Steinbock, October 27, 1948, HKC-LBI, box 14, folder 10; Kohn diary, December 12 and 16, 1948, HKC-LBI, box 20, folder 3; "Memorial Honors Dr. Judah Magnes: Foundation to Perpetuate His Ideas, Ideals Announced at the Meeting Here," *New York Times*, December 17, 1948.

32. Kohn, diary, January 6, 1953, HKC-LBI, box 20, folder 5; Hannah Arendt to Hans Kohn, January 7, 1953, HKC-LBI, box 8, folder 11; Robert Weltsch to Hans Kohn, November 12, 1953, HKRW-LBI; Georg Landauer to Hans Kohn, November 20, 1953, HKC-LBI, box 8, folder 12; Hans Kohn to James Marshall, December 21, 1954, February 12, 1955, HKC-LBI, box 4, folder 5.

33. Dorothy L. Bernhard, Edward S. Greenbaum, Hans Kohn, Savid Sher, and Eric M. Warburg, "Plea for Arab Refugees Backed," *New York Times*, February 5, 1956.

34. Kohn's "Zion and the Jewish National Idea" was first published in the autumn–winter 1958 issue of *Menorah Journal*. The quote here is from Hans Kohn, *Reflections on Modern History: The Historian and Human Responsibility* (Princeton, NJ: Van Nostrand, 1963), 211.

35. Kohn, *Reflections on Modern History*, 208–9.

36. The editors of the *Mitteilungsblatt* to Hans Kohn, September 7, 1961, HKC-LBI, box 25, folder 15. See also Hans Kohn, "Martin Buber achtzigjährig," *Deutsche Rundschau* 84, no. 2 (1958): 158–61; and "Ein Kämpfer für das Judentum," *Mitteilungsblatt*, June 23, 1961. For Yekke letters of complaint about Israel, see Helmut Schmidt to Hans Kohn, July 7 and

August 21, 1950, HKC-LBI, box 8, folder 11; Martin Buber to Hans Kohn, October 11, 1961, HKC-LBI, box 25, folder 15; Bergmann, *Tagebücher und Briefe* 2:386 and 531.

37. Hans Kohn to Immanuel and Vera Kohn, January 4, 1953, HKC-LBI, box 11, folder 4.

38. Hasia R. Diner, *Jews of the United States, 1654 to 2000* (Berkeley: University of California Press, 2004), 278.

39. "According to his wishes," Wallace Sokolsky said in his speech at a tribute to Kohn at the Goethe House, "his cremated ashes are to be dispersed. I'd like to think that, appropriately, they are to be scattered over the earth" (untitled speech, March 16, 1971, HKC-LBI, box 25, folder 16). Bergmann was shocked both by Kohn's death and "the manner of his burial (Art seines Begräbnisses)" (*Tagebücher und Briefe*, 2:623).

40. Grodzensky, "Im Sgirat Tiko shel Hans Kohn."

41. Zalman Shazar to Robert Weltsch, April 28, 1971, RWC, box 2, folder 7.

42. Shmuel Hugo Bergmann, "Hatragedia Shel Hans Kohn," *Davar*, May 14, 1971.

Afterword

1. Shmuel Hugo Bergmann, "Hatragedia Shel Hans Kohn," *Davar*, May 14, 1971.

2. Taras Kuzio, "The Myth of the Civic State: A Critical Survey of Hans Kohn's Framework for Understanding Nationalism," *Ethnic and Racial Studies* 25, no. 1 (2002): 20–39.

3. André Liebich, "Searching for the Perfect Nation: The Itinerary of Hans Kohn (1891–1971)," *Nations and Nationalism* 12, no. 4 (2006): 579.

4. Hans Kohn, *World Order in Historical Perspective* (Cambridge, MA: Harvard University Press, 1942), 93.

5. "Grandfathers of the field" would probably been a more apt term, as there were very important scholars also in the generation between the three authors listed in the text and Kohn and Hayes—particularly Karl Deustch (who was Kohn's student and later his colleague) and Elie Kedourie. On Deustch, see especially Andrei S. Markovits, "From Prague to America—Karl W. Deutsch between Experience and Knowledge," in *Disseminating German Tradition: The Thyssen Lectures*, edited by Dan Diner and Moshe Zimmermann (Leipzig: Leipziger Universitätsverlag, 2009), 101–22; Jan Ruzicka, "A Transformative Social Scientist: Karl Deutsch and the Discipline of International Relations," *International Relations* 28, no. 3 (2014): 277–87.

6. Benedict Anderson, *A Life Beyond the Boundaries* (London: Verso, 2016), 126–28.

7. Anthony D. Smith, *The Ethnic Origins of Nations* (Oxford: Blackwell, 1986).

8. Hans Kohn, *Die politische Idee des Judentums* (Munich: Meyer and Jessen, 1924).

9. Hans Kohn, *Living in a World Revolution: My Encounters with History* (New York: Trident, 1964), 21.

10. Hans Kohn to Martin Buber, December 10, 1929, in Martin Buber, *Martin Buber, Briefwechsel aus sieben Jahrzehnten*, edited by Grete Schaeder (Heidelberg, Germany: L. Schneider, 1972), 2: 357–60 (the translation is based on Martin Buber, *The Letters of Martin Buber: A Life of Dialogue*, edited by Nahum N. Glatzer and Paul Mendes-Flohr and translated by Richard Winston, Clara Winston and Harry Zohn (New York: Schocken, 1991), 372–73; Hans Kohn to Robert Weltsch, May 3, 1930, HKRWC. See also Kohn, diary, April 11, 1930, HKC-LBI, box 18, folder 4.

Archives

American Jewish Archives (Cincinnati, OH) ·
  Henry Hurwitz/Menorah Association Collection
Central Archive for the History of the Jewish People (Jerusalem)
  Judah L. Magnes Collection
Central Zionist Archives (Jerusalem)
  Arthur Ruppin Collection
  Brith Shalom Collection
  Leo Hermann Collection
  Moshe Jacob Ben-Gabriel (Eugen Hoeflich) Collection
Harvard University, Harvard University Archive (Cambridge, MA)
  Carl J. Friedrich Papers
  William Ernest Hocking Correspondence
Hebrew Union College, Klau Library, Special Collections (Cincinnati, OH)
  Hans Kohn Collection
Leo Baeck Institute Archives (New York)
  Hans Kohn Collection
  Hans Kohn–Robert Weltsch Correspondence Collection
  Hugo Knoepfmacher Collection
  Koppel S. Pinson Collection
  Robert Weltsch Collection
Library of Congress (Washington)
  Waldemar Gurian Collection
National Library of Israel, Archives Department (Jerusalem)
  Hugo Bergmann Archive
  Martin Buber Archive
Princeton University Library, Department of Rare Books and Special Collections
(Princeton, NJ)
  Council on Foreign Relations Records
  Fight for Freedom, Inc., Records
Royal Library: National Library of Denmark and Copenhagen University Library
(Copenhagen)
  David Simonsen Archives, Correspondents–Comité des Délégations Juives
Smith College Archives (Northampton, MA)
  Neilson Presidential Collection

Stanford University Libraries, Special Collections and University Archives (Stanford, CA)
    Salo W. Baron Papers
University of Massachusetts, Amherst, Libraries, Special Collections and University
Archives (Amherst, MA)
    W. E. B. Du Bois Papers
Wisconsin Historical Society, Library-Archives Division (Madison)
    Merle Eugene Curti Papers
Yale University Library, Manuscripts and Archives (New Haven, CT)
    Dwight Macdonald Papers

Index

Page numbers in *italics* indicate photographs. All titles of works by Hans Kohn appear without the author's name appended.

Bar Kochba, 31; assimilation, 27, 44–50, 271n152; blood/race, 15, 36, 38–43, 48, 50, 52–53, 255; cultural Zionism, 15, 25, 37, 44–53; East vs. West, 36–37, 128; identity, 14, 27–28, 31–32; Jewish renewal, 26–29, 120; militarism, 26; national soil, 15, 34–38, 53, 255; WWI, 58. *See also* spiritual Zionism

Barrès, Maurice, 98

Basheer, Tahseen, 8–9, 245

Beard, Charles, 188–89

Ben-Gurion, David, 109–10, 242

Bergmann/Bergman, Hugo: on assimilation, 45, 49; Brith Shalom, 107, 109, 110, 112; criticism by HK, 149, 156; critiques of HK's works, 37, 118; friendship with HK, 14, 246, 314n30; on Hebrew, 37; on HK's death, 250–51, 253, 315n39; on identity, 32, 266n79; influence of, 15; on language, 51; Palestine visit, 37; on Vietnam War, 236; on Weininger, 47; works with HK, 121–22, 125

Biemann, Asher, 27

Bieri, Ernst, 226–27

Bildung, 15

binationalism: HK's call for, 4, 85–86, 94, 103–13, 121, 123, 131, 145–49, 293n21; in Israel, 246–47; and UN, 205

Birnbaum, Nathan, 37–38, 124

Bloch, Jean-Richard, 98

blood, national, 15, 19–20, 36, 38–43, 48, 50, 52–53, 239, 255

Bohemia. *See* Prague

Böhm, Adolf, 44

"Books on the History and Literature of Judaism," 51–52

Borgese, Giuseppe Antonio, 174, 188, 191

bourgeoisie, 28, 126, 128

Britain, 100–105, 131, 136, 147, 163, 171, 174, 178–79, 232

Brith Shalom, 103, 106–13, 131, 143, 146–50, 152, 283n40, 284n54, 285n74, 293n21, 294n27

British nationalism, 174

Brubaker, Rogers, 18, 116–17, 154, 307n13

Bruges Conference, 223, 224–27

Brüning, Heinrich, 173, 299n43

Brutents, Karen, 8

Buber, Martin: addresses, 24–25, 39–41, 47–49, 52, 121, 182, 288n28, 301n72; on Arab Question, 150; *Der Jude*, 80–87; East vs. West, 36, 267n92, 279n114; HK's break with Zionism, 146, 150–52, 294n34, 294–95n38; influence/friendship and HK, 14, 15, 25, 28, 33, 150, 246, 265n61, 286–87n14; on Jewish renewal, 27, 41, 121, 264n52, 288n28; on land, 34–35, 36; mysticism, 29; on nationalism, 33, 104, 117, 286–87n14; in Nazi Germany, 170; on spiritual Zionism, 119, 262n32, 278n97; Tsvat, 103; on Weltsch, 294n34; on WWI, 59, 60; Zionism of, 124–25. *See also Martin Buber*; *Vom Judentum* (Bar Kochba)

capitalism, 71, 163, 181, 184

Carr, E. H., 210

Charles-Ferdinand University, 14, 24. *See also* Bar Kochba

Chatterjee, Partha, 5, 200, 255

Christianity, 186, 191, 302n90

CIA, 214

citizenship, 79

City of Man, 188–92, 202, 216, 219, 223, 255

civic nationalism: criticism of, 2, 254, 255; Enlightenment, 6; vs. ethnic, 2, 4, 121, 254, 255, 291n86; HK's move to, 120; as modern, 211–12; U.S., 197, 204–6

Cohen, Hermann, 119

Cold War, 5, 8, 190–91, 208–19, 221–38, 249–50, 255, 307n5, 310–11n72

colonialism: Arab nationalism, 130, 131, 290n66; British, 136; and Cold War, 212, 221–23; and Eastern nationalism, 132; and Israel, 244; nationalism as, 8, 236, 254;

and non-alignment, 221, 222; post-WWI, 97–98, 102; WWI experience, 3, 57, 61, 64–65, 83, 88. *See also* anti-colonialism; imperialism

Comité des Délégations Juives, 96–100

Committee of Fifteen, 188, 192, 302n90, 302–3n98

communism, 94, 180–81, 209, 223, 228, 300–301n66. *See also* Soviet Russia

"Communist and Fascist Dictatorship," 180–81, 300–301n66

concentration camps, 168, 179–80

"Concerning the NATO Conference," 225

Congress for Cultural Freedom, 5, 214

conservatism, 94, 133–35, 165, 191, 192, 217, 223

cosmopolitanism, 45, 77–78, 145, 155, 197, 296n54

Council on Foreign Relations, 157

cultural nationalism, 132, 176, 291n87

cultural Zionism, 15, 25, 37, 43–53

Czech, 18, 22

Czech nationalism, 7, 16–20, 22–23, 43, 51, 79, 95, 218–20

Czechoslovakia, 79, 94–96, 178, 179, 291n83

Czechoslovak Legion, 61, 73, 75, 78–79

Dannhauser, Werner, 229–30

decolonization, 187, 224, 225, 226, 232–34

democracy, 4, 163, 175, 177–78, 180–95, 204–6, 255

Deutsch, Karl, 315n5

Diaspora, 28, 30, 34–35, 37, 38, 41, 48, 122, 248, 263n45, 276n66

distinctiveness, 43–44, 121–22

Dostoevsky, Fyodor, 201

Du Bois, W. E. B., 9, 175–76

East, the/orientality: Arab affinity, 84; blood/soil, 34, 35–37, 41; of Jews, 64, 72, 128; political modernities, 126–41, 158, 290n66; radical orientalism, 130–31; vs.

West, 36–37, 41, 228, 267n92, 307n13. *See also* East/West nationalism

East and West, 153, 169

East/West nationalism: colonialism, 132; development of, 2, 196–200; history, 129–37, 165, 201–2, 208–10, 290n66; imperialism, 120, 131, 136, 201, 291nn83–84; and individualism, 197, 198, 199, 200; irrationality of the East, 199; vs. spiritual nationalism, 260n5

economics, 216–17

education, HK's, 13, 14, 23, 24, 66–72, 74, 76, 80, 88, 274n41, 276n60, 277n79

Egypt, 131, 221–22

Einstein, Albert, 154–55

Eliot, T. S., 6, 201–2

emancipation, Jewish, 21–22, 266n79

Encyclopaedia of the Social Sciences, 175

Enlightenment, 6, 24, 102, 182, 227, 230

Epstein, Oskar, 41, 42, 47

Epstein, Yitzhak, 83, 108, 112

Eretz Israel. *See* Israel; Palestine

ethnic nationalism: vs. civic, 2, 4, 121, 254, 255, 291n86; conflicts in Prague, 7, 16–20, 23, 218–20; criticism, 254, 255; Enlightenment, 6; as failed modernization, 211; Judaism as, 156, 186, 296n57

Die Europäisierung des Orients, 140–41

fascism, 4, 180–84, 228, 300–301n66, 301n75

federalization/federations: Austria as multiethnic, 21, 67–68, 104, 192; Cold War, 219, 235; economics, 216; vs. totalitarianism, 4, 186–87, 190, 202–3, 302n93

Federal Union, Inc., 203, 306n148

Fichte, Johann, 25–26, 38, 58, 69, 77, 263n41, 289n57

Force or Reason, 182–83

Foreign Policy Research Institute, 5, 223–27, 311n74, 311n79

France, 96–100, 129, 234–35, 281n15, 282n22